# *THE EXPERIENCE*

# *OF*

# *HINDUISM*

REFERENCE MAP OF
MAHARASHTRA
Scale
0 25 50 100 Miles
0 25 50 100 Km.
GUJARAT — State/Union Territory
KHANDESH — Region
Sangli — City of 250,000+ population
Bir — Other cities, towns, and villages mentioned in text
Rugged terrain
Mountains
MADHYA PRADESH
SATPURA RANGE
GUJARAT
DADRA & NAGAR HAVELI
KHANDESH
Tapi R.
Jalgaon
Akola
Amraoti
Buldana
Ramtek
Bhandara
Nagpur
Wardha
VARHAD / BERAR / VIDARBHA
Wainganga R.
Wardha R.
Penganga R.
Matapur/Mahur
Nasik
Shirdi
Ellora
Aurangabad
Jalna
MARATHWADA
Paithan
Thana
Panchaleshwar
Parbhani
Ahmednagar
Bir
Bombay
MAHARASHTRA
Godavari R.
ANDHRA PRADESH
Dehu
Chinchwad
Alandi
Pune
Saswad
Jejuri
Shrigonda
Ambajogai
Rashim
Theur
Morgaon
Phaltan
Indapur
Wadapuri
Tuljapur
Mahabaleshwar
Shingnapur
Satara
Wakhari
Sholapur
Pandharpur
Akalkot
Gangapur
Bhima R.
DESH
SAHYADRI / WESTERN GHATS
KONKAN
ARABIAN SEA
Ratnagiri
Audumbar
Sangli
Kolhapur
Krishna R.
KARNATAKA
GOA, DAMAN, AND DIU
22°
20°
18°
16°
74°
76°
78°
80°
J.E.S./U. of M./'87

Sri Garib Dass Oriental Series No. 138

# The Experience of Hinduism

## ESSAYS ON RELIGION IN MAHARASHTRA

*Eleanor Zelliot and Maxine Berntsen*
*EDITORS*

Sri Satguru Publications
*A Division of*
Indian Books Centre
Delhi-India

*Published by :*
**SRI SATGURU PUBLICATIONS**
Indological and Oriental Publishers
*A Division of*
**Indian Books Centre**
40/5, Shakti Nagar,
Delhi-110007
(INDIA)



**First Indian Edition : Delhi, 1992**

**ISBN 81-7030-314-1**



Printed in India

# Contents


Preface / Maxine Berntsen vii

Acknowledgements xiii

Introduction / Eleanor Zelliot xv

Notes on the Writing of Marathi Words xxii

I. THE CONCEPT OF THE SACRED

1 ▪ "Boy-Friend?": An Essay / Irawati Karve 3

2 ▪ "The Vow": A Short Story / Shankarrao Kharat 7

3 ▪ One Face of God / Maxine Berntsen 17

4 ▪ Gods, Ghosts, and Possession / John M. Stanley 26

5 ▪ Scattered Voices: The Nature of God / R.N. Dandekar, Anonymous, Narayan Surve 60

II. THE PRACTICE OF FAITH

6 ▪ "A Town without a Temple": An Essay / Irawati Karve 69

The Ganesh Festival in Maharashtra: Some Observations / Paul B. Courtright 76

▪ The God Dattatreya and the Datta Temples of Pune / Charles Pain with Eleanor Zelliot 95

9 ▪ The Religion of the Dhangar Nomads / Gunther-Dietz Sontheimer 109

10 • The Birth of a God: Ram Mama of the Nandiwalas / 131
K.C. Malhotra

11 • "On the Road": A Maharashtrian Pilgrimage / 142
Irawati Karve

12 • The Gondhali: Singers for the Devi / 174
Ramchandra Chintaman Dhere

13 • My Years in the R.S.S. / V.M. Sirsikar 190

14 • Scattered Voices: The Experience of Ritual / 204
D.B. Mokashi, Vitthalrao Ghate, Anasuyabai Koratkar, Anonymous, Anutai Wagh

III. REFORM AND REJECTION

15 • "All That Is You": An Essay / Irawati Karve 213

16 • The Last Kirtan of Gadge Baba / G.N. Dandekar 223

17 • Orthodoxy and Human Rights: The Story of a Clash / 251
Kumar Saptarshi

18 • The Orthodoxy of the Mahanubhavs / Anne Feldhaus 264

19 • The Birth of a Rationalist / K.N. Kadam 280

20 • Scattered Voices: Refuge in the Buddha / 291
Bebi Kamble and Ulpabai Chauhan

IV. CODA

21 • Bhakti in the Modern Mode: Poems and Essays / 297
Ashok R. Kelkar and Sadashiv S. Bhave

V. APPENDICES

A • Glossary / 323

B • Gods, Goddesses, and Religious Festivals / 334

C • The Hindu Calendar / 341

D • Castes / 342

Contributors / 345

Selected Bibliography on Religion in Maharashtra / 350

Index / 371

# Preface

We have titled this book *The Experience of Hinduism: Essays on Religion in Maharashtra.* The title is intended to indicate that the book is not a technical treatise on Hinduism but an attempt to convey what it means in human terms to be a Hindu in one particular area today. The limitation of our subject to one area we feel essential, for while Hinduism in one area shares many features with Hinduism in other parts of India, the experience of each one is shaped by its own ecological setting, history, and traditions.

To talk about people's experience of religion is, first of all, to talk of their conception of the sacred. "The Concept of the Sacred" is the theme of the first section of this volume. Irawati Karve begins the theme in "Boy Friend?", a personal essay. In it she starts out lightly playing with the concept that Vithoba is her boyfriend, but ends by confessing the great gulf which separates her from the divine. In my essay, "One Face of God," I touch on the vast range of objects of worship and deal in particular with the conception of God as a harsh power demanding ritual worship. Shankarrao Kharat's story, "The Vow," vividly portrays the anxiety people feel in meeting the demands of such a deity.

John Stanley's essay, "Gods, Ghosts, and Possession," deals with the most dramatic encounter with the sacred—possession by gods and ghosts. Though from the standpoint of Marathi culture the experience of possession by a god and by a ghost are polar opposites, both types of possession, Stanley argues, are religious experiences. The experience of possession by a ghost is in his view an experience of defilement, of disorder; and being cured is an experience of "coming right," of cleansing and restoration of order. If this is an accurate account of how the possessed understand their experience it is highly significant, for it comes closer to the Christian understanding of sin than any other account of Hinduism I have seen. The section closes with the first of three "scattered voices," which here are brief statements on the nature of God. The first selection is an excerpt from an article on Hinduism by the noted scholar R.N. Dandekar. The next two, the voices of ordinary, uneducated people, are short statements remarkable for the beauty and power of their expression. The section ends with a poem by the *dalit* poet Narayan Surve.

The second section of this volume, "The Practice of Faith," deals with religious institutions—the rituals and practices which give expression to faith. It opens with an Irawati Karve essay reflecting the Tamil saying that "one should not have a house in a town without a temple." A temple, Karve says, "is the focus of a community's faith, a symbol of its hopes and aspirations. . . . A temple gives form to the formless. It is where that which has no beginning is installed, and on occasion where that which has no end is destroyed." We see this function of the temple clearly in Anutai Wagh's brief statement in the second group of "scattered voices" telling how the worship of Ganesh served to unite her home town of Morgaon. In their essay on the increasingly popular worship of the archetypal guru, Datta, Charles Pain and Eleanor Zelliot reveal not only how the temple is the venue for moving communal worship but how the sect as a whole brings God close to man in a series of gurus, some of whom are incarnations of Datta. Paul Courtright's article deals with the Ganpati festival, an extravaganza that dominates the life of urban Maharashtra for ten days each year. Irawati Karve's classic essay "On the Road" deals with her personal experience of that most typically Maharashtrian institution—the pilgrimage to Pandharpur.

Dhere's article on the *gondhaḷ*, a dramatic performance in honor of the Devi, is especially significant as an account of an institution that preserves and transmits religious traditions. Sontheimer's essay on the nomadic Hatkar Dhangars is a richly-textured account which shows the close interweaving of the shepherd's life and their preoccupations with their religious practices and symbolism. To me one of the most moving details in the essay is that the Dhangar takes off his shoes before entering the sheep-pen; the sheep-pen is sacred ground.

The second essay on the religion of a nomadic people is Malhotra's study of the Nandiwalas. This study, which was initiated under the direction of Irawati Karve, recounts the remarkable story of a man who was murdered by his fellow tribesmen and then later venerated as a god. In addition to being a valuable contribution to the history and anthropology of religion, this story strikingly illustrates the ambivalence people have in regard to their deities.

In Sirsikar's account of his experiences in the R.S.S. we see the deliberated development of a modern institution using a broad Hindu identification as its ideological base.

Though the selections here deal largely with group practice, some of the most typical Hindu rituals take place in the privacy of one's home. The "scattered voices" in this second section include an account by Vitthalrao Ghate of his adolescent delight in the details of ritual—a delight shared by the adolescent K.N. Kadam, whose autobiographical account appears in the following section. We end with two much more austere comments from women on the function of ritual practices in inculcating discipline and attaining power.

The third section of this volume is "Reform and Rejection." An attack on the institution of caste—especially untouchability—and the ethical relation between person and person are prominent themes here, themes that may appear conspicuously absent from the earlier sections. Here Irawati Karve's essay "All That Is You" finds, in the Upanishadic doctrine of non-duality, a firm basis for a system of ethics:

> While you still have the feeling of duality, those who are outside you are "others," strangers. But really it is *ātmā* that pervades all.

Bebi Kamble and Ulpabai Chauhan, two Mahar women who have rejected Hinduism and become Buddhist, put their finger on a similar argument which they take to be the essence of Buddhism.

> Buddha wrote that we ourselves are God. There is no God in the world, and nobody should put any hope in Him. Nobody should feel that if he fasts or does other such things he will see God. A person should honestly follow his own path. The *ātmā* is God.

The doctrine of non-duality is also mentioned in Saptarshi's account of his confrontation with the Brahman priest who refused to let the Untouchables enter his temple. At one point Saptarshi asked the priest why the Hindu religion, which saw *brahman* in everything, was not ready to regard the Untouchables as men. In Saptarshi's account, and frequently in contemporary Maharashtra, the Upanishadic doctrine of non-duality shades imperceptibly into the modern notion of *māṇuskī*, a term that would best be translated as "humanitarianism" if the English word had not gotten watered down through time. The last *kīrtan* of Gadge Maharaj, a contemporary saint in the Varkari tradition, contains a thundering attack on untouchability, again based on the fact that human beings are one, that the only two "castes" are male and female.

Within the doctrines of Hinduism, then, there is a philosophical basis for ethical concern and the rejection of caste differences—for a kind of humanism. There are many Maharashtrians, however, who base their humanism on more

Western concepts of science and rationalism. K.N. Kadam's autobiographical account tells how he developed from a devout Mahar to disciple of Bertrand Russell and a militant atheist.

Of course, reform movements in Maharashtra are not new. The Mahanubhav sect rose in the thirteenth century as a protest against the casteism, ritualism, and polytheism of popular Hinduism. Anne Feldhaus shows how much of Mahanubhav religious practice today is in fact not very different from orthodox Hindu practice. Moreover, the sect has withdrawn into itself and has lost its potential for exercising a democratizing effect on Hindu society.

Our volume closes with a section we have called a coda—"Bhakti in the Modern Mode." This section presents a number of contemporary Marathi poems, followed by a discussion by Ashok Kelkar and Sadashiv Bhave. Both the poems and the discussion bring together many of the themes that have emerged in this volume. In the poems we find again and again the same sense of distance from the divine that we saw in Irawati Karve's "Boy Friend?". Kelkar's broad sketch of the strands of Hindu tradition gives a useful overall structure to which we can relate various ideas of the sacred and various religious institutions. Kelkar and Bhave differ in their assessment of the relationship of these poems to earlier traditions. According to Bhave the poems under discussion are bhakti poems, and, moreover, the bhakti tradition is not opposed to Advaita Vedanta philosophy, but is part and parcel of it. Kelkar, on the other hand, contends that one must be wary of too facile and unhistoric identification of the attitudes of one time with those of another. The argument is unresolved, but it is stimulating and provocative.

The essays in this book contain many themes not discussed here. Often the themes repeat themselves so that the essays illuminate each other. Whatever lacunae there may be, or deficiencies in scholarship, we feel that the material is rich enough for the specialist to find something of interest and for the general reader to get some sense of what Hinduism in Maharashtra is today.

*—Maxine Berntsen*

# ACKNOWLEDGEMENTS

*Special thanks are due to Philip C. Engblom, who proofread, prepared the index, and made almost countless helpful suggestions in the final preparation of this volume. Anne Feldhaus has contributed to the process of transliteration and definition as well as written her own article and translated another. We are also grateful to the many other contributors to the volume, who have waited patiently for their stories and essays to appear in print. Among them, the work of Jai Nimbkar should be singled out, since her translations of Irawati Karve's essays bring important material into English for the first time. Grants at various times from the American Institute of Indian Studies and Carleton College have furthered our work. We have many other obligations, and not the least of these is to our students, whose attempts to grasp the complexities of Maharashtrian culture have inspired us. For the rest, how can we properly thank all those who encouraged, questioned, stirred our imaginations, answered our questions, and spurred us on to finish a project which has taken much of our scholarly and personal lives for the better part of the last two decades?*

# ACKNOWLEDGEMENTS

Special thanks are due to Philip C[illegible], who [illegible] [illegible] and [illegible] suggestions in the final preparation of this volume. [illegible] to the process [illegible] [illegible] [illegible] to the many other [illegible] [illegible] [illegible] [illegible] [illegible] American [illegible] of Indian Studies and [illegible] have furnished [illegible]. We are grateful [illegible] and [illegible] students who [illegible] compiled [illegible] [illegible] [illegible] project which has taken much of our [illegible] and has [illegible] the greater part of the last two decades.

# Introduction

This volume is a tribute to Irawati Karve (1905–1970), an acknowledgement that all of us—anthropologist, sociologist, political scientist, historian, historian of religion, writer, and student alike—are in her debt. Her classic article on the Maharashtrian Varkari pilgrimage, "On the Road,"[1] illustrates why. This essay offers a fresh approach to the complexities of Hinduism. Her viewpoint is that of a participant-observer—emotionally and intellectually part of that Pandharpur pilgrimage, but also emotionally and intellectually somewhat distanced. The result of that perspective sheds brilliant new light on the annual pilgrimage of the devotees of the god Vithoba. It gives a sense of the actuality of that all-important, uniquely Maharashtrian religious phenomenon; it gives a new way of looking at the reality of religious belief and practice.

Irawati Karve was best known as an anthropologist. She received her Ph.D. in Anthropology from the University of Berlin; she taught in that field for many years at the Deccan College Postgraduate and Research Institute in Pune.[2] In her scholarly writing, Irawati Karve dealt with religion in an academic way, as part of the phenomena of Hindu society, caste, group relations, etc.[3] She did not consider her essays on religion part of her scholarly work. In fact, "On the Road" and her three other essays in this volume were written as *lalit nibandha* (artistic essays—in a sense, *belles-lettres*) for a popular Marathi-speaking audience.[4] Their initial purpose was to share her individualistic attitudes and personal reactions with others equally involved in Maharashtrian life and letters. In this volume, we have attempted to build on the insight of Karve's essays rather than the academic findings of her scholarly work. The material collected here forms a multi-colored image of contemporary religion in the Marathi-speaking area. The degree of our success in shaping this image is largely due to Irawati Karve's curiosity and energy, to her honesty, to her ability to probe new ways of thinking, to her impatience with the trite or the obvious.

The beginnings of this volume were in a seminar held under the auspices of the American Institute of Indian Studies in 1971, the year after Irawati Karve's death. An unconscionable amount of time has elapsed since that first planning session. I can only hope the volume's concept and contents have matured during the time lapse. It should be noted, of course, that some of our contributors have also matured. In the cases of Anne Feldhaus and Paul Courtright particularly, the material here was written when they were beginning to probe the fields in which they have now published mature work.

Our approach to this volume was to invite scholars working in Maharashtrian religious matters to shape an article that would be based on observation or experience, utterly realistic and down-to-earth. To that collection of essays we have added translations of some material already available in Marathi. Such an approach has limitations, since the result is by no means an inclusive study of all of the most important aspects of Hinduism in Maharashtra. Some of the gaps are heartbreakingly apparent: there is no study of any of the important Devi temples nor an analysis of what the goddess in her many forms means in Maharashtra, although she is often mentioned in these essays. There is no description of a traditional village pilgrimage-fair, a *jatrā*, nor of the major holidays of Dasara, Holi, and Nagpanchmi. Discussion on the household ritual or the life-cycle rituals of Hindus is too brief. Neither the ashrams of the world-famous gurus situated in Maharashtra (although their mother tongue is not Marathi)—Muktananda, Meher Baba, and until recently Rajneesh—nor those of the less famous, more typical Marathi-speaking gurus are described. The non-Hindu religions of Maharashtra—Islam, Christianity, Buddhism, Jainism, Zoroastrianism, the Lingayat sect, the animism of the tribes—are mentioned only in relation to Hinduism. There is also a Pune bias in this selection, due in part to our connections with Pune, in part to the dominance of Pune in literary matters, and in part to the fact that scholars have not roamed the Vidarbha, Marathwada or Konkan areas[5] in the way that they have moved in the Desh area around that great city.

But with all its limitations, it seems to me that our approach offers at least two rather exciting insights. One can see not only the synthesis of Shaivism and Vaishnavism, which is the hallmark of Maharashtrian Hinduism, but the interrelationships between sect and sect, between one school of thought and another. The Datta cult is urban and Brahman-dominated; the Varkari cult is rural and non-Brahman in character. Yet these two cults come together in such things as the use of the *bhajan* (group devotional singing), and they share past history: both are associated with the shadowy figures of the Naths from the North[6] and both have great centers near the Karnataka-Maharashtra border in the south. Possession, healing, and *navas* (vows made to a deity in the hope of wish-fulfillment) are not part of the cult of Vithoba, but do appear in connection with Datta, Devi, Khandoba, the Mahanubhavs, and the Nandiwalas. Hindu-Muslim interaction, an area not directly touched upon, is suggested in the history of the Varkari and Datta sects, reappears in the autobiographical statement of K.N.

Kadam, and is totally rejected by the Rashtriya Swayamsevak Sangh.

Reading these essays as a whole brings to my mind a sense of the constant change in Maharashtrian religion, which of course is combined with the phenomenon Sontheimer notes—nothing is ever completely lost. One must question the meaning of modernity in religion as one reads. The Ganpati or Ganesh festival in its current form and the Rashtriya Swayamsevak Sangh are the products of the modern period, indeed of the same militant Hindu political tradition. But, on the one hand, the Ganpati festival has become a joyous event for entire communities, where the benevolent traditions of the elephant-headed god are combined with themes of international solidarity as frequently as those of national unity. On the other hand, the Rashtriya Swayamsevak Sangh has, if anything, become more Hindu, more militant, and more political in the fifty years since its birth.

Most of the Datta temples in Pune described in Pain's essay were built in this century, and avatars—reincarnations of that God—continue to appear. The seven-hundred-year-old tradition of the Varkari sect produced a saint in this century: Gadge Maharaj. A figure out of the past in appearance, he was totally committed to the old forms of devotion, and yet with a social philosophy more modern than that of many urban intellectuals. "The Birth of a God" tells of a recently created deity, worshipped by a tribe which is an anachronism in this most industrialized of Indian states. But the events described are indicative of a process that may have produced many of the regional deities of this area in the distant past, deities now linked to the larger Sanskritic tradition. The wealthiest, proudest, and most thoroughly integrated of all the nomads—The Dhangars—still move through this area. They exhibit in some ways the least adaptation to this century of any group—yet we and they know change must come. Settlement seems inevitable as irrigation spreads and pasture lands are depleted; we look to see the ways in which they are already close to the settled agricultural community, as in the case of the worship of Khandoba.

The Gondhali, a prime example of religious functionaries adapting through the ages, may survive in the modern world through the commitment of elite musicians to tradition, through the power of a government bent on communicating modernity to the rural areas by traditional forms, and through their own dynamism. Is there an exception in the Mahanubhavs? Surely this heterodox sect made its accommodation with mainstream Hinduism long ago and survives by its very inconspicuousness and its clearly delineated areas of service in the form of healing. And yet there seems to be a new intellectual interest in the Mahanubhav philosophy and practice, perceptible on the Maharashtrian scene in novels as well as purely scholarly work.

It is clear that modernity and change do not necessarily involve Westernization. The dynamic within Hinduism itself seems sufficient to create new thought and new forms. And Westernization itself may not be a secularizing force. Indeed, the most exclusively Hindu of all the new movements, the Rashtriya Swayamsevak Sangh, is at the same time the most Western in its organization and psychology. And at the same time, a contemporary Datta guru finds the Rashtriya Swayamsevak Sangh too unorthodox in its attitude toward untouchability. And those Untouchables who reject Hinduism completely find both solace and intellectual legitimation for rationalism, equality, and humanitarianism in the religion of the Buddha, twenty-five hundred years old.

Something about the soil of Maharashtra produces fascinating religious continuity and profound and unusual religious reform. Perhaps it is its function as a bridge between North and South India, its ability to absorb and combine influences from Aryan and Dravidian cultures. Perhaps it is due in part to an unusual cultural cohesion, a sense of a regional ethos sustained in spite of the newness (1960) of the Marathi-speaking areas as the single state of Maharashtra. Or perhaps it is related to the economic mix of the modern period—an exceptionally wealthy trading and industrial world centered in the city of Bombay, with a hinterland in which rainfall is unpredictable and a hardy peasant tradition has learned to cope with scarcity as well as plenty. Whatever the reason, the traditions of Maharashtra are inextricably mixed: they cut through social and caste layers from high to low and exhibit a lively pattern of change and adaptability. It is our hope that these studies of facets of a living religion in a single language area may offer a better understanding of that region and also stimulate comparisons of the ways in which traditions appear, change, and blend in other areas of Indian culture.[7]

*—Eleanor Zelliot*

## NOTES

1. See page 142.

2. This volume, however, is not a memorial by her students. Indeed, the work of some of her finest students and closest associates, Y.B. Damle, Vidyadhar Pundalik, Sumati Kirtane, G.V. Dingre, Vijay Bhanu, R.K. Mutatkar, Savitri Shahani, is not in a form which suits the purpose of this volume.

3. See, for instance, I. Karve and J.S. Ranadive, *Social Dynamics of a Growing Town and Its Surrounding Area* (Poona: Deccan College Research Institute, 1965). The *Bulletin of the Deccan College Post Graduate and Research Institute* 31–32 (1970–1972) contains a listing of the 122 published works of Irawati Karve.

4. The *lalit nibandha* or artistic essay is an important genre in Marathi literature, meriting much critical attention. An example of other serious *lalit nibandha*s is Irawati Karve's *Yuganta: The End of an Epoch* (Poona: Deshmukh Prakashan, 1969), a series of essays on the *Mahābhārata*, which in its Marathi version won the Sahitya Akademi's prize as best book of Marathi literature in 1967. A Sangam reprint of the English translation appeared in 1974.

5. Vidarbha, the eastern part of the Marathi-speaking area, was part of Berar and the Central Provinces during British days; Marathwada was under the political hegemony of the Nizam of Hyderabad; the Konkan is the coastal area stretching south of Bombay. The Desh, the plateau east of the Sahyadri Mountains (Western Ghats) which includes Pune, was the heart of Marathi consciousness before the State of Maharashtra was created in 1960.

6. There is almost nothing in English on the history of the Naths in Maharashtra, although clearly they were of importance in the past. The Nine Naths (*nao-nāth*) can be found in religious pictures and some are remembered by small shrines. Ian Duncan of Massey University in New Zealand is now working on the place of the Naths in Maharashtra.

7. The new *Encyclopedia of Religion*, edited by Mircea Eliade (New York: Macmillan, 1986), contains articles on religion in India by linguistic region. The essay on "Marathi Religions," written by Eleanor Zelliot and Anne Feldhaus, is an attempt briefly to touch all facets of religion in Maharashtra, noting what seems to be unique or unusual.

# NOTES ON THE WRITING OF MARATHI WORDS

To help the reader understand Marathi pronunciation, we have adopted a somewhat original approach to the writing of Marathi words. Throughout the text, italicized Marathi words are written with the diacriticals described below. As in most northern vernaculars, the short *a* inherent after a consonant is frequently eliminated in pronunciation, and we have omitted it in transliteration as warranted. The sounds peculiar to Marathi—*ç* which is pronounced *ts*, *ĵ* which is pronounced *dz*, and *ḷ* (retroflex)—are all marked in a way not found in orthodox transliteration of Sanskrit words. We have, however, used standard transliteration for quoted Sanskrit and Pali words and Marathi and Sanskrit book titles. Also, in the appendices at the end of the volume, we have added standard transliteration in parentheses after the Marathi word. These are the policies we have followed:

1. Indian words commonly used in English are not italicized or written with diacritical marks.
2. Frequently used proper nouns and all place names are not italicized or written with diacritical marks in the text.
3. A glossary and appendices (lists of gods, goddesses, festivals and castes; and the Hindu calendar) appear with both standard transliteration as well as our system of writing Marathi words where these differ.
4. Some words from Persian or from nonelite groups are used in Marathi but do not appear in any Marathi dictionary; these words have been given diacritical marks only as a guide to pronunciation.
5. Words have been used in English plural and possessive forms.
6. Recent governmental policy has resulted in changes in place name spellings, such as Pune (old Poona) and Thane (old Thana). We have retained the old spellings when appropriate and all spellings currently used are given in the Index.

7. Our guide to the pronunciation of Marathi words:
   *a* is a short vowel pronounced as the vowel in English *but* or the first *a* in the midwestern pronunciation of *American*.
   ā is pronounced as in English *father*.
   *e* is pronounced as the vowel in English *day*.
   *c̣* is pronounced as English *ts*.
   *j̣* is pronounced as English *dz*.
   *ch* is pronounced as in English *church*.
   *j* is pronounced as in English *judge*.
   *ṛi* is used to indicate a sound midway between *ri* and *ru*.
   *h* is used following another consonant (and the diagraph *ch*) to indicate aspiration.
   A dot under *ṭ*, *ḍ*, *ṇ*, and *ḷ* is used to indicate retroflexion; *t*, *d* and *n* without a dot indicate dental sounds, while *l* without a dot indicates a normal lateral.
   The letter usually transliterated as *v* is given as *v*, *w*, or *o* in our writing system, according to pronunciation.
   *dny* is used in place of the standard *jñ* since it is closer to Marathi pronunciation.
   The nasal dot (*anuswār*) is rendered as *n* or *m*, as pronunciation demands.
8. As with all caste names, "Brahman" has been used throughout without italics or diacriticals. It must be distinguished from the name of the god, Brahma, and from *brahman*, which is generally translated "the absolute."

# *I.*
# *THE CONCEPT OF THE SACRED*

IRAWATI KARVE
TRANSLATED BY JAI NIMBKAR

# 1

# "Boy-Friend?": An Essay*

I was just back from Pandharpur, resting on the sofa. My daughter was reading something in a chair near me, and her husband was walking back and forth from the verandah to the room and back to the verandah. People were coming to see him on various kinds of business. When someone came he went out, when they went away he came in and talked to me. Our conversation went on like that.

He came in, took a chair and sat down in front of me. He said, "Well, did you see your boy-friend?"

For a few moments I was baffled by the question. Then it dawned on me that the boy was asking me about Vithoba. I said, smiling, "Yes, I saw him."

---

* "Boy-Friend?" from *Gaṅgājal* [Ganga Water] (Pune: Deshmukh and Company, 1972).

Some people came then and he went out.

But his question had jolted me out of my doze. In a way, boy-friend was a new term; but its sense was not new. People have called Vithoba their mother, father, friend, in-law, lover, and many other names. Doesn't boy-friend mean the same as lover? Haven't many devotees addressed him as a lover?

He came back in. Heaven knows how he could keep track of our conversation, when he kept going out and talking about something else in between. He said, "Doesn't your husband mind your having a boy-friend?" I said, "Husbands don't mind this kind of boy-friend." Even before I had finished answering, some more people came. He went out but my mind kept going over our conversation.

What did I mean by *this* kind of boy-friend? The kind that is made of stone? No, a stone lover is not necessarily acceptable to a husband. Meera's husband, Sakhu's husband, Bahinabai's husband, all objected even to a stone lover.[1] So a husband's acceptance of a lover depends not on whether he is made of stone or flesh and blood, but on how well the god is loved. Meera could not live without Giridhari. Bahinabai and Sakhu left their homes and husbands to go to Pandhari. I am not like them. I take the car on a holiday when it won't cause my husband any inconvenience. I make sure that the streams on the road to Pandharpur are not in spate. I also make sure that it is not a special day—*ekādashī, dvādashī, gopāḷkālā* and so on—so that there won't be a crowd in the temple and I can take *darshan* without a long wait. I think of all these things before I go to Pandharpur. As far as my husband is concerned, not only is this boy-friend made of stone, my involvement with him is not very great either. Then why shouldn't he put up with him? He even asks me now and then, of his own accord, "How come you haven't been to Pandharpur for a long time?" Then for a day at least he is free from my nagging and chattering. So this kind of boy-friend is not merely acceptable, he is often very convenient.

My son-in-law came back in and sat down in front of me

again. "Well, and what did your boy-friend have to say?" I smiled. "He said, 'So you have remembered me, I see.' "

Before my sentence was completed this whirlwind had left his chair and gone out again. "So you have remembered me." What does this mean? Vitthal stands on the same spot day and night. He always remembers. He is waiting. I only think of him once in a while. Even when I think of him I don't immediately go to see him. I go in my own time, at my own convenience. What else can he ask when I go on one of these once-in-a-while visits? There is really another question implied in this "so you remembered me," and that is, "Why have you come, my dear? What do you want? What's lacking in your life?" Meera had become obsessed with the love of God. She wanted only him. I am not like that. Only when I have to carry a burden that is too heavy for me do I remember him. I run to God only when I feel alone, when I have to face a difficult situation, or bear some hardship. I have not gone beyond the first two levels of devotion—that of the desperate devotees and the ones who want something. So really what God should ask me is, "Why have you remembered me now?"

The door opened again. The people still waited outside. He came out again. "Couldn't you go tomorrow?"

"No, I have a lot of work waiting for me. I must go today."

"I am going to the farm with these people. I'll be back late. By the time I return you'll be gone. Take care. You are looking very tired." He ran his hand tenderly over my face and went away.

I thought, devotees have imagined themselves as having every kind of relationship with Vithoba; but they have never made him a son or daughter. He is mother, father, brother, sister—everything. Then why isn't he ever a son? Why doesn't Jani[2] say,

> Vithuraya of Pandharpur, like a son to me
> A strong stick to lean on in old age.
> Vithuraya touches me with a tender hand,
> Saying as my own son would, Mother you are tired.

But no, neither Jani nor Tukaram[3] could possibly call

Vithu a son. I don't think any devotee has imagined Vithoba as his child. Even though all the familial relationships have been used to describe God, he is never thought of as inferior to the devotee. As a lover he is an equal, but even here God is always the man, and the devotee, whether he be a woman or man, always takes the role of the woman. A well-known saint from Varhad[4] wore black beads around his throat and bangles on his wrists in the name of Vitthal. In the bhakti known as *madhur* (sweet) bhakti, the male devotees imagine themselves to be Radha. Whichever relationship has been imagined, Vithoba has always been assigned the roles considered superior by the Hindu tradition. The baby Krishna is worshipped among the household gods, but I don't remember anyone having called Vithoba a son. Only Yashoda has the right to call Krishna a child. She earned it by sacrificing her own child. She did not give birth to God, but she kept him alive against tremendous odds. Who am I to call God anything like this? I am not that close to him. We had used the words "lover" or "boy-friend" only in joke. Unfortunately, the distance between him and me is great—very great.

## EDITORS' NOTES

1. Meera (Anglicization of Mīrā) was a bhakti saint-poet in the Rajasthani/Hindi tradition who was devoted to Krishna (here Giridhari); Sakhu and Bahinabai are women saints in the Varkari tradition whose center is the god Vithoba at Pandharpur or Pandhari.
2. Jani or Janabai, the serving-maid of the great Varkari Namdeo, was a poet in her own right.
3. Tukaram was the seventeenth-century saint-poet of the Varkari tradition, now the most beloved and most quoted of all the poets in that seven-hundred-year tradition.
4. Varhad is an older name for the eastern area of Maharashtra called Berar in British days, part of Vidarbha traditionally.

SHANKARRAO KHARAT
TRANSLATED BY MAXINE BERNTSEN

# 2

# "The Vow": A Short Story*

Full-moon day, the day to keep the vow to the goddess. Midnight had passed, the night was almost over. Under its basket the rooster crowed. And Tatya Naik sat up with a start. His wife Sarji sat up too. Tatya got up and walked to the corner of the room. He leaned down and felt with his hand under the basket, listening to the muffled *krr krr* of the chicken inside. He rose again, took the board leaning against the door and put it on top of the basket. Then with a sense of relief he sat looking at the door. Without getting up he turned his head and spat into the corner. He called softly, "Sarji, are you awake?"

Sarji immediately awoke from her doze. "What do you mean? Of course I'm awake!"

---

* "Navas," from *Sāṅgāwā* [It Must Be Told] (Pune: Continental Prakashan, 1962).

"Look here, it's almost morning. Didn't you hear the rooster crow?"

"Of course, that's what woke me up."

"Well then it's better to get started early making the food offerings."

"Yes, but it's still night. That's the first time the rooster has crowed and everybody is still asleep."

"Are you sure?"

"Why, I haven't slept all night. I've been half awake. Look, it's not quite dawn yet."

Though Sarji had tried to reassure him, Tatya was still worried. "But the sooner we get started for the temple the better."

Sarji answered quickly, "Yes, yes, that's true, but there's not a drop of water in the house. And this is the full-moon day of the goddess. How can I start cooking without taking a bath?"

"Are you going to follow all those rules and waste time and not be ready to leave for the fair till everybody else has gone?"

"It won't take any time. You put a little water in the jar and I'll get my work done in a hurry."

So husband and wife talked in the early hours of the morning.

Then Tatya got up, opened the door, and went out. He stretched and cracked his joints. He walked behind the house and looked up at the moon. It was still high in the sky. Tatya looked around at the Naikwada.[1] The whole neighborhood was still fast asleep. There was no movement anywhere, no sound of voices. The trees by the doorway were silent. Somewhere in the distance the bark of a dog fractured the silent moonlight. Tatya looked around again. Seeing that everything was still quiet he said to himself, "Hey, it's still the middle of the night." He went back inside the house.

Today was the fair of the goddess Mariai[2] at Degaon, six or seven miles from Tatya's village. It was held once a year on the full moon of Chaitra. Huge crowds always gathered.

People came like thousands of ants. In bullock carts or on horseback they came from miles around. A rich man might bring a goat as an offering to the goddess, a poor one might offer a cock to keep his vow. Some would bring food-offerings, along with a green blouse and a coconut for the goddess. Others would come prostrating themselves at each step or rolling their bodies through the dust; and when they arrived they would bathe the image in curds and milk. Some came to keep the vow they made the previous year.

Throughout the area the goddess of Degaon was known as a harsh and powerful deity. If a man did not keep his vow, it is said, the goddess would raze his house or cast thorny branches in his door. So on the full moon of Chaitra people would go with fear and devotion and would try at any cost to keep their vows. Last year Sarji had made a vow, "Mother goddess, let the crops grow well and watch over my children. And next year I will offer a cock and give a feast at your door."

Sarji kept firmly in mind that she had to keep her vow. So when the full moon of Chaitra drew near she set about making preparations. Begging a little from this farmer and that, she had managed to collect a *pāylī* of *jawār* and a few measures of wheat. The spices for the curry were ground and ready, and she had brought a measure of rice and a little jaggery from the grocer's shop.

Sarji had taken care of getting all the little things they needed, while Tatya had promised to bring the cock. He had kept his word and now they had no anxiety on that account.

She lay down again, keeping an ear open for the next crowing of the cock. Tatya opened the door, and hearing the sound Sarji called without getting up, "Are the neighbors up yet?"

"No, it looks like it's still night. The whole place is quiet. Even the birds are quiet. The moon is still up."

"Then why don't you lie down for a while? Why are you staying up?"

"Do you think I could still sleep? I'm worried about today."

"What are you worried about?"

"Well, there's nothing really, but I was wondering who all we'll find at the fair. We'll have to round up people for the feast. Every now and then they've invited us for meals, and now we'll have to pay them back."

"You don't have to worry about that! They'll all come flocking like crows."

"But it's a big fair. And everyone is involved in their own business."

"Don't worry, two weeks ago I sent a message to everyone—Maushi's daughter in Charegaon, your nephew in Limbuda, and there'll be someone from my family. And we'll meet the people from Itlapur and Ranjangaon there."

"Why, you've lined up so many! And how are you going to feed them all with one chicken?"

"So what if there are a lot of people? I'll make a big stack of *bhākrīs*. You put some water to boil in a big pot. The chicken is nice and fat. We can let the kids eat their fill. They never get a chance to eat meat otherwise; at least let them get a taste in the name of the goddess!"

"But all those people, besides you and me."

"Don't you worry. I'll take care of everything."

"All right. Do as you please."

Their conversation was suddenly interrupted by a loud, long crow from the rooster. Tatya started. Sarji was shaken. Immediately Tatya called to his wife, "Sarji, get up, the rooster has crowed again."

"I'm up. That rooster must have been sent by the goddess. It wakes us up just in time." Sarji got up and opened the door. She looked at the white moonlight and said to her husband, "Now get up. Go down to the stream and have your bath, then bring me some water from the spring before there's a whole line of people there."

"You look after your work and I'll take care of mine," Tatya said, taking a dhoti from the clothesline. He went outside. Putting a waterpot on his shoulder he went down to the stream. He washed himself clean in the water, while reciting the name of the goddess. Then making rapid trips from stream to house he filled the water jar in the house.

By then day had dawned. The sky became bright. The Naikwada awakened. The birds began to twitter. Doors of the surrounding houses opened and people came out. The dogs that had been sleeping in the doorways came out into the yards. They stretched and ran about. In some houses the cooking fires were lit. Smoke started coming out of the roofs. The men and women from the *wāḍā* filed down to the stream. A crowd gathered at the spring. Everyone was in a hurry to go to the fair.

Sarji plastered the earthen stove with cowdung, lit it, and put an iron pot on to boil. In the shed at the back of the house she sat on a stone and poured warm water over herself. Then she quickly scoured the pots and pans until they shone, put some sticks into the fire, and sat down to make *bhākrīs*. She worked rapidly. *Bhākrī* after *bhākrī* fell onto the griddle. A stack of puffed *bhākrīs* grew on the piece of cloth at her side.

Full-moon day had dawned. Tatya looked at the light and folded his hands in worship. As Sarji saw the mild rays of the morning sun cross the threshold she called to her husband, "Say, you'd better get the kids up." She looked angrily at the children, muttering, "Brats, they run around all over the place chasing birds, then sleep like the dead." She raised her voice again, "Did you hear me?"

"I can hear you. What do you want?"

"Get those kids up and wash them. It's full-moon day." Again she muttered to herself, "Damn kids, look at their hands and feet. You'd think a dog had peed on them."[3]

"Why don't *you* give them a bath? There's a whole jar full of water."

"Just listen to him! I've got to make a whole *pāylī* of *bhākrīs* and I've got to get the offerings for the goddess ready. And besides, these sticks won't stay lit. I'm half dead from blowing on them."

"Take your time, and when you're done with everything else wash the kids."

"Here I've already got my hands full and you just go on without even paying attention to what I'm saying. Now take some water in a pan and wash those kids!"

As the sun grew warm, Sarji's hands worked faster. The *bhākrīs* were more than half done. Tatya got the boys up and gave them a bath. He took out their new clothes from the bundle in which they were tied.

Delighted with their new clothes, the kids frisked about like lambs, then sat down by the stove watching their mother with avid interest.

Just then the rooster crowed and began to call *ko ko*. The wily youngsters were suddenly alert. They immediately spotted the basket. They ran toward it and started to lift it up. Sarji raised her flour-covered hand and shouted, "Why are you looking under that basket? Are you going to go outside or shall I give you both a good whack?" The older boy, six years old, answered, "Mother, there's a chicken under the basket. When did Baba bring it?" At this Sarji got wild, "Damn you to hell! Why are you getting after that rooster? Are you going to go outside or shall I call your father?"

At that moment the rooster screamed again and began to cackle. The youngsters wheeled around from the door and dashed up to the basket. With their ears to the basket they listened intently. They began beating on the basket. Out of her mind with their antics, Sarji picked up a brass pot full of water and poured it on one child's back. He let out a yell and ran outside. Tatya came in and asked angrily, "What's going on? Here it's full-moon day and you're making the kid cry!"

"Let both of them go to hell! They're getting after the rooster!"

"They're just kids, you know."

"I know, I know. But you'd better throw a gunny sack on top of the basket. That rooster keeps crowing and people are passing by our house all the time. Can't you imagine what will happen?"

Tatya tried to reassure her, "What is there to worry about? We're practically ready to go. Once we're on our way we're as good as there."

Sarji retorted, "Have you forgotten that we still have the cooking and everything to do?"

"It won't take long," he answered.

Suddenly Sarji thought of something, "Oh, go to the store and bring a coconut, incense, and camphor. Otherwise we'll forget it in all this rush."

"Now you're ordering me around. And how am I supposed to pay the shopkeeper—knock out my teeth?"

"Ask him just this once to let us buy it on credit. And don't say unlucky things!"

"But we still owe him some money."

"So what? Tell him we'll pay him everything at harvest time."

"You mean he's going to take my word for it?"

"Instead of just talking back, why don't you at least go and see?"

"You always bring up something at the last minute!" Tatya grumbled and got up to go to the store. Just at that moment Pandu Naik walked in, and hearing Tatya's angry voice said, "Sounds like a fight going on!"

"You said it! Half the people in the *wādā* have already left and we don't even have the offerings or the camphor, incense, and coconut yet."

Pandu casually poked his head inside the door and saw Sarji at the stove. "Vahini,[4] you're making a lot of *bhākrīs*," he said. "Looks like there's chicken or mutton for the fair."

Sarji laughed easily and answered, "No chicken or mutton, Dajiba—we're just getting ready a coconut and food offerings for the goddess."

"Just thought I'd ask." Hardly had Pandu gotten the words out than the rooster crowed loudly and began to cackle in fright. Hearing the crowing Pandu said, "Well, Tatya, so there *is* a chicken for your fair. Hope I'm included."

"That's right, ol' friend, it's the rooster we promised the goddess."

"Whatever it may be, don't leave me out."

"Of course not, you know we wouldn't do that!" Tatya answered and left hurriedly for the store in town. By then Sarji had finished everything. She sprinkled water on the stove and leaned the griddle against it. She took a dhoti and started tying up the food, putting the stack of *bhākrīs* at one end and the offering at the other. For cooking the chicken she took a big nickel plated pot. Into it she put two brass plates and a water pot, and tied them all together in a big cloth. She cleared everything up. And then, because she was going to the fair, she put on her best sari, the one with tiny checks. After she put on her new blouse with an embossed design, she stood at the door looking toward the town and waiting for Tatya's return. Keyed up with excitement, the kids kept jumping around, running to the basket to listen to the bird, and slapping the basket with a stalk of fodder. "Mother, show us the rooster," they kept begging, while Sarji in her turn kept scolding them.

Meanwhile Tatya had climbed the bank of the stream and was hurrying toward the house. When Sarji saw him she went inside. Tatya handed her the incense, camphor, and coconut. She took them and tied them in the bundle with the food-offering. Everything was set. Just then Tatya said, "Sarji, bring the stuff out to the door. I'll go and say a prayer before our Khandoba and be right back."

"Don't take too long. We'd better get started before the sun gets too hot."

"I told you I'd be right back," Tatya answered and hurried off to the temple at the western side of the Naikwada to take *darshan* of Khandoba.

Sarji quickly picked up the bundles one by one and carried them out to the door.

Meanwhile three men coming from the town left the main path and headed toward Tatya's house. They walked straight to his door. By then Tatya had returned from the Khandoba temple. His face fell when he saw Nana, owner of the big farm down below. He started to sweat. When Sarji saw the men she hung her head. She recognized the *pāṭīl*[5] and the policeman and was scared.

As soon as he saw Tatya, Nana demanded loudly, "Tell us, Tatya, did you come to my farm last night?"

Nana raised his voice even more, "It's all right to ask for grain, that we'll give. But that doesn't mean you can steal a rooster right out of my pen."

At the mention of the rooster Tatya quaked inwardly. His eyes turned toward the house. Still he answered calmly, "How would I know, Nana? After all, it's open land. It only takes a split second for a fox to run away with a chicken!"

"True enough! But how could he manage to get a chicken in the pen? Come on now, admit it!"

"Nana, I swear by my child I'm telling you the truth! If you say so, I'll place my hand on my son's head and swear before the *pāṭīl* here."

At that moment the cock crowed loud and long. The cramped and frightened bird cackled noisily. Tatya was speechless. He sat down heavily, as if all the strength had drained out of him.

Hearing the crowing, both kids jumped with glee and ran to the basket, saying, "Mother, show us the chicken!" Meanwhile the policeman and the *pāṭīl* had taken custody of Tatya and set off for the police station. Nana went along, taking his rooster as evidence. Both kids went dancing behind him.

Watching this whole performance Sarji was struck dumb. She was at a loss as to what to say or do. Finally she picked up the bundle of *bhākrīs* and started after her husband. As she set off she made a silent vow, "Goddess Mariai, get my husband out of this! And next year I'll give you a cock!" She put the end of her sari to her eyes to dry her tears.

## EDITORS' NOTES

1. Naikwada indicates the section of a village in which Naiks predominate. The term Naik is usually used for the low but not Untouchable castes of Ramoshi or Berad, but Kharat does not make the caste clear.

2. The goddess Mariai is found in every village and usually is served by Mahars, although as the goddess of pestilence she is worshipped by all.

3. The author, himself an ex-Untouchable brought up in a village, delights in the detail of village life, making the harshness of existence in rural Maharashtra clear through description and dialog.

4. Vahini, lit. brother's wife, is used here in the way that neighbors would use family terms to indicate a respectful familiarity with each other.

5. The *pāṭīl* is the village headman.

# 3

# *One Face of God*

In Shankarrao Kharat's story "Navas" (The Vow) the narrator says:

> Throughout the area the goddess of Degaon was known as a harsh and powerful deity. If a man did not keep his vow, they said, the goddess would raze his house or cast thorny branches in his door. So on the full moon of Chaitra people would go with fear and devotion and would try at any cost to keep their vows.

The devi is harsh and powerful. In Marathi these two adjectives are summed up in a single word—*kaḍak*. The devi of Kharat's story is by no means unique. The picture of a *kaḍak* deity is common throughout Maharashtra and, indeed, throughout India. Many of these deities are goddesses, though some are male gods. Two of the major deities of Maharashtra, the goddess Bhavani and the god Khandoba of Jejuri, are known for being *kaḍak*, in contrast to deities like

Ram and Vithoba who are known as *saumya*—benign or gentle.

Although the *kaḍak* face of god is only one of the faces of god seen in Hinduism, it is an important one for understanding the religion of the ordinary Hindu. To say that a god is *kaḍak* means, first of all, that he is especially powerful. Power, in fact, is the key concept underlying the Hindu concept of divinity. The bewildering range of objects of devotion in Hinduism—extending from a stone uncovered in a field or a gush of water, to rivers, tools, animals, gurus or divine images—becomes comprehensible when we see them all as manifestations of power. Some of these sources of power are transient, others are permanent. Of the latter, the traditional shrines are the most important. Each of them is a center of power—a center with a precise geographic location. This center is the *devasthān*, a word often translated simply as "temple" but meaning literally "the place of the god." Thus a powerful god is not identified simply by his name but by his location as well—such as Bhavani of Tuljapur or Khandoba of Jejuri. Worshippers may build temples and install images of these gods elsewhere, but in most cases these temples will not become as important sources of power as the original shrine.

In other words, though all *devasthāns* are by definition sources of power, in some the power is particularly alive and active. Such *devasthāns* are known as being *kaḍak*, or *jāgṛit* (wakeful), or *jājvalya* (efficacious, powerful). The god of such a place has under his control, or perhaps himself constitutes, the forces of order and chaos that control human life. If he is the *kuladaivat*—the family deity—his worshippers look to him to ensure the well-being of the family, to provide sufficient food along with freedom from sickness and accident. The *kuladaivat*, generally though not always a *kaḍak* god, has in his hands not only the family's well-being but its very continuity. Thus, every major event in the life of the family requires his blessings. A wedding invitation usually bears the inscription, "By the grace of the *kuladaivat*." The first duty of a new bride on entering her in-laws' house for the first time is to do *pūjā* to the *kuladaivat*. The birth of a son and the undertaking of a new business are usually occasions for a visit to the *devasthān* of the *kuladaivat*. Although a family may be spread out geographically, it retains its unity as long as its members acknowledge the gods of one household shrine as their own.

If the worshipper looks to a god to preserve the order and continuity of his own life and that of his family, he is in the greatest need when a crisis threatens that order. A woman who has not borne a son, for instance, may be in a desperate position, for from the family's point of view her chief function is preserving the continuity of the family by bearing sons. Until she has done so she has no standing in the family. Thus she feels under intense pressure and may go to the *kuladaivat* or to some other powerful god to make a *navas*. Along with childless women, people suffering from diseases or from *karṇī* (black magic) also frequently go to make a *navas*. Similarly, a person looking for work or a student about to take an examination may make a *navas* that he may be granted success.

In return for the beneficent use of his power the god demands ritual worship. This may include daily and special worship in the house but it primarily means an annual visit to the *devasthān*. It is here that the annual offerings must be given and any *navas* must be fulfilled. Depending on the means of the worshipper and the preference of the god the offerings may range from coconut and camphor or coconut and a blouse-piece to a chicken or a goat, or a large sum of money or ornaments for the image. For most deities known to be *kaḍak* the preferred offering is the sacrifice of a chicken or a goat. To make such a sacrifice the worshipper takes the live bird or animal to the temple, slaughters it before the god, then cooks it and shares it with his family and friends as *prasād*, a gift from the god.

In performing the ritual, the worshipper must take care to avoid ritual pollution. One of the chief characteristics of a *kaḍak* god is that he will not tolerate ritual impurity. A person who has not taken his morning bath, a woman in her menses, someone who has been in contact with childbirth or death, a member of an Untouchable caste—all are sources of pollution. Even the accidental touch of a worshipper's feet on the image or the offering results in defilement. Of course, the strictness with which these rules are observed varies a great deal from caste to caste and family to family. The lower castes and the poor generally follow a less elaborate code of ritual purity, probably simply because they do not have the leisure or money required for elaborate daily ritual. But, as Kharat's story illustrates, even the poor take care to bathe before preparing food offerings and taking *darshan* of the deity at the *devasthān*.

In looking at the list of what the *kaḍak* god requires, the reader might well have been struck by the absence of any reference to ethical behavior. In the traditional view, the god is concerned only with the individual's worship, not with how that person relates to his fellow-men. People have explicitly told me that rules regarding human relations are a part of *dharma* (right conduct) or a part of *vyavahār* (practical dealings); they are not the concern of the god. The god is not concerned with sin but with the ritual obligations of his followers.

If a person fails to fulfill his obligations, either by not making the required offerings or by defiling the deity, the deity reacts with anger and punishes the offender. The most common punishment is sickness, and it usually takes the most dramatic forms—fever, diarrhea, vomiting, cholera, plague. Even an unintentional act can call forth the wrath of the deity. In talking about the cause of ringworm, one young man said:

> The devi brings it on. If somebody is a devotee and is on his way to make an offering to the devi—if he is busy talking and his foot happens to touch the offering, the devi will show her anger with a sign. She won't stand for pollution.

With such a forbidding picture of the nature of god, one

might imagine that people live in constant fear. Some commentators, in fact, have felt that this is the case, and indeed it cannot be denied that an element of fear—or perhaps anxiety is the more accurate word—exists in some peoples' relations to the *kaḍak* gods. For instance, several years ago in a village in western Maharashtra the head was knocked off the image of a certain rajah's family deity. It is said that the rajah was extremely frightened and hastened to have the image repaired. In Kharat's story the narrator says that people would try at any cost to keep their *navas* to the devi; and Tatya goes to the extent of stealing a chicken for that purpose.

Along with this anxiety goes secretiveness. I had an experience of this several years ago. A woman came and sat down beside me on the bus. In her lap was a basket tied up in a cloth. On top of the basket were a brass tray and two polished bamboo sticks that she told me were required for doing *pūjā* to the devi. From inside the basket came the smell of camphor. The woman had obviously just returned from fulfilling a *navas* but she parried my questions on the subject and clearly did not want to discuss it. Later I inquired and found out that indeed one does not tell anyone about a *navas*.

Still, however, the cases cited above are probably not typical. The average person does not appear to feel a great deal of anxiety about his relationship to any god, however *kaḍak* he may be. There are several factors that serve to mitigate his anxiety. To begin with, the *kaḍak* god—who is usually the *kuladaivat*—is only one of the objects of a person's worship. Along with the *kuladaivat*, more benign gods like Vithoba, and often a god-like person such as a saint, *bābā*, or guru claim a portion of the worshipper's time and attention.

Moreover, the very complexity and sophistication of people's conception of their relation to a god helps to mitigate anxiety. Even the uneducated feel that a god is what his worshippers make him. There is a saying in Marathi *bhāv tasā dev*, "as the belief, so the god." Thus, a god is *kaḍak* only if his believers think he is. When asked about a god's being *kaḍak* some people told me, "It depends on how you feel about it" or "That's just a notion."

Not only does the worshipper determine the nature of the god, but by his act of worship he makes the image into a god. One illiterate man made this clear when he said of an image:

> It's a stone, a piece of rock, an image.
> That image is cast in the shape of a god.
> If we believe in the image it is a god, if
> we don't believe, how is it considered a god?

This same attitude was expressed by an elderly Untouchable. When I asked him what it meant for a god to be *kaḍak*, he answered:

> People mention various gods and then get scared of them. They say, "Let's go to such-and-such a god. Let's give him an offering. Does the god eat the offering? We do, don't we?"

At first I took this to be an expression of complete disbelief, especially as he went on to say:

> What is Khandoba like? Why, do you think we can see him? There's just a rock there and people call it Khandoba. Does it appear before us? No, the god that's set up there they just call Khandoba.

At this point I was convinced that he was a complete skeptic. I asked, "Then you don't believe in Khandoba?" His answer was swift and rather scornful, "Why, do you think I'd set up a stone without faith?"

Such an attitude may at first appear self-contradictory, but further examination reveals that this is not the case. What the man is saying is that he is perfectly aware that it is his faith which invests divinity in a stone, but that this does not make the divinity any less real. This awareness, however, must keep him from being overwhelmed by any sense of anxiety or fear in relation to the god.

The man quoted here might be a little more reflective than many others, but his attitude is probably not much different from that of most average people. Hard-headed and practical, they are very much aware that they are offering worship to a stone which somebody has given the name of Khandoba or some other deity. They know that when they give an offering to the stone the stone doesn't eat it, they do. Still, the stone is not merely a symbol; it is somehow related to the power that determines the well-being of themselves and their families. This power demands worship and they offer it. Because they believe in the efficacy of ritual they need not feel anxious. Some people have told me they are not afraid of a god's anger. Once they have fulfilled their ritual obligations, they say, what is there to worry about? The god is not going to punish them. Casual as this attitude seems, it reveals an important truth—that ritualizing a worshipper's obligations to a god decreases the worshipper's anxiety. If all the god demands are certain acts of worship, then once these are performed the worshipper is secure. Even in a situation of crisis the worshipper is encouraged by the fact that there are active measures he can take—making a *navas*, going on a fast, giving up something. He has, in other words, tools to aid him in facing his fate.

In the ordinary course of life, the worshipper approaches the *kaḍak* god perfunctorily or anxiously, according to his temperament and situation. In either case the encounter tends to be impersonal, since it is mediated by ritual, and the power of the god is a matter of faith rather than experience. But at times some people have what they feel is a direct experience of the beneficent power of a god, and they ever after approach the deity with personal devotion. The young man who talked about the devi's causing ringworm later told of his own experience:

> When I was in the eleventh grade I was very sick and was afraid that I could not pass my examination. But through the blessing and grace of the devi of Tuljapur, our *kuladaivat*, I passed, and since then I have been going to Tuljapur. Unless a person goes there for two or three days he has no peace of mind.

It is perhaps in the experience of possession that a person

has the most direct experience of the power of the god. Though it is generally the *kaḍak* gods who possess people, many of the people possessed feel that the power entering them is beneficent rather than fearful. They feel, as John Stanley has reported, that a special favor has been granted them and has utterly changed them. They strive to keep themselves in a state of readiness so that the god may return. This attitude, of course, is poles apart from fear or anxiety.

Within the framework of belief in a *kaḍak* god, then, a great variety of religious attitudes is possible. The very conception of a *kaḍak* god is, however, by no means universally accepted. It is under attack from a number of quarters. First of all, there is a large number of people who reject polytheism altogether, so for them the conception of a *kaḍak* deity has no relevance. Others accept polytheism but vehemently reject the idea that a god can be *kaḍak*. "A god is *kaḍak*," declared one man. Others said, "My own feeling is that a god is never *kaḍak*," "God is not *kaḍak*, men are," or "I have no experience of this."

Some of these people feel that a god has no power to punish man. As one said, "If I don't go to a temple, what is the goddess going to do?" Others, however, reject the idea of a *kaḍak* god out of the conviction that god is *shānta* (calm and peaceful). A horse-cart driver said emphatically:

> It's false to say god is *kaḍak*. God is *shānta*. What does god require? He doesn't ask for anything. What we offer is for ourselves. We say it's for god and we eat it ourselves.

On the public level too, the *kaḍak* god—or perhaps, the *kaḍak* conception of god—is ignored or played down, perhaps because it smacks of a primitivism that is no longer acceptable. Vithoba, the focus of bhakti in Maharashtra, is patronized by government officials and by All-India Radio. The public neglect of some of the *kaḍak* deities might be explained in terms of caste and class, for some of these deities are those of the lower castes and classes. But this is certainly not true of Khandoba or Bhavani. Yet they also do not have the public prestige of Vithoba, and even when they are presented in the mass media their *kaḍak* aspects are played down and their benevolence emphasized.

Thus the *kaḍak* conception of god is being attacked by those monotheists who reject idol worship, by those polytheists who believe god is *shānta*, not *kaḍak*, and by those public figures who are embarrassed by the "primitivism" of the *kaḍak* conception of god. These attacks are not new. They have been part of the tradition of Hinduism for at least hundreds of years. Yet the *kaḍak* conception of god persists, undoubtedly because it expresses man's deepest anxieties about his fate and gives him tools that offer at least the hope of influencing it.

JOHN M. STANLEY

# 4
# *Gods, Ghosts, and Possession*

There are two phenomena in the popular religion of Maharashtra that bear close comparative examination. One is known as *bhūt bādhā*, the possession of a person by a ghost; the other is *angāt yeṇe*, the possession of a person by a deity or a saint.[1] On first examination there seem to be good reasons to assume that the two phenomena are closely related. Indeed the observable actions of *bhūt bādhā* (ghost-possessed) victims are strikingly similar to those of many *angāt ālelī* (god-possessed)—a fact which has not infrequently led to a confusion of the two phenomena by casual observers. And the subjective feelings reported by many possessed people, especially in the early stages of possession, indicate some ambiguity as to whether it is a god or a ghost that has taken possession of them. Moreover, several scholars of the same type of phenomena in other cultures have emphasized their similarity.

Curious about the relationship between these two phenomena, I carried out field work for several months in the cities and villages of four districts in Maharashtra—Ahmednagar, Pune, Satara, and Aurangabad. Aided by a most valuable interpreter and research assistant, S.V. Patankar of Pune, I made observations at fifteen different healing centers and interviewed over one hundred people including *pujārīs* at healing temples, monks of the Mahanubhav *panth*,[2] *mujāvars* of *dargās* (tombs of Muslim saints, many of which are considered powerful healing centers), *bhūt* victims, relatives of *bhūt* victims, and former victims now cured. I also made observations of seventy instances of *angāt yeṇe* and conducted interviews with twenty *angāt ālelī* representing possession by eleven different gods or saints. On the basis of these observations and interviews I conclude that, though there are some clear surface similarities, Maharashtrian culture makes a sharp distinction between the two phenomena. Moreover, when the phenomena are analyzed as religious experience, they can clearly be seen as polar opposites.

### *Bhūt Bādhā—Possession by a Ghost: Traditional and Present Day Beliefs*

The traditional Maharashtrian beliefs regarding *bhūts* and *bhūt bādhā* have been recorded with exceptional thoroughness by a variety of nineteenth century ethnographers. Especially helpful are a series of reports submitted by hospital assistants and assistant surgeons at hospitals in the Deccan districts of the Bombay Presidency. These reports have been gathered together in the appendix to the Poona district volume (1885) of the *Gazetteer of the Bombay Presidency*. R.E. Enthoven (1924) has also catalogued a great deal of folklore about spirit possession that is relevant to Maharashtra as have William Crooke (1896 and 1968) and Sir James Campbell (see the Kolhapur volume of the *Gazetteer*), who gathered together material based on questionnaires submitted to school children about belief in ghosts and ghost possession. According to the beliefs recorded in these reports, *bhūts* come into being either as the result of inadequate or incomplete funeral rites[3] or through the untimely death of a person who dies with intense unfulfilled desires (e.g., a pregnant woman, a woman who dies in childbirth, a miser who dies suddenly without having a chance to spend his money, etc.). Though they can assume a great variety of forms at will (e.g., a blaze of fire, a whirlwind, various forms of animals, monsters, etc.), *bhūts* most often take some kind of human or semi-human form. They cast no shadow, speak with a nasal twang, cannot stand the odor of burning turmeric, and usually have reversed feet; they generally inhabit unused or polluted wells, cellars, woods, old tanks, privies, cemeteries, and generally any defiled or polluted place. Since, according to traditional beliefs, the earth has the power to frighten away evil influences, *bhūts* never sit on the ground; rather they perch in trees, on grave stones, or on pegs or bricks. *Bhūts* are not immortal; they continue in existence for approximately four human generations after which they are reborn according to the law of karma, the actions done as *bhūts* affecting their lives no less than actions performed during their human lives.

The popular tradition in Maharashtra developed an elaborate system for identifying and categorizing varieties of *bhūts*. The *Gazetteers* list over twenty such varieties which are organized into three categories: *bhūt* (in the narrow sense), *pishāça*, and *pret*. A *bhūt* in the narrow sense is thought of as any ghost resulting from a violent or sudden death; a *pishāça* is a ghost of an immoral person such as a liar, adulterer, or criminal; a *pret* (literally corpse) is thought of as a monstrous or deformed ghost, the result of incomplete burial rites. *Bhūts* are further sub-divided into *gharçe bhūt* (house *bhūts*) which attack only members of their own family, and *bāherçe bhut* (outside *bhūts*) which can attack and possess anyone.

When planning to attack a victim, the *bhūt* assumes a pleasing and desirable form to attract the attention of a passer-by, changing suddenly into a monstrous form in which it attacks and enters the body of the victim. Such possession by a *bhūt* results in some form of sickness—occasionally physical, more often emotional, and sometimes both. In the reports of the nineteenth-century ethnographers most cases of *bhūt bādhā* are attributed to the volition of the *bhūt*. *Bhūts* are assumed to attack either because they are provoked (e.g., by someone bumping into their tree or grave stone or peg, or because they need to possess a body to carry out certain intense desires that they were not able to fulfill in their lifetime). On certain occasions, however, according to traditional beliefs, some *māntriks* (practitioners of black magic) or *devṛishīs* (professional shamans) will use their magical powers to influence a *bhūt* to possess a specific person.[4] When this is done, the process is referred to as *karṇī*. *Karṇī* is looked on as a form of "black magic." It is socially unacceptable, and apparently in the nineteenth century it was quite rare.

Present day beliefs among Maharashtrians about the existence and actions of *bhūts* correspond in many ways to the beliefs outlined by the nineteenth-century ethnographers. There are, however, some interesting and noteworthy differences. One difference is that the many distinctions between different kinds of *bhūts* are no longer made. *Pret* is no longer used at all, and no functional distinction is made between *bhūt* and *pishāça*. Only a few of the people I talked to recognized any distinction between *gharçe bhūt* and *bāherçe bhūt*. Those who did thought the house/outside distinction unimportant. Moreover, the numerous different varieties of *bhūts* mentioned in the *Gazetteer* are no longer even recognized by most informants. When I would ask someone what kind of *bhūt* was possessing their friend or relative, the typical answer would be "some *bhūt* or *karṇī*—how can one know?"

A second difference between traditional beliefs and present day beliefs is that *bhūts* are no longer thought to be visible. They can, of course, be heard speaking through the mouths of their victims. Their actions can be observed in the actions of the possessed bodies of the victims. But, with two exceptions, none of the people I talked to claimed ever to have seen a *bhūt*. One exception was an *angāt ālelā* who specialized in exorcising *bhūts* and claimed that when he looked into the eyes of a possessed person, he saw the *bhūt* that was possessing him rather than the person. He never, however, saw *bhūts* except in the bodies of possessed people. The other exception was an old woman who reported she had seen *bhūts* when she was between the ages of twenty and twenty-five (1925–30). During those years she saw *bhūts* on several different occasions: once at a river at night, once immediately after she had given birth, once in a woods near a burning ghat, etc. On one occasion she saw the *bhūt* very clearly and noticed that its feet were turned backwards. She has not seen any *bhūt* since she was a young woman and thinks that now all *bhūts* have become invisible. She still, however, believes that they exist and she continues the observance of practices to guard her children against *bhūt bādhā*.

A third difference between traditional beliefs about *bhūt bādhā* and current beliefs is that present day beliefs place much stronger emphasis on *karṇī*. A rather elastic term, *karṇī* literally means "something done," the connotations of the term being that some black magic has been done against one. Sometimes the term *karṇī* can be used to refer simply to a curse or a spell such as love magic. Most often, however, the term is used to refer to *bhūt bādhā* which has been magically induced by a *devṛishī* or *māntrik*.

*Karṇī* is mentioned in the *Gazetteers* only briefly and the reports clearly imply that it was considered rare. This is still the case in small villages where people know each other well, and where none of the *devṛishīs* are suspected of practicing black magic. For example, in the village of Chambli near Saswad and again the village of Wadi Bolhai near Theur, villagers reported several cases of *bhūt bādhā* in the past year. They insisted, however, that all the cases were caused by people carelessly disturbing *bhūts* and that the possessions were the result of the *bhūt's* own volition. They were indignant that I should even think that any of the village *devṛishīs* or *māntriks* would do *karṇī* against anyone in the village. Nor did they think it likely that any evil influence of this kind could have come from someone outside the village. Except in these small villages, the people I talked to about *bhūt bādhā* attributed the majority of the cases to *karṇī*. There are, to be sure, exceptions. One victim thought that he had carelessly provoked a *bhūt* attack by disturbing a *bhūt* while going near his tree to urinate. Another informant reported that his friend had virtually invited a *bhūt* attack by crossing a river near midnight while in an unclean state. Another attributed his own *bhūt* attack to his having carelessly stepped over an offering at a three cornered *çauk* (a crossroad where three roads meet), which is considered an excellent place to get rid of a *bhūt* once you have successfully exorcised it from the body of a member of your family by a home cure. The belief is that by carrying an offering of rice balls, lime, and *kunkū* to the three cornered *çauk* you can lure the *bhūt* to accompany you. It is believed that the offering will hold the *bhūt* at the *çauk* for a short time and then it will "go on its way." I have observed many such offerings at Baba Jan Chowk in Pune camp and at other three cornered *çauk*s throughout Pune. Most Maharashtrians, however well educated, will avoid stepping over these rice ball, lime, and *kunkū* offerings lest the *bhūt* lingering by the offering attack and take possession of them.

But these instances of *bādhā*, as the result of the *bhūt's* own volition, though not rare, are not nearly as prevalent, especially in urban areas, as *bādhā* induced by *karṇī*. Moreover *bādhā* that is initiated by *bhūt* is generally believed to be much more easily exorcised because the *bhūt's* will by itself is usually not as strong as a person's will. One trip to a healing center normally suffices, and often even that one trip is not necessary since home cures are relatively effective against the unaided will of a *bhūt*. *Karṇī*, however, is quite a different matter, for in these cases the *bhūt's* will is strengthened forcefully either by the power of a *devṛishī* or a *māntrik* or by a vow (*navas*) to a god. *Bādhā* induced by *karṇī* is extremely hard to cure, the average case requiring from one to two months at most healing centers.

There are two ways that *karṇī* can be done. First, some *māntriks* and *devṛishīs* are willing to use their magical powers for evil or anti-social ends. One can go to such a person and pay him to perform *karṇī* against an enemy. The strength of this kind of *karṇī* depends on three things: the power of the *devṛishī* over ghosts, the weakness of the will of the person having the *karṇī* worked against him, and that person's susceptibility to *bhūt* entry. *Karṇī* can, however, also be effected without the assistance of a *devṛishī*. Any individual can go to a temple of any god who receives vows (*navas*) and make a vow to give the god something or to go through some ordeal if the god will send a *bhūt* to possess his enemy. Most of the people I talked to held that gods would seldom use their influence over *bhūts* in this way. Many, however, thought that if the bhakti (devotion) of the person was strong enough or the ordeal the person vowed to go through intense enough, the god would do as he was requested. *Karṇī* of this second type is thought to be extremely strong and very difficult to cure. Its strength depends on four things: the power of the god over the *bhūt*, the extent of the bhakti of the person asking the curse (the severity of the vow taken is usually thought to be an outward sign of the extent of the bhakti), the weakness of the will of the victim, and again, his susceptibility to *bhūt* entry.

The susceptibility of persons to *bhūt* entry requires some additional explanation. Answers to my questions about how *bhūts* can enter people provided a wealth of explanations. An examination of all the answers indicates that the crucial variable affecting susceptibility to *bhūt* entry is the purity-pollution status of the individual—especially as that is affected by the menstrual cycle, childbirth, sexual intercourse, and urination. Repeatedly it was explained to me that women are more susceptible to *bhūt* entry than men, that women are especially susceptible during their menstrual period or immediately after childbirth, and that anyone is especially susceptible immediately after urination because spirits frequently enter the body through the urinary passages. Some claim that newly-married couples are especially liable to *bhūt* attack for as long a time as any *haḷad* (turmeric powder used at weddings) still clings to their bodies. Frequently it was mentioned that a married person who takes up his daily duties without bathing after sexual intercourse is inviting *bhūt bādhā*. One man, a Muslim, claimed that *bhūts* nearly always enter the body through the urinary passage and that any uncleanness there, even the smallest drop of urine remaining on the body after urination, would invite *bhūts*. The male is fortunate in that circumcision can protect him against such uncleanness, and this is the reason, my informant claimed, that all Muslim men are circumcised and explains why among men more Hindus are possessed by *bhūts* than Muslims and among both Hindus and Muslims more women are possessed than men.

How prevalent are these beliefs in present day Maharashtra? In large villages, even those near cities, active belief in *bhūt bādhā* and *karṇī* is very high. In all of my interviews I was able to find only one outright skeptic. This man, a resident of the village of Kharpudi near Nimgaon, believed unquestionably in the ability of gods to possess people, but laughed at my question about *bhūt bādhā*. He said, "Some people in the village think that they are suffering from *bādhā* when they have a headache or a backache, but it is not so. I know many people now who go to the cemetery at night and even sleep there all night without being affected by a *bhūt* or a *pishāça*." For the most part, however, villagers not only believe in the existence of *bhūts* and the possibility of possession, they actively use the notion of *bhūt bādhā* to explain many of the problems and illnesses that they encounter in daily life. In cities such active belief in *bhūt bādhā* is considerably less prevalent than in villages; it is, however, more prevalent than I had expected it to be. The average daily attendance at one healing center in Pune is two hundred or more. On Fridays it is slightly higher; on Thursdays (a special day for this healing center) crowds are as large as nine hundred. In Bombay several hundred come daily to the Mira Datar healing center near Reay Road Station while each Thursday between four and five thousand people come between four-thirty in the morning when the center opens and midnight when it closes.

While a relatively small percentage of city dwellers seem to be active believers in *bhūt bādhā*, there are indications that passive credence in *bādhā* is considerably higher. One Western trained doctor who does not believe in possession by gods does not doubt at all the existence of *bhūts* and their power to possess people. Many highly educated Indians, though reluctant to admit active belief, refuse, when pushed, to say that they do not believe in *bhūt bādhā*. A typical response to my questions was, "I would not usually explain what seems to be for the most part neurotic problems that way, and I am sure those cures would never work for my own problem; still, it must be that 'these people' are taken over by something and that they are cured at the *dargā* (healing center)."

In one case I found confirmation about belief in *bādhā* where I least expected to find it. A highly educated Shankaracharya monk was in Pune giving a series of lectures on yoga. In an interview I asked him what he thought about *bādhā*. He answered, "I have seen a great deal of this so-called *bādhā*. In ninety-eight percent of the cases it is a psychic disorder. After a few sessions with breathing exercises and elementary concentration I would cure them so that they would never have the trouble again." I asked about the other two percent. He answered, "In two percent of the cases there is actual possession by a power (we might as well call it *bhūt*). It is the psychic substance of a dead person. In rare cases when one dies with a great unfulfilled longing for another person, the psychic powers of the deceased do not disperse immediately, and, if the situation is right, these powers will enter the body of the desired person." I asked, further, if he had any direct evidence of this. He answered, "I have seen a possessed person who had knowledge that was private to the deceased. I have seen another person who, when possessed, could speak a language which he did not know but which the deceased person did."

### *Bhūt Bādhā and Karṇī: Discovery, Prognosis, and Cure*

The first signs of *bhūt bādhā* or *karṇī* are usually noticed only by the victims. They will begin to feel "wrong," they may have headaches or backaches, or just feel "bad" or "not right." Frequently there will be specific pains such as sharp pains like pin pricks in the mouth or throat or, more commonly, in the urinary passage. At this stage, though they feel "wrong," there is nothing in their overt behavior to indicate *bhūt bādhā* to others.

At the next stage, the effects of *bhūt bādhā* can be noticed by others as well as the *bhūt* victim. Everything the victim does starts going wrong; his business falls off or he loses his job for no apparent reason. He may quarrel with close friends or have frequent or severe arguments with his wife and children. The "wrongness" seems to come in waves. At times the victim feels quite all right and begins to think there was nothing to it after all. Then things go wrong again. Most victims even at this stage will refuse to believe that they are victims of *bhūt bādhā* unless they actually experience a cure. A businessman from Bombay put it this way, "I didn't really think that there was any *bādhā* or *karṇī*. I had headaches. My business was going wrong. I didn't feel right. Then my brother convinced me to come here (Mira Wali Darga, Ahmednagar). What harm could it do? As soon as the *āratī* (ceremony of lights) began, I became unconscious. Later people told me that I was shaking all over and acting just like that (pointing to another person who was shaking violently). I think now it must be *karṇī*." For many victims these will be the only symptoms. Both their pain and illness and their feeling of "wrongness" will become progressively worse as the *bhūt* or "spell" (it will be difficult at this stage to tell which it is) takes hold of more and more of their personality. Many victims, however, will experience further symptoms and enter a third stage, where they will become very depressed and "sit quietly" for long periods of time. They will not follow orders, frequently fail to respond when spoken to, and often sit and stare straight ahead. If you ask them to do a task or errand, they may go to the place you ask them to go, but they will not complete the errand. They will just sit down at that place or somewhere along the way and stare at something. Then, as the *bhūt* gets a deeper hold on the personality, the person will lose all control of his emotions and begin to weep and sob.

In the final stage the symptoms become even more severe. The entire body shakes and shivers uncontrollably. The shivers become progressively worse, ending in wild gyrations and thrashing movements which often result in physical harm. Usually before the *bhūt* victim has reached this stage, he has sought medical aid of some sort, found that it did not help, and has been persuaded by relatives or friends to go to a healing center.

There are three different kinds of healing centers in Maharashtra: (1) *Dargās* or *chillas* of Muslim *pīrs* and *samādhīs* of Hindu saints, (2) temples of the Mahanubhav sect, and (3) temples of certain healing gods such as Kal Bhairav and Dattatreya.[5] A *dargā* is a burial place of the body of a Muslim *pīr* (a saint in the Sufi tradition who, because of the degree of his spiritual realization, is believed to possess great powers, which continue to emanate from his burial place). Although all *pīrs* are believed to have developed great powers, only a few *pīrs* developed powers over *bhūts*. Consequently only a few *dargās* are centers of exorcism. A *chilla* is a memorial to a *pīr*. The *pīr* is not buried in the *chilla*, but, through some association with the *pīr* such as an article of clothing, the *chilla* holds some of the *pīr's* powers, though less of them than the *dargā* does, and releases them in the same way as the *dargā*.

Though each healing center will have its individual characteristics, the basic pattern of cure and the behavior of spirit victims is strikingly the same at all healing centers.

The god or *pīr* at any center is known as "*bābā.*" The *bābā* is believed to have a special power over *bhūts*—a power which both stimulates the *bhūt* to greater activity and causes it intense pain. This power is present at the healing center all of the time and continually flows forth, disturbing and punishing any nearby *bhūt.* Anyone possessed by a *bhūt* (even if he didn't know he was possessed) would feel this power merely by walking near a *dargā* or a healing temple.

Normally the *bābā's* power flows forth at a relatively low intensity, but that power increases at special times. Each healing center has one day each year when its power is believed to be greatest. In addition, *pūrṇimās* (full moon days) and *amāvāsyās* (no moon days) are especially powerful healing times at Hindu temples; every Thursday is a special day at all *dargās* as is every Friday at Mahanubhav *maṭhs* and temples. More important than these weekly, monthly, and annual variations, there are certain times each day that the *bābā's* power reaches its highest intensity. Each of these times (the frequency varies from one center to another) is marked by certain ceremonies. *Āratī* is performed, drums are beaten, gongs are rung, and, at *dargās*, incense is burned in large quantities. It is during these special times, marked by *āratī*, that the *bābā's* power reaches an intensity sufficient to drive out *bhūt* and cure *karṇī.*

The *bābā's* power over a *bhūt* is also increased by the faith of the *bhūt* victim. In some cases, when *karṇī* is not involved or *bhūt bādhā* is exceptionally weak, *bhūts* can be driven from people without their active faith. Indeed it is believed that *bābās* drive out many minor *bhūts* without the possessed person even knowing it. In more severe cases, however, faith is required to raise the intensity of the power to a level sufficient to cure *bhūt bādhā.*

Spirit victims arrive at healing centers either by themselves or, if the case is severe, accompanied by friends. In some of the more severe cases, they begin to tremble and moan as soon as they come near the *dargā* or temple. Most, however, do not manifest this symptom until the *āratī* begins. At the first sound of the drum or gong marking the beginning of *āratī*, nearly all *bhūt* victims begin shaking, twisting, and moaning. Some faint and fall on the ground where they remain unconscious. Some writhe on the ground in apparent pain. Many swing their head and torso in a circular motion. Most do this while seated, some while standing. I observed one man, feet placed wide apart, bend from the waist and swing the upper half of his body in a circle at an incredibly fast rate. At each gyration his head very nearly touched the ground. Several victims throw their heads violently up and down letting their long hair fly and snap like a whip. Some become frozen in a rigid cataleptic trance. Several roll slowly over and over on the stone paving of the courtyard. It seems a miracle that they are not trampled. "Baba takes care of them," I am told; "only the *bhūts* are hurt." There is a great deal of screaming and moaning. Indeed, the impression is that the entire crowd is experiencing tremendous pain. As soon as the *āratī* ceases, most of the screaming and writhing stops and most victims abruptly regain normal consciousness. They appear puzzled for a moment, then smile, brush themselves off and begin normal conversations with people around them.

How can this behavior be explained? It would seem on the surface that *bhūt* victims are possessed only during *āratī* and that the *bhūt* abruptly leaves them as soon as the *āratī* ceases. Indeed this phenomenon causes some observers to come to the erroneous conclusion that it is the *bābā* or god who has possessed the person during the *āratī*. But this is not at all how the situation is perceived by those experiencing it. It is just that the *bhūt* has become exceptionally active during the *āratī*. Normally, a *bhūt* possessing a person occupies only a small portion of the person's personality. Upon nearing a healing center, however, the *bhūt* begins to feel the effect of the *bābā's* power and becomes agitated and aggressive. Then under the intense pain inflicted on him by the *bābā* during *āratī*, the *bhūt* becomes very active and takes over the entire personality of the victim, leaving him totally unconscious. When the *āratī* is over the *bābā* relaxes the punishment and the *bhūt*, exhausted, withdraws into the recesses of his victim's personality, thus allowing the person to regain consciousness feeling somewhat better. But it is not thought that the *bhūt* leaves the victim altogether when the *ārati* ceases.

As for the nature of the pain, every spirit victim that I interviewed insisted that he was totally unconscious during the entire time that he manifested the symptoms of hyperactivity and pain, that he was absolutely unaware of anything that he did, and that he would never know what he did unless people told him afterwards, and that, when told, he was, at first, quite surprised that he had acted in that way. The *mujāvars* and *pujārīs* of the healing centers told me that it was absolutely essential that the victim be totally unconscious during this period because, if he were not unconscious, he would die, so great is the pain. The more powerful a *bābā*, the more extreme the pain. But all of the pain, all of the writhing and all of the agonies are experienced only by the *bhūt*. The person himself, entirely unconscious, feels nothing.

In some cases these agonies are not merely psychic, but quite palpable. On two occasions I observed cases where there seemed to be a real danger that what appeared to be the *bhūt's* actions would do physical harm to the body the *bhūt* was apparently filling. In one case, a girl about twelve years old began to throw herself head first against a stone pillar. She would take several running steps, put her head down and butt it into the pillar with a sickeningly loud crack. At the time, I was interviewing another girl who had been possessed by a *bhūt* seven years earlier and had been cured. She saw my anxiety for the young girl and immediately assured me that the girl felt nothing and would come to no harm. "*Bābā* will take care of her," she assured me, adding that striking one's head against stone was a very effective punishment for a *bhūt* and that she herself used to do that during *ārati* when she was possessed. She explained that she would be completely unconscious and would not feel anything, but later people would tell her that she had pounded her head many times against the stone.

As soon as the *āratī* stopped she would feel quite all right and experience no pain even though her head was occasionally bruised and lacerated. The bruises and cuts would heal quickly upon the application of water from the tank at the healing center. Indeed, twenty minutes later, I observed the same young girl who had been bashing her head against the pillar. *Āratī* was over. She seemed quite normal. She was smiling and talking with a friend.

All healing centers claim a high percentage of cure for *bhūt bādhā* victims who come regularly to *āratī* sessions. Most of the cures are said to require only a few weeks; some, as long as a year. Although I was not able to test these claims in any rigorous way, my conversations with spirit victims and friends and relatives of victims, as well as with people who had been cured, confirmed the claims without exception. Nearly all who come regularly are, after a certain period of time, fully restored to feeling their former selves. Some few do come to sessions regularly for years without complete recovery, but even in these "incurable" cases the relatives and friends of the *bhūt bādhā* victim report that the sessions help the individual a great deal—especially that they feel much better immediately after an *āratī* session.

### *Angāt Yeṇe:* Possession by the Divine

*Angāt yeṇe* is ecstatic possession by a god, *pīr*, or saint. It is a religious phenomenon that plays an important role in the cults of several Maharashtrian gods as well as the cults surrounding a number of Hindu saints, Muslim *pīrs*, and Hindu-Muslim saints. Not all Maharashtrian gods possess their devotees. Khandoba, Mhasoba, Mhaskoba, Vetal, Kal Bhairav, Jyotiba, and Dattatreya occasionally possess their devotees, but not Ganesh, Ram, Shiva, Krishna, Vithoba, Hanuman, or Vishnu. The goddess Ekvira does possess her devotees, as does Bhavani, Janubai, Kalubai, Ambabai, Jogabai, Banabai, Yamai, Mahalaxmi; but Parvati, Saraswati, Sita, and Gauri do not.[6] Few Muslim *pīrs* possess their followers, but among those who do are the seventy-two Shi'ia Muslim saint-heroes of the massacre at Karbala. At the time of Muharram, and, in some cases, frequently throughout the year, these *pīrs* possess the bodies of some of their devotees. During their possession, the devotees carry a *panjā* (a wooden pole about five feet high garlanded with flowers and capped with an image of a large hand cut out of cardboard and covered with silver paper). The *panjā* symbolizes the *pīr*. Interestingly, in spite of the fact that Muharram is a Shi'ia celebration and that the seventy-two *pīrs* are Shi-ia saints, in Pune some of the *panjā* bearers are Hindus and most of the others are Sunni Muslims. Very few Shi'ias carry *panjās* in Pune, though some keep them in shrines in their homes during the six days from the fourth to the tenth of the month of Muharram.

The observable symptoms of *angāt yeṇe* vary somewhat both from cult to cult and from individual to individual. There is usually some form of ritual preparation. This may be very simple and brief such as burning some incense and eating a lime. The incense purifies the temple or shrine, and the lime purifies the body of the *angāt ālelā* so that the god can enter. Or the preparation may involve recitation of mantras and prayers, singing of *bhajans*, or, in the case of the *pīrs*, brushing of the face with peacock feathers which are also believed to have purifying powers. After this ritual preparation, possession, for some *angāt ālelī*, will come very suddenly. They may shout out the name of their god and immediately lose consciousness, or they may simply collapse into unconsciousness. For others possession will come more gradually, accompanied by a great deal of stretching of the arms and back, and yawning. Whatever the pattern, once it is established for an individual, it usually remains the same for future possessions.

The nature of the trance also varies considerably. Some *angāt ālelī* will become absolutely rigid, every muscle tensed, head to one side in a cataleptic trance. Some will sit quietly and stare straight ahead. Some will shout and scream; some will make no sound at all except to speak in a low toneless voice when they are functioning as mediums. Most *angāt ālelī*, however, exhibit hyperactivity usually manifest in some kind of dance, such as jumping up and down in short hops like a boxer in training jumping rope, or rocking back and forth in a shuffling motion like a dancer doing a slow samba, or spinning around in circles, either individually or two at a time, facing each other and holding hands. In nearly all cases there is a rapid increase in breathing. In the case of most devi *angāt yeṇe* this rapid breathing is accompanied by a sputtering sound produced by forcing the breath out between the lips which are held tightly pressed together. Although the rapid breathing seems to be involuntary, the sound is (at least sometimes) intentional and can be used as technique to bring on possession more rapidly. Devi *angāt ālelī* also seem to especially enjoy the trance itself. Those who are semi-conscious speak of it as an experience of great joy. Some admit that they use the sputtering-breathing technique to try to sustain the trance when they feel it slipping away. Others say they use the technique, when they feel the trance coming on, to reach out to the goddess and hasten her arrival. Devi *angāt ālelī* speak of the trance as the "play" of the goddess with them and their facial expressions are nearly always rapturous and joyous, which is not at all the case with other *angāt ālelī*.

The places where possessions occur also vary a great deal depending both on the individual and on the cult. Some *angāt ālelī* become possessed only at the temple of their god, some only in front of their family shrines in their homes; some can be possessed anywhere. Khandoba possession seems to be especially dependent on certain locations. Most of the Khandoba *angāt ālelī* interviewed said they were possessed only at or near a Khandoba temple or during a procession while close to the *pālkhī* (palanquin).

The ages of the *angāt ālelī* I interviewed varied from seventeen to fifty-five years (average thirty-five years); the ages at which they were first possessed varied from five to forty years (average seventeen years); the educational level varied from second to twelfth standard (average seventh);

1. Murlis (women dedicated to Khandoba) chant Khandoba's one hundred names to protect John M. Stanley from ghosts as he studies possession in Maharashtra. *Photo courtesy of John M. Stanley.*

2. A Khandoba *pujārī* puts on his ceremonial clothing, preparing to invite Khandoba to possess him. *Photography by John M. Stanley.*

the length of possession each time varied from two minutes to four hours (average forty-five minutes); the frequency varied from twice a week to once a year (average about once a month). Castes represented were Maratha, Chitpavan Brahman, Saraswat, Koli, Dhobi, Vanjari, and Muslim. Nearly all were reasonably well to do and highly respected members of their community.

About two-thirds of the *angāt ālelī* I interviewed claimed that they were completely unconscious during possession. They claimed they could hear nothing, see nothing, feel nothing, and remember nothing afterwards. They said that they felt that the god took over their body completely and that it was as if they had died for that period of time. One (a *panjā* bearer) claimed that he had some sensation of existing and moving about, but could hear nothing and feel nothing and could see only an image of a *panjā*. This he could see clearly but it appeared to be some distance off. About one-third of the *angāt ālelī* I interviewed claimed that they remained semi-conscious during their possession. One, possessed by Khandoba during a procession, claimed he could see the procession, see where he was going, vaguely see faces of other pilgrims that he recognized, but that it was as if he were not really there, but dreaming it. The visions were unreal to him; moreover he was totally unaware of anything the god said to others through him. Another claimed that he could see quite clearly and would recognize faces until someone possessed by a *bhūt* would come before him. Then he would see the *bhūt* instead of the person. My observations indicate that some, such as the *panjā* bearers, are indeed totally unconscious most of the time and must be led to keep from injuring themselves. Others (including some who claimed to be totally unconscious) are clearly able to see where they are going, to shout at people in their way and to focus their eyes when they need to (e.g., to move people out of their way or to give a menacing look to a foreign scholar who has become too curious).

A distinction must be made between *angāt yeṇe* and

power infusion. In some cases, especially in the Khandoba cult, a person will gain sudden extraordinary powers sufficient to run great distances in front of the god's *pālkhī* or to break heavy iron chains. Or, occasionally, one who has never before been possessed may be suddenly overcome if the god's *pālkhī* passes near him in procession. These religious experiences, though closely related to *angāt yeṇe*, are not usually considered *angāt yeṇe* by the people who experience them. They are rather considered a momentary infusion of the god's power, a gift to them because of their faith. For example, Vaghyas (men dedicated to life-long service of Khandoba) in the Khandoba cult become filled with Khandoba's power and perform feats of chain-breaking at festivals, but they insist that no Vaghya is ever possessed by Khandoba. The breaking of the chains is possible for them because, through their faith, Khandoba fills them momentarily with his power. The god himself, however, does not enter their bodies.

Nearly all *angāt ālelī* perform some extraordinary feats or mighty works as a result of their possession, such as holding burning camphor in their hands or mouths or performing a material manifestation, causing *kunkū* powder to magically appear in their hands or *pān* to suddenly appear in their mouths. An extreme example of this kind of mighty work is walking or dancing on fire. Though it no longer plays an active role in the Khandoba cults, this rite is still an important part of the religious experience of several of the *panjā* bearers at Muharram. I was able to observe a performance of the fire walking rite on *Kattal kī rāt* (the first night of Muharram) in March, 1971, and again in December, 1978, in Pune Camp between Baba Jan Chowk and Mahatma Gandhi Road. Shortly after becoming possessed, the *panjā* bearer, holding his *panjā* cradled in his arms and swaying forwards and backwards in a rocking motion, approaches a bed of coals about six to eight inches deep. The coals are red hot, the ashes having been fanned away. He steps directly onto the coals and stamps his feet gently and continues swaying in a rocking motion. Attendants brush away the live coals that continue to cling to the top of his feet and ankles. He experiences no pain. More amazingly, his feet are not burned at all. The concentration resulting from the possession has not only rendered the *angāt ālelā* insensitive to pain (not difficult to understand) but has apparently (and this far more difficult to understand) altered the kindling point of the flesh on his feet. Within three weeks after observing this rite I interviewed two of the *panjā* bearers I had seen walk on the fire (interestingly one was a Hindu and the other a Sunni Muslim). I also talked briefly to four others whom I had not observed, and I examined all of their feet very thoroughly. There was absolutely no trace of either burn or scar on any of the feet. All claimed that they had continued to walk on their "burned feet" for from two to four hours that night and from four to six hours the next day. When they emerged from the trance, their feet, they said, were quite normal; there was no pain at all—only a slight feeling of tiredness.

The mighty works that I've just described are not to be confused with tests of possession. Like the tests, they signify possession but they are informal indicators; in themselves, outside the formal context of a test of possession, these indicators are considered neither a necessary nor a sufficient condition of authentic possession. Most of the *angāt ālelī* performing these feats have already passed formal tests. If they haven't, these feats are no substitute; if they have, these feats are considered further signs of the power of the possessing god or *pīr*.

In addition to performing the mighty works as signs of possession, most *angāt ālelī* also function as mediums and, in that role, perform mighty works that are socially useful, such as healing sickness, casting out *bhūts*, etc. All of the *angāt ālelī* I interviewed regard the power to perform mighty works of this type as a great gift from their god and the most important aspect of their possession. During possession the *angāt ālelā*—or, more correctly, as he would see it, the god who has possessed him—gives advice about personal and business matters, finds lost articles and stray animals, and sometimes cures sickness and casts out *bhūts*. In most cases those persons seeking help must come before the *angāt ālelā* and put a question to the god or *pīr*. In some cases, however, the *angāt ālelā* reads the thoughts of the person even before he speaks, tells him why he has come for help, and provides the necessary assistance. Some *angāt ālelī* specialize in certain types of mediumship. For example, one Khandoba *angāt ālelā* I interviewed in Khondapur had become a specialist in finding lost articles and stray animals. He had developed his powers to the extent that by going to the Khandoba temple and praying he could successfully invite the possession of Khandoba whenever his services were needed to find things.

Those *angāt ālelī* who become well known for their correct answers, good advice, and powerful cures develop a large following. The Khondapur *angāt ālelā* just mentioned, for example, is highly regarded in his own and nearby villages. Indeed, according to the villagers, he had just the day before I interviewed him found a boy and two bullocks who had been lost for some time. There was great relief throughout the village.

Of all the *angāt ālelī* I interviewed the most highly regarded for her powers was the wife of a high court judge in Bombay. She is possessed from time to time by three different goddesses. Banabai (one of the wives of Khandoba) and Bhavani possess her when personal advice and answers to questions are needed. Kali possesses her if her powers are needed for *bhūt* exorcism. Her powers are widely known and people come to her from all over Maharashtra. Each Friday (interestingly not the usual day for devi possession) there is a long queue outside her Bombay home.

*Angāt ālelī* are not professional shamans. They accept no payment for their services. Indeed, most feel that their powers are a gift that they must share. Some express the belief that they would lose their power if they ever accepted payment. Others indicate that their powers are increased in proportion to their willingness to share them and their ability to help others.

## *Comparisons and Analysis of the Two Forms of Possession*

*Bhūt bādhā* and *angāt yeṇe* can be analyzed and compared on two levels: as ordinary human experience, and as religious experience.

On the level of ordinary human experience there seem to be several good *prima facie* reasons to stress the similarities between the experience of *bhūt bādhā* and that of *angāt yeṇe*. The physical actions of *angāt ālelī*, for example, are similar in many ways to the actions of *bhūt* possessed persons who have come under the influence of a *bābā's* power. In both cases the body usually shakes uncontrollably; the person loses consciousness; there is hyperactivity to the point of incredible physical exertion; the person in question does not seem to be himself; he performs actions that he could not or would not perform if he were himself; indeed he seems to be (and firmly believes that he is) taken over by another being. Then, too, there are two facts about the experience of the people I have studied that indicate that there is a possibility of the two phenomena being subjectively confused: the fact that the culture provides tests for *angāt yeṇe* (one of the reasons for the tests being the fear that the possessing agent may be a *bhūt*) and the fact that some *angāt ālelī* testify that when they first experienced possession, they feared that it might be a *bhūt*. They were not subjectively certain that it was not a *bhūt* until they passed a test. These cases are, however, relatively rare. Only three of the twenty *angāt ālelī* I interviewed spoke of such fears. For most people *angāt yeṇe* is immediately subjectively self-authenticating. Still, that some *angāt ālelī* are initially uncertain and that culture provides a test to distinguish between the two phenomena indicates that the two experiences are similar enough to be confused.

Moreover, scholars examining parallel phenomena in other cultures have pointed to certain similarities of causes and functions. Some psychologists and psychological anthropologists have found indications of similarity in the psychodynamics of the two experiences. Thus Anthony F.C.

Wallace sees both possession by evil spirits and possession by gods as obsessive-compulsive neuroses. He sees no significant psychological difference between the two types except that evil spirit possession might be more dangerous to the psyche because, and to the extent that, it threatens one's ego-ideal.[7] Also, some sociologists and social anthropologists studying other cultures and other areas in India have stressed that the two phenomena seem to have the same sociological causes. Thus Pressler (1965: 92) in his study of ecstasy and *ṭonā vidyā* (black magic) in Jabalpur finds that both phenomena are found primarily in the high poverty areas of the city. And, although Metraux does not comment on the source of the phenomenon of evil spirit possessions, he writes that one of the functions of god possession is to give pleasure "to poor souls ground down by life." "They are able," he adds, "by virtue of such a mechanism, to become the center of attention and play the part of a super natural being, feared and respected" (1960: 417–20). Simone de Beauvoir (1968: 530–32) has made a similar observation with regard to the god and saint possession among the blacks of Bahia in Brazil.

On the other hand, even on this level of analysis there are strong reasons to stress the differences between the two experiences as they are known in Maharashtra. For one thing the correlations suggested by Pressler's study, and partially confirmed by the observations of Metraux and de Beauvoir, do not seem to be applicable to the phenomena of *bhūt bādhā* and *angāt yeṇe* in Maharashtra. To be sure, in the two large cities (Bombay and Pune) it may be that active belief in *bhūt bādhā* is more prevalent in high poverty areas. Certainly the Mira Datar Chilla in Bombay, where hundreds come each day and thousands each week, is situated in a high poverty area. Other healing centers, however, are not so located; and, though the average economic level of those who attend them seems somewhat low, it is not as low as Pressler's study indicates it should be. Moreover the pattern that Pressler, Metraux, and de Beauvoir indicate for the explanation of god possession does not at all correspond with my observation of *angāt yeṇe* in Maharashtra, where most *angāt ālelī* seem to be relatively well-to-do and highly respected members of their communities. And, although there is a possibility of occasional subjective confusion, most *angāt ālelī* experience possession immediately as beneficent and have no doubts that it might not be their god who possesses them, while most spirit victims experience *bhūt bādhā* immediately as illness or trouble or "wrongness" and have no hopes that it might be a god who has taken them rather than a *bhūt*. Further, and perhaps most important, in Maharashtra a clear cultural indication of the difference between the two kinds of possession is provided in the Marathi language. As I have shown, Marathi employs two different phrases to denote the two different kinds of possession. One of them, *angāt yeṇe*, has only positive connotations. The phrase carries no connotations at all of attack or of anything malevolent or inauspicious and could never be used to refer to possession by a *bhūt*. On the other hand, the other phrase, *bādhā*, has only negative connotations. Although there is no precise English equivalent of *bādhā*, the dominant connotations are of something "wrong" happening to someone, or something adversely affecting someone. The term is never used in Marathi except to refer to something unpropitious and malevolent. One could never use the term *bādhā* to speak of possession by a god or *pīr*.

Thus, although there are some clear surface similarities between the two phenomena when compared on the level of ordinary human experience, there are also, even on this level of comparison, some clear indications of distinct differences. It is when the two phenomena are analyzed as religious experience, however, that the true depth of those differences is revealed.

The essential quality of a religious experience is "specialness," or to use a more precise term, "sacredness." Every religious experience is an opening up of a person to the sacred and a revealing of the sacred to the person.[8] The religious experience itself drives a wedge into the continuity of experiences that a person has come to know as his life, dividing the ordinary from the special, causing him to see the rest as ordinary but *this* as extraordinary, special, or sacred. All of my interviews and observations in Maharashtra indicate that *angāt yeṇe* is such an experience. Indeed *angāt yeṇe* could be considered a prototype of a religious experience. In most cases the *angāt ālelī* I talked with did not consider themselves especially religious before the experience of their first possession. To be sure, they participated in the usual family *pūjās* and some observed special days for their gods, but they considered themselves no more religious than the average person in their village or neighborhood. Some considered themselves less religious than average. Then something happened to them. Suddenly, unexpectedly, something occurred that was wholly outside their normal range of experience. They felt that their body was taken over by a god.

All of the *angāt ālelī* emphasized that they felt that their power was a gift from their god—a special favor given to them. They did not originally seek the experience, but once it happened they felt utterly changed and sensed an obligation, even a desire, to keep themselves "ready" for it to happen again. The key to the "readiness," they believe, is "devotion" (bhakti), or better, "continued diligence in devotion." As they put it, they must "always remember" their god. If they fail to do this, the god ceases to come. I talked with one middle-aged man who had lost his power to be possessed and who regretted the loss deeply. I asked him why he had lost his powers. He answered, "I didn't remember Khandoba and he stopped coming." Will he come back? "Only if my faith becomes so strong. If we have complete faith, if we are always remembering him, he comes; if we don't have faith he stops coming." Another *angāt ālelī* tells what she does to "always remember" her goddess: "I don't eat anything. I keep a strict fast. At the time of *āratī* I take only one spoonful of *tīrtha*. I stand on one leg for hours concentrating on Janabai, singing her songs, praying, doing *āratī*. I celebrate Navratra by holding a clay pot on my head for twelve hours; during that time I continue my worship without any break. I don't even stop for the call of nature. There is no break in my bhakti."

In the course of my interviews I asked each *angāt ālelā* to describe what happened when he became possessed. What did he feel like? All had some difficulty answering. They seemed surprised that the question had been asked and even more surprised that they were having trouble answering. One response was as follows: "How can I describe it?" (long pause; then very slowly), "I feel that the god Khandoba comes into my body. That is why I take a lime—to keep my body pure so that he can come in." This response provides a direct insight into *angāt yeṇe* as religious experience if we interpret it in light of Eliade's treatment of the body-temple-cosmos homology.[9] The body of the *angāt ālelā* is the temple of the god; it is also the cosmos in microcosm. The god enters the body just as he would enter a temple; or, again, he comes into the body as he came into the world. The *angāt ālelā* is the vessel purified, being filled; the temple, purified, which the god enters; or, on the appropriate special day, the cosmos which the god creates, saves from disaster, or frees from demons. Thus, just as Khandoba on Champashashthi enters the world to restore order by destroying the demons Mani and Malla, so also Khandoba enters his *angāt ālelī* and through them restores some order to a little piece of the cosmos by solving a neighbor's problem or by finding a lost bullock or by driving a *bhūt* out of the body of an old woman from the next village.

The religious dimensions of the ritual of the *panjā* bearers who walk in the fire also becomes clear when seen in this light. I asked all four of the *panjā* bearers I interviewed why they walked on fire. The answer was slow in coming. I waited patiently. Then eventually, "It is our duty," (long pause) then finally, "It is to remember what happened to the saints of Karbala. They were made to walk on fire there and so conquered evil and made Islam great. It is our duty to do it each year." Does it matter to them that their historical account is not quite accurate? Does it matter that they don't even belong to the same community as the saints of Karbala, that they are Sunnis and not Shi'ias? Not at all. For they are not telling me history. They are telling me a myth—a myth that has become the basis of their annual ritual. They are the vessels, purified, for the *pīr* to enter and do again each year what he did once long ago (in *illo tempore*). They are vessels who by the *pīr's* favor are filled. Thus they become the *pīr* triumphing over evil, making Islam great. They are, in Eliade's words, "living close to the center"; they are "communicating with the gods" (Eliade 1957: 72).

*Angāt yeṇe* is clearly an experience of the sacred *par excellence*. The *angāt ālelā's* body becomes for the god either a momentary temple for him to enter, or, more often, a cosmos for a momentary incarnation.

### *Bhūt Bādhā as Religious Experience*

In the case of *bhūt bādhā* it is much more difficult to get at the religious dimension of the experience through interviews and observations. There are two reasons for this. First, it is a more complex experience and it is never so unequivocally related to the subject's religious life as is *angāt yeṇe*. In the second place, when *bādhā* itself is perceived as a religious experience, it is an experience of defilement, wrongness, and disorder, and it requires considerable time and patience to reach a point of intimacy with informants sufficient for them to speak with frankness of these feelings. On the basis of my interviews and observations thus far, two things are clear: first, there are many for whom the experience seems to be other than a religious experience, tangential to their religious life, ordinary. There are some, for instance, whose attitude toward the *bābā* and the healing center is quite casual. Some say something like, "I was persuaded by my brother to come and try it. I thought I had nothing to lose." Others seemed more serious in their attitude toward the healing center but are clearly forming only a temporary association. They will become vegetarians only while they are at the Mahanubhav temple. They will make an initial indication of their faith in the *bābā*, but after they are cured they will not come back. Moreover, for some, the faith expressed is more like confidence in a doctor than faith in a god. Indeed, for some, the whole experience from *bhūt* attack to cure is more closely analogous to a physical illness or a wound, the subsequent diagnosis, and convalescence than it is to defilement and cleansing. In these cases the *bābā* is seen primarily as a healer. People in this category would speak easily of one healing center in comparison to another as if they were comparing hospitals or doctors. They would speak of the reputation of this *bābā* or the power of that one compared to another. Several had visited many healing centers but "preferred" this one to others or found this one "more convenient." For many, however, indeed for the majority, the experience of *bhūt bādhā* is primarily perceived as a religious experience, as an opening up of the person to the realm of the sacred. In these cases there are two phenomena to consider: *bhūt bādhā* itself as a religious experience, and the cure of *bhūt bādhā* as a religious experience.

There is evidence that *bhūt bādhā* itself is perceived by some victims as a religious experience. In the same way that an *angāt ālelā* feels himself to be a vessel filled and exalted, the *bhūt bādhā* victim feels himself to be a vessel defiled; he feels as if evil, defilement, chaos, wrongness, disorder have entered him and taken him over. Moreover, he identifies himself with the world and feels his "wrongness," chaos, and defilement as part of the wrongness, chaos, and defilement of the world. This can be seen both from the observed actions and speech of the victims while unconscious, i.e., while (from their point of view) their body is taken over by the *bhūt*, and form the testimonies of those interviewed when they are conscious. Many of the unconscious actions of *bhūt* victims are confined to certain violent motions of the body and crying and moaning under the punishment of the *bābā*. Most of the phrases recorded are something like "Baba, don't hit me; don't burn me; Baba, please leave me, etc." Frequently, however, the victims will become quite articulate or perform more complex actions, such as acting out the role of a rebellious agent of chaos or of a polluted or defiled being. Frequently they will grovel in dirt or filth or some particularly defiled place or they will walk or crawl in an abnormal manner, assuming the posture of a deformed monster. One dramatic example of this kind of behavior is the attitude assumed by the *bhūt* victims who come before a well-known Bhavani *angāt ālelī* in Bombay. As a *bhūt* victim approaches her, he immediately falls on the ground and puts his neck against her right foot (i.e., against the foot of Bhavani). She then puts her foot on the neck of the *bhūt* victim in the classical position of Bhavani conquering a demon. Thus, unconsciously, the spirit victim has identified with the traditional agents of disorder and chaos and, in the presence of Bhavani, has submitted to being conquered, thus restoring order to the personality.

In some cases evidence is verbal as well as visual. Occasionally a *bhūt* victim becomes quite articulate and carries on a long dialogue with the *bābā*. In these cases nearly always the victim plays the role of a rebellious agent, rebelling against the *bābā's* power and determined to continue to cause what chaos he can. The twelve-year-old girl (possessed by the *bhūt* who strikes her head against the stone wall) addresses the *bābā* thus: "Who are you? Who do you think you are that you are so strong? Are you a *dādā* (slum boss)? Are you going to fight with me now? If you are a *dādā*, I have seen so many *dādās* like you. (Pause) Please stop! Please don't hurt me! I will leave her! (Short pause) Why are you laughing? If you laugh I will stay and disturb her. I won't leave her! (Several screams.) I will leave now, but I will come again to disturb her."

Interviews with spirit victims when they are conscious and with previous victims after they are healed provided another source of evidence that *bādhā* is sometimes experienced as being taken over by wrongness and chaos. They speak of being overcome by a general feeling of wrongness. They can't seem to do anything right. Even things they know how to do well (e.g., cooking) are frequently spoiled. They fight with friends for no reason. They can't understand what has come over them, or what has gotten into them, but something extraordinary has radically changed their life, making it all wrong. One former victim put it this way, "I don't know how to say it. Then *everything* was wrong—not only with me but my sister, and all the family was sick. It was all wrong. Now I am fine and my sister is happy and everything is all right."

As I have shown, some spirit victims seem to experience their cure (as they did their treatment) largely as a profane or secular experience. They were sick; they went to a healing center; now they are well. They are pleased; they return to their normal life. For many, however, the experience of "becoming right" results in a lasting bond of loyalty and devotion between the victim and his *bābā*—loyalty and devotion that can only be understood in religious terms. In all of my interviews I would ask informants their opinion of other healing centers. As I have shown above, some would readily make comparisons and give reasons for preferences. From many, however, I would get nothing but more praise of their *bābā*. A typical response is this one of a man at Mira Wali Darga, Ahmednagar: "I have absolute faith in this *bābā*. There may be others. I don't know about that. Through this *bābā* I became all right. I have faith only in him." The man is a Hindu. He was cured several years ago after having a *bhūt* for several months. Since then he has come at least once a week and climbed the long hill to take *darshan* of his *bābā*. This pattern is repeated again and again. Several former victims come daily to the Mira Datar Chillas in Pune and Bombay to take *darshan* of the *bābā*, and many more come at least once a week. One of my most helpful informants, a young woman nineteen years old, had been cured of *bhūt bādhā* seven years ago and has come to the *chilla* to take *darshan* without fail at least once a week for the last seven years.

In some cases the experience of taking *darshan* or being present for *āratī* can still be, years after their cure, a very moving religious experience. On a Thursday night at the Mira Datar Chilla I was interviewing the young woman mentioned above. We had retreated to the sitting room of the Mujavar's house to escape some of the noise. I had just asked a question and I looked up when she didn't respond. Unheard by me, the first few beats of the *āratī* drum had sounded a block away. My friend, a Roman Catholic, held up a small hand signaling me to wait for a moment. She had heard the very first beat of the drum, which for so long had signaled for her the beginning of the punishment of her *bhūt* by her *bābā*. Her eyes half closed, her lips forming the one silent word, "Baba," she crossed herself. Then she smiled and said: "It begins, *āratī*!" For these people the pattern of loyalty and devotion established by their cure has, in effect, formed a new religion. Without leaving their former faith, without ceasing to be a Hindu or a Roman Catholic, the former spirit victim has become initiated into a new faith—his treatment, cleansing, and cure form an informal *rite de passage*.[10]

Thus, both *bhūt bādhā* itself and the cure of *bhūt bādhā* are often perceived as religious experience. When *bhūt bādhā* itself is so perceived, the experience is the polar opposite of the experience of *angāt yeṇe*. It is an experience of wrongness, chaos, disorder. The body as temple or vessel is entered and taken over by a defiling agent, or the body as microcosm is entered and attacked by agents of chaos and disorder. When the cure of *bhūt bādhā* is perceived as religious experience it is experienced as "coming right," as cleansing of defilement or a restoring of order, and it frequently results in informal initiation into a new faith.

## NOTES

1. *Bhūt* means ghost; *bādhā* means harmful effect. *Angāt yeṇe*, literally "to come into the body," refers to the phenomenon of possession itself. One who is possessed is called an *angāt ālelā* (*f. angāt ālelī, n. pl.*

*angāt ālelī*). The author has preferred, in the case of this usage, to use the indicated Marathi plural form rather than the English "s."

2. See Anne Feldhaus' article in this volume.

3. This is also the view that is stressed in the *Agni Purāṇa* and the *Garuḍa Purāṇa*. For a summary of the Puranic material see Thomas (1966: 11–13; 48–49).

4. *Devṛishīs* derive their power from *angāt yeṇe*; *māntriks* derive theirs from the chanting of incantations (mantras).

5. Kal Bhairav is a form of Shiva; see also Sontheimer's article in this volume. For Dattatreya, see the article by Charles Pain with Eleanor Zelliot.

6. It would seem that the list of Hindu gods who do possess people corresponds closely to those ancient non-Aryan Maharashtrian gods who are gradually being assimilated into the great tradition as avatars of Shiva and Parvati (see Kosambi 1962: 139–43 and 121–22).

7. Wallace 1966: 141–49; cf. 209. Though Wallace may be overstating the case, Metraux's findings in Haiti (1959: 419–20) give some support to the notion that the psychodynamics of the two phenomena are sometimes similar. Metraux's study shows that in the culture of Haiti god possession (or *loa* possession) sometimes seems to satisfy obscure cravings which have a masochistic tendency. He cites as examples the hurling of the self to the ground, the banging of the head against the wall, etc. Metraux's findings in this regard are confined to *loa* possession which parallels *angāt yeṇe*. He does not make a similar observation about possession by evil spirits, which would parallel the Maharashtrian phenomenon of *bhūt bādhā*. It should be noted that Metraux discounts the claim that ritual possession in Haiti can be entirely explained as compulsive neuroses or hysteria (421–22), pointing out the stylized and controlled nature of the phenomena as well as its frequency. It should also be noted that other scholars emphasize a distinction between the two phenomena. Thus de Waal Malefijt (1968: 251) labels the one (analogous to *angāt yeṇe*) "spirit intrusion" and the other "spirit possession." She suggests distinguishing between the two on the basis of whether they are voluntary or involuntary. Cf. Lewis (1971: 46–47; 64) who prefers the terminology of controlled and uncontrolled to denote this distinction.

8. See Eliade (1957) for the development of this concept.

9. See Eliade (1957: 1–72).

10. The concept of informal initiation has been developed by Pressler (1965) to denote initiation into a new religion which is unexpected and unintended and accomplished without leaving any of one's former religious affiliations.

## REFERENCES

Beattie, J.H.M. 1967. "Consulting a Nyoro Diviner: the Ethnologist as Client." *Ethnology* 6:57–65.

Crooke, W. 1896. *The Popular Religion and Folklore of Northern India*, second edition. Westminster: Archibald Constable & Co. Third reprint in 2 vols: Delhi: Munshiram Manoharlal, 1968.
Das Gupta, S. 1969. *Obscure Religious Cults*. Calcutta: K.L. Mukhopadhyay.
de Beauvoir, S. 1968. *Forces of Circumstances*. Translated by Richard Howard. Middlesex: Penguin. First published in 1963.
de Waal Malefijt, A. 1968. *Religion and Culture*. New York: Macmillan.
Dowson, John. 1926. *A Classical Dictionary of Hindu Mythology*. London: K. Paul, Trench, Trubner.
Dube, S.C. 1955. *Indian Village*. Ithaca, NY: Cornell University Press.
Dubois, J.A. 1906. *Hindu Manners, Customs and Ceremonies*. Oxford: Clarendon Press.
Eliade, Mircea. 1937. "Cosmical Homology and Yoga." *Journal of the Indian Society of Oriental Art* 5:188–203.
———. 1958. *Patterns in Comparative Religion*. Cleveland: Meridian.
———. 1957. *The Sacred and the Profane*. New York: Harper.
Enthoven, R.E. 1924. *The Folklore of Bombay*. Oxford: Clarendon Press.
*Gazetteer of the Bombay Presidency*. 1885 (Vol. 18, part 1, Poona) and 1886 (Vol. 24, Kolhapur). Compiled by James M. Campbell. Bombay: Government Central Press.
Ghurye, G.S. 1962. *Gods and Men*. Bombay: Popular Book Depot.
———. 1953. *Indian Sadhus*. 2nd ed. Bombay: Popular Prakashan. Reprinted in 1964.
Kosambi, D.D. 1962. *Myth and Reality*. Bombay: Popular Prakashan.
Lewis, I.M. 1971. *Ecstatic Religion: An Anthropological Study of Spirit Possession and Shamanism*. Middlesex: Penguin Books.
Metraux, A. 1959. "A Selection from Voodoo in Haiti." *Anthropology of Folk Religion*. Edited by Charles Leslie. New York: Vintage. Reprinted in 1960.
Pressler, H.H. 1965. "Informal Initiation Among Hindus and Moslems." *Initiation*. Edited by C.J. Bleeker. Leiden: Brill.
Thomas, P. 1966. *Incredible India*. Bombay: Taraporevala.
Underhill, M.M. 1921. *The Hindu Religious Year*. Calcutta: Association Press.
Wallace, A.F.C. 1966. *Religion: An Anthropological Approach*. New York: Random House.
Whitehead, Henry. 1921. *The Village Gods of South India*. London: Oxford University Press.

# 5
# *Scattered Voices: The Nature of God*

## Editors' Introduction

Studies of Hinduism tend to fall into either of two categories, those dealing with philosophical Hinduism and those dealing with popular Hinduism—the latter usually on the village or tribal level. The casual student often gets the impression that the "great" philosophic tradition is uncompromisingly monistic and sees the Absolute only in impersonal, negative terms, while the "little tradition" of the Hindu populace involves primitive faith and practices untouched by "higher" speculation. The reality, as always, is more complicated. The traditions are not rigidly compartmentalized but are constantly interpenetrating.

The "scattered voices" presented here show a striking convergence. In the excerpt from his article "The Role of Man in Hinduism," Professor Dandekar shows how in Hinduism "absolute monistic idealism and passionate devotionalism . . . abide side by side without any conflict."

The next two selections, brief comments by people of

little or no education, show the ease with which ordinary people handle the difficult concept of the nature of God. These comments, taken from interviews conducted by Maxine Berntsen, come out as spontaneous poetry.

The last voice is that of the *dalit* poet Narayan Surve. In his poem he juxtaposes his identification with *Brahma*, Marathi for *brahman*, the absolute, with the reality of his homeless condition—a juxtaposition raising social irony to a cosmic level. (*E. Z. and M. B.*)

## *The God-Consciousness of Hinduism**

The consideration of the role of man in relation to god is relevant to our discussion of the Hindu concept of man. Just as the philosophical approach to the problem of the role of man gives rise to the dualism between the essential self and the empirical self, so the religious or theistic approach presupposes the dualism between man and god. Philosophically, this dualism between man and god is inadmissible for essentially man is god. The very concepts of man and god cannot be said to possess absolute reality; they belong to the realm of the world of experience. That is why many philosophical systems in India are essentially non-theistic or supertheistic. They are not required to posit the existence of a personal god in order to answer the various cosmological, psychological, metaphysical, and even ethical questions which they have raised in the course of their spiritual quest. This does not, however, mean that Hinduism has nothing to do with god. On the contrary, Hinduism, particularly popular Hinduism, is crowded with gods. Hinduism is certainly god-conscious, indeed very much so.

It redounds to the glory of Hinduism that in it absolute

* From "The Role of Man in Hinduism," in *The Religion of the Hindus*, edited by Kenneth A. Morgan (New York: Ronald Press, 1953) 131–33.

monistic idealism and passionate devotionalism should abide side by side and without any conflict. What is still more creditable is that Hinduism has achieved this marvelous feat in a more or less rational manner through the assumption of the possibility of two points of view in philosophical matters: the absolute point of view and the relative point of view—the one not spurning the other, each possessing reality in its own way, and each independently leading to the final goal. The proverbial catholicity of the Hindu mind is also, in no small measure, responsible for what would appear to a casual observer to be the paradoxes of Hinduism. Indeed, one of the most beautiful of such paradoxes is to be seen in the fact that a staunch monistic idealist like Sankara has composed some of the sweetest and most stirring hymns in praise of personal divinities.

To put it in broad but philosophically not quite precise terms, god stands in the same relation to the Supreme Being as an individual does to the essential self. Thus the relation between god and man is in many ways influenced by the relation between the Supreme Being and the essential self. Theistically, the goal sought by man is either to live in the same world as god, or to be nearest to god, or to assume the same form as god, or, finally, to achieve intimate union with god. It will be seen that, while the first three goals more or less represent the stages leading to the last goal, the last goal is but a reflection of the philosophical goal of the mystic union of the essential self with the Supreme Being. The philosophically accepted identity between the Supreme Being and the essential self is sometimes qualified in theism by suggesting that god and man are identical in essence but different in form. What sparks are in relation to fire, men are in relation to god. A further development of this partial separateness of man from god is that god is described as being not really external to man, but as being the inner controller in man. Theism describes god as the efficient directive cause in man's life.

This theistic approach conceives of god as the creator and moral governor of man and the universe, the dispenser of the law of karma. It is interesting to note, in this connection, that even though he accepts the complete separateness and the awe-inspiring distance between man and god, the Hindu seeks to achieve a direct personal communion with god through a complete surrender of his whole being to god. This is the ideal of a Hindu devotee. Devotion, bhakti, according to the Hindu view, implies dedicating all one's actions to god, rendering service to him, and meditating on him in single-pointed concentration; devotion requires that man rid himself of all consciousness of "I" and "my," and develop an attitude of being the same to all god's beings, whether friend or foe; and, paradoxical as it may seem, devotion requires that the devotee create in himself a peculiar mystic power through surrender, humility, and faith. Prayer, worship, ritual, and religious observances have places in the Hindu religious practice, but the doctrine of true devotion must be regarded as the most potent factor which governs the role of the Hindu in relation to god.

*—R.N. Dandekar*

## *What is God Like***

The saints have said, "I am weary from thinking about the nature of God." Why? Because the truth about God is that He is like the covering of the sky, without form, quality, or color. . . . God has no name, no form, no color. He is unseeable and unknowable, fixed, unmoving, without form. Then what can we say about Him? Can we describe the shape of happiness? If I went out of this room and found a hundred-rupee note I would be happy. And if someone asked me what this happiness is like—is it green, yellow, turquoise, blue? I'd say no. "Well, is it ten feet long, five feet deep, and three feet wide?" "No, not that either." "Well, blue,

** This and the anonymous statement that follows were collected in taped interviews by Maxine Berntsen.

yellow, purple?" "No, not that either." "Salty, hot, sour?" "No, not that." "Then what is it like?" "It's just happiness," I answer. Happiness has no length or width. No one can say what God is like.

—*Anonymous*

*Can the Wind be Seen?*

Parmeshwar is One,
He is called by different names,
He is in everything.
What is Parmeshwar like?
Why, have we gone to see?
He cannot be seen.
Can the wind be seen?
We can feel it, that much is sure.

—*Anonymous*

*For I Am Brahma****

I will protect all that belongs to Brahma,
all that is Brahma.
I'll undo the knot of time.
I'll bring the world to my door,
where it will frolic like a child.
I'll play *lagorī* with the sun.
I'll tie up big clouds like cows outside my house.
I'll milk them to fill pots with ambrosia.
I'll hold the wind in my yard,
where it will spin like a top.
I'll raise the rooftops of heaven.

*** "Aisā gā mī Brahma (For I am Brahma)," from the book of the same title (1962; Bombay: Popular Prakashan, 1971). In this direct translation we have kept the Marathi *Brahma* for the Sanskrit *brahman*.

I'll straighten out the bending sky,
single-handed,
and punish whoever bent it in the first place!

The mole's mountain, the mountain's mole—
they're both inside of *me*.

For I am Brahma. I hold the world together—
I, the helpless one,
without even a room to call my own.

*—Narayan Surve*
*translated by Jayant Karve and*
*Eleanor Zelliot with the assistance*
*of Pam Espeland*

# II.

# THE PRACTICE OF FAITH

IRAWATI KARVE
TRANSLATED BY JAI NIMBKAR

# 6

# "A Town without a Temple": An Essay*

We had been walking down that road every day for some time. There was a new colony being built, and we saw small new houses gradually taking shape. Finally the colony was finished. Many of the houses were now occupied. On one side of the colony an empty lot was left. One day a foundation was dug on it which looked different from the foundations of the houses. In a very short time a small temple was erected there. One day we saw a crowd in the temple yard. An image of Maruti was being installed. By the time we came back, the Maruti was standing in the temple facing us!

"Another new temple! As though Pune doesn't have enough temples."

---

* "Devaḷāvinā gāo," from *Gangājal* [Ganga Water] (1972; Pune: Deshmukh and Company, 1977).

"But you see, this new colony did not have a temple. Now these people have a place to come for *darshan*, to come and sit in the evenings."

"Nonsense! What's the need for a temple in every little new colony that comes up? The *bhajan* in the early mornings and evenings will only drive people out of their minds."

I smiled and said something softly to myself.

"What are you mumbling?"

"Nothing. I was thinking of an old Tamil saying." I said it again, and translated it literally, "One should not have a house in a town without a temple." I went on, "Who knows who the ancient man was, but he felt that he couldn't live in a town where there was no temple. It doesn't seem as though there could have been a town without a temple in the old days when this proverb came into being. That time is past now, but the old habits of thinking have taken root in the mind. The people who are building this new colony in Pune probably don't know the Tamil proverb but their pattern of thinking is the same."

"What is this pattern? What sort of form does it take?"

I thought for a minute. I realized that this was a good opportunity to show off my learning. I said, "Last year I was reading an old book, probably from the thirteenth or fourteenth century. It was written in Sanskrit and was all about town planning and the planning of a house. I couldn't quite understand all of it, but some things in it were clear. In planning a town you first determined the directions and drew a quadrangle. Then you divided each side of the quadrangle into eight equal parts and drew sixty-four quadrangles inside and named each of these after a deity. The biggest building was the temple and its yard was in the center. Then came the palace or the residence of the royal family. Then the street with big houses belonging to the noblemen. Then, starting from very wealthy merchants, merchants who dealt in diamonds and precious stones, the plan went on to indicate the placement of the greengrocers' shops, shops selling salt and spices, shops of the middleclass traders, then outside the quadrangle of the city, the houses of the Untouchables, and even further away, the houses of the engineers and the carpenters.

"The temple in its quadrangle was always the reference point to indicate the location of any place in the town. Making use of gods and temples in this way, to assign locations in a town, was a new idea to me. However, I realized that the science of engineering had not created these gods. The writer of this book had merely made a very clever use of already existing gods. The book not only specified where each person's house should be, it also decreed that all houses on one street should have the same height, and specified how tall, that is, how many stories, the houses on each street should be. It said that the temple at the center of the town should be its tallest building.

"There was a rule that the palace should be lower than the temple and the Brahmans' houses lower than the palace. However important the Brahmans considered themselves, the king, who was the representative of Vishnu, was naturally more important than they. And God himself was more important than his representative. A traveller coming from afar should know by a glimpse of the temple spire that a town is near. The temple spire was symbol of the existence of the town, of its wealth and pride. In Maharashtra, if you discount the hill temples, the temples built in towns on level ground are not very grand. But in the South we still see such very tall and grand temples. The *gopuras* of the temple of Meenakshisundaram at Madura can be seen from anywhere within a radius of five to ten miles. Christian churches are also built on the same lines. The book I mentioned has used temples to fix the location of places. Formerly, temples were used in the same way in Pune too. There were Bhangya Maruti (Hashish Maruti) and Pasodya Vithoba (Vithoba of the quilts). In the prostitutes' colony there was even a Chhinal Maruti (Whoring Maruti)."

"Was that all the temples were for?" came the sarcastic question in response to my lecture. "So that one can give the accurate address for one's house by a reference to a temple?"

"No, a temple is the focus of a community's faith, a symbol of its hopes and aspirations. A town which does not have a temple is a place without faith, a place where people have no collective aspirations. That is why one shouldn't live there. This is how you have to interpret the proverb."

"What exactly do you mean by a temple? It's a building constructed in the name of something that doesn't exist, isn't it? What can it symbolize?"

"In a way what you say is true. A temple gives form to the formless. It is where that which has no beginning is installed, and on occasion that which has no end is destroyed. There is something called *'sat'* which we are not, although we are aware of its existence. We give this *'sat'* various forms. That is God. We ask from God what we cannot ask from man. We ask for a permanent haven, justice, security, peace—or ask for help for the need of the moment. If nothing else, we go to a temple to get a moment's respite from the turmoil of daily life. Some people don't approve of the idea of such refuge; some feel the need of it. They feel that there is something which is unquestionably superior to them and that the temple is a symbol of it."

"You were describing the height and grandeur of a temple. But aren't palaces, and the Taj Mahal, also grand? Aren't they also symbols of some kind of grandeur?"

"They are not only grand, they are also beautiful. But they cannot become places of worship. Some people had nursed the silly hope that educational institutions could become the symbols of this kind of noble and divine feeling, but they couldn't. There are religions which destroy the temples of others, there are people who shatter their own temples and sever their own association with the past. In such times a man who says one shouldn't live in a town without a temple will undoubtedly be judged as foolish. Even so there are many people who feel the way he does. As far as they are concerned, the grandeur or beauty of a temple has secondary importance. It is the idol inside which has been for centuries the repository of people's pain, compassion, peace, and sanctity. Our feelings are quite different when we see the Taj Mahal or the Jaipur palace, and when we see the image of Vitthal at Pandharpur. This Tamil man seems to say that there are no feelings where there isn't a temple, and that is why one shouldn't live there."

"Things like drainage, shops, clean residential areas, roads, a hospital are necessary to a town. Parks and means of entertainment are also needed along with these, and schools, colleges, and libraries. But what's the point of a temple? These other things make life pleasanter. What does a temple do?"

"When you have all the good things in the world, do you wish for nothing more? Even when you have everything you still feel a longing for something. You are aware that there is something beyond physical comfort. Even if everybody were happy, some problems would still remain. This is not a facetious question, like asking, if there are no poor what would happen to the people who are trying to better their lot, or, if there are no ignorant people, what will happen to those who are trying to educate them. I am also not claiming that God has kept the world imperfect just so man can have something to aspire to. Even if the world were perfect, we would still continue to feel that there is something lacking. And a temple is the symbol of our desire to rectify the lack."

I thought of a new idea. I said, "Our saints have called the body 'bodytown.' They maintained that there should be a temple in this town too. They felt that there must be a god inside you even if there wasn't one in the town outside. Even when you have attained everything that is attainable in life, your mind still strives for something. A kind of restlessness eats at you. There is something that makes you feel insecure."

She stopped me and asked, "Isn't all this due to an awareness of death? Even when you are very happy, the thought that there is an end to this happiness torments you. However many close friends you have, the feeling that you are alone, that you are going to remain alone and die alone, overwhelms you. The mental struggle, restlessness, helplessness, all of it may be because of this. It may not represent the thirst, the struggle, to find the god in your heart at all."

"That may be true. There are both kinds of people. Some are looking for God within themselves, for some meaning in existence. And some believe that life is totally meaningless, but that they should nevertheless make it as happy as possible, live and let others live with dignity. In a way these idealists have found some kind of god. Some don't have even this idealism. They live only for themselves. They go on taking whatever they can from the world, and one day—one moment—they perceive their own loneliness, helplessness, and uselessness with such intensity that it becomes impossible for them to continue living and they commit suicide.

"You know about my young friends, Bal and Lahani. What fine children they were! They had everything. On the surface both seemed enviable. Both lived completely and enjoyed life. One of them committed suicide in a foreign country, far away from his family, alone. All that remained was a letter he had written to father.

"The other committed suicide one day in a house full of people. The helplessness and loneliness in her last letter was heartrending. She had everything—mother, brothers and sisters, husband, children, wealth, education, looks, friends. Then why this loneliness? These two made those left behind forever guilty. Why? Why?

"I have been asking this question for many years. Now I think that in their town there was neither God nor temple. In the midst of a full life they must have suddenly had this overwhelming sense of aloneness."

Without a moment's delay came the question, "But why then did Dnyaneshwar die? He certainly was not without God, was he?"

I replied just as quickly, "His God and his temple had become so large that his small body could no longer contain them. The bonds of the body became impossible to bear. It was not possible to exist within the body and become as great as God. That is why he died."

The thread of the conversation was broken. Each was engrossed in her own thoughts. I was trying to find an answer to a puzzle.

Bal, Lahani, and Dnyaneshwar had been brought together, even if only in the course of the conversation. They had all committed suicide before the age of twenty-five.* Was this the only similarity among them? Behind the similarity, didn't they also have in common the intensity of awareness and the impatience to translate the awareness into action? All three had run to embrace death.

And the rest of us? Have we ever wondered whether there are gods in our town? Have we ever asked ourselves whether we are empty or full? We have been alive since birth, slowly walking the road without giving it any conscious thought, until we collide with death.

She heard my sigh and asked anxiously, "What is the matter?"

The answer came out of my bottomless emptiness, "Nothing, nothing at all."

---

* Editors' note: Dnyaneshwar, the thirteenth century saint-poet, entered *samādhī* at the site of the temple in Alandi after completing his commentary on the *Bhagavad Gītā*. *Samādhī* is almost untranslatable. At times, scholars have used "religious suicide" to indicate that the saint has deliberately ended his earthly duties. Devotees, however, believe the saint still lives, and *samādhī* is never synonymous with suicide or death. Irawati Karve here deliberately uses the word suicide, we feel, to startle her readers into reflection.

PAUL B. COURTRIGHT

# 7
# *The Ganesh Festival in Maharashtra: Some Observations*

The tradition of devotion to the god Ganesh or Ganpati among Maharashtrian Hindus can be divided into two component parts: the sectarian and the general or universal. Sectarian Ganesh devotees (Ganpatyas or the Ganesh *sampradāy*) can be traced back as early as the sixth or seventh centuries.[1] As a sectarian movement, the Ganpatyas were small in number and confined, for the most part, to Brahmans who worshipped Ganesh as their family deity (*kuladaivat*), or devoted themselves to Ganesh for reasons of personal choice (*ishṭadaivat*). To Ganesh sectarians, Ganesh was the symbol for the transcendental monistic principle, *brahman*, and devotion to him was reputed to yield the fulfillment of one's desires and protection against obstacles. The Ganesh cult in Maharashtra fully bloomed during the rule of the Brahman Peshwas, rulers of the Maratha Kingdom in the eighteenth century. They themselves worshipped Ganesh as *kuladaivat* and supported the major cult centers at Morgaon, Theur, and Chinchwad, all of which are located in Pune District. In addition they sponsored Ganesh festivals, principally the festival during the Hindu month of Bhadrapad (August/September) in a quasi-public manner to demonstrate their religious sentiments and to invoke Ganesh to protect them from obstacles.

Today the Ganesh cult remains, as it always has been, small and principally confined to Deshastha and Konkanastha Brahmans and oriented around eight cult and pilgrimage centers, the *Ashṭavināyaks,* located mainly in Pune and Thana Districts. The cult center at Chinchwad, near Pune, is not one of these eight but remains an important Ganpatya center. In addition to these sites, there are approximately eighty Ganesh temples in Maharashtra.[2] While they are scattered over the state, the greatest concentration of them is in Thana, Kolaba, Ratnagiri, Pune, and Satara Districts.

The general or universal devotion to Ganesh is expressed by Hindus of all castes and sects on a more intermittent basis. Ganesh is worshipped along with other deities and is exhorted on numerous occasions for protection from misfortune. Hindus regard him as Lord of Obstacles or Overcomer of Obstacles. Exclusive worship of Ganesh occurs during the Bhadrapad festival which lasts for ten days. This festival, originally confined more to sectarian Ganpatyas, was brought into public and general observance through the efforts of Bal Gangadhar Tilak in Pune in 1893 and after (Barnouw 1954; Cashman 1970, 1975) and given an explicit political role as a means of mobilizing large numbers of Hindus behind the objectives of religious revival and political independence. The festival continued to increase in size and importance both as a religious and political event during the years of struggle for independence. Since 1947 it has shifted its emphasis away from the political to the more religious and social. The Ganesh festival today is the largest Hindu public religious performance in Maharashtra and is regarded by Maharashtrian Hindus as particularly expressing their regional religious ethos.

How is the vitality of the festival to be accounted for? What sorts of religious values and emotions find expression through it? What can an examination of the festival tell us about specifically Maharashtrian Hindu sensitivities? In an attempt to suggest some possible answers to these questions, we shall look at the operative mythology of Ganesh from a structural perspective,[3] and then turn to the patterns of social organization which are employed to carry out the festival's celebration. We shall try to show that the mythological and ritual structures are homologous and represent a consistent and coherent religious pattern. In the discussion of the festival's social organization, the author will draw upon his own field research carried on principally in Ahmednagar District.

### *The Mythology of Ganesh*

Ganesh, "Lord of Divine Hosts," "Son" of Shiva and Parvati, is the improbable deity who is portrayed as having a corpulent human body and an elephant's head. He is usually represented iconographically seated or standing, having four arms and carrying in his two left hands a tray of *modak*, a sweet preparation used in his worship, and a noose of rope used in binding an adversary's hands. On his right side, one hand holds either an elephant's goad or a *parashu* (a battle-axe); the other hand is in the *varadahasta mudra* or "boon conferring" posture.

Ganesh is known by a number of names in Maharashtra. The most frequently used are Ganpati, "Leader of the Divine Hosts"; Gajanan, "Elephant-faced"; Vighneshwar, "Lord of Obstacles"; Vinayak, "Remover of Hindrances"; Mangalmurti, "Auspicious Image"; and Moreshwar, "Lord of Moraya" or the "Lord of the Shrine at Morgaon." Of these names, only the last two, Mangalmurti and Moreshwar, are regional and particular to Maharashtra. The others are Sanskritic and recognized throughout India. All of these names relate to Ganesh's mythological functions, to his physical description, or to his cult.

Most of the Puranic myths about Ganesh tell about his birth, how he acquired his elephant head, and how he took on his divine role. An examination of the structure of these myths in terms of how their themes are related will give us a clearer idea of Ganesh's role. The first two myths we shall consider are from the *Śivapurāṇa* and the *Skanda-purāṇa* respectively, and they have been confirmed by this author to be currently known, with minor variations, in Maharashtra.

> Once upon a time, Jaya and Vijaya, the two companions of Pārvatī, suggested to her that, though she had Nandi and Bhṛingi and the others among Śiva's attendants as his servants, still it would be better for him if she had a person as her own servant. Pārvatī took the advice in good part and it so happened subsequently that, on the occasion when she was bathing in the inner compartments of her mansion, Śiva, not knowing where she was at that moment, went into the place where she was bathing. Pārvatī realized the value of the advice of her friends fully and then resolved upon creating a person who would be her faithful servant. She took a little dirt from her skin and created out of it a lovely being and ordered him to keep strict guard at her gate so as not to allow anyone inside without her permission. Once, Śiva himself happened to go to meet his consort, but could not get access to her apartments as the new gate keeper would not allow him in. Śiva tried entreaties and threats, none of which proved effective. Then he resolved upon forcing his way in somehow. On noticing this, the new gate keeper administered a few cuts to Śiva with his cane and drove him out. Incensed at the behavior of this insignificant servant of his consort, he ordered his host of demons to kill him at once. In the fight that ensued, Śiva's host of demons were completely defeated and driven away. Then Viṣṇu, Subramanya and the others tried on behalf of Śiva, but their strength with Vighneśvara did not meet with better result. Then Pārvatī, upon seeing that her son Vigneśvara was fighting single-handedly against powerful opponents, sent two minor goddesses to his help. By their mysterious power they drew toward themselves all the missiles aimed against Vighneśvara and protected him from injury. Finding that direct methods of attack did not succeed, Viṣṇu,

through his *māyā* (divine power), caused confusion. Thereupon, the two minor goddesses, finding their presence no longer of use there, returned to Pārvatī. Then it became easy for Śiva to cut off and remove the head of Vighneśvara.

The news of the destruction of her son was conveyed to Pārvatī by the sage Nārada; and on hearing it she became so angry that she created a thousand fighting goddesses to bring trouble on all those who took part in the destruction of Vighneśvara. These goddesses attacked the gods and made them feel very miserable. To rescue gods from this pitiable condition, Nārada and the other sages prayed to Pārvatī, who promised to restore peace as soon as her son was brought back to life. Śiva, on hearing this, ordered the gods to proceed to the north at once and bring back the head of the first living being they met and fix it on the neck of the beheaded son of Pārvatī. The gods immediately proceeded and came across an elephant; they cut off its head and brought it and attached it as directed to the trunk of Vighneśvara. When Pārvatī saw her son brought back to life in this manner, she felt pleased and took him into the presence of Śiva. Vighneśvara apologized to Śiva and the other gods for his past remisses in conduct and bowed in deep reverence to his divine, adopted father. Śiva was thereby highly gratified and conferred upon Vighneśvara the commandership over his own demon hosts and anointed him as Gaṇapati. (Gopinatha Rao 1968:37–39)

The second myth contains all the same structural elements but in reverse order.

The immortals and holy sages, observing that, whatever the action which they or others commenced, whether good or bad, no difficulty occurred in accomplishing it. Consulting together respecting the means by which the obstacles might be opposed to the commission of bad actions, they determined to have recourse to Rudra (Śiva). They accordingly proceeded to Kailāsa and thus with reverence addressed him: "O Mahādeva, God of gods, three-eyed one, bearer of the trident, it is thou who canst create a being capable of opposing obstacles to the commission

> of improper acts." Upon hearing these words, Śiva looked at Pārvatī and began to consider in what manner he could effect the wishes of the gods; and as he was immersed in thought, from the splendor of his countenance (which represents the *ākāśa* portion of his divine form) sprang into existence a youth shedding radiance around, endowed with the qualities of Śiva, and evidently another Rudra, and captivating by his beauty the female inhabitants of heaven. Umā (Pārvatī) regarded him, and when she saw him thus lovely, her natural disposition was excited, and incensed with anger uttered this curse: "Thou shalt not offend my sight with the form of a beautiful youth, therefore assume an elephant's head and large belly, and thus shall all thy beauties vanish!" Śiva thus spoke to his son, "Thou shalt be the chief of the Vināyakas, Vighnarāja, the son of Śiva; thou shalt be the chief of the Vināyakas and the Gaṇas; success and disappointment shall proceed from thee; and great shall be thy influence amongst the gods, and in sacrifices and all affairs. Therefore shalt thou be worshipped and invoked the first on all occasions or otherwise the object and prayers of him who omits to do so shall fail. (Gopinatha Rao 1968:40–41)

The first myth may be condensed into the following themes: Ganesh born in unnatural manner from Parvati's impurities; assigned the function of guarding her bathing place, Ganesh blocks Shiva's attempt to reunite with Parvati; quarrel ensues; Shiva mutilates Ganesh by depriving him of his head; Parvati becomes incensed with Shiva's action; she creates chaos in the universe, the immortals approach Shiva for a solution, Shiva replaces Ganesh's head with that of an elephant; Parvati is reconciled, the universe is returned to order; Shiva confers on Ganesh his mediatory function as lord of the divine hosts.

The second myth may be similarly condensed into the following themes: threat of chaos due to lack of distinction between good and evil actions; immortals approach Shiva for a solution; Shiva creates Ganesh in an unnatural manner from his thought; Parvati incensed at Ganesh's sexuality because he was regarded as a duplicate of Shiva himself;

Parvati mutilates Ganesh and gives him an elephant's head; Shiva confers mediatory functions upon Ganesh as lord of the divine hosts.

We can see the similar structural elements in both these myths if we set up a diagram in the manner illustrated on page 83. Even though these two myths are opposite in many respects (in the first myth Parvati creates Ganesh and Shiva mutilates and restores him with the elephant's head, while in the second myth it is Shiva who creates Ganesh and Parvati mutilates him and restores him with the elephant's head), the overall structure of the two is the same. Oppositions are set in conflict, they are mediated by a "mutilated" third category which remains ambiguous and unnatural, but nevertheless remains the necessary link between the oppositions. The creation of Ganesh and his mutilation is necessary to restore the balance in the universe. In the first myth Ganesh is created to prevent Shiva from uniting with Parvati, and in the second he is obliged to create obstacles such that the polarities of good and evil will remain in opposition and not become united thus causing confusion. In both these myths Ganesh's mutilation is necessary for the two polar principles of the universe to remain oppositional. His mutilation may be interpreted as a sexual one if we consider that his subsequent appearance and role is an asexual one. Although he is recognized as the "son" of Shiva and Parvati, his sonship is unnatural and asexual. The paradoxical oppositions (in the first myth, male-female and the second, good-evil) can be tolerated only through the mediation of a third element which is neither of the two but in some sense both. For his pains Ganesh is assigned a mediating position as the "son" of Shiva and Parvati and as the one who mediates between success and failure by means of creating or overcoming obstacles. His visual form as a man-elephant illustrates his ambiguity. He is neither man nor animal but something else, a category unto itself. Because he is a mediating figure, neither male nor female, his character is ambiguous and unpredictable.

Related to this essential ambiguity in Ganesh's character

**First Myth**

Shiva (Male) ⟷ Parvati (Female)

← Secondary Male (Ganesh) unnatural birth-prevents Shiva's reunion with Parvati

Shiva "mutilates" rival Male →

← Parvati creates chaos in the universe

Sages appeal to Shiva

Shiva "restores" Ganesh with elephant's head →

← Parvati appeased

Male (Shiva) ⟷ Mediator (Ganesh) ambiguous sexuality Lord of divine forces (ganas) ⟷ Female (Parvati)

**Second Myth**

Shiva (Male) ⟷ Parvati (Female)

Universe in chaos-Immortals appeal to Shiva

Secondary Male (Ganesh) unnatural birth Duplicate of Shiva-prevents his reunion with Parvati →

← Parvati incensed-gives Ganesh elephant's head Mutilates "rival" male

Shiva restores Ganesh by conferring mediatory function on him as Lord of divine forces (ganas) →

← Parvati appeased

Male (Shiva) ⟷ Mediator (Ganesh) Sexually ambiguous Lord of divine forces (ganas) ⟷ Female (Parvati)

and sexuality as a result of his mediatory role is the theme of Ganesh-as-trickster. This motif has been pointed out particularly by Leach (1962:91). In order to illustrate this theme, we can cite two additional myths:

> Gaṇeśa and Skanda were both courting the same two girls, Siddhī and Buddhī. It was agreed that the brother who could first circumnavigate the world would win the two girls. Skanda made the journey, but Gaṇeśa stayed home and proved through his logical talents and aptness for quotation that he had already completed the journey. (Wilkins 1913:334)

> Women, barbarians, and Śūdras and other workers of sin obtained entrance into heaven by visiting the celebrated temple of Somnāth. Sacrifices, ascetic practices, charitable gifts and all other prescribed ordinances ceased, and men thronged only to the temple of Śiva. Hence old and young, those skilled in the Vedas and those ignorant of them ascended to heaven. At length it became crowded to excess. Indra and the gods sought Śiva's help in alleviating this situation. Śiva could not help because he had promised that all who visit this temple at Somnāth would reach heaven. The gods approached Pārvatī with the same request. She created Gaṇeśa by rubbing her body, and said to the gods, "Desirous of your advantage have I created this being who will occasion men with obstacles, and deluding them will deprive them of their wish to visit Somnāth, and thus they shall fall into hell. (Getty 1936:5–6)

Ganesh's ambiguous behavior is consistent with his ambiguous appearance as a man-elephant and his ambiguous sexuality. This ambiguity is expressed in terms of his cunning and quick-wittedness. Because he behaves in unpredictable ways, he must be propitiated before the devotee can have any hope of achieving his religious aims. Ganesh's trickster tendencies must be brought under control through the devotee's ritual actions.

From what we have seen so far, Ganesh functions as the Lord of Obstacles, the god of the threshold, the keeper of the gate leading to the divine worlds. He mediates between human and divine realms. He must be approached with reverence and respect for his unpredictable disposition. He must be placated and persuaded not to place obstacles in the devotee's path. One dare not to presume his behavior, for if it is the deity who can overcome obstacles, he is also the one who can create them. The Lord of success is also the Lord of failure.

Ganesh's ambiguous mediator role is brought into clearer relief when we examine the occasions upon which he is invoked or the situations in which his help is sought. He is invoked at the beginning of all rituals, *samskāric* or otherwise, before all other deities (with the exception of funeral rituals). His image is placed at entrances and doorways to symbolize his role as gate keeper and mediator between one order of space and another. His blessing is sought at the beginnings of any new undertakings, such as building a house, writing or publishing a book, opening a new business, beginning a journey. Students frequently invoke Ganesh or write his mantra at the beginning of an examination.[4] From this partial list of occasions when Ganesh is called upon, it will become clear that his primary role is that of mediator, bringer of good fortune, expeller of bad fortune. In addition, Ganesh is sometimes referred to as a god of wisdom, a role usually assigned to Saraswati. This role can be accounted for either by Ganesh's association with the writing of books or by his more general mediator function if one seeks the aid of Ganesh to prevent obstacles and failure in achieving wisdom.

From this examination of the structure of the Ganesh mythology and the role he plays in the Hindu devotional system, we can see that Ganesh is fundamentally a mediating figure between the divine realm and the domain of human concerns and aspirations. Through devotion to Ganesh, who is at once the Lord of Obstacles and the Remover of Obstacles, the devotee hopes to pass beyond such incumbrances to an experience of temporary religious fulfillment, or minimally to achieve success in a specific undertaking.

## *Social Organization and the Celebration of the Festival*

It must be pointed out initially that the Ganesh festival is predominantly an urban phenomenon. Most Maharashtrians regard Pune as the center of the festival for historical reasons as well as the fact that in Pune the most lavish decorations can be seen. However, the festival is also observed on a large scale in all other Maharashtrian cities and is increasingly filtering into the rural areas, principally as a festival introduced through the village schools where it tends to be observed as a "cultural program."

Before discussing the forms of social organization which are pertinent to the festival itself, we should briefly look at the various subevents which together make up the festival. For reasons of space, we shall not take up the private or domestic ritual which are part of the total festival but which need not be included in order to understand the overall pattern of the public festival.

A few weeks before the beginning of the festival, the various voluntary associations (*maṇḍaḷs*) collect subscription contributions, from their own membership or from the neighborhoods in which their members live, to pay for a clay image (*mūrti*) of Ganpati, the decorations and materials for the image's exhibition, and any entertainment and ritual expenses. On the fourth day of the bright half of the month of Bhadrapad each *maṇḍaḷ*, usually as a group, collects the Ganpati image from the artist who shaped it or from a merchant and carries it, frequently in a musician-led procession, to the place where it will remain in exhibition for the duration of the ten days of the festival. During this period the exhibition is made increasingly elaborate by decorations placed around the image itself, such as cloth background, flowers, other clay-carved figures, loudspeaker systems for playing recorded devotional and cinema music. The exhibits are usually adjacent to the public street or in a heavily traveled area where they will have maximum exposure to the public. In the evenings during this ten-day period, the *maṇḍaḷs* sponsor "cultural programs" which might include:

singing devotional songs (*bhajans*); sponsoring elocution contests, lectures, films, or Marathi dramas (which might be either legitimate Marathi plays or *tamāshā*, the traditional folk theatre); or the putting on of lavish religious rituals (*satyanārāyaṇ pūjā*), after which consecrated food (*prasād*) is distributed to the assembled crowd. The extravagance of the programs any *maṇḍaḷ* can sponsor depends on the funds it is able to raise from members or patrons. There is a good deal of competition for public attention among the various *maṇḍaḷs*. The Marathi press devotes an enormous amount of coverage to the festival and the various *maṇḍaḷs'* exhibitions. The ten-day period of public festivity culminates on the ninth night with all the *maṇḍaḷs* having fully decorated their exhibitions. The streets become filled with crowds circulating around to see the *maṇḍaḷs'* decorations and to attend the various programs. Because of the large crowds, a heavy police contingent is visible to prevent disorder. On the ninth evening, two hours are specifically set aside for women to circulate around, and men are prohibited from being in the streets during that time. (In 1970, Ahmednager police officials estimated the total crowd on the ninth evening at between 50,000 and 75,000, which was nearly three-fourths of the population of the city.)

The tenth and final day of the festival begins mid-to-late morning with a procession of the *maṇḍaḷs'* images through the length of the city to a river at the city's edge where the images are worshipped for a final time and ceremoniously immersed in the water. The procession, like the events of the previous evening, draws enormous crowds. The women remain off the streets during the procession and watch from the balconies. The *maṇḍaḷs* mount the images atop profusely decorated carts and trucks and march before them dancing, throwing red powder (*gulāl*), singing, playing instruments (drums, horns) and *leḷīm* (a folk dance with sticks), and performing different types of acrobatics. All the forms of entertainment involve a high degree of cooperation and group solidarity. The order in which the *maṇḍaḷs* appear in the procession is set, to a certain degree, by tradition, the rest by a first-come-first-served arrangement. In the 1970 festival procession in Ahmednagar, there were 167 *maṇḍaḷs* who participated, and the procession lasted over eighteen hours. In Pune over 600 *maṇḍaḷs* participated.

Participation in the voluntary festival associations is restricted to males. The *maṇḍaḷs* involved conform to the instrumental-expressive typology.[5] Some *maṇḍaḷs* are drawn exclusively from other types of voluntary associations which are purely instrumental: i.e., labor unions, employees of private companies, government workers associations, etc. Most of the *maṇḍaḷs* are either permanently constituted neighborhood organizations, which carry on other activities during the year such as *bhajan* singing, travel-pilgrimage, or social service projects; or they are neighborhood associations which are brought together expressly for the purpose of celebrating the festival. In both these cases the associations are expressive in character. In the case of instrumental organizations, they take on an expressive function when they are celebrating the festival. The great majority of the neighborhood associations are made up of males between the ages of twelve and thirty. Many of these *maṇḍaḷs* call themselves "youth associations" (*tarūṇ maṇḍaḷ*). Festival participation is a great favorite of school boys. Caste does not play a visible part in the festival, and the *maṇḍaḷ* organization reflects caste organization only to the degree that the neighborhood from which the *maṇḍaḷ* membership is drawn reflects caste exclusiveness. Of twelve *maṇḍaḷs* surveyed in a predominantly Maratha-Mali neighborhood, all of them had a majority of members from those castes, but were not exclusively caste organizations. Many informants emphasized that they were not conscious of caste as a factor in membership and some indicated that they explicitly encouraged intercaste membership. Some also expressed the view that the festival is *particularly* a time when caste loyalties should not play a role. The festival is conceived of as a time of unity among people of all stations in the society.

Members of the *maṇḍaḷs* believe the chief values of the

3. A contemporary Ganesh image in a Pune temple. *Photography by Eleanor Zelliot.*

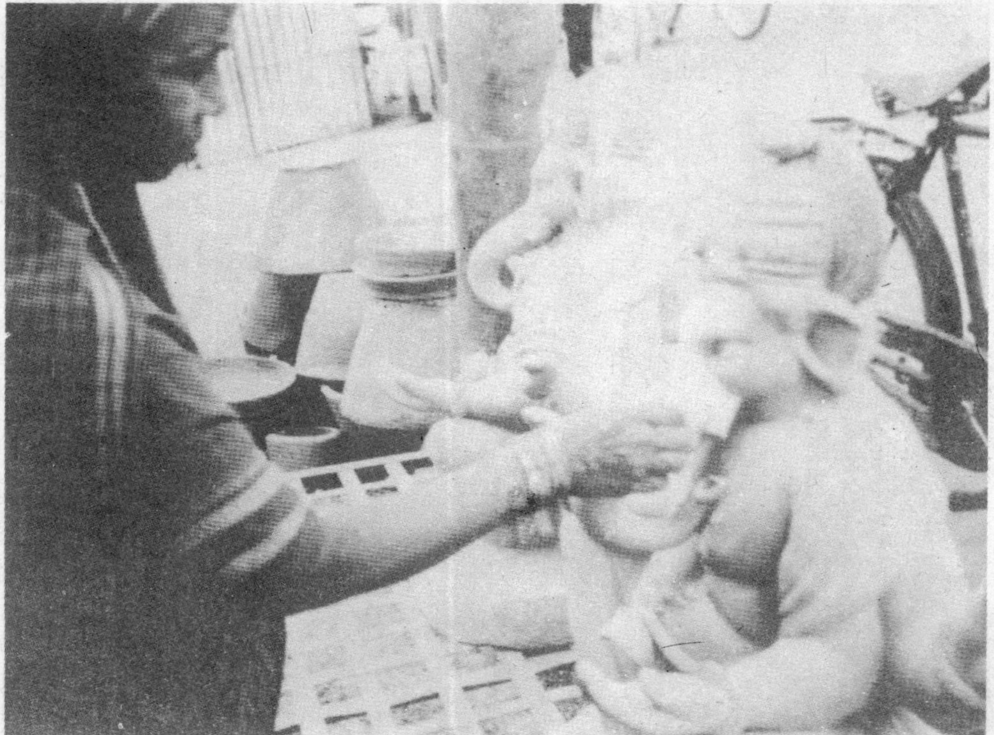

4. A woman puts the finishing touches on a clay image of Ganesh which will be painted and sold for the Ganpati Festival in Pune. *Photography by Eleanor Zelliot.*

festival are (1) the worship of Ganpati, (2) achieving and expressing unity of society, and (3) providing a context for exhibiting "culture." On the second point, several informants interpreted Ganpati to mean Lord (*pati*) of the People (*gaṇa*) and saw the festival as a demonstration of India's democratic ideology and commitment to social progress. On the third point, participants felt the festival was an opportunity for artists, playwrights, and musicians to express their creativity. Many of the *manḍaḷs* depicted themes from Maharashtrian religious traditions, such as representations of incidents from the lives of Marathi poet saints or scenes showing holy sites in Maharashtra. Some political themes continue to be expressed and tend to focus on obstacle or conflict situations, such as the "Indicate-Syndicate" split in the Congress Party, the Maharashtra-Karnataka border controversy, or the achievement of a manned landing on the moon. These themes are artistically depicted in the *manḍaḷ* exhibitions and the image of Ganesh is always to be found somewhere in the background.

Because of the enormous degree of enthusiasm generated by the festival and the young age of the majority of participants, the social fabric of the urban areas is placed under unusual stress. The festive context relaxes the normal social interaction. Police authorities are apprehensive about the potential exploitation of this "liminal" situation by "antisocial elements" who might take this opportunity to stir up communal grievances, but usually the festival remains a time of untroubled gaiety.

If we apply the structural model observed in the Ganesh mythology to the festival itself, we can see the following pattern emerge. The voluntary associations are structurally in between the involuntary family-caste set of relationships on the one hand and total individuality and isolation on the other. The *manḍaḷs* provide a mode of association which is particularly supported by males in a transitional stage between the dependence of childhood and the independence of adulthood. We can further illustrate this with the following diagram.

| *More Structured Situation* | *Mediation* | *Less Structured Situation* |
|---|---|---|
| Caste/Family ⟷ | *maṇḍaḷ* | ⟷ Individual autonomy |
| Childhood ⟷ | *tarūṇ maṇḍaḷ* | ⟷ Adulthood |

On the festival level the fragility of order and less inhibited modes of behavior such as throwing *gulāl* and ecstatic dancing would correspond on the mythological level to Ganesh's ambiguous and "trickster" role. In addition, the modes of relationships among members within a given *maṇḍaḷ* are characterized by a high degree of informality and comradeship, or in other words, by a relative suspension of structures and status-recognizing modes of interaction. This comradeship is seen by its members as highly desirable and one of the values of celebrating the festival.

To return to the question of why the festival has caught on in Maharashtra particularly, we can perhaps suggest some tentative answers. Clearly, the factors of Tilak's charismatic leadership at the initiation of the public festival and the association the festival has had with the independence struggle are important in accounting for the festival's continued popularity. But an additional explanation might be suggested in terms of the structural observations we have made so far. We have observed that the pattern of opposition/mediation has been characteristic on the level of myth as well as ritual. If we consider that Maharashtra is a geographical and cultural unit which lies in between an "Aryanized" north Indian cultural unit and a "Dravidianized" south Indian one and contains many aspects of both yet not all of either, we might see how a myth-ritual complex which articulates a mediation structure at a number of levels would have a particular appeal to a cultural unit which itself plays a mediating role in the larger all-Indian cultural situation. This may also help to explain why so many Maharashtrian cultural themes are believed to be most appropriately expressed through the festival. Of course, this mediating structural pattern is not a conscious aspect of the festival so far as the participants are concerned. But it does seem to emerge as a pattern visible from the outside and may help us to understand one reason why the festival continues in vitality and increasing numbers of participants.

## NOTES

1. See Yoroi 1968:8; Ghurye 1962:99-113; Bhandarkar 1965:147-50.
2. See Gadgil 1967.
3. For a structural analysis of the Pilliyar (Ganesh) mythology of South India and Ceylon, see Leach 1962; for a more theoretical discussion of a structuralist approach to the interpretation of myth, see Levi-Strauss 1955.
4. Personal communication from Professor Norvin J. Hein, Yale University.
5. See Jacoby and Babchuk 1963:461-71; Sharma 1969:579-94; Owens and Nandy 1971.

## REFERENCES

Barnouw, Victor. 1954. "The Changing Character of a Hindu Festival." *American Anthropologist* 56 (Feb.):74-86.

Bhandarkar, R.G. 1965. *Vaiṣṇavism, Śaivism and Minor Systems.* Varanasi: Indological Book House. First published in 1913.

Cashman, Richard. 1970. "The Political Recruitment of God Ganapati." *Indian Economic and Social History Review* 7(Sept.):347-73.

———. 1975. *The Myth of the Lokamanya.* Berkeley: University of California.

Courtright, Paul B. 1985. *Gaṇeśa: Lord of Obstacles.* New York: Oxford University Press.

Gadgil, Amerindra. 1967. *Śrī Gaṇeś Koś* [Encyclopedia of Ganesh]. Vol. 2. Pune: Shriganesh Kosh Mandal.

Getty, Alice. 1936. *Gaṇeśa: A Monograph on the Elephant Faced God.* Oxford: Oxford University Press.

Ghurye, G.S. 1962. *Gods and Men.* Bombay: Popular Book Depot.

Gopinatha Rao, T.A. 1968. *Elements of Hindu Iconography.* Vol. 1,1. 2nd ed. New York: Paragon. Originally published in 1914.

Jacoby, Arthur and Nicholas Babchuk. 1963. "Instrumental and Expressive Voluntary Associations." *Sociology and Social Research* 47:461-71.

Leach, Edmund. 1962. "Pulliyar and the Lord Buddha: An Aspect of Religious Syncretism in Ceylon." *Psychoanalysis and the Psychoanalytic Review* 49:80-102.

Levi-Strauss,Claude. 1955. "The Structural Study of Myth." *Journal of American Folklore* 68:428-44.

Owens, Raymond and Ashis Nandy. 1971. "Voluntary Associations in an Industrial Ward of Howrah, West Bengal, India." Paper presented to the 23rd Annual Meeting of the Association for Asian Studies, Washington, D.C., March 29-31, 1971.

Sarma, Jyotirmoyee. 1969. "Puja Associations of West Bengal." *Journal of Asian Studies* 28:579-94.

Wilkins, W.J. 1913. *Hindu Mythology: Vedic and Puranic.* Calcutta: Thacker. Originally published in 1882.

Yoroi, Kiyoshi. 1968. *Gaṇeśagītā.* The Hague: Mouton.

CHARLES PAIN WITH ELEANOR ZELLIOT

# 8

# *The God Dattatreya and the Datta Temples of Pune*

## *The God Datta*

The god Dattatreya or Datta has been described as "enigmatic and fascinating,"[1] his legends as "profound and shadowy."[2] But in Maharashtra, he is not only exceptionally popular, he is clearly the ultimate syncretistic god, an *avatār* (incarnation) of Brahma, Vishnu, and Shiva. The image of Datta usually seen in pictures and temple images in Maharashtra shows not only the three heads of the three gods attached to one figure, but also six hands which hold the emblems of all three gods: the trident and drum of Shiva, the water pot and lotus (or rosary) of Brahma, the conch and wheel of Vishnu. Datta is dressed as a Shaiva ascetic, accompanied by a cow which represents Mother Earth, and by four dogs, which are said to represent the four Vedas.

This image of Datta has been familiar at least since the seventeenth century and has been described by Tukaram, the Varkari saint-poet:

I fall prostrate before the one with three heads and six hands
A bag of alms hanging from his shoulder
Dogs in front of him.
He bathes in the Ganga daily.
A staff and water-pot are in his hands;
On his feet are clanking wooden sandals;
On his head a splendrous coil of hair;
On his body beautiful ashes.
Tuka says, I bow to him who is clad in space.[3]

The vision of Datta as wandering ascetic is a reflection of the popular belief that he travels to various holy places in the course of a day. Thus he takes his morning bath at Hardwar on the Ganga River or at Panchaleshwar on the Godavari River, which represents the Ganga for Maharashtrians. He meditates at Girnar in Gujarat; he begs for alms at midday in the courtyard of the great Mahalakshmi temple at Kolhapur in Maharashtra; he sleeps at Mahur, center of the goddess Renuka in eastern Maharashtra. Most of these places are centers for Goddess worship; Hardwar is a place frequented by Shaiva ascetics. Connected to the idea of his daily wandering is the belief that he is an eternal *avatār*; unlike other *avatārs* whose stay on earth is limited to a period of time, Datta remains on earth in an invisible form, appearing only to a few.

This popular image of Datta, however, represents only a portion of the complexities which surround him. Ian Raeside has indicated something of the difficulty of comprehending the totality of Datta:

> Dattatreya, like so many of the gods of Hinduism, swims up into our awareness from mysterious depths, makes and breaks connections of which we scarcely know the hundredth part, acquires and discards legends and philosophical attachments of which only a small fraction have reached us and still today he is gaining and losing attributes, shrines, doctrines, swamis and devotees at a rate which an outsider can only hope to follow by persistent anthropological fieldwork and a devoted attachment to the hagiographic ephemera of the Deccan cult centers.[4]

While much has been written on the Datta cult in Marathi, very little has been published in English, aside from translations and discussions of philosophical texts.[5] However, the general history of the development of the Datta image and legend in Maharashtra can be broadly sketched. The first references to Datta in Marathi literature are in the very earliest literature in Marathi, that of the Mahanubhavs. Here Dattatreya appears as one of the five incarnations of the Supreme Being, Parmeshwar, along with Krishna and three sect figures. Current popular worship of Datta in Maharashtra, however, is not due to the Mahanubhav source. The Mahanubhav accounts of Datta as well as references to him in Sanskrit Puranas point to a tradition of Datta worship existing in northern Maharashtra (or, to be more specific, in the Sahyadri and Godavari region) well before the thirteenth century.[6] At some point Datta became connected with the traditions of the Nath yogis and Dasnamis, both pan-Indian Shaiva ascetic orders. Datta has only minor importance in the Nath tradition of northern India, and his connection with the Maharashtrian Nath tradition appears to come rather late. However, he attains prominence in the eighteenth-century Marathi Nath work *Navanāthabhaktisāra,* where he is regarded as the founder of the Nath *sampradāy* (tradition) and guru of Gorakhnath and Matsyendranath. The connection between the Datta cult and Nath tradition continues to be very strong.

Datta is also connected with the Varkari cult of Pandharpur through Janardan Swami, the guru of Eknath (a pivotal figure in the development of the Varkari tradition and a devotee of Datta). According to legend, Janardan brought the young Eknath into spiritual realization by calling up an appearance of Datta, who came in the form of a Muslim fakir. Only when Eknath recognized God in the fakir could he achieve spiritual maturity.[7]

The connections between Datta and the Varkari tradition continue after Eknath; for example, Tukaram's guru, Sri Raghava Chaitanya, received initiation by Datta in a vision at Girnar. However, Datta's importance in the tradition has remained secondary to that of its main deity, Vithoba.

In the sixteenth century, several streams of the Datta tradition emerge, each inspired or centered around the idea that Datta, himself an *avatār,* incarnated as a particular saint. Thus the sixteenth century Datta bhakta, Dasopant, believed in sixteen avatars of Datta.[8] Another stream, which has become the dominant stream nowadays, is represented by the highly revered Marathi text *Gurucaritra* (Life of the Guru). According to this work, Datta incarnated as two holy men, Shripad Shrivallabha (1320–1350), who was born in Pithapur in (present-day) Andhra Pradesh, and Narasimha Saraswati (1378–1458) who was born to a Brahman family in Karanjangar (Akola District). At the age of ten, Saraswati was initiated into the Dasnami order in Varanasi, and spent the next thirty years at various *tīrthas* in the North. He then returned to the Deccan, spent some time at Narsobaci Wadi and Audumbar on the banks of the Krishna, and spent his last twenty-three years at Gangapur in northern Karnataka, now the most important pilgrimage place of the Maharashtrian cult. It should be noted that these saints are considered to be *avatārs* of Datta; they were *not* devotees of Datta.

This seems to be the key to the popularity of Datta today. Not only is he three gods in one, he is the divine archetypal guru, reincarnating himself as guru time after time. He also combines three figures highly revered in Hinduism: the *sannyāsī,* the guru, and the *avatār.* In addition to Shripad Shrivallabha and Narasimha Saraswati, many other saints are regarded as *avatārs* of Datta by their own particular group of followers; however none of them has gained the same degree of recognition as these two saints. Many of the Datta *avatārs* lived during the past one hundred and fifty years. The most prominent are Manikaprabhu (1817–65) and the Swami of Akkalkot (d. 1878). Some of the Datta *avatārs* belong to other traditions or sects; for example, Shridhar Swami (1908–) belongs to the Ramdasi tradition but is considered a Datta *avatār* by some of his followers. The Datta *avatārs* include several Muslin saints, such as Noori Maharaj and Alamprabhu, as well as saints with no definite

Hindu or Muslim affiliation, like Sai Baba of Shirdi. Most of the Datta *avatārs* represent the advanced type of ascetic known as *avadhūta* or *paramahamsa,* typified by Datta.

In his introduction to *Avadhoota Gita,* a text which bears the signature line of the Guru-God Dattatreya, Shankar Mokashi-Punekar summarizes the diverse meanings of Datta:

> A study of the profound and shadowy legend of Dattatreya shows him ... as the patron of many Indian religious cults. For the Natha sects ... he has been the fountain-head of asceticism and *siddhis* (supernatural powers), besides being the initiating and interceding deity. He often leads the ascetics to Shiva or leads Shiva to the ascetic. He often grants them initiation himself. In Western India, he has been all of this, and more. He has inspired a number of domestic virtues and disciplines, arts, poetry and music.... Dattatreya means many things to many people. There are local redactions of his image. These seem to be capable of bringing about personal transformation.[9]

The following essay on the Datta temples of Pune[10] indicates some of the meanings of Datta and illustrates the contemporary growth of the sect. True, the temples are probably less important than the places of Datta pilgrimage in Maharashtra and Karnataka, and certainly less ubiquitous than the presence of the Dattatreya name or picture. But they are the places where the various associations of Datta meet, where the continuing guru tradition can be seen by all, and where song and story herald the significance of Datta to his worshippers.

## *The Datta Temples of Pune*

For many Hindus, including Datta worshippers, the local temple plays a subordinate role in their religious life in comparison with the household shrine and the pilgrimage places. This is especially true in Pune, where there are no imposing, ancient temples. It seems that many Datta de-

5. (L) An image of Datta as incarnation of Shiva, Vishnu, and Brahma in a Pune temple. *Photography by Eleanor Zelliot.*

6. (R) Gods and gurus in the god-house of a Pune Brahman family. The top-most image is that of Datta. *Photography by Eleanor Zelliot.*

votees rarely visit a temple, and when they do it is only to take *darshan,* or view the deity briefly.

The Datta temples of Pune are characteristically small, and many are inconspicuously hidden behind storefronts. Some are merely roadside shrines which can be viewed only from the outside. The larger temples consist of a small meeting hall or *sabhāmaṇḍap,* in front of an inner shrine or *garbhagṛiha,* generally a small cubicle which contains the central image of the deity and the utensils used in worship. From the ceiling of the hall hangs a bell which is rung by visitors to announce their arrival to the god. As is characteristic of Shiva temples, there is usually a well-defined corridor surrounding the inner shrine, with small shrines and pictures along the way, built for circumambulation (*pradakshiṇā*) of the god, which is a popular act of Datta worship.

The daily program of worship at Pune temples follows a general pattern observed at other temples. M.S. Mate told me that in Maharashtra many differences in temple *pūjā,* which once existed among various cults, have been diminished due to Maharashtra's peculiar tendency toward religious syncretism. The daily ritual, or *pūjā,* at Datta temples consists of an early morning session of bathing, dressing, and anointing the image and offerings of food, incense, and flowers, and in the evening a brief waving of lights (*āratī*) performed by one or two householder priests or *pujārīs.* With some exceptions, the *pujārīs* at Datta temples in Pune are Deshastha Brahmans, some working part-time and salaried by the temple management to perform morning and evening worship. On Thursday, Datta's auspicious day, a more elaborate *pūjā* is performed.

During my time in Pune in 1969, I was able to locate seven Datta temples, plus one dedicated to the nineteenth-century Datta incarnation, the Swami of Akkalkot. Ghurye reported in 1956 that there were eleven Datta temples in Pune, nineteen Rama temples, twenty-six Ganpati, fifty-two (of at least fourteen forms of) Devi, and fifty-four for Vithoba. At the beginning of the nineteenth century, however, there was only one Datta shrine, which was inside the private house of a merchant.[11] Most of the Datta temples in Pune were built shortly after the turn of the century, the most popular one, the Dagadu Halwai Datta Mandir, being consecrated in 1904. New temples continue to be built. One Datta temple in the Cantonment area of Pune was built as recently as 1960; and a new *āshram* center near Karve Road is dedicated to Julavani Maharaj, an art teacher in Pune who became a renowned Datta bhakta. If one observes the pictures of the god in homes, tea shops, storefronts, and motor rickshaws, it would seem that in this city Datta is a deity almost more important than any other, except for the ubiquitous Ganpati.

The three-headed image of Datta is found in most of the Datta temples in Pune, though one-headed (*ekmukhī*) images are found at the Math of Ganganath Maharaj and the Kala Datta (Black Datta) Mandir in Kasba Peth, which seems to be a particularly old temple. The six-armed *ekmukhī* image of Datta is found at several important Datta temples in Maharashtra. Usually in Datta temples, in front of the main image, are found representations of Datta's wooden sandals, or footprints, called *pādukās*. These are the main object of worship. I have been told by several devotees that the importance of the *pādukās* is connected with the idea that Datta is constantly moving and never in one place for very long.

By the use of various symbols and images, Datta's Vishnu or Shiva aspect may be emphasized. For example, in the inner shrine of one temple, a large metal image of Vishnu is situated below the standing Datta image and there are wall paintings of Vishnu on both sides of the entrance hall, indicating a strong emphasis on Datta's Vaishnava aspect. The inner shrine of the Datta mandir on Parnakuti Hill houses an image (*mūrti*) of Datta with three heads and *pādukās* but is significantly connected to a Shiva temple built into a rock cave, with a small shrine of Shiva's wife, Parvati, nearby. There is a full-time *pujārī* in residence here, but as far as I can tell there is no special worship on either Thursday, Datta's day, or Monday, Shiva's day.

In the courtyard of Rasta Wada in Pune's Rasta Peth is another Datta temple which is part of a Vaishnava complex that includes Ram and Hanuman. However, each temple has its own *pujārīs* and there seems to be little interaction between them. In fact, the Ram temple seems to be nearly out of use. An interesting feature of this temple is its bearded and mustached three-headed bust of Datta. Though Datta is usually clean-shaven in iconographic representation, in many older pictures he has a long, matted beard. There is a story that a noted classical singer and Datta devotee, Hirabai Barodekar, had a dream in which Dattatreya appeared as a bearded man. She searched for a temple with this image and, finding it, returned once a year to sing a concert to Dattatreya.[12]

The Datta temple in the courtyard of a Someshwar (Shiva) temple in Ravivar Peth has a connection with the Nath ascetic order. Across from the temple is a Nath ashram and nearby are shrines of Ram, Ganpati, and Parvati. In this temple, Datta is depicted as the guru of the nine legendary Naths (in Marathi called *nao-nāth*) and their pictures are hung along the walls of the *sabhāmaṇḍap*. Inside the ashram is a sacred fire (called a *dhunī*) and pictures of Shiva, Dattatreya, Hanuman, and Gorakhnath. The wandering Nath ascetics that I met there were Hindi-speakers and appear to have come from the North. Once I met an English-speaking Nath ascetic from the center at Nasik (Maharashtra) who performed some magic and offered me *gānjā* (marijuana).[13]

Halfway between Pune's City Post and the central market, behind an arcade of shops, is a temple dedicated to the Swami of Akkalkot (d. 1878), considered by his followers to be the third historical Datta *avatār* (after Shripad Shrivallabha, and Narasimha Saraswati). Judging from the rich interior of the temple and the large number of visitors at the place, it seems that the Swami of Akkalkot has attracted a particularly large following and widespread recognition in Pune. Inside the main shrine is an image of the Swami marked by a frowning expression and a prominent Vaishnava *tilak* mark on his forehead. A large metal *nāga* (serpent) hood, a Shaiva emblem, rises behind his head. In front of the image are several large elliptical stones which the *pujārī* said were *banalingas,* stones naturally shaped by the abrasion of river water into the phallic symbol of Shiva.

As is typical of Datta temples, there are large brass *pādukās* of the Swami, placed during the morning and evening in front of the inner shrine as the chief object of worship. On the walls of the front hall are pictures of Dattatreya, Narasimha Saraswati, the Swami of Akkalkot, and his successor Gajanan Maharaj, as well as a picture of Dnyaneshwar, the Vaishnava Varkari saint. Outside in the courtyard is a small shrine of Datta's *pādukās* and image at the base of an *audumbar* tree, which is particularly sacred to Datta. Many devotees circumambulate the tree as a devotional act. Two full-time *pujārīs* are in residence at the temple to attend to the morning and evening *pūjā* as well as to the influx of visitors who come to take *darshan.* Usually, on late Thursday afternoons and evenings, a group of women assemble here to sing devotional songs to Datta and Akkalkot Swami.

The most popular Datta temple in Pune is the Dagadu Halwai Datta Mandir, named after the famous Pune sweet merchant who built this temple. Datta at this temple is believed to be particularly *jāgṛit* (awake); his presence is particularly felt here. The facade of the temple is ornately carved and painted,and the temple is open to the street. (A site very near the temple is used for a Ganpati booth during the Ganpati festival; the Dagadu Halwai Ganpati is probably the most popular in all Pune.) The three-headed image of Datta inside is easily visible from the street, and in the evening there is usually a crowd of people pausing outside to take *darshan.*

The front of the inner shrine is plated with silver and carved with images of Datta and the sun-god Surya. On the wall in back of the *garbhagṛiha* (inner shrine) are pictures of Ganpati, the incarnations of Narasimha Saraswati and Shridhar Swami, and Shiva.[14] Many people who come here are middle-class Brahmans, though other groups and castes come too. Occasionally *sannyāsīs* visit and often, particularly on Guruvar (Thursday, Datta's day), there is a group of beggars sitting outside in front.

It is a curious feature of the god Dattatreya that he is also the patron god of prostitutes in Maharashtra. It is said that Dagadu Halwai, who was something of a social reformer, had this temple built on the edge of Pune's red light district so that the prostitutes would have a place to worship. That Datta can be both a god of Brahmans and ascetics and a god of prostitutes is explained by the fact that he is an *avadhūta,* an advanced type of ascetic, who is untouched by purity or impurity and who looks upon all beings impartially.

The *pūjā* at the Dagadu Halwai Datta temple is performed in turn by five Deshastha Brahman householders from three families. The temple opens at five-thirty in the morning and unlike the other Datta temples in Pune has a complete *mahāpūjā* consisting of sixteen acts of service to the deity. A short *āratī* is performed at noon to the accompaniment of drums and flutes. The inner shrine is then closed until five-thirty, when it is open again for *darshan.* A daily evening program of *āratī* and devotional songs (*bhajan*) begins at nine-thirty.[15] This *bhajan* program is attended chiefly by Brahmans who live near the temple. Clearly, for these people the temple plays an important role in their religious lives. The program begins with several short songs and then, to the accompaniment of drums and cymbals, a small procession of devotees led by the *pujārīs* circumambulates the inner shrine three times, pausing in front of the deity and the sacred pictures, performing *āratī* and singing songs. The drums sound loudly, and holy water is thrown by the *pujārī* over the group of devotees. *Prasād* of *panchāmṛit,* a mixture of milk, ghee, honey, sugar, and the water with which Datta's *pādukās* have been washed, is distributed to the devotees. A second session of *bhajans* follows. One of these songs, a mercy-invoking song by Vasudevananda Saraswati,[16] indicates more than others the

Brahmanness of Datta (who is the son of the Brahman sage Atri and his wife Anasuya):

> Hail glorious Shri Guru Datta
> Do not be hard-hearted now.
> Let the mind that grieved when thieves beat the Brahman grieve now.
> Let the mind that grieved when the Brahman suffered pain grieve now.
> Let the mind that showed compassion when the Brahman's son died not be aloof now.
> Let the mind that showed compassion when the widow grieved turn to me now.
> O Shri Guru Datta, leave aside this callousness and turn your tender heart toward me now.

The evening worship draws to a close around ten-thirty; the deity is put to sleep and the doors of the inner shrine are closed.

On Thursday evenings, the service begins later and is more elaborate. A palanquin containing Datta's *pādukās* and pictures of Datta and Narasimha Saraswati is brought out by the *pujārīs,* and carried in a procession around the inner shrine three times, to the accompaniment of *bhajans, āratī,* incense, and drums. The atmosphere is charged with the spirit of the devotees and a strong sense of power.

At the time of Datta's birth anniversary, the Datta *jayantī* (in mid-December), this temple and others observe a seven day celebration. Special *bhajans* are held, and at Ananda Ashram in Budhwar Peth a continuous twenty-four hour a day reading of the *Gurucaritra* is performed by about two hundred devotees. Other sacred texts are read by devotees on this occasion—the *Datta Prabodh,* composed in 1860 by Kavadi Bova, and the *Datta Māhātmya* by Vasudevananda Sarasvati. Both works are in Marathi and describe the deeds (*līlā*) of the *avatār* Datta, as drawn from the Puranas and other sources. Both works are relatively late, attesting to the continuing development of the cult in modern times.

## NOTES

1. Shankar Mokashi-Punekar, "An Introduction to Shri Purohit Swami and the Avadhoota Gita," in *Avadhoota Gita* (New Delhi: Munshiram Manoharlal, 1979), p. 7. Mokashi-Punekar's long introduction to the text is one of the best sources in English on the Datta cult.

2. I.M.P. Raeside, "Dattātreya." *Bulletin of the School of Oriental and African Studies* 45:3 (1982):489.

3. Translated by Charles Pain. This *abhanga* of Tukaram's is found in most Marathi pamphlets on Datta worship and in the *Śrīdattātreya-jñānkoś* by P.N. Joshi (Bombay: Surekha Prakashan, 1974), p. 15.

4. Raeside, "Dattātreya," p. 500.

5. On the Datta cult and philosophy, see Jaya Chamarajendra Bahadur Wadiyar, *Dattatreya, the Way and the Goal* (London: George Allen and Unwin, 1957); Hariprasad S. Joshi, *The Origin and Development of Dattatreya Worship in India* (Baroda: Maharaja Sayajirao University of Baroda, 1965). For a description of a major pilgrimage place, Gangapur, see M.S. Mate, *Temples and Legends of Maharashtra* (Bombay: Bharatiya Vidya Bhavan, 1962). For Marathi sources, see C. Kulkarni, *Gaṅgāpūr Māhātmya aṇī Śrī Datta Upāsanā* (Belgaum: Saraswati Book Collection, 1969); R.C. Dhere, *Dattasampradāyācā Itihās*, 2nd ed. (Pune: Nilkanth Prakashan, 1964); and the encyclopedic *Śrīdattātreya-jñānkoś* by P.N. Joshi.

6. See Raeside, "Dattātreya," p. 496.

7. See *Eknath: a Translation from the Bhaktalilamrita*, trans. Justin E. Abbott (Pune: Scottish Mission Industries Co., 1927). verses 149-208. The author is Mahipati, although this information is not given in the volume until the introduction of the translator.

8. The biography of Dasopant, the *Dāsopanta Caritra*, has been translated by Justin Abbott as *Dasopant Digambar, The Poet-Saints of Maharashtra*, no. 4 (Poona: Scottish Mission Industries' Orphanage Press, 1928).

9. Shankar Mokashi-Punekar, "An Introduction to Shri Purohit Swami," p.7.

10. Charles Pain's essay on the Datta temples of Pune was written during his first visit to India as an undergraduate in 1969. Footnotes indicate changes he noticed subsequently, but we have left his essay substantially in its original form as a fresh and unusual observation. Eds.

11. G.S. Ghurye, *Gods and Men* (Bombay: Popular Book Depot, 1962), p. 125-26, 218.

12. The importance of music in the Datta cult has been mentioned by many writers including Dhere and Mokashi-Punekar; music is said to be very pleasing to Datta. Ghurye (*Gods and Men*, p. 112) notes that one chapter of the *Gurucaritra* is devoted to a classification of *rāgas* and their deities. The importance of music in the cult points to the influence of both the Nath and Sufi traditions.

13. On a subsequent visit in 1986, I found that the ashram had been converted to a storeroom.

14. Since my visit in 1969, the large picture of Narasimha Sarasvati has been replaced by one of Adbanginath ("Lord of Idiots"), who is included among the nine Nathas according to one tradition. There is a *samādhī* (tomb) of Adbanginath in the form of a Muslim tomb at Dudulgav near Alandi, which in recent years has become a popular place of pilgrimage.

15. I was told in 1986 that the evening procession and *bhajans* had been discontinued some years back, probably because of the street's greatly increased motor traffic.

16. Vasudevananda Saraswati (1854-1914) was a Datta devotee. The translation of this song, heard at both the Dagadu Halwai Mandir and at Gangapur, was made by G.V. Ketkar and Charles Pain.

GUNTHER-DIETZ SONTHEIMER

# 9
# *The Religion of the Dhangar Nomads*

In western Maharashtra, in the districts of Pune, Ahmednagar, and Satara, well inside the Deccan Plateau and in a region traversed by the west-east flowing Bhima, Karha, and Nira rivers, we come across the scattered monsoon camps of the nomadic, pastoral Hatkar Dhangars. The region is broken up by spurs emanating from the western mountains, which separate the plateau from the coastal area of Maharashtra. These spurs slowly descend from west to east until they are lost in the vast plateau. Today the monsoon camps are well within these hill ranges or close to them, where the agricultural expansion of the last one hundred fifty years or so could not dislodge them. Here the Hatkar Dhangars, with their typical red turbans, heavy sandals, black woolen blankets, staff often held horizontally behind the neck on the shoulders to provide a rest for the arms, and their women folk—with a more generous amount of ornaments than found amongst the agricultural castes—are still very conspicuous.

In places here the annual rainfall does not exceed two inches. Agriculture in the river valleys is nowadays well secured by dams, canals, or wells, but the rocky hills and stony heaths are only fit for grazing sheep and goats, and the cultivation of millet crops during the rainy season. Some hardy farmers have made a dent in this rocky area wherever there is a suitable depression, allowing for local village dams and wells. But farming remains hazardous. The whole region was traditionally given to pastoral activities rather than to regular plough cultivation. Spreading agriculture has naturally pushed pastoralism back and has led to overgrazing of the remaining pastures.

The seasonal monsoon camps are mostly inhabited by members of one patrilineal clan, who live separately in nuclear families, each having a flock of fifty to a hundred fifty sheep. Present day campsites are fixed. A symbiotic relationship exists between the farmers, some of whom also own sheep, and the Dhangars: the Dhangars help the farmers to shear the sheep (a poor Dhangar may even find employment as a shepherd), and the farmers buy the heaps of sheep manure at the end of the Dhangars' stay. The farmers also ask the Dhangars to pen their sheep in the fields and sometimes even entrust them with the sale of their sheep in the coastal area. Dhangars and farmers have an equal status in the hierarchy within the area of their monsoon camps.

The pastures around the campsites are owned by the Dhangars. Sometimes a meager millet crop may be grown and harvested on a sharecropping basis by members of the agricultural castes. The camps have huge sheep pens and the loosely piled-up stone walls are crowned by the dried thorny branches of the *bābhūḷ* tree to protect the sheep against the rare wolves and, hopefully, against the more common thieves. Some Dhangars have small tents of canvas, but more and more huts and houses are being built. There is no dearth of stones and boulders around the camp as building material. The roofs consist of corrugated tin sheets which somehow do not manage to convey the dismal look of slums in the big cities. If the roofs are not fixed to the huts they are deposited with farmers in a nearby village as long as the Hatkar Dhangars are on migration.

The length of stay in the seasonal monsoon camps or settlements is determined by the southwestern monsoon and the marginal influence of the northeastern monsoon. The rainy season lasts from the beginning of June up to the beginning of October. During this period the Hatkar Dhangars normally remain in their monsoon camps. But if the monsoon is insufficient and the stay in the camp is seriously disturbed, the Dhangars are forced to migrate into an area with more rainfall. But too much rain there drives them away again. They may also turn to areas protected by canal irrigation; here they pen their sheep in the fields of the farmers. If the rain is good—which means not so much as to create diseases among the sheep but enough to somewhat regenerate the pastures—the four months' stay follows. It is devoted to a leisurely grazing of sheep and to a comparatively easier life, full of social and religious activities.

After the monsoon the annual migration begins towards the west on a traditional route with fixed camping sites. This becomes increasingly more difficult as the spreading industrialization encroaches on camping sites, and the bottlenecks of towns and cities get narrower and narrower. Moreover, heavy truck traffic is not favorable to the little caravans of pack horses and the huge flocks of sheep. The horses, or rather ponies, are packed to capacity with household utensils, little children, chickens with baskets to house them during the night, lambs unable to walk, nets for penning sheep, long sticks for pitching the tent, and so on. The women go ahead while the men drive the flocks with considerable skill along the road or on some shortcut over a hill, taking a diversion ever in search for a chance to graze their sheep. But this also becomes difficult as grazing is foiled more and more by the ubiquitous ragweed,[1] which is shunned by the sheep and is a cause of allergies to people. By the time the men arrive at the camping site the women have pitched the small tents, if the weather makes this

7. A Dhangar herds his sheep through the streets of Pune. *Photography by Frances Bressman.*

8. Dhangar men dance on the festival of Krishnamai during the month of Shravan. *Photography by S. Y. Waghmare.*

necessary, and prepared the simple evening meal consisting mainly of millet bread. The next morning at about ten the camp will set out for the next halting place. Thus the Dhangars migrate one hundred to two hundred miles until they reach the rice area and their patron villages in the west. Here they will break up into smaller groups, which shift from field to field and village to village in order to pen the sheep. Sheep manure is very much in demand amongst the farmers, and the Dhangars are paid in kind (rice) or cash. Generally vegetation is much richer in the west and one can graze the sheep on harvest fields—if no second crop is introduced with the help of new irrigation facilities as in parts of the Konkan—or take them to nearby forests, if this is permitted. As soon as the monsoon approaches, the Hatkar Dhangars are on their return journey to the drier east, hoping intensely that sufficient rains have revived their pastures and filled the water places.

The traditional difficulties and anxieties may be decreasing with the new age. There are fewer wild animals and fewer dangerous rivers to cross and some of the human and animal diseases are checked by modern medicine, which is, however, made use of somewhat sluggishly. Modern times do bring some material advantages as well. For instance, with industrialization in the big cities and thriving agriculture around them, the sale of mutton increases.

## *The Influence of Shaivism*

The religious beliefs of the Hatkar Dhangars are very much their own and also at the same time shared by many other pastoral groups in the Deccan. The compartmentalization of traditional Indian social life does not mean that religious beliefs and rituals are the exclusive property of a particular group, but rather that certain aspects are predominant and emphasized in each group. Variations in the emphasis of the religious outlook may depend on, for instance, whether a group is settled or nomadic. Generally the religious beliefs of the pastoral groups have been enriched by the contact with Shaivites, e.g., the saints of the Nath[2] sect (*siddhas*) with their supernatural powers (*siddhis*) from the North of India and the Shaivite Lingayat[3] saints from the South. There is little direct influence of Brahmanical outlook. Vishnu and Krishna, the shepherd god *par excellence* of the Vaishnava bhakti movement, better known to the settled Dhangars,[4] are hardly known to the nomadic Hatkar Dhangars. If one goes, for instance, on the birthday of Krishna to their camps, one will find that the day passes without notice. One of the major cults of Maharashtra is devoted to the god Vithoba of Pandharpur. This cult developed first in a Shaivite context before it was taken over by Maharashtrian Vaishnava bhakti. In the traditions of the Dhangars, Vithoba is a brother of their god Biroba and their attitudes towards him remain rather "Shaivite" than "Vaishnava."

## *The Ancestors*

The ancestors, though "deceased," are not just remembered, but are very much part of the life of the Hatkar Dhangars. They do not interfere obtrusively and at all times, but they *are* there, contributing towards the unity of their descendants and rewarded with the respect shown to them at every religious function. They live on the border of the monsoon camp where little shrines are built to house them. Important ancestors, especially the eldest known, are installed here in the form of stone tablets which often show the ancestor riding a horse with his wife or wives astride and accompanied by his dog.

The Dhangars normally burn their dead. When a corpse is taken to the funeral place, the son of the deceased carries with him an earthen pot filled with water. A stone nearby is selected, worshipped, and then used to break the waterpot. After the body is burned the bones are collected and thrown into the river. The stone is again worshipped and kept at the border of a field or in the ancestor shrine.

The dead man (*māṇūs* "man" or *jīv* "soul") ascends to

heaven or to Shiva's abode, the Kailas mountain, or "somewhere"—there is generally no pronounced view about where he goes. But he may return by god's order to the living and appear in a dream demanding a shrine, a *mūrti* (image), and a feast. Then a date has to be fixed and on the appointed day he possesses or "enters the body" of one of his descendants and speaks: "Install me, I have come." A shrine is made and a *mūrti* is installed in it beside the original stone. After this a communal dinner follows which includes non-vegetarian food. First an offering (*nived*) is given or "shown" and some morsels are placed before the *mūrti*. After the dinner a dance (*kheḷ*) follows during which the ancestor enters the body of one of the Dhangars who is asked whether his, i.e., the ancestor's "soul," is satisfied. Thereafter the deceased is elevated to the position of a deity; that is, he has become a deified ancestor and has some obligation to favor his living descendants. Along with other ancestors he watches the doings of the living from the border of the camp. The Dhangars are under a special obligation to honor the ancestors in a ceremony which takes place once a year after the full moon day in the month of Kartik (October/November). During other festivals, if the Dhangars are not forced to migrate because of failing rains, the ancestors also partake of the food, a little of which is placed before the ancestor stones. These stones are washed at least once a week, usually on Sundays.

Some would make a distinction between the "soul" (*jīv*), which ascends to Kailas, and the "mind," "desire," or "unfulfilled wish" (*man*)—a kind of shadowy soul. The *jīv* which goes to Kailas will be judged by the god of death, Yamaraja, simply called Yam, who weighs merits and sins. Accordingly, the *jīv* will be reborn as a human being or in an animal form. But this view plays a marginal role. The others who do not distinguish between *jīv* and *man* also have the idea of retribution, though here the emphasis is on the return of the ancestors, who become deified after proper worship and form a cluster near the monsoon camp. This points to a tendency also common among tribals in

Middle India to worship the ancestors of a clan clustering not far from the living on the border of the settlement. The notion of the ancestors' living in Kailas or in some heaven is rarely in the foreground of Dhangar thought. Likewise the notion of retribution and incarnation—which Max Weber called one of the few real dogmas in Hinduism[5]—is rather casual and does not preoccupy the minds of the Hatkar Dhangars.

### *The Devṛishī: Medium of the Ancestors and the Gods*

An important link between the dead, or the gods, and the living is the *devṛishī*. A Dhangar god may be directly approached by the worshippers and may even indicate answers to questions by appropriate sign like a flower or a betelnut falling to the right or the left from the *mūrti*, but normally gods, goddesses, and ancestors communicate through the *devṛishī*. The *devṛishī* of a monsoon camp does not look different from the other Dhangars, nor can we affirm that he is mentally predisposed to be the medium of gods and ancestors. He may be a young lad and a great-grandson of the camp's original ancestor, who possesses him, initially indicating his presence by some illness. A sonless ancestor may possess a brother's son, which amounts to a kind of *post mortem* adoption. The *devṛishī* has to be confirmed in a ritual test. A person may also be a special devotee of the god Biroba or another Dhangar god. He gets possessed during the festival or on some other occasions demanding communication with gods and ancestors, e.g., in cases of illness caused by a ghost or if any other inexplicable untoward event takes place.

There is little fear of ghosts. If the ghost is a dissatisfied ancestor, he can be set at rest by installing him in an ancestor shrine and giving him a feast. Really malignant spirits usually come from outside the community. One Dhangar, for example, was caught by the ghost of a deceased Muslim while he was on migration in the Konkan and had gone to defecate in the morning—a typical moment of impurity and danger likely to attract ghosts. After prolonged illness he was healed when during the *kheḷ* (dance) the drums attracted the family god. A virtual fight between the god and the ghost took place in the body of the Dhangar and the ghost was driven out at last. Ever since, the family god has taken possession of the Dhangar, and he has become an acknowledged *devṛishī*.

The special devotion and the powers of the *devṛishī* will attract members of other castes who come and consult him in cases of an unusual illness and persistent mishaps. His powers are remembered and live on even after his death, and he is specially worshipped in a shrine beside his god. The *devṛishī* himself has, in fact, turned into a god, who possesses more prestige and power than a simple ancestral *dev*. His son would normally assume the functions of a *devṛishī* if he has the capacity of getting possessed. If not the son, some other male descendant may inherit the powers. Eventually an annual festival, called *jatrā*, will develop and at the height of the festival the god enters the body of the son or other relative, who now also tends to become a *pujārī* (temple priest) and will permanently attend the god. The power of the god established by the deceased *devṛishī* will attract other devotees not belonging to the patrilineal clan, and the *jatrā* may grow, attracting people from other castes as well. There may be more reasons for the origin and growth of a cult and a *jatrā*, but the deep devotion of a *devṛishī* or a *siddha* attracting a powerful god is often said to be the root.

### *Biroba and Mhaskoba: The Jatrā in Honor of the Gods*

The desire to meet a powerful god, the joy of taking part in the festival and its ceremonies, the religious merit deriving from them, the sacrifice of a sheep for the god (perhaps in the fulfillment of a vow) and the ensuing feast in which he partakes, the appreciation of his help, the feeling of having reassured the continuing bond between god and man and his group, and the fun involved in a fair—all these motives mix inextricably. Thus the famous Biroba of Arevadi in

Sangli District attracts twenty thousand Dhangars to annual *jatrā*. Another god, the Mhaskoba of Vir in Pune District, originally a simple pastoral god who had been brought there by a Hatkar Dhangar, has gathered more and more devotees from other castes, especially agriculturists. Some may even doubt that the god has a special connection with the Dhangars. But since a religious belief hardly ever gets lost in India we find that the story of the origin of the god is preserved in the oral tradition of the villagers and the Dhangars. There are many accretions and interpretations of the cult, especially by Shaivite Gosavis who have turned Mhaskoba into an incarnation of Shiva, namely Kal Bhairav. But the descendants of the original Dhangar devotee who brought the god to Vir still get "hereditarily" possessed by the god.

The fourteen-day *jatrā* at Vir in the month of February culminates in one or two Dhangars getting possessed by Mhaskoba. They first "play" with a long sword as if with a threat to kill themselves lest the god not come and enter them. This reminds us of the *siddhis*, the supernatural powers acquired by the Naths or Siddhas, who could slash their bodies without causing any injury. And, in fact, these Dhangars are called *shids* (from Skt. *siddha*). In the middle of a huge crowd the god then makes his appearance in the form of the Dhangar. He (the Dhangar) ascends a horse, that is, he rides on the shoulder of a man, and a royal parasol is held over him while he makes his forecasts about rain and crops to the gasping devotees.

Naturally most of the festivals in honor of Biroba are held during the four months' stay in the monsoon camps. The temples of Biroba are always well outside the villages in some stony pasture. They are whitewashed and crowned by a spire which makes them look somewhat like Muslim tombs. The "images" of Biroba are rough boulders coated with red lead and fashioned somewhat into a face, with inset eyes. The god is said to have manifested himself in the boulder or stone when he came to the particular spot.

If one attends a *jatrā* of a Biroba belonging to the nomadic Hatkar Dhangars, one will first see Dhangars with their red turbans flocking in, along with their women, who lead the ponies. For once the ponies are not overburdened with household goods as during the migration, but carry the few utensils and provisions which are needed for the *jatrā*, which lasts one and a half days. Each family brings, if possible, one or two sheep for the feast, sacrificing it in honor of Biroba. One of the main ceremonies consists of circumambulating the temple in a procession. During this procession the shrines of other deities attached to the temple are also visited, e.g., that of Biroba's wife (if the particular Biroba is married) and of the founder of the cult. The sounds of drums, cymbals, and flutes make the air vibrate. When the procession reaches the front of the temple, the Dhangars break into a dance. The rhythm of the drums starts slowly and grows faster and faster, determining the speed of the dance until the rhythm reaches a peak and suddenly drops to a halt. That is the moment when the special devotee and priest may get possessed by the god. The Dhangars may occasionally smoke hemp (*gānjā*)—so does the god Mhaskoba—but not to get possessed. As in all rites of possession, not only in shamanistic seances, the drums are important—they are the dangerous, magical instrument for the achievement of possession. (We hear in a story from a settled Dhangar group that a devotee, possessed by the god, was killed when his enemy suddenly changed into the wrong rhythm.) Dense clouds of turmeric thrown by the Dhangars descend on the special devotee/priest, covering him with a thick layer of yellow powder. The god is present in the substance of the turmeric powder and slowly but steadily the devotee/priest (*bhakta/pujārī*) and the other participants assume a yellow-golden color—the god and his devotees merge.

Meanwhile the sheep have been sacrificed by the individual families and the meal has been cooked by the women. The patrilineal descendants of the original ancestor who set up the cult, sacrifice near their ancestor stones, which are in front of the temple and either face Biroba or, like him, face the East. A share in the meal, consisting of liver, millet bread, and rice, is "shown" to the god, whereas the ancestors are actually fed. Sometimes one may see that some morsels of food are placed near the mouth of an ancestor stone as if he is to eat it—a visible expression of the fact that we have to think of the ancestors' stones as more than just "symbols." As the god very much resides in the *mūrti* so the ancestors *are* present in the stones.

In some places, among settled Dhangars, the god tends not to partake of the non-vegetarian offerings; here he may have been joined by Vithoba as his brother and we have, for once, the influence of Vaishnava or Lingayat vegetarianism.

Another typical Dhangar religious institution which should be mentioned in this context is the *dāvaṇ*, literally a "rope" to which five rams are tied. Each year for five years a ram is set aside for the family god. In the fifth year the rams are freed and the first which reaches the herd has a lease of mercy. The others are brought to the temple and one is given to the priest. In the case of Khandoba, the non-Brahman priest (Gurav) will sell the ram, because he is vegetarian. The other three sheep are sacrificed in the name of the family god, who is shown the *nived*. The relatives by blood and marriage as well as friends are invited for the dinner. After a few days the remaining fifth ram is sacrificed in the camp in the name of Biroba. A little closer to the fervent, unconditional devotion to Shiva, Shiva-bhakti, is the tradition of identifying oneself with sacrificial animals. The traditions of the god Mhaskoba remind us vaguely of this type of *dāvaṇ*. In this story, the five sons of the Hatkar Dhangar who brought the god to Vir are demanded by the god as a sacrifice in order to test their true devotion. One of them hides himself and is saved. The other sons are sacrificed. But, as a true Shaivite god, Mhaskoba brings death *and* life—one conditioning the other—and revives the children or rather replaces them by lambs.

### *The Ovīs:*<br>*The Oral Traditions and Their Performance*

The dance at the *jatrā* may last deep into the night. Some Dhangars may join together to sing their *ovīs*—ballads which are intoned in the memory of their family god and all other gods and goddesses worthy of being remembered. One singer leads together with another and they sing two lines. The same are repeated by two other Dhangars, who in this way learn to sing the *ovī*. Such *ovīs* may not only be sung at the *jatrā*, but also late into the night in the camp or in the open field while penning the sheep, without a glimmer of light except perhaps the stars and the moon. The Dhangars are seated on felts and woolen blankets. The singing of the *ovīs* assures wakefulness in two ways: it keeps the man awake to watch the sheep and keeps alive the awareness of the presence of God. The melody is simple, based on five tones, and reminds us of Gregorian chorals. It seems much more in consonance with the pastoral surrounding and the perpetual rustling of the wind during the monsoon period than the *ovī* among settled Dhangars elsewhere. There the *ovī* is performed with the accompaniment of all kinds of instruments and measured dance steps to underline what is a kind of dramatical show.

Though very much in touch with the routine of rituals and the religion of the group, the *ovīs* are almost unmarked by ritual and religious obsession. They transcend these as the reflections of a religiously-inclined, sensitive composer, who also has the talents of an entertaining poet. The *ovīs* thus act as a leaven to the routine of rituals and make daily life more meaningful. There are few modern, "progressive" strains in them. Dhangars of settled groups, on the other hand, are literate and some of them highly educated. Amongst the settled Dhangars' texts of the "Great Tradition" are the *Rāmāyaṇa* and *Mahābhārata* in Marathi, turned into *ovīs*. One even hears of Mahatma Gandhi.

The contents of the *ovīs* of the Hatkar Dhangars often relate to the Satyayuga—the Golden Age of Truth—which seems at times still present in out-of-the-way camps not touched by the influence of the cities of Pune and Bombay. Many of the *ovīs* tell the adventures of Dhangars, sometimes funny, sometimes serious: the taming of a tiger, the crossing of rivers and the encounters with river goddesses (an incident as old as the Rigveda), drought, and the search for pastures. But religious and ethical teachings are also present in an unobtrusive way. For instance, Shiva comes as an old haggard mendicant afflicted with leprosy and the Dhangar offers him hospitality, though the Dhangar has not yet recognized him: God is ubiquitous.

A typical *ovī*—which actually comes from a settled Dhangar but could be translated into a nomadic Hatkar Dhangar context—describes a Dhangar watching the morning prayers of a Brahman standing in the river. He questions the Brahman, who explains the significance of the ritual in the Dhangar's terms: if I take this dip in the water the god shows himself. The simple Dhangar threatens to drown himself unless the god shows himself. The god appears, the Dhangar is not sure whether it *is* the god or not. He binds the god with his red turban to a tree lest he disappear and runs to the Brahman who has to identify the god. The Brahman is a little worried that the god should yield to the simple devotion of the Dhangar rather than to his kind of worship. Ultimately the god grants a boon, but the Dhangar does not wish for anything. Hasn't he got everything? Four brothers, mother, father, wife, children, a hundred sheep (in that order)—what more could the god possibly give him? But he has one wish, namely, that the god should come every evening to the sheep pen to drink an offering of milk. Hospitality and self-negation—not exaggerated asceticism—are two of the subtle points which emerge, plus a touch of *identificatio Brahmanica* otherwise less conspicuous among the Hatkar Dhangars.

*Ovīs* also give the origin of cults. Take, for instance, the famous god Babir in the Indapur Taluka of Pune District. A big *jatrā* in honor of this god is attended by ten thousand Dhangars—not all of them Hatkars. The god Babir was said to have been a cowherd of the Gavli caste. (The Gavlis were the predecessors of the Hatkars in this particular area when pastures still sufficed for big cattle herds.) Babir was killed by Ramoshis, but the cult that emerged is more than a simple cult for a cowherd boy who died a violent death and is set to rest in a simple stone. The *ovīs* connect Babir with Shiva as Mahadev (the Great God) of Shingnapur not far away. The *ovīs* tell this story: a Gavli woman assiduously worshipped this Shiva, and he had to concede her wish for a son. But he confronted her with a choice: either she could have a son who would be wise, but who would live only up to the age of twelve, or she could have a son who would be stupid but live a normal life. The Gavli woman chose the wise, short-lived son. Mahadev tried in vain to substitute the child of another woman for himself but ultimately had to incarnate himself to keep his promise. The woman gave birth to a son. When he had grown up enough he grazed his cows and let them stray into the fields guarded by Ramoshis, who tried to steal his cows. But they couldn't steal his cows. He had a flute, and when he played a happy tune the cows came running and gathered around him. After twelve years his life as a human being came to an end. The Ramoshis killed him and stuffed him into the den of a porcupine. On that spot a neem tree grew and Babir appeared in his mother's dreams pointing out the spot. And the *ovī* ends:

> In the month of Kartik
> On the festival of lights
> The boy Babir was killed.
> A great light descended,
> He became a god,
> He would help poor people.
> It was given to him
> To fulfill wishes.

In the previous *ovī* about the Dhangar and the Brahman the message is that the god comes to the simple and guileless—he is Bholanath, the lord of the simple and truthful. And in this *ovī* it is the poor to whom he attends.

The *ovī*-singer is mostly, as we have said, one of the more religiously-inclined members of the camp. In some cases, however, it is a priest who makes his round in different camps to visit the devotees of a particular clan or god. He may initiate an *ovī*. He is probably closer than others to the "Great Tradition" of regional and general

Shaivite beliefs, and the *ovī* transmitted through him pronounces religious attitudes and ethical notions. The terms "karma" and "dharma" may appear, and instances of devotees' fearless and sincere bhakti are narrated. But the god himself is sometimes not above reproof and also has to prove his *sattva*, which may be translated "clarity, sincerity, reliability, and straightforwardness."

## *Khandoba and Banai*

One of the most famous gods of Maharashtra is Khandoba. He is traditionally a warrior god, an "incarnation" of Shiva, and a version of a proto-Indian god of whom the Rudra of the Vedas, the Shiva of the Puranas, and the Murukan of the old Tamil literature are the best known. Khandoba's first wife, Mhalsa, comes from the Shaivite Lingayats, once a dominant agricultural and trading community in southern Maharashtra and one still to be found in Karnataka. His second wife is from the tribes and the pasture/forest. Some say she is from the fishermen caste, some say that she is a Gavli, but the overwhelming view—and that of the Hatkar Dhangars—is that she comes from the Dhangars. Through his two wives the god not only combines two basic communities, the pastoral and/or hunting and fishing communities, but also two ecological areas, the settled area under the plough and the pastoral/forest area. According to the *ovīs*, Khandoba appropriately meets Banai during a hunt and takes her to Jejuri, the main center of Khandoba worship in Maharashtra. Another version of the myth says that he came as a haggard old man in tatters to Banai's camp. She was a tremendously rich shepherdess. Unrecognized, he was employed by her, and when the vanity of the shepherds and Banai grew too great, he killed all her sheep. When she implored him for forgiveness, he revived the sheep on the condition that she would become his wife. In a simple, unbrahmanical rite they were married: sheep droppings were thrown on the couple instead of rice. Other versions stress the erotic component in the union of Khandoba and

Banai. Since then, the goddess Banai has resided in Jejuri—much to the chagrin of Mhalsa—and the Dhangars have been worshippers of Khandoba. Banai looks after their well-being and the increase of their herds; non-vegetarian offerings for Khandoba are actually shown to her.

The rites of the Hatkar Dhangars for Khandoba are many. For instance the Hatkars accompany Khandoba for a ritual hunt on the day of the conjunction of the sun and the moon (Somavati-Amavasya). On the *jatrā* days, e.g., on full moon days, and on Somavati-Amavasya, the breaking of chains is a special rite practiced by the Dhangars.[6] The heavy chains with joints somewhat thinned are kept in the ancestor shrines in the camp along with the spear which is said to be Khandoba. The spear, which has a small woolen wreath just underneath the blade representing Lakshmi, the goddess of wealth, and the chain are brought to the *jatrā*. The chains are to be broken with powerful jerks. The god empowers the Dhangars to break the chain, and, indeed, the breaking is accompanied with sighs of relief and expressions of joy by the onlookers. The breaking indicates the presence of the god. This folk rite reminds us of the temporal fetters in Shaivite belief and philosophy which have to be broken to enable the soul to be near to or join Shiva.

### *The Stay in the Monsoon Camp and the Khel*

During the stay in the camp the sheep are washed and shorn in the sheep pens. After the sheep are washed in a pond or river, the seven water goddesses or water nymphs are worshipped in the form of seven chalcedony flints on the bank. They receive offerings of turmeric powder and *gulāl*. Then the herd is taken to the sheep pen. The Dhangars remove their heavy sandals in order not to offend Lakshmi, who resides invisibly in the sheep pen. The wool of one sheep is set aside as an offering to one or the other god. All these rites are done not so much in apprehension of the wrath of the deities as in respect, giving everybody what is due. The desire to ensure the enduring help of the gods and nature is the guiding motive.

During the stay, weddings are also performed. These are solemnized by a Brahman, but also contain features of fertility rites not practiced anywhere else. For instance, one Dhangar family buries the womb of a sheep with an unborn lamb under the seat of the couple.

After the Dasara festival, in the month of October, the *kheḷ*, the dance before the ancestors and gods, is held on a traditionally fixed date which varies from camp to camp and thus allows relatives and guests to participate. The *kheḷ* foreshadows the departure for the migration. It can be seen as a miniature *jatrā*. In the *kheḷ*, however, the emphasis is more on honoring the ancestor.

The *kheḷ* is primarily an internal affair of the members of a camp. It strengthens the relations between the living and the dead and between the living. A successful *kheḷ* adds to the prestige of the camp in the eyes of the members of the surrounding camps and honored guests who participate in it. Failing to participate in a *kheḷ* would be unthinkable. Each member has a role or, if he is too young, a potential role to play while sharing the labor involved in the preparation and performance of the festival. The *jatrā* for a family god or any other god is, on the other hand, an act of voluntary faith, though at least a few members of the camp would try to participate, because the *jatrā* is also an appeal to a higher and more powerful authority than the ancestor could possibly be. The *jatrā* is an affair which transcends the involvement of one clan. It has many more elaborate rituals of various origins. In the *jatrā* privileges and duties of many groups are involved and orchestrated in a well-ordered whole so that the god may be pleased.

On the evening before the *kheḷ*, the waving of five lights on a platter is performed before gods and ancestors. The rites are more or less the same in each camp. We shall describe the *kheḷ* in one particular camp. First, Mariai, the goddess living in an unhewn stone and housed in a shrine, is bathed and clad in a new sari; then Biroba, housed in a miniature shrine in the camp, is visited. He is "junior" to the family god Biroba who has his center somewhere else, but is of the same substance. He is also bathed and receives a new turban. Every god receives a bit of turmeric powder and *gulāl*. Our particular camp has a curious "ancestor" to worship. He was a religious Dhangar, without a son, belonging to a different clan. After his death he came into a dream of the eldest sonless clan member and promised that a son would be born to his wife. He asked this man to assume his name, i.e., to function as some kind of "son." After the intruder is worshipped in the form of a stone set up *ad hoc* at the border of the camp, the eldest ancestor receives his bath and new clothes. One of the descendants shapes a small turban, skillfully winding it around his bent knee, and then places it on the head of the ancestor, i.e., on the ancestor stone.

The next day a fixed number of sheep are sacrificed in honor of the ancestors and for the communal dinner of the ancestors, their living descendants, and the guests. Biroba, as we have seen, receives his sacrifice at the place of his chief temple during the *jatrā*. A dance of the men and boys takes place before the ancestor shrine, and then the whole camp including the women moves to Mariai, who possesses the *devṛishī*. Then the procession visits the "junior" Biroba and moves in front of those houses where the gods are displayed in the form of silver plaques on a blanket. These gods—all of whom one knows and finds important enough to worship—are shaded by another blanket which has been formed into a small tent. They are worshipped with turmeric powder, *gulāl*, coconut, water, and pieces of coconuts broken in front of them. The *devṛishī*, a young man, gets possessed by Biroba, and he locates another possessed Dhangar who behaves like a horse. The "horse" (from another camp) is caught by "Biroba" by the neck with a horse-whip which he has formed into a sling. He then mounts the "horse" and is carried in circles in front of the gods, accompanied by the sound of the drum. He normally makes some utterances about the future migration, especially about the rains. Then the horse with his rider suddenly rushes away to the shrine of the eldest ancestor where "Biroba" changes his form, now personifying that ancestor. He holds his spear like a lance and carries his chain over the shoulder; the eldest known ancestor of the camp was a special devotee of Khandoba, and these are his signs.

When the day of the departure comes, the spear, the chain, and the silver-plaque gods wrapped in a cloth are loaded on the ponies. They accompany the Dhangars but the ancestors remain at home in their shrines. If somebody dies on the route, a shrine is set up for him and will be worshipped whenever the Dhangars pass by. This ancestor may also be "called" to the monsoon camp and his shrine installed there. When some feast is celebrated during the migration, an offering is made in the direction of the ancestors far away in the monsoon camp.

This short account cannot reflect in detail the richness of religious beliefs and wealth of oral literature of the Hatkar Dhangars. What may seem remarkable to the observer is the absence of fear or undue obsession in their rites and attitudes. Sincerity in belief and proper worship yields a life in harmony with nature and its dangers, with ancestors and gods. The communion with ancestors and gods in the *khel* or the *jatrā* is a matter of joy, if not fun, as well as an act of faith, devotion, expiation, and merit for the group and individual.[7]

## ACKNOWLEDGMENTS

*Field research among various groups of Dhangars in Maharashtra was carried out in the years 1967-68 and intermittently between 1969-79. I am grateful to the German Research Association (Deutsche Forschungs Gemeinschaft) for financial help. I am also grateful to the late Professor Irawati Karve who had discussions with me on the Dhangars, to Mr. R. P. Nene, Dr. S. N. Bhavsar, who helped me in the first stages of my research, and to Mr. R. S. Atkar and Mr. R. B. Zagade. I owe special thanks to many Dhangar friends and informants.*

## EDITORS' NOTES

1. The ragweed seems to have been brought into Maharashtra from the United States during the days of the wheat export to India.

2. The Nath cult was important in Maharashtra until, it seems likely, the eighteenth century, and is still remembered in folk ritual for the nine Naths (*nao nāth*) who are pictured as Shaiva ascetics and through tombs or *samādhīs* of those nine Naths.

3. The Lingayat or Virashaiva cult began as a bhakti movement in the twelfth century in Karnataka, becoming a somewhat heterodox Shaiva cult with its own priests and caste-like identity. For the saints' literature, see A. K. Ramanujan, *Speaking of Shiva* (Baltimore: Penguin, 1973).

4. There is little literature on the settled Dhangars or on the problems involved in moving from a nomadic to a settled lifestyle. There is, however, a novel by Vyankatesh Madgulkar which deals with a village that is almost completely composed of settled Dhangars. See *The Village Had No Walls*, trans. Ram Deshmukh (New York: Asia Publishing House, 1958).

5. See Max Weber, *The Religion of India*, trans. and ed. by Hans H. Gerth and Don Martindale (New York: The Free Press, 1958).

6. See John M. Stanley, "Special Time, Special Power: The Fluidity of Power in a Popular Hindu Festival." *Journal of Asian Studies* 37:1 (1977): 27-43.

7. For a discussion of Dhangar practice and the origins of contemporary Hindu belief and ritual, see D. D. Kosambi, "The Living Prehistory of India." *Scientific American* 216:2 (1967): 104-14.

## REFERENCES

Leshnik, Lawrence Saadia and G. D. Sontheimer, eds. *Pastoralists and Nomads in South Asia*. Wiesbaden: O. Harrassowitz, 1975.

Murty, M. L. K. and G. D. Sontheimer. "Prehistoric Background to Pastoralism in the Southern Deccan in the Light of Oral Traditions and Cults of Some Pastoral Communities." In *Anthropos* 75 (1980): 163-184.

Sontheimer, G. D. "The Dhangars: A Nomadic Pastoral Community in a Developing Agricultural Environment." In Leshnik, Lawrence Saadia and Gunther-Dietz Sontheimer, eds. *Pastoralists and Nomads in South Asia*. Wiesbaden: O. Harrassowitz, 1975: 139-70.

———. *Biroba, Mhaskoba und Khandoba. Ursprung, Geschichte und Umwelt von pastoralen Gottheiten in Maharashtra*. Weisbaden: Franz Steiner Verlag, 1976. (Contains a German translation of the traditions of the Mhaskoba Cult, *Śrīnāth Mhaskobā Devāce Caritra*. 4th ed. Vir, 1972.)

———. "King Vikram and Kamatu Sinde, the Shepherd. Bhakti Episodes from an Oracle Epic of the Dhangars of Maharashtra." In *South Asian Digest of Regional Writing* 6 (1977): 97-128.

———. "Popular and Scriptural Religion in India: The Case of Rudra, Siva and Khandoba." Paper submitted to the International Seminar on Folk Culture, Cuttack, December 1978.

———. "Some Incidents in the History of the God Khandoba." In *Asie du Sud. Traditions et changements*. European Conference on Modern South Asian Studies 6. Paris, 1978.

———. "Some Notes on Biroba, the Dhangar God of Mahrashtra." In *Prof. D. D. Kosambi Commemoration Volume, Science and Progress*. Bombay: Popular Prakashan, 1974.

K. C. MALHOTRA

# 10
# The Birth of a God: Ram Mama of the Nandiwalas

## Editors' Introduction

The question of origins for most of the gods of the Hindu pantheon at its sophisticated level becomes very complicated. Any one deity is likely to be the result of a long history of splitting or coalescence of a large number of deities over hundreds of years. In some cases it is possible to guess the existence of a historical figure behind the gods, but because of the overlay of myth the human figure is difficult to perceive. Occasionally, however, we can actually document the transformation of a historic figure into a god at the folk level. Malhotra's paper gives an account of such a transformation among the nomadic Nandiwalas.

Of course, the connection between death and deification is common to many facets of religion everywhere. But this paper is especially significant in light of the current work being done on the oral folk tradition in South India where much evidence points to the deification of those who have undeservedly died a violent death.[1] Malhotra's article adds a curious twist to this universal theme, since the death of

Ram Mama was a result of his evil nature, not of a heroic stance. (*E. Z. and M. B.*)

### *The Nandiwalas of Maharashtra*

Among the Nandiwalas of Maharashtra one of the most important religious events is the celebration of the *yātrā* of Ram Mama. A study of the origins of this *yātrā* and its socio-religious significance can shed light on the process by which a historical personage takes on the attributes of deity.

The Nandiwalas, numbering about eight thousand, are found chiefly in western Maharashtra. They have migrated from Andhra Pradesh and are bilingual, speaking Telugu among themselves and Marathi with others. They are divided into two groups. One group, all of them true nomads, assembles once every three years near Wadapuri, a village in Indapur Taluka of Pune District. The remaining five thousand are scattered in thirty-eight villages in the Districts of Ahmednagar, Aurangabad, Bhir, and Nasik. While most of these are true nomads, some are semi-nomads. In the past there were some marriages between the Nandiwalas who assemble at Wadapuri and the others, but in the last fifty years or so they have stopped. In recent years the Nandiwalas have started contracting marriages with the Devwalas, a distinct but similar caste who have also migrated from Andhra Pradesh.

The Nandiwalas traditionally move in small bands throughout a set of villages which are their territory by heriditary right. They move with their sacred bull, the *nandī*, the vehicle of Lord Shiva, performing tricks with the trained *nandī* and in turn getting grain, *bhākrī* (unleavened bread of sorghum or millet), cash, and other articles. In addition they trade in bulls and frequently act as moneylenders to the local farmers. Their womenfolk sell or barter trinkets and indigenous medicines. The Nandiwalas are excellent hunters; with the help of their trained dogs they hunt hare, iguana, porcupine, mongoose, pig, deer, and other animals. They also trap partridge and other birds and catch fresh-water fish.

Though their wanderings are limited to Maharashtra, the bands encounter a wide variety of socio-cultural and ecological settings. Since each band has a different set of villages, it is exposed to somewhat different settings than the other bands.

Despite their wandering in small bands the Nandiwalas do maintain contact with each other. Often a number of them meet in weekly markets, where they exchange news. During the rainy season the whole group assembles in one place. The people of Wadapuri assemble once in three years, while the other Nandiwalas assemble yearly. It is during this period that they perform all their socio-religious ceremonies, worship their gods and their ancestors, perform marriages, and settle the disputes that have arisen since they last met (Hayden and Malhotra 1976). Disputes are settled by the *panchāyat*, the caste council.[2] As far as possible, the Nandiwalas avoid the government courts.

The Wadapuri Nandiwalas are comprised of four strictly endogamous hierarchical groups: Patils, Chougules, Komtis, and Daundiwalas.

The family among these people is nuclear, patrilineal, and patrilocal. It consists of parents and their own children, but married daughters are not regarded as members of the family. Children are married young, and it is common for a man to marry more than one wife. The preferred type of marriage is of a man to his mother's brother's daughter, his father's sister's daughter, or his sister's daughter. While a widow can remarry, divorce is not permitted.

## *Religious Beliefs and Practices*

Though more information on the Nandiwalas' religious beliefs and practices is needed, the main outlines are fairly clear. Most of their worship falls into either one of two categories—worship of ancestors or of deities. The worship of Ram Mama, which is the subject of this paper, does not fall unambiguously into either of these two categories. We will consider later the question of whether Ram Mama is worshipped as an ancestor or a god.

The Nandiwalas' ancestor worship is based on a belief in life after death and the immortality of the soul. Apparently the Nandiwalas also believe in reincarnation though this is not entirely clear. Most of them believe that the ancestral spirits return as members of the kinship system. The spirits of the dead contact only those among the living who are related to them. These spirits may be either benevolent or malevolent. A malevolent ancestor can visit sickness, poverty, or distress on his descendants.

Sacrifices are made to the dead on two occasions. On the thirteenth day of the death rites a pig is sacrificed, and once a year each family sacrifices a pig to their ancestors. The ceremony is rather simple and there are no symbolic objects representing ancestors.

The Nandiwalas worship a large number of deities. All of these deities, interestingly enough, have their main shrine in Maharashtra, not in Andhra Pradesh. These deities include Ambaji-Limbaji (Bapu Saheb), Navnath, Shivnath Maharaj, Mumbadevi, Nana Saheb, Firisti Mariba, Ranabai, Satwai, Mhasoba, Gumasta dev, Sahebrao dev and Maruti. Some of these gods, like Ambaji-Limbaji, are worshipped by all Nandiwalas. There are others which are specific to certain clans; many families or lineages have their own deities. There is, however, no deity which is associated with a particular endogamous group. All of these deities are propitiated at least once a year.

Most of the deities are connected with disease and malevolent spirits (ghosts, witches, etc.). Belief in evil spirits fits in very well with the kind of life the Nandiwalas lead—camping in remote, isolated places, passing through hilly and jungle tracts, going out on hunting expeditions during the night.

Before the advent of the Ram Mama *yātrā*, the Nandiwalas invoked Ambaji-Limbaji for the protection of the family, for aid in sickness and adversity, and for the granting of children, especially sons. To repay a *navas* (vow) to Ambaji-Limbaji they offered a goat or a fowl. For success in hunting expeditions and protection from evil spirits they worshipped Firisti Mariba.

### *Possession by a God*

In addition to the regular worship of gods and ancestors, an important part of the religious life of the Nandiwalas is the phenomenon of possession by a deity, the same phenomenon that has been described by John Stanley and G.-D. Sontheimer elsewhere in this volume. Among the Nandiwalas a person who is in distress and wants to know what to do goes to an *angāt ālelā*, a person who is known to get possessed by a certain deity. He explains why he has come and offers liquor to the *angāt alelā*. The other drinks a bit, sits down, and closes his eyes. He begins to murmur, swaying his body from side to side. Though most of his utterances are audible, their meanings are unclear. Within fifteen to twenty minutes the person is in a state of trance. This is the indication that the god has entered his body. The consulting person then tells his difficulties to the deity and asks for his blessings: "Please be kind to us, if you take us out of this difficulty we will do what you want us to do" (or "we will sacrifice a pig/goat/fowl" as the case may be). The deity then reveals why the person is in distress, the usual reason being that the consulting person has failed to fulfill a vow. The person is told to first fulfill the missed vow and then to make another sacrifice. With folded hands he promises to fulfill the missed vow. Then he touches the feet of the *angāt ālelā*. After a little while the *angāt ālelā* opens his eyes and returns to normal.

These consultations are carried out in the open and the vows are made aloud. The possessed person does not use any props in divination, in the sense that no guidance is taken from flowers, grains, or other objects as is done by many other groups. For the services provided by the person possessed nothing other than the liquor is given.

It is also worth noting that there exists a hierarchy among those who get possessed. Some people are known to experience more genuine possession than others. Consequently there is a rivalry between the possessed persons, and they will often say privately that so-and-so only pretends to be possessed. A person's status as an *angāt ālelā* is liable to fluctuation, depending on how often he has given correct advice.

### *The Story of Ram Mama*

Although Ambaji-Limbaji and other gods are still worshipped, they have in the last seventy years been overshadowed by Ram Mama. The status of Ram Mama, as we have already indicated, is somewhat ambiguous. The Nandiwalas assert that he is a god, while some features of his worship indicate that he is worshipped as an ancestor rather than a deity. Before attempting to answer the question of whether he is regarded as an ancestor or a deity we must look at the history of Ram Mama and the development of his worship.

Ram Mama, who was originally known as Ramu, was a member of the Chougule caste of Nandiwalas. He was still alive some seventy years ago and is recalled by a few of the elderly Nandiwalas. Adept in black magic, which he had learned from a non-Nandiwala, he had extra-ordinary powers: he could kill someone's *nandī*, stop running water, make people ill, and even kill them. Because he often used his malevolent powers people feared and hated him. Finally one night during a hunting expedition in the hills near Bhor in Pune district, the people of Ramu's own clan cut off his head with an axe. His departure brought peace to the group.

But the peace did not last long. Some of the murderers fell sick, the *nandī* of others died. The people propitiated Ambaji-Limbaji but to no avail.

Then a Chougule woman of the clan of Ramu had a dream in which Ramu appeared and told her that he had been killed by his own people. He warned her that he would take revenge and destroy the entire community. She narrated the dream to the people. The atmosphere became tense and the people approached Ambaji-Limbaji, asking what they should do, but they received no guidance.

A few days later the woman who had had the dream was possessed by Ramu. People knew how to respond to a possessed person; they gathered around her and some of the elderly people said to her, "Please do not get angry, we are prepared to do all that you want us to do." The woman spoke, "I am Ramu. Some of you have murdered me, but I am alive and I will not rest in peace until I punish you all." The people begged, "Please forgive us; we shall do all you say, Ram Mama." The woman answered, "All right, I will pardon you on condition that every year each family offers me a pig, liquor, and *gānjā* (hemp)." Then the possessed woman gradually returned to normal.

Since then all four castes of the Nandiwalas refer to Ramu as Ram Mama, or simply Mama, and perform a *yātrā* to him at least once a year.

### *The Yātrā*

To begin with, the people performed the *yātrā* once a year during their assembly at Wadapuri. But now many people perform it twice. The *yātrā* is very systematic and well-organized. First the caste council fixes the day for the sacrifice. This may be any day except Sunday or Tuesday, Sunday being market day and Tuesday sacred to Hanuman, to whom only vegetarian offerings are given.

Then arrangements are made to get pigs. Sometimes traders bring the pigs, but usually people go and get them themselves. As many as five hundred pigs may be sacrificed. Generally each nuclear family sacrifices its own pig; sometimes, however, the sacrifice is done by the extended family. The ceremony is collective in the sense that all sacrifice on the same day and in the same place.

On the specified day, the Nandiwalas load the pigs on their shoulders and go to an open field, generally a bit away from their own settlement and from the village. Although there is no fixed time, the *yātrā* usually starts about nine in the morning. First the pigs are killed by hitting their jaws with iron or wooden rods or with stones. Occasionally they are suffocated by holding their snouts in a small pit. The pigs are then put on a fire. After half an hour they are removed from the fire and the hair is scraped off with stones or a scythe. Then they are washed.

In the meantime a small place is cleared and plastered with cow dung. Several small stones representing Mama and his family are placed on it, and *kunkū* (red-dyed turmeric powder) and *gulāl* (red powder) is applied to all the stones. In front of the stone representing Mama are placed two lemons, five betel leaves, betel nut, liquor, incense sticks, cigarettes (in place of *gānjā*), and *bhākrī*.

The pig is then laid face down, the snout facing Mama. The legs, tail, and head are chopped off and put aside. The fat is sliced off, the viscera removed, and the blood collected in a vessel. The pig is then cut into small pieces with an axe. The liver and blood are cooked on the spot, and the head, feet, and cooked liver are placed before Mama as a *nivedya* (food offered to an idol). Then, after folding their hands and bowing down to Mama, the members of the family partake of the *prasād* (food received from a god): first a little of the liquor, then the liver cooked in blood. The remaining meat and fat are taken to the tent where part of it is cooked and the rest boiled, sun-dried, and stored. The fat is converted into oil to be used later in cooking.

### *The Status of Ram Mama*

In the details of the Ram Mama *yātrā* just described, we find a mixture of the elements of deity and ancestor worship. First of all, as for ancestor worship, a pig is sacrificed to Ram Mama. The sacrifice of a pig is not associated with the worship of any of the deities of the Nandiwalas. Unlike ancestor worship, however, the Ram Mama *yātrā* is very elaborate and Mama is symbolically represented. Moreover, he is worshipped by the whole group rather than just by his kinsmen.

On the other hand, the *yātrā* lacks a number of features common to the Nandiwalas' deity worship—a priest, flags, and a shrine. (However, at Jat-Deole in Ahmednagar district a small shrine for Mama has recently been built alongside the shrine for Ambaji-Limbaji.)

Despite the lack of these features, the evidence we have indicates that indeed Ram Mama is regarded not only as a deity but has become the major deity of the Nandiwalas. It was mentioned earlier that the Nandiwalas formerly invoked Ambaji-Limbaji for family welfare and Firisti Mariba for success in hunting and protection from evil spirits. The situation has radically changed now. In all these situations most people prefer to make a *navas* to Mama. Mama, in their opinion, cures, brings prosperity, and protects against evil spirits. Mama, they say, is very powerful and looks after them better than any other deity. One can affort to fail to fulfill a *navas* to any other deity—even Ambaji-Limbaji—but not to Mama; the consequences are invariably bad.

Another indication of the popularity of Ram Mama is thc number of people who are possessed by him. The number of persons, both men and women, who are possessed by Mama is far greater than the number possessed by all other deities combined.

The popularity of Ram Mama is not confined to the Wadapuri Nandiwalas. The Nandiwalas of Ahmednagar, Bhir, and Nasik, and even the Devwalas worship him. However, the worship of Ram Mama has not spread to a single indigenous Marathi-speaking group.

It is clear from the preceding discussion that while Ram Mama is not completely established as a deity, he is in the process of becoming one. Unlike the Nandiwalas' other ancestors, he exerted during his lifetime a malevolent power over the whole group. By murdering him and then worshipping his spirit, the Nandiwalas transformed him into a beneficient deity. As the Nandiwalas experienced the power of Ram Mama they spread the news of him to the other groups to which they were allied. But the worship of Ram Mama has remained confined to those who share a common way of life and Telugu as a mother tongue.

## AUTHOR'S NOTE

*This paper is based on research originally conceived and partly carried out by Irawati Karve. The study of the Nandiwalas was a multi-disciplinary project of the Deccan College, Pune. The field work in July-August 1969 was carried out under the direction of Dr. Karve. After her death further field work, under the direction of K. C. Malhotra, was carried out among the Wadapuri Nandiwalas in 1972 and 1975, and among the other Nandiwalas in 1976. Only participant-observation methods were used; no questionnaire was administered. In 1975 the research team sacrificed two pigs along with the Nandiwalas.*

## EDITORS' NOTES

1. See Stuart Blackburn, "Death and Deification: Folk Cults in Hinduism," in *History of Religions* 24 (1985): 255–74, for an analysis of the deifying of the dead, with special emphasis on Tamil culture.
2. The Nandiwala's colorful tradition may be seen in the documentary film *Court and Councils: Dispute Settlement in India* (produced by Ron Hess of Worldview Productions and the University of Wisconsin's South Asia Center). A segment of the film shows the caste council in its triennial meeting at Wadapuri in Maharashtra debating in traditional style various cases of violation of caste rules.

## AUTHOR'S REFERENCES

Hayden, R. M., and K. C. Malhotra. 1976. "Dispute-processing among a group of non-pastoral nomads: the Nandiwallas." *Indian Statistical Institute Tech. Report No. Anthrop/5/76* (June 28): 1–32.

Malhotra, K. C. 1974. "Socio-biological Investigations among the Nandiwallas—a nomadic caste-cluster in Maharashtra." *Bulletin of the International Committee on Urgent Anthropological and Ethnological Research* 16: 63–102.

———, S. K. Hulbe, S. B. Kolte, and S. B. Khomne. 1976. "A preliminary report on the socio-biological survey among the semi-nomadic Nandiwalas and Devwalas of Maharashtra." Mimeographed: 1–9.

Misra, P. K. and K. C. Malhotra, eds. 1982. *Nomads of India*: proceedings of the national seminar. Calcutta: Anthropological Survey of India. (Proceedings of National Seminar at Mysore, 1978.)

Thambi-Dorai, K. and K. C. Malhotra. "The Nandiwalas, an account of their native customs and beliefs." In preparation.

IRAWATI KARVE, TRANSLATED BY D. D. KARVE AND FRANKLIN SOUTHWORTH

# 11

# "On the Road": A Maharashtrian Pilgrimage*

People impatient to get out were pushing me from behind; people anxious to get in pulled me out. Somehow I landed on my feet on the dusty platform. I gathered my few packages and made my way out of the railway station through a crowd. The reasons for the crowds became clear: today was the day of the weekly market, and the "god" on his journey had reached this town to make a day's halt. My guide and I picked our way through heaps of millet and wheat and rice, through pots and pans, through bales of cloth and saris, toys and hand-mirrors, vegetables and

---

* Originally published in English in the *Journal of Asian Studies* 22:1 (1962): 13-29; reprinted in *South and Southeast Asia*, Association of Asian Studies 30th Anniversary Commemoration Series Vol. 3 (Tucson: University of Arizona Press, 1972). Originally published in Marathi as "Wātcāl" in *Paripūrti* [Fulfillment] (Pune: Deshmukh and Company, 1951). The translation used here is slightly changed from that used earlier.

sweets—everything displayed on both sides of the road. Farther on, there were amusements—the revolving cradles and merry-go-rounds, gramophones shrilling loudly, a snakecharmer, a troupe of tight-rope dancers.

Today, as once every year, the image of Saint Dnyaneshwar rested for one day here on its fifteen-days' march from Alandi in Pune District to Pandharpur in Sholapur District. People from far and near had flocked to pay respect to the great saint. Whole families had come. They would "visit" the "god," then buy in the market, amuse themselves, and go back. Thousands walked from Alandi to Pandharpur with the image of the saint, some joined later on the way, some hiked the twenty miles from Pune over the hills, then joined the others at this station and walked for twelve days over the plains. We cut through the crowds. My companion pointed toward the open space, "That's the way to 'Mother's' tent; we will be there within minutes." I was slowly getting used to the vocabulary. Saint Dnyaneshwar was referred to as *Dev* (God) or *Māulī* (Mother). His god Vithoba[1] was also *Dev* or *Māulī*. It is rather confusing at first but becomes quite clear because the context tells which *dev* or *māulī* is meant. I looked up and saw above the heads of people a dirty white canvas tent, with a shining golden pinnacle. The saint was represented by silver images of his wooden sandals, *pādukās*. Everyone was elbowing his way to put his head on the feet of the saint. I did not hurry; I had ample time, for after all, I was to be with the saint for the next twelve days. We went to our quarters and were welcomed by an old man. My companion, a well-known preacher and devotee, was given a seat among the men. I was led inside to a room for the women.

This was but a small hut. From where I sat, I could see Brahman women, wearing special ritual garments, cooking food in the open courtyard. There was a small brick wall, and beyond it, just a few feet away, Maratha women were cooking food for their party, without ritual clothes.

"What time is it?"

"Half-past eleven," said somebody.

"We must hurry," said the first voice. "The pots and pans have to be scoured and washed and packed in the truck before the god starts moving."

"The meal is ready" (this from the courtyard).

Apparently the party was waiting for my companion. He and the other Brahman man of our party put on their silk garments and took their meal. After them the women who had cooked filled their own plates and sat apart to eat; the rest of the food, with the pots, was handed over to those who, like me, were in ordinary clothes. After the meal, we washed the pots. Beyond the wall, the Marathas were also having their meal, all together and without ritual. They also finished washing their pots. As we went to load the truck, I discovered that the Marathas and we belonged to the same walking group or *dinḍī*, which was to keep together and share the truck, but of course not the food nor the accommodations every noon and night. Because there was a little time before the god's palanquin could start, the older women lay down for a few moments of rest. I sat against the wall and had a good look at my companions of the next few days.

There were about nine women: three were past middle age and were widows with shaved heads; about six were middle aged; and one—Tai—was very young. At the next stop, two or three more joined us. Beyond our room, in the men's group, was a gentleman whom we called Kaka. He was a member of the group singing devotional songs, and he kept accounts and generally looked after the provisions. The actual shopping was done by the women, but he rendered any help that was necessary. Then there was another gentleman, the one with whom I had come. He was famous for his religious discourses and was "Guru" to everybody in the group.

I was quite new and eager to learn whatever Tai had to tell. Some things I already knew from literary sources. I knew that in the thirteenth century, when Dnyaneshwar wrote or rather composed and sang in Marathi the meaning of the Sanskrit *Bhagavad Gītā*, the cult of Vithoba was already well established. Even then the shrine of Pandharpur was a famous place of pilgrimage. Neither my father's family nor my husband's family belonged to this cult, and so I had never gone to Pandharpur. The pilgrimage starts from Alandi where Dnyaneshwar "died" (i.e., took *samādhī*) voluntarily at age twenty-two in the presence of hundreds of people. The silver images of his sandals are taken every year in a palanquin to Pandharpur so as to reach the town the day before the first Ashadhi Ekadashi, the eleventh day of the waxing moon in June-July. Simultaneously, different "saints" born between the fourteenth and the seventeenth century and belonging to this cult also start—that is, their foot-images start—for this pilgrimage from different parts of Maharashtra. Each palanquin is accompanied by pilgrims. The pilgrims are those who belong to the cult and go to Pandharpur each year—the Varkaris—as well as those who are not members of the cult, but who have a wish to visit the god in the company of the saints.

"But what did you mean when you pointed out that woman as the mistress of our group?" I asked Tai, in my ignorance.

"Well, you see it is like this," she explained as one would to a child, "The singers, the drummer, and the old lute-player belong to a sacred school in Alandi; they and Guruji are the core of our *diṇḍī*-group. But taking these people to Pandharpur, feeding them, carrying their things, all cost money. Lay people like us want to be attached to such a group. So, people like that lady and her sister, devotees who have money and a large circle of friends, undertake to organize. We pay contributions while she and her manager hire the truck, buy the provisions, and make arrangements for the nightly halt. It is time for us to start now; the men have already left to take their place in the procession."

We got up and stood by the road. I heard the bugle. The procession had started. Our *diṇḍī* came along. Tai bent down and took up the dust on the road. God's saints were passing today on this road. The dust under their feet was sacred. I too dipped my finger in the dust and put it to my forehead. The ritual was followed every day. We joined our own group. The *mṛidang* drum gave the rhythm, the *vīṇā* lute strummed the tune, the men with two small cymbals tied to a string around their necks marked time and sang one of the multitude of sectarian songs composed since the thirteenth century:

> The quality of compassion is to love—
> To love without thought of return,
> As a mother loves her child.

Easier said than done! How is it possible? Or—is it so impossible? That sparrow which built its nest, which fed the little ones all day long—what did it expect in return? It mourned pitifully when my cat ate the fledgling, but what did it lose? Can one order one's love at all? Does love ask one's permission before it appears? It weaves itself into the warp and woof of the heart without asking permission; the threads are pulled all the time this way and that, and may cut deep. Then men cry out with bleeding hearts, "O God! Please rescue us." Not only the love of the mother, but all love is without any thought of gain; that is why it is so painful . . . or . . .

Suddenly, my neighbor gave me a nudge, "Look at the women with the lamps." All along the main street, women were standing with lamps, rice, and coconuts on brass plates held in their hands to pay homage to the palanquin. I was jerked out of my thoughts and I looked around. The road was a sea of human beings. From all sides, one heard the chant of the saints' names, "Dnyanoba Tukaram," "Dnyanoba Tukaram."[2] We crossed through the town and began to walk along the open road. The speed of our walking increased somewhat. The sun was covered with clouds. A strong wind was blowing, and the dust raised by thousands of feet made the atmosphere hazy. The hilly region of Alandi, Pune, and Saswad was left behind, and we were slowly entering a high plateau. Still one saw a few low hills and some high mountains in the background. This year, there had been a lot of rain during the Rohini constellation in early June, and the weather was neither too dry nor too hot. Off an on, some words of the songs came to my ears—

"Bring Hari speedily to me"—
"Placed his hand on my head to caress me"—
"Vithai come soon, come soon"—

Different *dinḍīs* sang different songs, and snatches came to my ears while I listened to our own group. Suddenly the procession stopped.

"What is wrong?"

"Nothing, this is the place for the 'straight' ride."

I did not understand but kept mum, watched, and did what others did. The songs had stopped. All chanted the name of the god and his divine spouse—"Vithoba-Rakhumai"—"Vithoba-Rakhumai." The singers kept rhythm with their feet. The women behind them were also moving their bodies to the rhythm—ever louder, ever faster the cymbals clashed. The crowd parted, leaving a wide straight lane; on came two horses at a gallop, one riderless, the other with a richly dressed rider holding a silver staff. Both horses stopped near the saint's palanquin, dipped their heads, and went back again. The lines of people joined as the procession started.

"Do you see how even dumb animals are filled with devotion?" said the woman.

"But what have these horses to do with the procession?" I asked.

She pitied my ignorance and explained, "Did you see the riderless white horse? It is God's horse and has a silken saddle on its back. And the rider with the staff is God's rider. Both horses are part of the paraphernalia presented to the god [i.e., Saint Dnyaneshwar] by Sardar Shitole."

I acknowledged the information and realized that the "straight" ride was over and the palanquin was moving off.

Soon we reached the place where we were to stay overnight. It was the open courtyard of a big house. Our Maratha companions lived in the open porch of the next house. Tai and I ate things left over from the morning meal and spread our beds. The older women had prepared some fresh stuff for the men, but before these arrived, I had fallen fast asleep. The other Brahman women in our *diṇḍī* were going to eat later. Right up to Pandharpur, this was our routine. Tai got very hungry in the evening. She took her food early and I joined her. The others had various ritual regulations about eating. Some had a fast; others ate the usual food prepared in a special way, calling it a ritual diet and not then putting on the ritually pure clothes; some ate only peanuts, while still others ate sago. In this way, each evening there was almost more variety than the number of women; at the morning meal, it was the same. Some had the usual one-meal fast, some would not eat salt on Mondays, some had a regular whole-day fast on Monday, and some ate only in the evening. Moreover, special food was prepared in the evening for the men. I could not understand all this complicated business and the enormous amount of extra work it involved. I could not explain how the women did all this and why. As we proceeded on our way, the hot sun burnt our faces and left everybody looking tired and parched. The daily toil left everyone exhausted. All complained about aching feet and legs, but hardly anybody protested about the work. The older women were very lovingly looked after. The hard work and cheerful attitude of the women always surprised me.

We got up at 4:30 in the morning and finished our toilet in the dim light of a lantern. One woman drew water from the well, another took a bath, a third washed her sari. There was only one hand-wheel for drawing water from the well, and there were a hundred men and women wanting to bathe. You had just time to pour a little water over your body and wash clothes by beating them on stones and rinsing them quickly. I never had occasion to use the soap cakes, which I had brought in my vast ignorance, for bathing or washing. I was accustomed to do my hair and put the red mark on my forehead in the dark and so felt no need of a mirror. I was ready before everybody else. I packed and put my bag and bedding into the truck and went out with the idea of paying homage to the sacred silver sandals. The place where the palanquin had stopped for the night was about half a mile farther on from our shelter. As usual, crowds of villagers were going towards the place. The palanquin was resting in a big fallow field, and thousands of people had made their beds at night around it. Some bullock carts and pedestrians were already on the way while others were collecting their bedding, clothes, and utensils. These were the better-class farmers. There were hundreds of professional beggars and poor people. They ate whatever people gave them, spread their mat wherever they found room, and walked with the palanquin. They suffered if it rained. Fortunately this year there was not much rain; also the sky was cloudy and so there was not much sun either.

I put my head on the *pādukās* and turned to go away but a woman stopped me, "Watch the *pūjā*. Don't go yet." The silver sandals were taken out of the palanquin, put on a silver plate, and handed over to the priest. The worship was gone through in full detail, but rapidly, because this was only a short halt on a long journey. At the end of the *pūjā*, the worshipers sang devotional songs and performed *āratī*, the waving of lamps. The hereditary servants then stood up and held a screen around the god. "What is all this now?" my ignorance queried again. The woman said, "God has been offered food. He is now having his meal. The screen is to prevent the evil eye of the onlookers from affecting him." I was amazed at this extreme humanizing of god, of imagining him to have qualities and form identical with man. "Formerly, the offering in the plate before the god was actually eaten. But nowadays nobody has faith, and naturally such miracles do not take place," the woman explained to me as I came out of the tent. The devotees waiting outside rushed in, and I heard the men round the palanquin crying loudly, "Ladies, please give your contribution." The thoughts of all those rushing in were directed to the feet of the god—while the thoughts of those near the palanquin were directed to the pockets of the people. I quickly got out of this oppressive atmosphere, and soon the bugle gave the signal to start. Every morning the god's palanquin started at 6:30, and this was the signal. I mingled with the women's group and began to walk.

We used to walk the whole day except for two or three hours around noon. Right in the front, there were the bullock carts loaded with luggage. Following them were hundreds of people in smaller or larger groups, chanting, singing, and playing various instruments. After that walked the main procession. In the vanguard was the *diṇḍī* of the Untouchables,[3] then came the god's horses, then hundreds of people carrying flags. Again I was supplied the information, "The huge orange flag carried on a pole is a sign that the man who carries it is a special type of devotee who goes to Pandharpur every month. A man hopes that when he is too old and feeble, a strong son will bear the pole and carry on his tradition." Following the banners came the wagon carrying the palanquin of the god and behind them a mile-long crowd of people on foot. There were as many women as men. The red, green, and blue saris of the women, with borders and ends of contrasting colors, the red turbans and other multicolored headgear of the men, the dull orange flags fluttering in the breeze, the black, freshly-ploughed fields spreading for miles on both sides, the hazy hills on the distant horizon, the grass on the roadside which had turned green from recent showers, and the blue sky peeping from behind the rain clouds—I could look at all this for hours and hours and still not be satisfied. In the early afternoon, thousands of people would stop at a roadside brook, and the moving scene would become stationary for a time. The first thing everybody did at a halt was to dry the clothes which had been washed at the early morning bath. Then all the fields would be carpeted by the colored saris spread out to dry. Blue smoke and reddish flames rose from hundreds of fires in the noon air. From morning till evening, one's ears were ringing with the sound of the cymbals and drums and the devotional verses of Tukaram, Dnyaneshwar, Eknath, Namdev, and other poet-saints. When we stayed in a house for the night, the singing within the four walls of a room often seemed discordant and the noise of the instruments unbearable. Indoors I felt oppressed, but out in the open, the sound of the bell-like cymbals was never too loud.

Except during a few still hours of early morning, all day long a stiff breeze was blowing. When I started from home, Haushi, my maid servant, had told me, "Bai, it is no use taking an umbrella. The wind is so strong that you can hardly hold it." She was right. I did not regret having forgotten my umbrella in the train. Everything was in motion in the wind-swept atmosphere—the ends of the saris of women, the branches of the trees, the stalks of millet in a few unploughed fields, the walking crowds, and the clouds overhead. I was walking on and on in a space filled with color, sound, and wind. When I looked down, I saw innumerable feet moving up and down, onward to the rhythm of *ṭāḷ* and *mṛidang*. I felt I was a drop in this vast stream of human beings; that instead of walking, I was being carried forward by the surrounding motion. Even at night when I slept, I dreamt that I was walking, and when I got up in the morning, I was surprised that I still lay at the spot where I had fallen asleep.

Today, the Brahmans and Marathas in our group were camping near each other. Every day we would walk together and camp near each other, but the food would be cooked separately. Today I said to the Maratha man who managed all on behalf of the mistress, "Buwa, please allow me to take my meals with you." Buwa agreed very readily to my request. As soon as the truck arrived, the big vessels containing the cooked food were taken down; the curry was warmed and the leaf plates arranged in two rows, one for men and the other for women. A few of the group served the food. All the women were chattering and laughing while the meal was going on. Wherever we camped for the night, the women got up in the early dawn, lighted the fire, and cooked the rice, vegetables, and chapatis. These were then packed in vessels and the mouths were tied tightly with cloth before being loaded onto the truck. The rice would still be warm when we reached the noon camp. This was easy on the women, for as the rice was warm, only the curry had to be heated. Thus people could sit down to their meals soon after we camped at noon. Then they could rest for a couple of hours till the palanquin moved, and they did not have to walk immediately after a meal. But the Brahman group would start cooking only after reaching the noon camping place. The Brahmans had to place the stones, light the fire, bring water, chop the vegetables, and then make rice, chapatis, and lentil curry; all this took at least an hour and a half. Then the men ate, after changing into special silk dhotis; when they had finished, the women in special clothes ate their food. Finally we others took charge of all the remaining food and ate without changing our clothes. By the time we ate, we would be hot and very thirsty. After meals, we had to take all the pots to the stream for scrubbing, put them into sacks, and load them into the truck as quickly as possible, because the truck was to go ahead to our evening camp. In this way we got hardly half an hour of rest before it was time to start.

In the Maratha group, the women did the cooking, but the men took over serving the food, bringing water, and loading the heavy baggage into the truck. Altogether, the men and women behaved more freely and openly with each other. Of course, they always sat in separate groups and there was no joking or laughing between them, but one noticed that there were no special inhibitions of behavior between the two groups. On the other hand, in the Brahman group, most of the work was done by the women. There were only two men, the guru and another. When the guru was about, everybody was very subdued and respectful. The other gentleman did carry out a few chores, but the women did most of the work. The routine the Marathas followed was uncomplicated. None of them put on special clothes, and nobody had different kinds of fasts. All sat down to their meal together and all finished together; so, even though there were about fifty or sixty people in the group, everything was done quickly. Every day I regretted the fact that one and the same *dinḍī* was divided into these two sections. All of the people were clean, and they ate their food only after taking a bath. Then why this separateness? Was all this walking together, singing together, and reciting the poetry of the saints together directed only towards union in the other world while retaining separateness in this world? This question was in my mind all the time. In the same way I had become friendly with the Brahman group, the Maratha women had also taken me to their hearts. As I could not bring the groups together, I joined now one group and now the other, trying to construct a bridge—at least as far as I was concerned. After I had taken my meal with them, I felt that they were more friendly. Many of them walked alongside of me, held my hand, and told me many things about their life. Towards the end, they called me "Tai," meaning "Sister." A few of the said, "Mark you, Tai, we shall visit you in Pune." And then one young girl said, "But will you behave with us then as you are behaving now?" It was a simple question, but it touched me to the quick. We have been living near each other thousands of years, but they are still not of us and we are not of them.

Why is this so? Are the Brahmans so heartless? On no! Most definitely not. If one of the Maratha women were hurt, the Brahmans would at once go to her aid and give her medicine. If some Maratha man had been hungry, the Brahmans would certainly have fed him well. But they would not take food sitting in the same row, or accept food or water from a Maratha. They had no feeling that they were doing anything wrong. Every one of them was caught up in the vicious circle of an old custom. Some were observing the traditional rules of behavior willingly and earnestly. Others were observing those rules just because otherwise society might consider them improper. But what I could not understand was that men who in their city life came daily into contact with Christians, Muslims, and others were also behaving in the same way as the women. The tradition of the Varkari pilgrims, the rebellion of the saints against giving importance to external matters and against the hypocritical following of prescribed behavior, the teaching of the oneness of man and deity, and above all modern city life—how could one reconcile these with regard for ritual purity and impurity?

On some occasions I was outraged. I do not remember the name of the town, but when we reached that place in the evening, we found that the well was far from our camp. I went there, washed my hands, feet, and face, and brought back with me a small pot full of water. Then I took out my bedroll from the truck and sat down on the veranda. Just then Buwa came to enquire if all the arrangements were satisfactory. I said, "Oh, the place is very nice, but the well is far away. Our feet are so sore from the long march that I do not know how we can bring water from such a distance." Buwa pitied our plight, made a servant scrub and clean a big copper pot, fill it with water, and place it in our quarters. I blessed him and drank from it to my heart's content. But for drinking and for making tea, the other women in my group used only the water which they themselves had brought; they employed the water sent by Buwa only for toilet purposes. The next morning we got up early as usual and went to the stream in the dark, in order to wash. A large number of people were there, cleaning their teeth, washing their mouths, and spitting into the stream. I could not bring myself to clean my mouth with the water, and took only a cursory wash. However, the women in our Brahman group apparently felt no hesistation, took their baths with the usual cries of "O Ganga! O Bhagirathi!" and even washed their mouths with the water. Apparently the spitting of members of other castes was not considered as pollution of their bathing water in the stream, while the clean well water was considered polluted because it had been brought by a man of non-Brahman caste!

It was the same story with conversation and ways of behavior. We were, on another occasion, bathing in a wayside stream before dawn. We had brought two kerosene lanterns with us. When I came up from my bath, I could not find the second lantern. It had apparently been taken away by some women from our group who came later, in order to light their way to the place where they had gone in the fields; but my companion and I did not know this. Just then another woman with a lantern in her hand came down to the bank into the stream and I asked my companion, "Can that be our lantern? Should I ask her?" But before I could say another word, my companion shouted to the woman, "Hey, you there, whose lantern are you taking away there?" The woman turned to us defiantly and said, "The lantern belongs to me. And who are you to shout 'Hey, woman' at me?" Naturally, we were in the wrong, but my companion was surprised at her sharp retort. She turned to me and said, "Do you see how angry she became? One cannot even say 'Hey, woman' to them now!" In order not to continue the quarrel by further exchange of words, I quickly started up the bank; but I could not help thinking for a long time how we do not realize the offending air of superiority in the way we speak. With all our keenness to bow down before God Pandurang and all our willingness to suffer much hardship on account of that desire, we daily show contempt for the living gods beside us.

But am I not being a victim of meaningless sentiment in my analysis of the existing situation? Brahmans and other castes are present in a particular social situation. Most people accept that situation; they do not feel any unjust discrimination in it. Am I making a mountain out of a molehill for nothing? No, definitely not. Have not many saints in the Varkari cult themselves exposed this degrading differentiation between Brahmans and the others by means of many poems and many similes? Did they not ask for justice at the feet of Pandurang? Only yesterday our *diṇḍī* was singing the song of the Untouchable devotee Chokhamela.

> Chokha is uncouth,
> but his devotion is not uncouth.
> Why judge him by his exterior?

Did we sing that without understanding its meaning at all? The revulsion against social injustice is bound to be translated into action soon and not remain as mere platitudes in the verses of the saints. Are we Brahmans going to remain blind to this future? Ritual purity, pollution by one person and not by another—are we going to keep up these outward pretenses? Are we going to continue to give up humanity and neighborliness in the name of ritual purity? "The pure love of God"—are we never going to be worthy of it?

Fortunately there was not much time for me to spend in these fruitless and bitter thoughts. The whole atmosphere was full of joy. Not that there were no quarrels, no abusive words, but such occasions were very few. If anyone used bad language or became angry, the others would say, "You must not do that while we are on the way to Pandhari," and the offender would be ashamed and fall silent. I saw this several times. Many of us used to walk a mile or so ahead of the palanquin and sit down to rest under a tree. Different groups got together under a tree in this way, and the women would press each other to sing a song. From the language and subject of the song and the way it was sung, I would try to guess from which part of the country the singer had come. Once, while I was sitting under a tree, I heard the words "*male, tule*" and I at once got up and joined the group. "Are you from Khandesh?" I asked one of the group. "No," she replied, "We belong to the Ghat." My companion, who was from Pune, remarked, "They do not speak like the people from Maval (the mountainous or *ghāt* area between the Desh and Konkan). How can they be from the Ghat?" I told her, "The 'Ghat' she means are the hills near Aurangabad or perhaps near Buldana." The women were very happy to hear this, and finding that I knew their country, they told me that they came from near Ellora in Aurangabad District. I asked, "What caste do you belong to?" One of them told me that they were of the Warik (barber) caste. Then I quoted the verse of a poet-saint, "We are Wariks and we shave very smoothly." At once the woman smiled at me with great satisfaction and said, "Oh, you know just the right thing." That group had nearly fifty men, women, and children all belonging to the barber caste. They had come by train to Pune and had been walking with the palanquin right from the start at Alandi. Some men and women had come from as far as Bidar, Bhid, Parbhani, Jalna, even Nanded. They always said they came from "Gangathadi"—the bank of the river Ganga. Every sacred river is "Ganga" and in Maharashtra the river Godavari especially is called "Ganga" or "Gangabai."

Once we were going along in the morning, and just in front of us was a bullock cart full of baggage with three or four children seated on top. One boy in the group was howling loudly because he did not want to sit in the cart as his mother was forcing him to do. He was making a racket and kicking with his feet while his mother held a millet stalk in her hand and pretended to threaten him, smiling all the time. "We went out to see the god in the morning and I thought that since the poor child had already walked a lot, he would be happy to ride in the cart. But now he has started this game! Wait, I will break your head for you," said the mother, and rushed at him. She was followed by the other woman shouting, "Oh, don't! Don't!"

While this chase went on ahead, a young woman came up from behind, holding a child whom she could scarcely carry. I asked, "Why is your child crying?"

She replied, "He just will not walk! All the time he says, 'Auntie, please pick me up!' I thought he should walk for a couple of miles in this cool morning. But he begins to wallow on the road, and so I am just dragging him along."

"The irony of it! That other child is crying because he wants to walk, and this one is howling because he does not want to walk. Let this one sit in the cart and let that one walk."

Meanwhile a man came along, took up the child on his back, and the woman began to walk with us. She was a

Maratha by the name of Pawar and came from Jogaiamba. The child was her dead sister's son. She had started for Pandharpur and was already out of town when her brother-in-law brought the child and asked her to take him along. The child had just one shirt, not even anything to cover himself with at night, and the poor girl would be carrying him along on the pilgrimage for a fortnight. Another day I saw her sitting with the child in a group of men and women. We also sat down for a little rest. She was massaging her arms. "Are you very tired?" I asked.

"What can I do?" she asked. "The whole day I have to carry the child on my back. I don't feel any pleasure in living."

"Oh! But he will repay all your troubles when he is older," I tried to console her.

"I don't think so at all! Yesterday he bothered me so much that when I reached our halting place in the evening, I gave him a sound beating. Do you know, he said, 'I will strangle you!' " She also joined in our laughter and the naughty boy turned his face away and smiled.

So, I was getting to know my Maharashtra anew every day. I found a new definition of Maharashtra: the land whose people go to Pandharpur for pilgrimage. When the palanquin started from Pune, there were people from Pune, Junnar, Moglai, Satara, etc. Every day people were joining the pilgrimage from Khandesh, Sholapur, Nasik, and Berar. As we neared Pandharpur, the pilgrimage was becoming bigger and bigger. All were Marathi-speaking people—coming from different castes, but singing the same songs, the same verses of the Varkari cult, speaking to each other, helping each other, singing songs to each other. The only Maharashtrian area not represented was Konkan, the District of the Maharashtrian seacoast. When I enquired about this, I was told that the Ashadh month's pilgrimage was for the plateau people; the month of Kartik would bring out the whole of Konkan. Ashadh was their time for work in the fields, so naturally, they could not leave. On the plateau, the fields had already been ploughed, and there was now spare time before the sowing. All areas were devoted to the god of Pandharpur, but neither the coastal people nor the plateau people neglected their fields to show their devotion.

I witnessed how the language and culture of Maharashtra had spread among all its social layers. The fine poetry of five centuries was recited daily. That poetry embodied a religion and a philosophy. People speaking many dialects sang the same verses and thus learned a standard language. Their learning was achieved in a massive dose but without pain or compulsion. Every one was laughing and joking during the march. Nobody pressed people to join the pilgrimage. No public announcement of the program was made, and the outside world might just as well not have existed. The pilgrims were intoxicated with happiness; anyone who had a heart, who had the insight, could have the same joy.

One day I became particularly aware of the difference between culture and literacy. While we were resting in our midday camp, I looked up the road and saw a pair of missionaries. They had little pamphlets in their hands and had come to spread the religion of the Lord Jesus Christ. After the first two or three days, they must have despaired and gone away, for I did not see them during the later stages of the pilgrimage. I was very angry with them, but the people in my group just laughed at the whole thing. The pair was certainly literate in Marathi but had not even a trace of understanding of Maharashtrian culture. Different human societies express their sense of beauty and sanctity and the goodwill in their hearts in different ways; to learn the value of these different manifestations and at least to try to understand what others believe before insisting that one's own beliefs are the only right ones—is this not the sign of wisdom? "The quality of compassion is to love—to love without a thought of return." To love humanity without any desire for gain—is not that the means to true wisdom? But the followers of monotheism—political, social, or ethical—

can never understand this. Particularly the servants of Christ, who for the last two or three centuries have conquered and ruled different human societies all over the world and trampled upon their cherished values, are not likely to realize this.

I could never really find out how many songs, poems, and stories these illiterate women knew by heart. During the whole journey, I never heard the same song twice. There was great temptation to take down the songs, but I had started from home with the vow that I would not touch book, notebook, or pencil. Besides the usual women's songs, others were of the devotional type common among the Varkaris. There was a surprising variety of songs— *gondhaḷ, kheḷiyā, gavḷaṇ,* everything was there. One woman who knew I was teaching at Pune taunted me, "This is better than your colleges. Have your students this education and this discipline?" Naturally I did not agree with her, but though this was not a college, three characteristics of education were present here: the preservation of traditional knowledge, its cultivation, and its transmission to the next generation. This education was also many-sided. Besides religion and philosophy, the three arts of music, dancing, and drama were included in it; and it also encompassed the living together for some time of the whole society. Not that the music was of a very high quality, but in addition to the traditional simple tunes, attempts were made to put them into classical *rāgas* with the rhythm of the *mṛidang* drum. I had already heard the Bhairavi, Kafi, Bhoop, Sarang, Jaijaivanti, Durga, and Malkansa *rāgas.* The day we left Phaltan, it was raining. A singer of that town had come with us for a couple of miles, and the morning's songs tunefully sung by him and repeated after him by our group are still fresh in my ears. So absorbed was I that only after the singer had gone back did I realize that we had been walking in the rain for over an hour.

Five times on the way we witnessed the horses paying homage to the saint in *rangaṇ* performances. For a *rangaṇ,* the palanquin is taken into the center of a large field while thousands of spectators sit or stand around it in a big circle. Leaving a wide circular passage round the spectators, the devotional singers form an outer circle and continuously repeat the names of the saints, or chant "Vithoba Rakhumai!" Both horses make three or five circuits through the passageway at a fast trot, bend their heads down in front of the palanquin, and go away. Then all the people play *jhimmā*, *phugḍyā*, and the like—games of hand-clapping, reeling, and leap-frog. The men's games are rather rough and fast, and women do not take part in them. Even if someone takes a tumble, he does not get hurt very much in the soft fields. Finally, all the members of the *dinḍīs* dance round the palanquin in a circle and then the palanquin moves on.

The performance of *bhārūḍ* stories also takes place in an open field. *Bhārūḍ* is a kind of folk-drama, in which the different actors explain some ideas of Vedantic philosophy.[4] A single actor may perform a series of roles, making lightning changes in his dress and make-up. Thus as a king's astrologer, he puts on an old pair of spectacles and a big turban two feet in diameter; as soon as that part is over, he throws away those paraphernalia and takes up another role and its costume. Adding to the original philosophic compositions of Eknath, the actor often puts a number of his own words into the *bhārūḍ* and accompanies them with gestures. The interpolated words are sometimes obscene, but the gestures may be particularly so. This crude form of theatrical art never lasts for longer than about half an hour. Men and women listen to it, laugh to their heart's content, and forget everything as soon as they take to the road again.

Erotic representations and imagery have been a part of religious festivals from very ancient times. In the old Brahmanical sacrifices which went on for days and months, there were always some parts which were purely for amusement, for sexual excitement, and for entertainment. In fact there are some who insist that all drama originates in religion and magic. Why should such entertainment be vulgar? It could well do without the sexual slant. Of course none of the well-known discoursers on religion, who are deeply learned and respected, participate in the *bhārūḍs*. The actors in these are half-educated persons. Their easiest way to make people laugh is to use shameless gestures and sentences with a double meaning. This has been going on from very ancient times, and if in a whole fortnight of continuous singing of devotional poetry there is a little—really very little—of this kind of diversion, one need not object to it. If the low thoughts that are present in everybody's mind can be given some outlet in this harmless way and for such a short time, and if they disappear from ordinary life at other times, occasional obscenity would be really a small price to pay.

There is always a considerable amount of latitude given to obscene or disgusting sentiments in poetry which praises renunciation. To give as offensive a description as possible of the worldly life while recommending renunciation is a very old trick, and the Varkari tradition is no exception to it. One such poetic song is a long composition known by the name of "Madalasa." The story goes that a royal lady named Madalasa advises her baby princes, while they are still in their cradles, to give up the temptations of this life; the sons thereupon renounce the pleasures of this life and become ascetics. The song brings together the advice Madalasa gave to her sons, punctuated by the refrain, "Madalasa spoke—'I am He.' Sleep child, sleep." I heard this song three or four times. The Varkaris may perhaps be inspired towards renunciation by it, but what I found disgusting was not the worldly life but the poem.

> The human body, under the attractive skin, is full of blood and flesh and such stuff; the body contains excreta, faeces, and urine; the nose is full of mucus; this beautiful body decays with disease and old age—and therefore, O men, give up this life of enjoyment, adopt celibacy, and retire from the affairs of daily life.

This advice is directed towards men, and rightly enough.

A woman brings into this world a shapeless mass of flesh, feeds the hungry being every three or four hours, washes its soiled clothes, and cleans its body; and when gradually the bundle of flesh begins to take on color and form and smiles at her, she feels herself the happiest being on earth. Such a mother knows quite well what the human body is made of, and a description is not likely to engender renunciation in her mind. When men become ascetic, the only thing they forgo is sex. Otherwise, they are being well looked after. Even in the absence of a wife, they get tasty and well-prepared food: a mother or sister by blood or by sentiment cooks for them. It is always women who come forward to serve a celibate with devotion and real attachment.

I found an interesting example of feminine devotion in this pilgrimage. As we neared Pandharpur, palanquins from different parts of Maharashtra joined the Dnyaneshwar palanquin. The camp before Pandharpur became a huge city of palanquins and *dinḍīs*. Every part of Maharashtra was represented there. There were the palanquins of Tukaram Maharaj from Dehu, Sopankaka from Saswad, Muktabai from Khandesh, Rakhumai herself from Amraoti—all of them were there. This year there was the palanquin of Ramdas[5] from Sajjangad near Satara, which joined us on the way. The carriers of the palanquin were all men, but accompanying it and waving the yak-tail brush (to keep away flies) were women. This man, Ramdas, who ran away in the midst of his wedding ceremony in order to escape leading the family life, was surrounded by women after his death! It made me smile. It is always women who come forward to render service to such renouncers. Very often such devotion is completely without ulterior motive. When I saw a woman whose life had been devastated by early widowhood, lacking a family of her own children, but caring for the Guru, seeing that he got warm, tasty food, then I valued more the tender heart of that woman than the strict celibacy of the Guru. "The quality of compassion is to love—to love without thought of return." Once I had heard the song of

Madalasa, I found myself bored with listening to it again and again. My thoughts used to wander into history. I wondered how and when the status of the householder in the Hindu social system had lost its honored place, and how celibacy and renunciation had assumed more and more importance.

The Varkari sect itself insisted that the transcendental *brahman* was too difficult a concept to grasp; one could reach it gradually through loving worship of an incarnate god. Its saints showed devotion to Vithoba on the level of human passion using the imagery of a lover towards his beloved. Its god was the dark Vithoba, who was none other than the Lord Shri Krishna, the lover of many women. They chanted the name Vithoba but always with the name of his wife Rakhumai, whose love story, too, is part of the Varkari literature. The *Gītā* that induced Arjuna to accept his duty in this world was the sacred book of the Varkari saints—and on the other hand, there was all this preaching of celibacy and renunciation! How were these two to be reconciled? The Vedas taught one to become immortal through begetting progeny and perpetuating the race. The land was once filled with smoke from the sacrifices of the tribes of the Kurus and Panchalas who wanted sons to be born to them; Manu, the ancient law-giver, told of several ways of obtaining a son if there was no son born to a person. Shabarswami, an old commentator, wrote, "One should remain at the teacher's house for twelve years after initiation for the usual education. If one wishes to become a specialist in some branch, one may remain with the teacher and devote oneself to study as a celibate. But one who preaches celibacy for a longer period is probably a eunuch."

While the merits of a married life were being praised on the one side, the life of seclusion in a forest and the philosophy of the Upanishads was developing on the other. Buddhism and Jainism based themselves on the latter philosophy, propagating the great value of the ascetic life and the worthlessness of the normal life of work and pleasure. But the popularity of the ascetic religion depended upon a peculiar social contradiction. The livelihood of the men and women who renounce the ordinary pursuits and lived the life of beggars with very few wants ultimately needed the support of wealthy royal houses or the rich merchants who lived in cities like Vaishali and Shravasti. A well-to-do and generous society of householders was the essential precondition for the edifice of a religion of renunciation and asceticism. The history of this great transformation in the value system of the Hindus is as important as it is interesting. But songs like that of Madalasa are neither entertaining nor ennobling.

The song of Madalasa had ended some time back. I felt there was some change in the atmosphere. In a moment, I heard the words of Dnyaneshwar's well-known song—

> Caw, Caw!
> A crow in the courtyard.
> Are you giving a good omen?
> Will the King of Pandhari be my guest?
> If you bring him,
> I'll put golden anklets round your feet.

Yes, the mood of the group had definitely changed. I too breathed more easily. The leader of our *diṇḍī* always showed this kind of judgment. Once, after the Madalasa song, he had started the verses of Dnyaneshwar's sister, Muktabai. In anger one day, the saint had locked the door of his room. In these verses, Mukta had begged him to open the door of his room and of his heart. The tenderness of this poem had dispersed my gloom. Another time, when the evening halt was some distance away and we were weary, the men could not find any enthusiasm in the usual hymns. But then our leader began the song—

> We'll tell no lies,
> Nor spread false news.
> An ant gave birth to a colt,
> And how much milk had she?
> Seventeen barrels full.
> And fourteen elephants drank
> All that was left over.

We'll tell no lies,
Nor spread false news.

And everybody at once smiled. That particular song, which all of us had heard as children, made everyone laugh, and we reached the camping place in no time at all. When there was a *rangaṇ*, I felt as if it was a circus. When the games started, everybody forgot the hardships of the journey. The *bhārūḍ* performances were given occasionally, always interspersed with devotional songs or absurd songs. The repetition of god's name was going on almost incessantly and helped to keep the spirit happy and calm in spite of the long and arduous marches.

This does not mean that all the pilgrims were happy. This communal living, this sharing, brought both joy and sorrow. So many unhappy and bereaved persons were walking the road to Pandharpur! On the way they opened their hearts and unburdened their sorrows to their travelling companions. They tried to get consolation and sympathy and hoped to gather the strength to bear their misfortunes. And what sorrows there were! Each of a different kind, but still each sharing much with the others.

One day, we were sitting under a tree, speaking about this and that. What else do women speak about but, "How many children have you?" and "What does your man do?" I asked the same of the handsome woman next to me. Her eyes filled with tears and she said, "No, there aren't any children to play in our house. Such a large house and just the two of us—he and I. No quarrels, nothing. But what can we say to each other all the time? So, I am going to the feet of Pandurang."

"I suppose you want to put your sorrow at his feet?" I asked.

"On no!", she said, "Doesn't he know it? He will do what he thinks is best. One must live as he wills."

Again one day we were resting from the hot midday sun. Near us was a group of three or four women. One of the women was feeding a boy at her breast and tears were rolling down from her eyes.

"What is the matter, my dear? Don't you feel well?" I asked.

"It's the little one," she answered.

She came from the region near Bhid. They had been on the road for a month. The poor child was hot with fever. In sun and rain and wind, the child had been carried on her back, and one would have been surprised if the child was not now suffering from anything.

"But how could you bring such a small child?"

"How can I explain?" she started, "All the neighbors were going. They wanted me to go with them. I said my baby was too young. They retorted, 'With all the care you have given to your home and children, have not many children died? Don't be afraid, come with the little one. Why not go to the feet of Pandurang while you have the strength?' So I came. But for the last two days, the baby hasn't even opened its eyes."

I pointed to the government medical van accompanying the pilgrimage and told her that they would give free medicine to her. She used to buy milk every day and give it to the baby. How could she know that it should have been boiled?

"Give hot tea with milk to the baby and it will perspire and the fever will go. Vitthal won't let you suffer."

She went to the medical van. Just then I saw an old man who was lying down with his head on his turban just beyond the group.

He said to me, "She is not the sort to do the pilgrimage. She cries when the child gets fever. One must be satisfied with whatever God gives us."

I was a little riled at this pontifical attitude and retorted, "You can talk like this, but only one who suffers really knows."

But the old man continued. "You know, Vitthal is a very hard god. If your heart gets entangled with something, he tears it out. Look at me. I had a wife and children and a home. But a single epidemic killed them all in a few days. Then I sold the house, sold everything, and said to God, 'You are the only onc I have.' "

As my *diṇḍī* was approaching, I got up, gave him some money for a cup of tea, and started walking, but not before I heard the words, "God, you thought I should drink some tea! O Pandurang, O Narayan!"

I also used to see an old woman off and on. Once somebody asked her, "Grandma, where are your children, your grandchildren? What do they do?" The old woman closed her eyes, her face became strangely desolate, and she began to shake. We all got frightened, went near her, and held her tightly with our arms.

"Grandma, please wake up. Drink this water," said I.

Her frail body was shivering in my arms. And then I remembered. I had a dog once and her puppy died; she had also shivered like that and I had drawn her to myself and felt her body quivering in my arms. How near we are to the animals, I had thought! After some time, the old woman stopped shaking. Tears streamed down from her closed eyes and the dumb grief found words. She told her story. And what was her sorrow? Hers was of the same kind as the others: her only son had died in his early twenties. These sorrows were not the result of any social inequalities, nor were they caused by any political turmoil or war. These were human sorrows, and would disappear only when human beings disappeared. They were there for the rich and for the poor, for the young and the old; they encompassed the whole of humanity. The old woman told her story, stopped, gave a deep sigh, and said, "O Pandurang, one must live as you will." I bit my lip and said to myself, "*Tena tyaktena bhuñjīthāḥ*—you can enjoy only that which he allows for your use." Only what this greedy, all-taking Lord does not take, remains for us. And the words of the old man came back to my mind: "Pandurang is a very hard god! If your heart gets entangled somewhere, he tears it out." But God! Why do you let it get entangled in the first place? You allow it to be completely enveloped and then cruelly tear it to shreds. What greatness do you find in this? What pleasure do you get in bringing such tired, torn hearts, shedding tears of blood, to your feet? Would it not be better if in the dawn of life, the blossoming flower in the mild early morning sun of happiness is plucked and used for your worship?

Oh but I was out of my mind! The agony of the old woman made me forget the world for a moment. Who brings whom to his feet? It is all a play of the human mind. First it creates a god with qualities out of a completely indifferent, formless, and attributeless principle, then makes him the author of everything that happens, makes him the Lord of the universe, and then says, "We can only have what he does not take."

Every one of us was deep in her sad thoughts when one woman started singing, "I care not if I live or die, for my heart is ever with thee, Pandurang." All of us mingled our voices with hers. A moment later, the woman also joined in with her shaky voice: "Pandurang, I swear, my heart is with thee." After some time, the shadows of sorrow melted away. All of us had our sorrows, and still we would bear them in each other's company.

Is religion a kind of opium? Human civilization has created many kinds of opiates and wines. Opium makes a man forget the world and become sleepy. Wine makes him offensive. Both are methods of forgetting the existing situation. Somebody creates a god, somebody a science, somebody a political *ism*. Have not all those thousands of scientists pursuing their studies, forgetting everything else, partaken of a kind of opium? The ones who let out the cry that modern science is the agency for making mankind happy are clearly intoxicated with the wine of knowledge. From Buddha to Marx, there have been many profound philosophers who wanted to eliminate the sorrows of society by social reorganization. Yet we see not only that the old sorrows have not been eliminated but that new sorrows have been added to the list. And then man takes opium or alcohol, forgets the sorrow, and says, "We have progressed. We are at the dawn of a happy world..."

That was the last day on the road. By evening the companions of all those days would part. Each one would go to his or her home. I had an uneasy feeling—my eyes were filling again and again.

Haushi had told me, "The last bit of the plateau is called, 'Weeping Plateau.' "

"But why?"

"Oh, you have got to cry when you walk there."

All around me, people were saying good-bye to each other. I could find no words—I could only nod to the companions in my *dinḍī* to say good-bye and start on ahead. I reached the entrance to the town. But somehow I was feeling restless. I could not see Him, who had been there, sometimes in the *dinḍī*, sometimes ahead of us, sometimes under a tree, and sometimes near the well. When I turned round, I saw His back and He was marching away in the opposite direction. "Why, Dark One, are You leaving too? Are You not coming into Pandharpur?" He smiled and shook his head. "Where are You off to?" Without a word, He merely waved His arm and began to walk fast. The black ploughed fields and the sky full of heavy black clouds soon engulfed that delicate dark figure with the blanket on His shoulder. And I stepped inside the gates of Pandharpur with streaming eyes, weary legs, and a heavy heart.[6]

## EDITORS' NOTES

1. Vithoba (Father Vitthal) is elsewhere in this account called by the regional names of Vithai (Mother Vitthal), Vitthal, Pandharinath (Lord of Pandharpur) and Pandurang (The White One) as well as by the universal Vaishnava names for god, Hari and Narayan.

2. Dnyanoba is a familiar name for Dnyaneshwar, the thirteenth-century founder of the Varkari tradition. Tukaram, a seventeenth-century poet and saint, is the most beloved of all the hundreds of saints. A bibliography on this Maharashtrian bhakti movement is included in the "Selected Bibliography" at the end of this volume.

3. Since this account was written, the Raidas *dinḍī* of the Chambhar Untouchables has won the privilege of marching behind the god's horses, as do all other *dinḍīs*, rather than in front. The change came about after much negotiation and represented to the Chambhars greater equality with other castes. Raidas or Rohidas was an Untouchable bhakti poet from the Hindi-speaking area who, like the Maharashtrian Chambhars, was a leather worker.

4. For a note on the *bhārūḍs* and some translations, see Eleanor Zelliot, "Chokhamela and Eknath," in the *Journal of Asian and African Studies* 14 (1980): 136–156, and her "Eknath's Bharude" in *The Sants* (Berkeley: Religious Studies Series, 1987). For an account of a *bhārūḍ* session, see Hugh van Skyhawk, "*Eknāthi Bhāruḍe* as a Performance Genre" in the *South Asian Digest of Regional Writing* 10 (1981): 48–56.

5. Ramdas (1608–81), a devotee of Ram, was the founder of a monastic order and a commentator on socio-political matters as well as religion. Nevertheless, he is included in most discussions of the Maharashtrian bhakti movement and although he himself did not go to Pandharpur as a Varkari, his *pālkhī* is part of the current pilgrimage.

6. Another personal essay on the pilgrimage to Pandharpur by a Maharashtrian intellectual offers an interesting comparison and contrast to Irawati Karve's account. *Palkhi* by D. B. Mokashi, trans. by Philip Engblom (Albany: State University of New York Press, 1987) is a book-length account of that author's pilgrimage.

9. Pilgrims carrying their Varkari flags on the road to Pandharpur. *Photography by Maxine Berntsen.*

10. A small boy insists on being photographed with a wall representation of Shivaji, seventeenth-century King of the Marathas, shown here with the sword called Bhavani. The Goddess herself is thought to have entered the sword. The legend reads, "Victory to Bhavani, Victory to Maharashtra." The painting is probably the effort of an R.S.S. member. *Photography by Eleanor Zelliot.*

RAMCHANDRA CHINTAMAN DHERE
TRANSLATED BY ANNE FELDHAUS

# 12

# *The Gondhali: Singers for the Devi*

## Editors' Introduction

Of all the colorful traditional performers in Maharashtrian popular Hinduism, the Gondhalis seem to have the best chance of surviving in the modern world. Their place in ritual now has been almost lost, although a few Deshastha Brahmans and Marathas still include a *gondhaḷ* performance in especially elaborate weddings. The *gondhaḷ* as entertainment retains such vigor and is so adaptable, however, that it may well continue with new functions and new audiences. Although the initiative comes from the sophisticated elite who treasure the meaningful forms of the past, the Gondhali himself, who has adapted to changing circumstances for over a thousand years, may find it possible and profitable to train his sons to use the old techniques of performance in new ways or to teach others.

Three recent *gondhaḷ* performances illustrate the continuance of the tradition. Bhimsen Joshi, probably the best-loved classical singer in Maharashtra, called a Gondhali to perform at his house-warming, which in this area is still a ritual occasion. A *gondhaḷ* performance was included in a great festival of traditional performers at Pandharpur sponsored by the Indian National Theatre in 1982; it was acclaimed as the most dramatic and effective performance among all those of the Vasudevs (colorful chanting religious mendicants), *lāwaṇī* singers, *bhārūḍ* groups, and others. The third instance may be the most important: the Central Government's Song and Dance Division has sent a Gondhali party to tour the rural areas of Nasik district, where they will incorporate advice on family planning and agriculture into their flexible traditional songs. The party consists of one traditional Gondhali and three non-traditional, highly-educated young musicians who serve as accompanists. The same combination of traditional and modern musicians serves Indian classical music well; perhaps it can extend the life and vigor of folk music.

What seems lost in this modernization of the *gondhaḷ* is the close tie with the worship of the Goddess. Although the devi phenomenon has been little studied in Maharashtra, there is no doubting the importance of the four great devi temples—Mahalakshmi in Kolhapur, Renuka in Mahur, Saptashringi near Nasik, Bhavani in Tuljapur—which ring the Marathi-speaking area, nor of the smaller temples dedicated to the goddess, nor of the non-sanskritic, formless, formidable Mariai and other "mother" goddesses whose rough temples are found in every village. There is little doubt that the goddess Bhavani was far more important than the gentle bhakti god Vithoba as a religious base for the dynamics of the great Maratha empire in the seventeenth century. Maharashtra does not pay such public homage to Mahalakshmi as Bengal does to Durga, but the goddess as *kuladaivat* (family deity) and the temples of the goddess as places of worship and festival still have a large part in the religious life of the Maharashtrian people. The contemporary attraction of the Gondhali may well be not only his skill in performance but also his attachment to the devi. Some of the power of his songs, even though they are bent more now than in the past to secular matters, may stem from his status as the devi's singer. (*E. Z. and M. B.*)

## *The Gondhali**

Among the great figures of Marathi folk religion—the Gondhali, the Vaghya and Murli, the Bhutya, the Vasudev, the Potraj, and so on—the most important is the Gondhali. The *gondhaḷ*, a dramatic rite of goddess worship, is a traditional family observance in Maharashtra. After weddings and thread ceremonies, Deshastha Brahmans and most Marathas traditionally sponsor a *gondhaḷ* in honor of their family goddess.

The Gondhali stands in the courtyard or on the verandah, a robe over his body, a string of cowrie beads around his neck, and a fancy turban on his head; with him are his accompanists with their *sambaḷ*-drums and their one-stringed *tuṇtuṇ*-drones; in front of them is a piece of blouse-cloth spread on a square stand, with grain arranged on it in a quadrangular design; the goddess is installed on a pot on top of this. Around the design is erected a frame of millet or sugarcane stalks. The goddess has been worshipped, the host has lit a torch, and, young and old, the audience is impatient to hear the *gondhaḷ*. This scene may now be rare, but at one time it had an important place in the life of the Marathi people. As long as the host kept pouring oil on the torch, the *gondhaḷ* performance would continue—often until dawn began to break. As the Gondhali wove puranic myths and heroic legends into songs interspersed with prose embellishments, listeners from all strata of society would be caught up in the emotions evoked by the stories.

It was through the story woven into the songs, the var-

---

* This article is an abridged translation of a chapter from Dhere's *Marāṭhī Lokasaṃskṛtīce Upāsak*. [Religious Performers of Marathi Folk Culture] (Pune: Dnyanaraj Prakashan, 1964). I am grateful to Dr. S. G. Tulpule for his help in checking the translation. A. F.

ious techniques of elocution and story-telling, the actions accompanying the narrative, and the accompaniment of the *sambaḷ* and the *tuṇtuṇ*, that the *gondhaḷ* captivated the minds of the people who attended it. The *gondhaḷ* lavishly illustrates the pleasure and fun of the institutions of folk religion. Because it is enjoyable, it is an easy and natural medium of instruction.

### *History of the Gondhaḷ*

Gondhalis are worshippers of Renuka and Tulja Bhavani. Gondhalis maintain that they originated from Jamadagni and Renuka and that their place of origin is Mahur. The *Reṇukā Māhātmya* relates that after Parashuram had killed a demon named Betasur, he cut off its head, threaded the sinews of the head through the aperture in the crown, put it on his shoulder, and went to his mother playing *tintṛiṇ tintṛiṇ* on it. This first homage which Parashuram paid to his mother, playing the stringed instrument fashioned from the body and the head of Betasur, is the origin of the *gondhaḷ*.[1] In his work *Svānubhavadinakara*, Dinkar Swami has recorded a similar story about the *gondhaḷ*:

> Since Sahasrarjuna tormented his parents,
> and wounded his mother twenty-one times,
> so twenty-one times did Parashuram
> rid the earth of Kshatriyas.
> He killed Sahasrarjuna and his retinue,
> and made a stringed instrument of his corpse.
> Parashuram gave a *gondhaḷ* at Matapur;
> "Come, Mother, come," he cried.[2]

Besides Renuka, another goddess of the Gondhalis is Tulja Bhavani. The two main types of Gondhalis, Renukrai and Kadamrai, are connected with Renuka and Tulja Bhavani respectively.[3] Kadams are officeholders who have a hereditary share in the worship of Tulja Bhavani; this seems to be the origin of the name Kadamrai.

It is difficult to determine when this honored tradition in the worship of Renuka and Tulja Bhavani originated.

Tulja Bhavani's antiquity extends to before 1000 B.C.,[4] and Renuka is even more ancient than that. The antiquity of the *gondhaḷ* is tied to the antiquity of Renuka.

However, from Old Marathi literature—particularly from the earliest, that of the Yadava period—we learn that the *gondhaḷ* must originally be linked with a goddess named "Bhutamata." Later the *gondhaḷ* was incorporated in the worship of Renuka because Bhutamata became incorporated into Renuka, a popular goddess in Maharashtra. The *Nṛtyaratnāvalī*, composed in A.D. 1240 by Jayan, the leader of Ganpati Kakati's elephant regiment, states that the Chalukya king, Someshvar III (Bhulokamalla) of Kalyan, gave a *gondhaḷ* program on the occasion of the great festival of Bhutamata.[5]

The great festival of Bhutamata is a semi-secular festival; it is described variously in the Puranas.[6] From the first day of the dark fortnight of the month of Vaishakh to the no-moon day, Bhutamata's festival was celebrated with great pomp and much noise, in order to drive away ill fortune and to obtain good progeny. The popular belief was that by celebrating this festival people were protected from the ravages of such ghostly and demonic creatures as *bhūts, prets, ḍākinīs, shākinīs, pishāças,* and *rākshasas*. After worshipping Bhutamata with devotion for four days, on the no-moon day they would hold an elaborate procession. The *Prabhāsakhaṇḍa* of the *Skanda Purāṇa* informs us that plays and dramatic performances would be held every night during the festival. According to the *Bhaviṣya Purāṇa*, Bhutamata's festival was celebrated enthusiastically in the month of Jyeshtha. In their exuberance, some people would sing and dance, laugh and play, pronounce forbidden words, make obscene gestures, roll in the dust, and even smear their bodies with mud as if they were possessed. From the textual references it appears that this festival of Bhutamata, which originated in folk culture, was celebrated with enthusiasm from the seventh to the thirteenth century.

In the *Jñāneśvarī*, the term "gondhali" is used in the sense of "demon" (*pishāça*) or "ghost" (*bhūt*). Dnyaneshwar uses the following analogy to illustrate the point that *purush,* when subject to *prakṛiti,* loses its brilliance: "Just as, when a Gondhali comes and drags him into his band, a saintly man's goodness is destroyed, and he begins to dance with the band, so does *purush* lose its brilliance when it becomes subject to *prakṛiti.*"[7] The association of Gondhalis with ghosts appears clearly in the following verse from Dasopant's *Gītārṇava*:

> One who's fallen into the ghosts' *gondhaḷ*
> is not our [kind of] man.
> His life has come
> to depend on sin.[8]

The references to the *gondhaḷ* that occur as allegories in the earliest Mahanubhav literature include such phrases as "a band of all the *shaktīs,*" "a *gondhaḷ* of a circle of *yoginīs,*" and "circle *gondhaḷ.*" In addition, the tumult of musical instruments preceding a corpse is brought into connection with the *gondhaḷ.*[9]

In view of these and many other such references, it can be stated with certainty that the *gondhaḷ* was originally connected with Bhutamata and, in fact, is a liturgical dance of Bhutamata's companions, the troops of ghosts (*bhūts*). In its original form, the *gondhaḷ* appears to have been a ritual in which a group of men dressed as ghosts formed a circle, made a clamor of songs and music, and danced. Later, it seems, this ritual was introduced into the worship of Renuka, and in time its ghost form was lost even to memory.

Yadava-period scholars who wrote books on music and dance included in their works many popular local musical and dance forms. The *gondhaḷ,* under the name *gaunḍalīnṛitya,* is included in *Saṅgītaratnākara, Saṅgītasamayasāra, Nṛtyaratnāvali, Aumāpatam, Bharatārṇava,* and other texts about music and dance. There are many Sanskrit variants of the name: *gauṇḍalī, guṇḍalī, goṇḍalī, kuṇḍalī.* In his *Saṅgītaratnākara,* Sharngadeva holds that his local dance form was "born in the Karnata land."[10] Descriptions of this type of dance are also found in the Telugu literature of the period.[11]

*Gondhaḷs* have a special place in the *bhārūḍ* literature of the saints. The *gondhaḷ bhārūḍs* of Eknath, the king of *bhārūḍ* literature, are extremely majestic and inspirational. Take as an example the following *gondhaḷ* of Eknath's:

1. We've set up your *gondhaḷ* at a good time on a good day.
   We've tied up the garland of knowledge and detachment.
   We've lit the torch of the moon and the sun.
   We've made a throne and installed a pot on it.
   Refrain: Say "Hail!", the "Hail!" of Mother the guru.

2. We've spread the clean seat of action and restraint.
   We've washed our feet with the object of meditation, the meditator, and the meditation.
   We've worshipped with our bodies, voices, and minds in unison.
   We've sipped water with faith in dualism and non-dualism.

3. We've worshipped Amba with devotion, detachment, and knowledge.
   Seeing our goodness and intelligence, Jagadamba is pleased.
   The crowd of your children take refuge in Eka Janardana.
   Save us, Amba, save us! Your servant stands before you.

The saints who understand Vitthal as the primordial goddess Bhavani have a particularly remarkable *gondhaḷ*.

The fact that the saints used Gondhalis as a medium for spreading their ideas gives us an idea of how respectable the Gondhalis once were. Contrasting Gondhalis' former popularity with contemporary indifference to them, S. T. Shaligram, a compiler of *povāḍās* (ballads of heroic deeds), has said:

> Just as the Bhats of Rajasthan caused a reawakening in that state by telling the stories of its heroes, so under the Peshwas the Gondhalis' *povāḍās* had the same kind of effect. Under the Peshwas the Maratha people would lose them-

> selves in the *gondhaḷ*. It's not so now. Maratha people say, "Who wants to listen to those pointless stories?" and so no one comes to *gondhaḷs*. It's the same as the way these new and undiscriminating people are bored with legends and with stories and myths. These days, even war news bores Maratha people. In the Peshwa period, there were so many *gondhaḷs* the Gondhalis hardly had time to catch their breath between one *gondhaḷ* and another. They had no leisure time at all. Under the Peshwas, Gondhalis used to get plenty of honoraria: various types of bracelets, bags of money, pairs of double earrings, and different types of shawls. At each *gondhaḷ* they would get at least one shawl and turban and an overabundance of food to eat.[12]

Gondhalis were at the same time bards and priests. Just as legends and myths were recited in connection with Vedic sacrifices, so, in the realm of Marathi folk religion, were legends and myths recited on the occasion of the family worship of the goddess. The role of these influential priests in the realm of folk religion needs to be studied.

### *The Performance of the Gondhaḷ*

There is an unpublished Sanskrit text named "Āmalikāgrāma Māhātmya." Amalikagrama is Mahur. At Mahur there is a black *āvaḷī* (*Phyllanthus emblica*) tree which is considered holy, and which has given Mahur the name Amalikagrama. In three chapters of this text on the glories of Mahur, the "*gauṇḍalī*-dance" is described:

> ... One should select an auspicious day, don a necklace of cowries, take a torch, and perform the *gondhaḷ*. Everyone should be invited to the place where the *gondhaḷ* is to be performed....
>
> *Gauṇḍalī* troupes are classified as superior, middling, and inferior, the superior troupes having thirty-two members: four chief singers, eight secondary, and four cymbal players. The middling troupes must have half as many, that is, sixteen; and the inferior ones, half again as many, that is, eight members. A warning is made that there should not be fewer than that.

> Since there are thus thirty-two people included in a Gaundali dance, there must also be a big enough space for them to dance in. A circular ground seven armsbreadths from east to west and seven from south to north should be adequate for the dance. Precise stipulations are made about how the dance is to be done, who should stand where, who should hold the torches, who should use which musical instruments, and what is an appropriate time for a *gondhaḷ*.[13]

In this description of the *gauṇḍalī*-dance, a troupe of eight members is considered inferior. But in *gondhaḷs* today there are only four. One of them has the *sambaḷ*-drum. One has the *tuṇtuṇ*-drone. One does the narration, with songs and stories; the fourth interrupts the narration with humorous questions, making the audience laugh and keeping the narration from lagging. The chief Gondhali, the one who does the narration, is called the leader.

The leader begins the *gondhaḷ* with a *gaṇa*, a verse in praise of Ganesh. After that the Gondhalis praise Jagadamba and invite numerous gods and goddesses to the *gondhaḷ*. Then the "musical storytelling" gets under way. The *gondhaḷ* ends with an *āratī* to Jagadamba.

The literature which Gondhalis use in their *gondaḷs* is a type of folk literature. To keep his audience of various classes and ages interested all night long, the Gondhali showers them with fascinating ballads and stories. These stories and ballads are, by virtue of their content and their form, a branch of folk literature. No major attempt has been made to collect the stories and songs of the Gondhalis, such as was made to collect their *povāḍās*. What is remarkable is that the Gondhali evokes the heroic mood with his *povāḍās*, he creates waves of various emotions with his stories and ballads, and at the same time, he brings forth bursts of laughter with his humorous songs.

The song program of a *gondhaḷ*[14] begins as we said with a *gaṇa*, just as Ganesh is praised at the beginning of a book or at the beginning of any auspicious ceremony. The Gondhali begins to sing a hymn of praise to Ganaraja (Ganesh):

Morya, Ganapati, O Ganaraja,
How much can we ask of you, O Maharaja?

Thirty-three crores there are of gods and goddesses;
Ahead of them all is the leader of the Ganas.

You beat the demons and put them in distress.
You sent them running in all directions.

You punish the evil one.
How much can we ask of you, O Maharaja?

After singing the *gaṇa*, the Gondhali praises Jagadamba and "invites" the gods and goddesses of many places to descend to the arena of his *gondhaḷ*. Included in the "invitation" along with the famous puranic deities known to everyone are the popular deities of Maharashtra; and so as not to skimp on his idea of the ubiquity of the gods, the Gondhali also does not fail to mention the gods living in water, on land, and in the sky. He says:

You seven oceans, come to the *gondhaḷ*!
You hundred thousand waves, come to the *gondhaḷ*!
Mother Earth, come to the *gondhaḷ*!
Mother Space, come to the *gondhaḷ*!
You company of devotees, come to the *gondhaḷ*!
Everyone else, come to the *gondhaḷ*!

Heeding this invitation, all the gods and goddesses descend into the "arena," and then with them as witnesses the Gondhali exhibits his great memory, inventiveness, eloquence, and story-telling style. Then he performs his combination of drama, song, and music, and the *gondhaḷ* is unfadingly brilliant—the night comes to an end, but no one feels that the *gondhaḷ* should stop.

In the song program of the *gondhaḷ* there are songs praising the goddess, there are "dairy-maid songs" (*gauḷaṇīs*) which string together stories of Krishna; there are *povāḍās* extolling the valor of heroes; there are songs which in ironic language throw light on the realities of village life; and there are also songs which are not sarcastic but purely funny. The *gondhaḷ* song which presents the story of Krishna killing the snake Kaḷiya is rhythmic, fast-moving, and evocative of a whirlpool of emotions:

> Said his mother Yashoda, "Listen, Yadunath,
> Don't you wander around the village now.
> The dairymaids practice calumny; they're accusing you with a torrent of lies.
> Go play outside; play
> Your flute, Shri Hari; go play *itidandu*."
> Shriranga collected the cowherd boys; they went to play ball.
> A crowd of cowherd boys came running; they encircled him all around.
> Shriranga was in the center; his face could not be seen.
> He divided his playmates, taking half for his team; boldly he said, "Come on, let's start the game."

So the cowherd boys begin to play catch. Krishna tosses the ball up high—as high as the sun—and, as they look on, it gets caught on the branch of a *kadamba* tree sticking out into the current of the Yamuna river. A boy named "Crooked," one of Krishna's playmates, stands in Krishna's way and tells him not to go home without freeing the ball. Krishna climbs up into the *kadamba* tree, but just as his hand is about to reach the ball, the branch it is caught on breaks off with a crash and falls into Kaliya's pool. And then—

> A cry went up in Gokul: "Yadunath is lost!"
> His cowherd friends came running.
> They dove into the water.
> They tried to see to the bottom, but they couldn't fathom the depths.
> They got tired out from diving again and again.
> "We can't find Hari anywhere," wailed the cowherds.
> "Hari's lost; we can't find him.
> At home, Hari's mother will ask where he is.
> What will happen if we tell her?"
> The cows came running,
> They were lowing for Shri Hari's feet.

As the cowherds and the cows were crying, his mother Yashoda came wailing; she stood on the bank of the Yamuna river and asked it:

> "How could you have done this, lady Yamuna?

Is Hari nowhere? Has no one seen him?
O fawn whose mother deer I am,
How can you have gone off and left me?"

As this lament was going on, Krishna himself came up, mounted on the great snake Kaliya. As soon as they saw him, Gokul was flooded with joy.

Young and old said, "Krishna! Krishna!"
They raised him to their hips.
All over, in front of Nanda's house,
They threw glass balls of red powder.

The hearts of the audience, at first gripped with fear at Krishna's predicament, cannot fail to be dyed by that red powder of joy.

To bring the *gondhaḷ* to life, the Gondhali often also uses the device of talking about individuals present in the audience, under the pretext of creating a scene from a puranic story. To get an idea of how this device works, take a look at this list of the names of the dairymaids on their way to see Krishna:

The oil-man's wife Thaki, the bangle-seller Sakhi,
Talked with Bhiki the Dhangar's wife.
They began to talk together.

The goldsmith woman Sangi, the clothier's wife Lingi,
And Gangi the wife of Kusha Gurav
Were startled.

The carpenter-woman Maina, the blacksmith-woman Gahina,
And Changuna the wife of the Koli
Were all three invited together.

They thought to themselves,
"Let's go to Hari. Come on, let's see him for ourselves.
Let's place our minds at his feet."

In the Gondhalis' songs about Nagpanchmi as well, there is a humorous and cleverly-drawn sketch of the women of the various castes of the surrounding society. As the women begin bustling together to go to the anthill on the Nagpanchmi day,

Here comes the Chambhar woman Ithi,

She always talks as if she's angry.
It's about no more than a guava.
She puts her friends aside.

Here comes the carpenter-woman Babi.
The way she talks is striking:
She holds a tobacco tin in her hand
And calls to her girlfriends.

Here comes the smith-woman Hiri.
Her sari's not over her head.
In her rush to get ready
She's put no *kunkū* on her brow.

Here comes the Dhangar's wife Nara
There's fresh green snot at her nose.
On her hip is her crying child.
Let's not take her along.

Here comes the Maratha woman Sali.
Her ways are plain and simple.
The gypsy woman wears no blouse.
How will she understand our talk?

Among this collection of women, only for the Maratha woman does the Gondhali show the least partiality.

Jokes, which are found only rarely in the Old Marathi literature of the saints and scholars, abound in *gondhaḷ* performances. Also worth hearing from this point of view are the Gondhalis' songs "The Fight Between Salt and Chili" and "The Jackal's Wedding." The song which presents "The Fight Between Salt and Chili" is satirical. When the quarrel between the two fails to get resolved, the housewife prepares to grind chutney, and then—

With the grindstone below and the pestle above,
Their quarrel finally ends.

In the song "The Jackal's Wedding," a human marriage ceremony is celebrated in all its details in the world of animals.

## *Conclusion*

We have seen that besides being a priest of folk religion, the Gondhali is also a bard. In this second role he disseminates heroic compositions and *povāḍās.* Gondhalis provided a valuable service for the Maratha kingdom by binding together in their songs stories of victorious ancestors and contemporary heroes. Even now, when the tambourine is beaten, people's ears prick up, their arms twitch, and their breasts are filled with emotion. So one can imagine how thrilling the *povāḍās* must have been at a time when the audience included many heroes who had themselves taken their lives in their hands and experienced heroic events. It was the Gondhalis who sang the *povāḍās* and brought them to life. Most of the *povāḍās* collected by Acworth and Shaligram came from the mouths of Gondhalis.[15]

Besides, when the Gondhalis went into *tamāshās,*[16] they were able to make full use of the dramatic character of the *gondhaḷ.* The humorous songs in the *gondhaḷ*s and the character who asks funny questions and makes the audience laugh play a part also in *tamāshās.*

Rama Gondhali, who was famous in Pune at the end of the Peshwa period (early nineteenth century), demonstrates the Gondhalis' effect on the *tamāshās.* About this man's fame, Shaligram has said:

> He was like a Gandharva.... His eloquence was incomparable. The city of Pune became so enamored of his sweet voice that thousands of people would crowd around his *tamāshās.* It is said that the crowd would extend for a quarter mile around his *tamāshā.* And he received honoraria which sound incredible now.[17]

After the Peshwas' rule was ended in 1818 by the British conquest, Rama Gondhali went to Baroda to take refuge with the Gaekwads.[18] Tukaram Gondhali, Madhav Gondhali, Udaji Pandu Gondhali, Ranaba Gondhali, Alekar Gondhali, and other Gondhalis who performed in *tamāshās* lived, like Rama Gondhali, under the protection of the Gaekwads.

This institution had at one time a great deal of influence over the Marathi mind. As an institution of folk religion it has a thousand- or twelve-hundred-year history. Since ancient times it has spread across the large southern regions of Andhra, Karnataka, and Maharashtra. It has had a great influence on the shape of our folk religion and folk literature. It is imperative that this important institution be thoroughly studied before it dies out.

## NOTES

1. *Reṇukā Māhātmya* (Marathi), chap. 10, verses 44-47.
2. *Svānubhavadinakara*, 1.6:75-81.
3. In the book *Mumbaī Ilākhyāṃtīla Jātī* (an adaptation of Enthoven's *Tribes and Castes of Bombay*; see Selected Bibliography, Castes IV), six subcastes of Gondhalis are given: Maratha, Kumbhar, Kadamrai, Renukrai, Brahman, and Akaramase (p. 76).
4. For further discussion of the antiquity of Tulja Bhavani, see my article "Tuḷajābhavānīcī Prācīnatā," *Indrāyaṇī* 1, no. 1.
5. *Bhārata Itihāsa Saṃśodhaka Maṇḍaḷa Quarterly* 20, no. 2:81-82.
6. Manmathray, *Hamāre Kuca Prācīna Lokotsava*, pp. 49-50.
7. *Jñāneśvarī*, 13.1004.
8. *Gītārṇava*, 1.2391.
9. *Śiśupālavadha* (Bhāskara), 446; *Rukmiṇīsvayaṃvara* (Narendra), 735, 810; *Saihādrivarṇana* (Ravalobas), 24.
10. *Saṅgītaratnākara*, 7.1287.
11. Suravaram Pratap Reddi, *Āndhrakā Sāmājika Itihāsa*, pp. 34, 63, 90, 208, 292, etc.
12. Acworth, Harry Arbuthnot and S. T. Shaligram, eds., *Itihāsaprasiddha Puruṣāṃce va Striyāṃce Povāḍe* (Bombay: Nirnayasagar, 1891). Introduction, pp. 3-4.
13. *Āmalikāgrāma Māhātmyam*, chaps. 74-76. This manuscript was given me by Mr. P. P. Dhamdhere. A manuscript of one chapter (74) of the text is in the collection of the Bharata Itihasa Samsodhaka Mandala. See *Bhārata Itihāsa Saṃśodhaka Maṇḍaḷa Quarterly* 20, no. 1:18-20.
14. Here selections have been made from the Gondhalis' songs published by Dr. Sarojini Babar in *Eka Hotā Rājā* (Bombay: Maharashtra Rajya Lokasahitya Samiti, 1965), and in *Navabhārata* (October, 1958).
15. See Harry Arbuthnot Acworth, *Ballads of the Marathas* (London: Longmans, Green and Co., 1894), for the translation of ten *powāḍās*, together with a lengthy introduction which includes notes on the role of the Gondhali in the late nineteenth century. (Eds.)
16. See Tevia Abrams, "Tamasha: People's Theatre of Maharashtra State, India," Diss. Michigan State University, 1974, for the lengthiest discussion in English on *tamāshā*, the folk theater which has appropriated the drama and humor, though not the religious purpose, of the

Gondhalis. Abrams' "Folk Theatre in Maharashtrian Social Development Programs," in the *Educational Theatre Journal* 27:3 (1975): 395-407, discusses the use of *tamāshā* and such religious professionals as the Vasudev and the Vaghya of the Khandoba sect in government social programs. (Eds.)

17. Acworth and Shaligram, Marathi Introduction, pp. 4-5.

18. The Gaekwads were princes of the Maratha Kingdom who retained much of their land after the British conquest, maintaining the princely state of Baroda, now in Gujarat, up until the time of Indian Independence. (Eds.)

V. M. SIRSIKAR

# 13

# *My Years in the R.S.S.*

## Editors' Introduction

The Rashtriya Swayamsevak Sangh (National Volunteer Corps), known as the R.S.S., has become an important part of a nationalistic Hindu ethos since its founding in Nagpur in 1925. Subject to controversy almost since its inception, it has been banned twice—once after the assassination of Mahatma Gandhi in 1948 by a militant right-wing Hindu and again during the Emergency declared in 1975, since it was identified with the opposition to Indira Gandhi. The head of the R.S.S., Balasaheb Deoras, together with some sixty thousand R.S.S. members and members of the Jan Sangh—a political party linked ideologically and through its personnel to the R.S.S.—spent the period of the Emergency in prison. The R.S.S. may have gained ground very recently through a number of related educational organizations, through new proselytizing work among tribal peoples, and through its association with members of the Janata Party coalition. The youth work of the R.S.S. can still be seen in the cities and towns of Maharashtra, as young boys perform their early morning or late afternoon drills with precision and decorum. Obviously a disciplined group, their brand of Hinduism is not sectarian but rather an austere nationalism based on glorifying the militant aspects of the Hindu—not the Mughal, Sultanate, or Buddhist—past of India. (*E. Z. and M. B.*)

## *The Program of the R.S.S.*

Although some of these things happened over five decades ago, I will try to recapture the feelings, experiences, and perceptions of the sixteen years I spent in the R.S.S. I remember very clearly the day I was introduced to the organization. The year was 1933 and I was studying in a high school in Nagpur, the home of the R.S.S. I was introduced by my brother-in-law to a slightly older neighbor who took me to an R.S.S. *shākhā* (branch) meeting one evening. A number of young boys like me had gathered there, most of them in a simple uniform of khaki shorts and a short-sleeved white shirt. While I was being introduced to the other boys there was a shrill whistle; the boys immediately formed lines according to their *pathaks* (companies of fifteen to twenty boys). With another shrill whistle, a saffron flag was hoisted on the flagpole. There was complete silence, and then the order came for a salute. The R.S.S. had developed a different kind of salute—neither the Western salute nor the Indian *namaste*. Everyone kept his right arm folded with his fist touching his heart. After a few moments there was a Sanskrit prayer in praise of the motherland and the flag.

> Salutation to thee, ever-affectionate Motherland! I was brought up in comfort by thee, O Hindu Land, O most auspicious Holy Land. May this body of mine fall for thee. Salutation to thee! Salutation to thee!

> O omnipotent God! We the members of the Hindu nation bow down to thee respectfully. We have girded our loins in thy cause. Give us thy sacred blessings for its fulfillment.
>
> Give us O Lord, such power as will be invincible for the whole universe; moral character, before which the world will bow down in respect; knowledge, which will make easy the traversing of the thorny path we have chosen.
>
> The one and the highest means of obtaining both worldly prosperity and spiritual liberation is the severe vow of the warrior; may it ever throb in us. May staunch and undecaying devotion to the Ideal be ever awake in our hearts.
>
> And may the victorious and efficacious power of our union defend this *dharma*, by thy blessings, and may it be able to lead this nation of ours to the highest glory.

After the prayer was over, each group went to its appointed place. Some played games, some performed calisthenics, and others did military drill. After an hour, all the boys reassembled in front of the flag, and with a salute and a prayer the flag was taken down.

Much impressed by the strict discipline and punctuality observed in the *shākhā*, the next day I started inquiring about the R.S.S. among my schoolmates. I found that nearly three-fourths of them were attending various R.S.S. *shākhās* in the city. Thus surrounded by my neighbors and classmates, I started my career in the R.S.S. in an atmosphere which was conducive to making me a devoted *svayamsevak* (volunteer) in a matter of a few months. I was invited to small informal parties and gatherings and was overwhelmed by the cordiality with which I was welcomed. The daily activity of games and athletics was fascinating since I had never known anything like this in the taluka town where I had grown up. The games and calisthenics were especially appealing because, except for the drill, they were all Indian. We never played volleyball, badminton, or other Western games, but our own games, *hu-tu-tu* and *kho-kho*, instead. The calisthenics were all performed with Sanskrit orders.

The whole week was filled with activity. Every evening,

of course, were the drill and games. Then once a week these were suspended and there were lectures on Hindu culture, some of which, I later realized, were repeated every year. These lectures largely eulogized the Hindu religion and the political heroes of the past, such as Shivaji and Rana Pratap.[1] They never emphasized religious orthodoxy. Brahman boys were not encouraged to do *sandhyā* or any other Brahman ritual, nor to go to a Hindu temple, nor to pray to any particular god or goddess. The emphasis was on an attitude toward a Hindu nation, not on Hindu religious rituals.

Every Sunday there was a parade. We assembled early in the morning at the main parade ground on the outskirts of the city, clad in dress uniform—khaki shirt and shorts, shoes, puttees, black cap, and a long staff. We drilled and then performed a route march for two or three hours. Orders for the drill were in English and a band played English music. After the parade, the usual salute and prayer marked the end of the Sunday routine.

These weekly parades served as preparation for formal occasions like Vijaya Dashmi day when all the *svayamsevaks* in the city assembled for a huge parade. Everyone looked forward to this occasion and prepared assiduously for it. Hair was cut short, shoes shined, uniforms pressed, and brass shoulder badges with the initials R.S.S. polished.

I later came to know that most of the practices in the parade, even the use of the military band, had been borrowed from the University Training Corps. This kind of formal march and the Sunday parade ground activities gave a certain militaristic tinge to the whole organization. I am not sure this was in the mind of Dr. K. B. Hedgewar when he began the organization in 1925, but eight years later when I joined, the major lines of activity had been drawn.

At this time I was also introduced to the R.S.S.'s novel method of fund collection. Once a year, on a day fixed according to the Hindu calendar, all the *svayamsevaks* were expected to place in front of the flag an offering of money called the *guru dakshiṇā* (offering made by a disciple to his teacher). Preparation for *guru dakshiṇā* day began almost a month earlier; there was a kind of competition among the *pathaks* as to which of them would contribute the most. I remember how later I too used to save every *paisā* of my pocket money in order to make a handsome *guru dakshiṇā*.

An interesting aspect of the whole procedure was that no one except the *karewār* (secretary) knew how much money had been collected that day. It was only after the contributions from all the branches had been pooled that the total was announced. Moreover, there was an air of secrecy about the expenses that were met out of the *guru dakshiṇā*. It was an unwritten rule that no *svayamsevak* was to ask for accounts of the organization. I think that for a long time no accounts were kept and everything depended on personal trust between the *svayamsevaks* and the leadership.

A few months after my introduction to the R.S.S. I was considered a regular member and assigned to the *pathak* of which my neighbor and friend was in charge. From then on I was slowly absorbed, stage by stage into the organization, moving into positions of increasing commitment and responsibility. After a year of membership, while still in high school, I was taken aside by the *shākhā kāryavāh* (head of the branch) and asked to take the oath of initiation to become a full-fledged member of the R.S.S. Only a few *svayamsevaks*, he told me, were considered good enough to take the oath, which committed one to the organization for life. Although too young to understand the implications of a life-long commitment, I was very much elated at being asked, and I readily agreed.

The dignity and solemnity of the oath-taking help to impress on the initiate the seriousness of the occasion. The ceremony is held in private with high dignitaries of the organization present. Every new member comes before the flag and repeats very slowly the Sanskrit oath dictated by the *kāryavāh*:

> I swear in the name of almighty God and my forefathers to protect our sacred Hindu *dharma*, Hindu culture, and Hindu society and to strengthen the organization. I have

> become a member of the Rashtriya Svayamsevak Sangh. I will carry out the work of the Rashtriya Svayamsevak Sangh honestly, selflessly, with all my physical, moral, and material powers. I will dedicate myself to this work for my whole life.
>
> Hail to the motherland!

After taking the oath, the initiate salutes the flag and the dignitaries. Following the oath-taking there is a short lecture. The whole ceremony serves to impress on the initiate that he now has new responsibilities and also a high status in the organization.

### *The R.S.S. Leadership*

For the next few years, as a full-fledged member of the R.S.S., I took part not only in the daily training and the Sunday parade but in the annual camp held every December and the six-week summer Officer Training Camps. The O.T.C.'s were started first in Nagpur but later were conducted at various centers in different states. There were separate camps for first, second, and third-year trainees, the third-year camps being held only in Nagpur. The training in all the camps emphasized physical fitness, moral uprightness, and indoctrination in the R.S.S. ideology.

The daily routine in the camps was quite strict: physical training in the morning, *baudhiks* (instruction sessions) in the afternoon, and military drill in the evening.

Here also the stress was on Hindu nationalism and the superiority of Hindu culture. There was not much emphasis on religious orthodoxy or scripture. As in the *shākhā* the *baudhiks* here also centered on Shivaji, Rana Pratap, and Hari Singh Nalwa, a Kashmiri king who opposed the Muslims. There was an undercurrent of anti-Muslim sentiment and a glorification of Bharat Mata—Mother India. The main speaker was M.S. Golwalkar, who had succeeded Dr. Hedgewar as the *sar sangh chālak* (leader of the whole Sangh) after the latter's death in 1940.

Another emphasis of the camps was leadership training. Most of the R.S.S. *prachāraks* (missionaries), who devoted themselves to lifelong celibacy, poverty, and service to the R.S.S., were selected from the members of these third-year camps.

This institution of the *prachārak* is the life-blood of the R.S.S. So far as I know, no other Indian organization has as dedicated a middle-range leadership. In the 1940s most *prachāraks* were highly-educated young men who could have made a success of almost any career, but they denied themselves comfort and family life and accepted a life of sacrifice and hard work. It was the band of *prachāraks* with their unbelievable devotion to the cause of the R.S.S. which spread the organization outside Nagpur and outside Maharashtra to all the states of the country. Wherever they went they picked up the language, culture, and social attitudes of the area. As a result, they were able to convert Punjabis, Tamils, Malayalis, Bengalis, and others to the R.S.S. ideology.

Not all *prachāraks*, of course, kept their commitment to life-long service. Some quit after six months or a year. Some worked for ten years or so and then became disillusioned or tired and gave up the work. Provided they remained loyal to the R.S.S., they were not criticized.

The *prachārak* institution itself contains several levels. At the state level are the *prānt-prachāraks* (area missionaries), under them, the divisional *prachāraks*, and under them, district, *tālukā* and local *prachāraks*. The exact number of all of these categories is not known, but the *prachāraks* together must number in the hundreds if not thousands.

During this period in the early 1940s I was getting more and more involved in the R.S.S. After completing my college education in 1941 I was given charge of a *shākhā*. In 1943 I was sent to Mysore State as a *prachārak* with my headquarters in Bangalore. I stayed there one year, with the duty of spreading the R.S.S. in the district and *tālukā* towns of the area. Gradually, however, I began to doubt that this life of a modern ascetic really suited me; after a year I came back to Nagpur and told the R.S.S. that I intended to lead a normal life.

By this time it was not only my unwillingness to remain a *prachārak* that had begun to alienate me from the R.S.S. I was also beginning to have serious ideological differences with the leadership. The R.S.S. under M.S. Golwalkar was a very different organization than that originally shaped by Dr. Hedgewar. As this difference was in part due to the character and personality of the two men, it may be helpful to describe them both briefly.

The R.S.S. founder, Dr. Hedgewar, had studied medicine in Calcutta but did not practice as a doctor. He was celibate and lived a spartan life, dressing in a dhoti, plain shirt, coat, and tall cap. He was not much of a speaker, nor, in my opinion, much of a thinker; but he was a warm, honest man and an organizer of first-rate caliber. Thus he was able to attract the young. His approach to the organization was more political than religious or cultural. He had participated in the independence movement *satyāgrahas* and had gone to jail for a year or two. It was a matter of pride for all of us that before his death he had met Subhash Chandra Bose[2] and had a long talk with him.

Dr. Hedgewar shaped the R.S.S. without a constitution. Under him everything just evolved, and when the question of succession came up, with his deteriorating health, there were many who aspired for the position. Dr. Hedgewar's choice fell on a comparatively new member of the organization, M.S. Golwalkar, who later came to be known as Guruji. Though there was no overt factional fight, Golwalkar was not completely accepted for several years by some of the old guard.

The new *sar sangh chālak* was cast in a different mold from the founder. He had received his M.Sc. and law degree from Benares Hindu University but did not practice law. He was religiously inclined and had been associated with the Ramakrishna Mission and other such organizations. Golwalkar Guruji definitely possessed more charisma than

Dr. Hedgewar. With his long hair, flowing beard, and dhoti and *kurtā*, he looked the part of a traditional guru. He had good command over English, Hindi, and Marathi, and was a powerful and emotional speaker who could keep his audience spellbound.

Under the leadership of Golwalkar the R.S.S. became a different organization, with greater cohesion and dynamism. It was at this time it expanded outside Maharashtra to become an all-India organization stressing Hindi rather than Marathi as its main language.

Golwalkar was more orthodox than Hedgewar in his view of Hinduism. (In fact, later in his life he almost created a hornet's nest by justifying the traditional four-fold division of castes known as *varṇāshrama*). He was also more dogmatic than Hedgewar about the idea of Hindu nationalism. In his book, *We, The Nationhood Defined*, he argued that Hindus are the only true nationals of this country.

Concerned with maintaining the cultural nature of the organization, Golwalkar tried to keep the R.S.S. out of the political struggles of the time. I still remember a stormy meeting in 1942 which lasted for eight or ten hours. The younger leaders, including the present *sar sangh chālak*, Balasaheb Deoras, were in favor of joining the Quit India movement.[3] Although Golwalkar had taken over the reins of the organization only two years earlier, he was successful in keeping the R.S.S. out of the movement. Five years later, when the country became independent, Golwalkar, like the communists, was not convinced of the worth of political independence or the national resurgence.

In 1948, Mahatma Gandhi was assassinated by Nathuram Godse, a member of a right wing party, the Hindu Mahasabha. That party was banned, and a ban was also put on the R.S.S., which had been critical of Gandhi, for a year. Although the Hindu Mahasabha and the R.S.S. had somewhat the same roots in Hindu nationalism, they disagreed in the 1940s about political participation. After Independence, however, some of the younger R.S.S. leaders from the North were anxious to start a political party. When the period of the ban was over, and Golwalkar was finally convinçed, the combined efforts of some Hindu Mahasabha leaders, especially Dr. Shyama Prasad Mookerjee, and the politicized activists of the R.S.S., brought the Jan Sangh into being. The growth and consolidation of this political party was really due to the trained cadres it had received from the R.S.S.

As for myself, I left the R.S.S. in 1949, after the ban on the organization was lifted. By this time I was becoming increasingly aware of socio-political reality in India and was convinced that what was required was a socio-economic and political program for the transformation of society. I was in fundamental disagreement with Golwalkar and the politicized younger leaders of the R.S.S., who, whatever their differences might be among themselves, agreed on their support for the *status quo* and the preservation of what they thought was good in the society.

Thus, intellectually, I had drifted away from both the old leadership of the R.S.S., and the elements that were to become the Jan Sangh. Under the circumstances it would have been dishonest to continue as a member of the organization. My colleagues and friends were extremely unhappy over my decision, but I had made it after thinking it over for many months, and there was no going back on it.

### *A Critique of the R.S.S.*

It is now over thirty years since I left the R.S.S. As I look back on the organization which for so many years formed the focus of my life, I have mixed feelings. To begin with, there is no denying that as an organization it was brilliantly conceived. The founder might not have known the modern jargon of political sociology, but he had understood the process by which young minds could be politically socialized. The combination of organized games, drill, and friendship groups, all with an ideological base, was a very powerful one. Moreover, the system of self-financing and the institution of *prachāraks* gave the organization an autonomy and dynamism seldom achieved in voluntary organizations in this country. It was, in fact, the example of the R.S.S. that served as an impetus for the founding of volunteer organizations by practically every political party in India.

Of course, even the critics of the R.S.S. concede its organizational strength. What they attack is the use to which the organization is put. The R.S.S. is often considered a fanatical religious organization and has been variously described as anti-intellectual, fascist, and anti-Muslim. Not all of these charges can be completely refuted, but neither can they be completely substantiated.

It is understandable that the R.S.S. has been looked upon as a religious organization. First of all, it is restricted to Hindus. Secondly, the saffron flag of the R.S.S. is the traditional Hindu religious flag; flags on many Hindu temples are of the same color, and a saffron flag is used by the Varkaris (pilgrims) of Pandharpur. But in my opinion, the R.S.S. is not fanatical. Moreover, unlike the Muslim League and the Hindu Mahasabha, it is not interested in religious orthodoxy or in strict adherence to the scriptures. The *svayamsevaks* were never asked to observe the traditional rituals of Hinduism. Even their zeal in the movement for a ban on cow-slaughter must be considered in the context of the general demand of Hindu society. (Prominent Congressmen too have been vociferous in demanding the ban.) What the R.S.S. did was to create an organization of modern youths believing in Hindu nationalism. Religious identity and loyalty were used to strengthen the organization. In its inception, at least, the R.S.S. was primarily concerned with the struggle for the freedom of the country. At that time its call for the protection of Hindu culture was primarily a camouflage for its main goal.

The charge that the R.S.S. is fascist is frequently made. In a way, the charge is understandable, for the uniforms, the military drill, discipline, and devotion to a leader and the motherland give the R.S.S. a superficial resemblance to the youth organizations of Nazi Germany or fascist Italy. However, in more fundamental ways the R.S.S. differs from the fascists. It has never prevented non-conformist opinions among its members and has never prevented any member from leaving the organization. Neither has it used methods to suppress its opponents.

The charge that the R.S.S. is anti-intellectual is correct. Youth organizations are mainly built on emotionalism and the R.S.S. is no exception. Anti-intellectualism was inherent in its ideology of loyalty to the Hindu nation and its technique of personal conversion of new entrants. No effort was made for a theoretical defense of the ideology; such an effort was not considered essential. To anyone who wanted theoretical explanations the standard reply was, "You don't require intellectual arguments to love your mother—the same thing is true of the motherland."

The charge that the R.S.S. is anti-Muslim has some truth in it. Though anti-Muslim attitudes were not officially encouraged, they existed as an undercurrent in the organization. The anti-Muslim attitude was the result of Hindu revivalist attitudes and of ignorance about the Muslims, and also a reaction to Muslim militancy and Muslim attacks on Hindus. Even more important, perhaps, was the feeling that Muslims—and Christians—do not regard Bharat (India) as their motherland and thus have no parity with the Hindus. Sometimes this anti-Muslim attitude expressed itself in the juvenile pranks referred to by S.H. Deshpande in his article on the R.S.S.[4] Though these things are certainly reprehensible it must be kept in mind that they do not constitute the main thrust of the organization.

My own criticisms of the R.S.S. are somewhat different from the foregoing. For one thing, I feel that the restriction of the organization to men has caused certain major distortions in the R.S.S. As an organization of young men, emphasizing athletics and feats of physical courage, it had an atmosphere of bubbling enthusiasm and bravado. Looking back, I feel that this fostered mistaken notions of manliness and virility and contributed to an undesirable type of personality development.

Moreover, I feel that while the organization began with

a laudable goal it must ultimately be judged a failure. What it set out to do was to transform Hindu society. It did succeed in building healthy social attitudes in some of its *svayamsevaks*, teaching them to subordinate their personal needs to social needs, but it never developed a clear idea of a socio-economic program to transform Hindu society. Moreover, in the more than fifty years of its existence it has only one major achievement to its credit—that during the time of partition[5] thousands of *svayamsevaks* gave their lives helping to save Hindu refugees. But that was forty years ago. Thus, as I look at the R.S.S. today, it is without bitterness or rancor, but with a sense of pity for the thousands of *svayamsevaks* who continue to cling to an organization that has lost its *raison d'etre*.

## EDITORS' NOTES

1. Shivaji was the seventeenth century Maratha King who founded the Maratha empire; his battles against the Mughal emperor Aurangzeb are often interpreted by Maharashtrians as Hindu-Muslim conflict. Rana Pratap ruled the Rajput kingdom of Mewar in the sixteenth century, resisting the efforts of the Mughal emperor Akbar to conquer his country until his death in 1597.

2. Subhash Chandra Bose (1897-1945), known as Netaji (the leader), was a Bengali nationalist who served in the Indian National Congress until his ouster in 1939. He joined the Germans and then the Japanese in the Second World War, leading the Indian National Army in an effort to free India.

3. The Quit India Movement was the third and largest of Mohandas K. Gandhi's non-violent, non-cooperation campaigns. Almost all Indian National Congress leaders were imprisoned after the Quit India declaration in 1942.

4. S.H. Deshpande, "My Days in the R.S.S.," trans. by Ramesh Deshpande, *Quest* 96 (July-August 1975): 19-30.

5. Even this action of the R.S.S. is subject to controversy. For a generally critical view, see Des Raj Goyal, *Rashtriya Swayam Sewak Sangh* (New Delhi: Radha Krishna Prakashan, 1979); for a favorable history, see K.R. Malkani, *The RSS Story* (New Delhi: Impex India, 1980). A Western scholar's view may be found in J.A. Curran Jr., *Militant Hinduism in Indian Politics: A Study of the RSS.* (New York: Institute of Pacific Relations, 1951). Curran indicates that the strength of the R.S.S. was

greater in Uttar Pradesh, Madhya Pradesh, and the Punjab at that time than in Bombay Province. The most recent study is *The Brotherhood in Saffron: The Rashtriya Swayamsevak Sangh and Hindu Revivalism* by Walter K. Andersen and Shridhar D. Damle (Boulder: Westview Press, 1987).

# 14

# Scattered Voices: The Experience of Ritual

## Editors' Introduction

Religious austerities and ritual worship form part and parcel of the fabric of daily life in many Hindu homes. Perhaps to many this daily ritual tends to become routine. There are some people, however, who find in the details of ritual worship a source of joy and even ecstasy. The first two voices below express this kind of delight in ritual worship. The first is a description of one of the characters in D.B. Mokashi's *Farewell to the Gods.* The second is Vitthalrao Ghate's account of his adolescent experience of worship—the extravagant vow to offer a hundred thousand *bel* leaves to Shiva.

The two women's voices here strike a very different note. Anasuyabai Koratkar's statement (recorded by Maxine Berntsen) tells in a matter-of-fact way how daily ritual—especially the observance of *sovḷa* (ritual purity)—teaches self-control and discipline. It is clear from her comments that these rules, in addition to their spiritual benefits, provide a framework that enables family to live within its means. The second voice is that of an anonymous Brahman woman who was interviewed by Carolyn Slocum. She talks of women's power—*shaktī*—as being derived from fasting and other ritual austerities. There may be in this brief statement an undercurrent of resentment against fathers and husbands who control women's wills, and a brief hint that she may at times explode, although the main thrust of the piece is a sense of self-contained strength.

The section ends with a description by Anutai Wagh of an entire town participating in the rituals of a Ganesh temple. (*E. Z. and M. B.*)

### *Ramu and the Godhouse**

Ramu sat cross-legged on the little foot stool and stared at the images in front of him. The day after tomorrow the gods would not be there. They would go to a new place and there they would feel lost. This Balakrishna was put here by grandmother's friend. This Vishnu was brought by another woman, who could no longer take care of him. These ten *shāligrāms* were brought by a wandering Brahman. Each one got himself a place on the ten steps below.

He looked at them carefully. He could see the *shāligrāms* and the idols smeared with spots of stale, faded sandal paste. Two-day-old, dark, wilted flowers and petals were strewn around. Vishnu-bhatji's son was given the job of doing the *pūjā*. This was his laziness, obviously.

He felt unhappy. Since his childhood he had been doing the *pūjā* with true devotion. When he cleaned the brass images, he cleaned them so well with tamarind that they glittered. He never let the *shāligrāms* stay wet. He always dried them lovingly, carefully. Aba had the force of his

* From *Farewell to the Gods* by D.B. Mokashi, trans. by Pramod Kale (Delhi: Hind, 1972).

money. Naru was free, and Jagu was an atheist. He had neither the force nor the freedom and atheism of these three brothers. Ever since he could remember, he felt pressured and scared. Even in his childhood he had needed god's grace, god's protection, as much as he needed it now. He needed it to pass tests, to play well, to make his kite fly high.

Should he take these gods? Who knows, fortune might smile on him. These gods had protected his home for eight generations. This house had lived on their grace. They might protect him. His poverty might go away.

Would he be able to uphold the burden of the gods in his poverty? Gods, they say, lose their power. Is it possible these gods no longer had the power they once had?

Shocked at his own sinful thought, he folded his hands to the gods and said to himself, "Narahare! I am poor. How can I take you? It's my poverty which makes me think this way. Don't get angry. Be merciful. I shall keep a small image of you in the house. I shall perform a small feast in your honour. Or shall I take you?..."

Even when he had concluded the *pūjā,* Ramu had not quite made up his mind whether he should take the gods with him. Getting down from the stool he said to Jagu, "Go! Call everyone here for the *āratī.*"

*—D.B. Mokashi*
*translated by Pramod Kale*

## *One Hundred Thousand Bel Leaves***

Bapusaheb had made a vow to offer a hundred thousand *bel* leaves to Shankar. Just at that time he had to go on a tour to do some urgent work. So I was given the task. It must have been Shivratri [the major Shiva festival]. In the morning I took my bath. Then I took the big basket of *bel*

** From *Diwas Ase Hote* [Such Were the Days] by Vitthalrao Ghate (Bombay: Mauj, 1961).

leaves and went to the Mahadev temple. I fasted all day and I sat offering the *bel* leaves, chanting in my broken Sanskrit, *eka bilvapatrāya shivārpanāya* (I offer a *bel* leaf to Shiva). I was tremendously exalted.

I was literally in a state of ecstasy. I was ten years old. In Ahmednagar I had gone through the magic world of the *Arabian Nights* and now I had entered this new magic world. In my mind, in my dreams, I saw innumerable visions of God—in various forms, various textures and fragrances. When I went into the shrine the air was heavy with incense. From whichever book I opened came the fragrance of sandalwood. My senses feasted to the full.

*—Vitthalrao Ghate*
*translated by Maxine Berntsen*

## *Sovḷa*

*Sovḷa* means cleanliness. For instance, not going into the kitchen in the morning without taking a bath. First you should wash your face and hands and feet and then go into the kitchen or into the shrine. It's all right to sweep or wipe the floor of the prayer room without a bath. But if you are going to touch the image you must bathe and put on freshly-laundered clothes. Then you can do *pūjā* in *sovḷa*. *Sovḷa* means cleanliness, extreme cleanliness. No dirtiness is permitted. If some food that has touched your mouth falls to the floor you must clean the spot and plaster it with cow dung. That's what's called *sovḷa*. . . . When a woman comes of age they make her start observing *sovḷa*. *Sovḷa* means you first bathe, then do *pūjā* and water the *tuḷshī* plant and then sit down to eat. In the evening you put on the *sovḷa* garments and then have your meal. You shouldn't be eating something every time you turn around. You shouldn't have meals four times a day. Just morning and evening. And when Chaturmas comes there are many rules of austerity to be followed. . . . You see, these are four sacred months. During this time you observe special disciplines, read sacred books, and do not have your meals until you have gone to the temple. "I won't do so and so until I have gone to the temple," "I have to do *pūjā* first," . . . "I won't eat until my Brahman has eaten"—each person has his own rules. The main thing is self-restraint. Not eating or drinking whenever you feel like it. You could say self-restraint or regulation. Say regulation. All these things are to control our eating and drinking.

*—Anasuyabai Koratkar*
*recorded by Maxine Berntsen*

### *Shaktī: Women's Inner Strength*

*Shaktī* is like steam: if you compress it, steam has the power to pull a whole train. If you don't bottle it up, it simply dissipates—but it could explode if you don't let some out. *Shaktī* is just like that. If you control your will, you can gain *shaktī* or inner strength. If you don't, your *shaktī* will just disappear.

Rituals and fasts are the most important ways to control your will. You have to suppress your desires and do everything for God. Everyone has some *shaktī*, but women have more of it because they do more rituals and fasts. Women also gain *shaktī* because of their place in the family. Husbands and fathers control women's wills. We must always be lower than men. You must control your own desires too. You must have perfect fidelity to your husband even in thought. When women have children, they bear pain and suppress their own desires for their children. That brings *shaktī* too. Young girls now aren't being taught self-control and aren't learning to do rituals and fasts. They won't have as much *shaktī* as older women.

Women use *shaktī* mostly to help their families. In the old days, women like Savitri could save their husbands from death. Because this is the Kali Yuga, women can't do that anymore, but we can give our husbands longer lives and bring prosperity to the whole family. Women can make their husband's and sons' businesses go better. Women with a lot of *shaktī* can cure illnesses. All women can bring happiness to their families through their *shaktī*. Women also use their *shaktī* for themselves—to help do all their daily work and to get peace of mind. It can even save you from harm. Sita's *shaktī* saved her from burning.

So a woman's *shaktī* can be really strong in helping herself and others. It's funny that you get more inner strength the more you control and suppress your desires and will. If it's suppressed too far though, it can explode and be a bad force. But mostly it's a good power. So you see, it's a lot like steam.

*—Anonymous*
*recorded by Carolyn Slocum*

### *Gaṇeshbhakti in Morgaon****

Our family is from Morgaon, in Pune District. Morgaon is the site of the most important of the *Ashṭavināyaks*—the eight major temples of Ganesh. At Morgaon, there is a clean, spacious, and beautiful temple of Morya (Ganesh). There the god is regarded as a king—so to mark the hours of the day, the kettledrums are played. The oil lamps are lit; *āratī* is performed morning, noon, and night. A large amount of *prasād* is prepared, and many young people receive it.

Everybody in town—young and old, rich and poor—people of all castes, sects, and religions, come at least once a day to take *darshan* of Ganpati. On Ganesh *chaturthī* everyone fasts. On the next day, everyone feasts. Nowhere today are Harijans refused entrance into a temple; but at Morgaon, everyone has had the freedom for many years to pour water on the god and to touch his feet on Ganesh *chaturthī*.

---

*** From *Kosbādcyā ṭekdīvarūn* [From the Hill of Kosbad], ed. by Ashok Chitnis (Bombay: Rich Publishers, 1980).

The land for the great Ganesh temple at Chinchwad was given to the Morya Gosavi sadhus by the Sultan of Bijapur four hundred years ago. Every year, on the fourth day of the bright fortnights of the months of Bhadrapad and Magh, the palanquin of Ganpati comes from that great temple in Chinchwad to Morgaon. On Dasara there is a big celebration of the god's ceremonial crossing of the town border. The procession lasts all night long. There are the fireworks and the firing of a cannon is permitted by the government. The honor of firing the cannon belongs to the Wagh family. . . .

All the Wagh family are fervent devotees of Ganesh, as if their family had been given the motto of "one god." Today Ganesh-bhakti (devotion to Ganesh) is increasing in society. Ganesh is the "god of the multitudes"—the protector of democracy. From this point of view, I feel that this symbol is very important and hope that its favor and protection will remain with us.

*—Anutai Wagh*
*translated by Maxine Berntsen*

# *III.*

# *REFORM AND REJECTION*

IRAWATI KARVE
TRANSLATED BY JAI NIMBKAR

# 15
# "All That Is You": An Essay*

"That's enough for today. My mind refuses to work any longer. Why don't you correct the part we have gone over today and come back tomorrow? Then we'll read on tomorrow."

"You are feeling all right, aren't you? I hope my coming every day doesn't put too much of a strain on you," she said anxiously.

"No, no. That's not it. It's just that I can no longer work the way I used to. You must try to finish your work before my health breaks down altogether."

"You care so much about me, Bai. It's really my work, but you bear all the burden of it. You do such a lot for others."

She said it very earnestly but without really thinking about it. I smiled. She said, "Did I say something funny?"

---

* "Te sarva tūç āhes!" from *Gaṅgājal* [Ganga Water] (Pune: Deshmukh and Company, 1972).

"You did. You said that I bear the burden of your work. You think that I take pains over you because you are my student and I am your teacher. . . . "

Before I could finish my sentence she interrupted, "But isn't that true?"

I shook my head. "You see, Tapi, it's true that you are a student, but what's significant is how I qualify that word. I say *my* student. I teach her. When she passes, I too pass. You pass as a student, I pass as a teacher. You have no idea how difficult this examination is. The remarks of the external examiners apply more to me than to you. Luckily for me, my disgrace is not too obvious. When students fail, I fail with them. That is straightforward enough. But even with those who pass I barely manage to pass. I have to struggle to pass this examination. I sometimes scold you, sometimes cajole you; I work hard to see that you write well. All this is not really for you, it's for myself. One of the many different roles I play in life is that of a teacher. I have formed a mental image of myself as a teacher. Each one of my students is I myself twice over. He or she is a symbol of me both as a teacher and as a student. So my striving is all for myself. I strive only for the endless 'I's' contained in my self."

I was silent for some time. Tapi was thinking over what I had said.

"Doesn't it say somewhere in the Upanishads that when you love a wife, the love is not really for her but for your own self?" I asked.

Tapi had read the Upanishads only recently and her memory was also sharper than mine. She took the *Bṛhadāraṇyaka Upaniṣad* down from my shelf and found the exact page:

> A husband is dear not because you love him
> but because you love yourself.
> Sons are dear to you not because you love them
> but because you love yourself.
> Gods are dear to you not because you love them
> but because you love yourself.

> All beings are dear to you not because you love them
> but because you love yourself.

"You see Tapi, Yadnyavalkya did not refer to a student-teacher relationship separately because the student he was teaching was his wife."

Tapi said a little doubtfully, "Do you mean that when a mother loves a child, cares for it, it is only an expression of her self-love?"

"Yes, Tapi. Out of all the examples that Yadnyavalkya gives, I think this one is the most apt. The mother's tiny self expands into being the ultimate self, the Creator. The little being which she has created is totally dependent on her. She feeds it, cares for it, she has the power to make it cry or smile. In short, she is playing the role of the omnipotent god. When she cares for the child, she casts herself in the role of the mother, a role recognized by society. It is she who teaches the child how to speak, how to behave, she who pats it on the back or punishes it. She is all-in-all to the child. While playing this role, she gets so intoxicated with the idea that the child is an expression of her own self, that she forgets that it is an independent being.She continues expecting, even from the grown-up child, the helplessness of infancy. She continues expecting it to cling to her, to be afraid of her and to obey her. When she is thwarted in this wish, she feels sad. She forgets that this grown-up child who is flouting her authority is also an expression of her self."

Tapi seemed to be convinced by my lecture. She said, "You don't have to wait for the child to grow up, Bai. Its independence becomes evident very early. Just as the mother has her expectations, the child has its own expectations. It also behaves as though the mother were an extension of its self. My four-year-old sulks if I go home late. And it's not as though he lacks anything when I am not there. His whole attitude is that by being late I am denying him what's his by right," she said laughingly. Then she left, promising to come back the next day.

She went away, but she had left my mind with an entertaining new game. My granddaughter fell down while playing. Not thinking of my own ill health, I ran to pick her up. My mind said, "She is you." With my dry old hands I held my small granddaughter whose smile is like the tender moonlight and who runs like a spring breeze. Smiling, I said, "Of course she is I." I went out into the garden and was greeted by our tail-wagging dog. "He is also you." "Yes indeed," I said. A cuckoo was sitting on the *bakul* tree eating the fruit. It flew away as soon as it saw me. "It is also you."

I went on playing the game. A few days later I went to Mahabaleshwar. From one of the viewing points I was watching the sun set behind the ranges of hills across the valley. Giant waves of frozen rock below, billowing multicolored clouds in the blue sky above, and I suspended somewhere in between. "All this is you." My mind was brimming over with joy. It revelled in the oneness with the sunset. One of the Upanishads came to mind to add to my joy. "O sun, you who regulate the lives of people, you who are the creator of people, bring your burning rays together and subdue them. Let me see your mild, beneficial aspect. The man who dwells in it is I." I said the lines of the old verse again and again, rolling the words around on my tongue, savoring them. I was drunk with the feeling of oneness with the universe.

Back in Pune, I was skimming over the newspaper as I did every day. It contained an account of the Eichmann trial. I had known of course that the Nazis had tortured and killed millions of innocent people—men, women, children. But I still could not bear to read this account of the atrocities committed by one single man. I thought of my German friends who had been destroyed in this holocaust, and of others who had escaped and been saved but whose lives were ruined, meaningless. My mind rose up in anger against their killers. "They are also you." I felt as though I had received an electric shock. No, no. Never. How can those for whom I feel nothing but loathing and anger be I? It is impossible. I hastily shook off this disgusting cockroach which was trying to cling to me. My poor mind was silenced.

My daily routine went on. I was lecturing about crime and society, enjoying my presentation. "The persons whom we label as criminals are also components of society. Social environment and the social system are also, along with other factors, responsible for crime. You and I are sitting in this room discussing criminals and criminal tendencies, as though criminals were some sort of strange creatures, perhap apart. But that's not true. Human tendencies are the same everywhere. Everyone wants to be able to live well, to have enough to feed and clothe himself, his wife, his children. The criminal shares these desires with ordinary people. Another natural tendency is to respect the wishes of those who are older, more educated, higher than oneself in social status, or in a position of authority. We see that in the social, religious, and political field, older people and leaders take advantage of this tendency that people have. It is not as though a murderer murders only for gain or out of revenge. People kill also out of religious fanaticism or patriotic fervor."

"Do you mean that a war means murder?" a voice in the classroom asked.

"It's an interesting point for speculation, but our subject today is crime in society, so we will confine our discussion to that."

"Do you mean that noble feelings like religious faith, love for one's father or for one's country can also motivate crime?"—a second voice.

"Sometimes people are taken over by emotions. They do something their teachers, leaders, or elders ask them to, without question. They forget that they have values of their own, that they have a right to weigh religious values and adopt only the ones which are acceptable to them. Other things like a job or the desire for a good life also make people forget this. In the old days a man in the king's service was proud to obey his protector's orders. Giving up his own life and taking someone else's was the same in his books. Being completely possessed by another is a mark of the highest devotion. In this state of mind it is possible to commit a crime. History has recorded many such atrocious crimes. In the Middle Ages in Europe many people were subjected to untold torture by the Inquisition. And this was all for the sake of religion. Even here in India people in Goa experienced some of the shock waves of the Inquisition. This was a horrible crime against humanity, and it was motivated by religious fanaticism."

The period over, the students had dispersed. But my thoughts went on. If it is true that criminals have all the normal tendencies of ordinary people, then it must mean that under special circumstances, any person can commit a crime. You can perhaps find one person among thousands of people who says, "I will keep my values intact even at the cost of my life," and one in a million who, when actually put to the test, will behave accordingly. When you consider crime, immorality, and crookedness as expressions of ordinary human nature, then criminality becomes merely a reminder of the extremes that are possible in human nature. Does crime present to us, then, our own hidden unrevealed face?

My mind recoiled in alarm.

We had finished the old topic and started on a new one. I was explaining the different kinds of social relationships. Without giving it much thought I was listing as if by rote, "superior-inferior, leader-led, cooperation-opposition. . . ."

"Is opposition also a social relationship then?" a voice from the classroom asked.

"Opposition is not possible unless a relationship exists. In fact, wherever there is cooperation, opposition also exists. Industrialist and laborer cooperate in manufacturing, and it is in this relationship that their opposition is implicit. In the process of learning society's rules and taboos and becoming socialized, opposition is always evident. Take the example of children. Isn't it hard to teach them the habit of brushing their teeth before eating in the morning? They keep resisting it but slowly their resistance weakens as their social consciousness develops and they imbibe the values of their society. Freud goes beyond this and says that often opposition is a sign of agreement. Deep down, the mind is in favor of something; the opposition is only on the surface. A mind which has awareness—in other words, a socialized mind—has been taught very unequivocally what things are good, what things are bad. But there is another mind buried deep inside this mind. That other mind possesses a wolf's cruelty, a tiger's hunting instinct, a deer's fear, a dog's servility, a pig's greed, and a monkey's mischievousness. This mind secretly admires the events or people that the other mind holds in contempt. There are thus two minds in one body. Ordinarily, in the case of most people, only one mind comes into play. The other one is repressed, but sometimes it boils up, and then the same man plays the contradictory roles of god and demon. This characteristic of human nature has been used in Western literature to make the story line interesting. In many stories and novels the man who is misunderstood, loathed, and hated ends up being loved. Here in this country bhakti writings and philosophy have deeply explored this idea, but other literary forms do not seem to have used it. Bhakti literature mentions *virodh-bhakti* (devotion through opposition) as a form of worship. Those who vehemently oppose god and hate him also reach him because their hatred itself makes them permeated with god. According to our philosophy, in order to become one with *brahman,* one must become totally indifferent. In this state of indifference one has no anger, greed, loathing, desire, love, or hate. Water has the same attitude towards a cow and a tiger. It doesn't say, "Let me quench the cow's thirst, but become poison to the tiger." The sun does not discriminate between rich and poor. That is what is meant by indifference, neutrality. It is the attitude that says that in one sense, everything is you, and in another, you are not bound up in anything. When you think of all this, you realize that opposition—extreme opposition—stems from not only social but also personal relationships, and it contains love. Love and hate are the two manifestations of the same self."

My mind refused to go any further. It stopped thinking.

Sometimes once you stub your toe you keep on stubbing it in the same place. That's what happened to me. A visitor highly recommended a book he was reading—Shirer's *Rise and Fall of the Third Reich.* I was familiar with the history of course, but it was presented from a different point of view. The book explains the rise of Hitler in Germany. After the First World War, Wilson had certain plans for rehabilitating Europe, but he got fed up with the devious political game which England and France were playing and opted out of the whole situation, leaving Germany in the clutches of this pair. These two enemies of that country wanted to punish Germany for having committed the crime of starting the war, by crushing her once and for all. It became impossible for German leaders to obtain justice in the League of Nations. Even her simple, reasonable demands were rejected out of hand. At the time when I was in Germany, that whole nation was smoldering with rage. When Hitler wrested by force what Germany could not get by begging, Germans declared with one voice that this was exactly what was needed. England, France, and even America would not respond to their just demands; they only understood a show of force. When Hitler had gotten away with this first act of bullying, he proceeded to swallow up innocent countries. At this time the big nations kept quiet. If they had rapped him and put Germany down in time, it would have saved the world from the awful consequences of Hitler's action. But they remained passive—at first out of selfishness, then out of fear. The result of all this was that all the tiny middle European countries, from Poland to Albania, lost their freedom to Germany and later to Russia, and millions of helpless Jews were inhumanly massacred. Was Germany alone responsible for this? Didn't all Europe, and actually the whole world, share the responsibility? And what is true of political crime must be true of social crime.

I was in torment because I had become aware of a terrible truth. My mind was pointing the finger at me, saying, "All that is you!" Trembling, I admitted, "Yes, all that is I. I am Eichmann, Stalin, Hitler, and I am also the people they killed."

But this flood of knowledge was not going to stop here. "Why are you talking of the people and events in other countries?" my mind mocked. "Why don't you come closer to home?"

"Do you remember what you said when innocent people got killed in the struggle for freedom?"

I remembered. "When a country is at war, these things occasionally happen."

"Is it possible for you to have nothing to do with those who are corrupt, who have made their money by crooked means?"

"No," I admitted.

"You believe that all castes, all religions should live together in harmony. But there are those who twist a situation, make strident propaganda, and enflame young people's feelings. Are such people among your acquaintances?"

I said yes, and asked, annoyed, "What must I do then? Go and live in a jungle? Or commit suicide?"

"You can pretend to be neutral only if you do one or the other. Even if you associate with such people only as far as absolutely necessary, you still share in their misdeeds. You know that this kind of propaganda was being made continuously against the Jews. The atmosphere here is not that tense yet, but there is no guarantee that what happened in Germany will not happen here. Wasn't Gandhi murdered as a result of a similar hate-campaign? And was not his murder used as an excuse to set fire to thousands of homes in Maharashtra? Didn't an insignificant reason lead to fierce communal riots in India?"

I was saying "Yes, yes," but this was not the end of it yet. "What effort have you made to destroy these seeds of hate? Haven't you lived in this same society by following the policy of saving your own skin? Then what is the point of saying that you share none of the responsibility for the crime in the world, in your own society? All of it is you. Remember what Yadnyavalkya said?"

Heavily I went over the quotation, "Thus *ātmā* is completely outside, and in the same way it is totally inside.

While you still have the feeling of duality, those who are outside you are 'others,' strangers. But really it is *ātmā* that pervades all. *Ātmā* is full of knowledge; *ātmā* is knowledge."

Is awareness or knowledge ever pleasant? I was being consumed by the fire that is knowledge. Painfully I said, "Yes, yes. My young granddaughter is I, the dog who wags his tail and looks at me with expressive eyes is I, the cuckoo that flies swiftly across the blue sky is I, the glorious evening is I, Eichmann, Stalin, Hitler, those who murder, burn houses, start riots, and those who burn in the burning houses, who die in the pits are also I. Yes, it is all I."

My confession was complete. I was reduced to ashes at the moment of knowledge.

G. N. DANDEKAR, TRANSLATED BY MAXINE BERNTSEN
WITH JAYANT KARVE

# 16
# *The Last Kīrtan of Gadge Baba*

## Editors' Introduction

Gadge Maharaj (also called Gadge Buwa or Gadge Baba) (1876–1956) left the life of a house-holder in Amravati Taluka when he was about thirty to spend fifty years wandering through Maharashtra preaching to the masses, his only possession a clay pot (*gāḍge*). His family belonged to the Parit (washerman) caste, and from early youth he was concerned with the poverty and indebtedness of the lower classes. His religious tradition was bhakti—the Varkari movement begun in the thirteenth century and still a strong force for piety and, sometimes, reform, in Maharashtra. Like other saints in the bhakti movement, he stressed devotion to Parmeshwar, the God above all who is also in ourselves. Unlike most contemporary Varkaris, he also stressed social reform. He would move from the praise of God to a stern injunction to be thrifty and to get an education. He advocated vegetarianism with passion and humor. He ridiculed the practice of drinking, not uncommon among the lower classes, telling sons to beat their drunken fathers and wives to consider their husbands gods only if those "gods" were sober. And, consistently, he scorned the idea of untouchability, not only lambasting the practice in his *kīrtans* but associating himself with the work of the Untouchable leader, Dr. B.R. Ambedkar, and himself cleaning latrines.

This last *kīrtan* of Gadge Maharaj was tape recorded by some stroke of fortune, and appears in a biography of *Śrī Gāḍge Mahārāj* by G.N. Dandekar. This is a slightly abridged translation of that recording. Although Gadge Maharaj's work was little noticed by the intelligensia in his lifetime, he has been the object of much writing in recent years. The Shri Gadge Maharaj Mission of Bombay runs more than thirty schools, orphanages, and missions all over Maharashtra, including a center in Pandharpur, the heart of the bhakti movement of which Gadge Maharaj was the most recent of the unorthodox, pragmatic, altogether human saints. (*E. Z. and M. B.*)

## *Gadge Baba's Kīrtan**

On November 8, 1956, there was to be a Satyanarayan *pūjā* at the Bandra Railway Police Station in Bombay. The devout police there had for many years wanted Gadge Baba to perform a *kīrtan* in front of the police station. They came to meet Baba and humbly expressed their wish.

Baba listened to them and said, "Look here, I'm not well. I'm down in bed."

Still the police officers insisted, "All right, Baba. Don't do a *kīrtan*. Just come to Bandra. We'll do a *bhajan*. You just listen. That will be enough for us."

* From Gopal Nilkanth Dandekar, *Śrī Gāḍge Mahārāj* (1976; Bombay: Majestic Book Stall, 1982).

11. Gadge Maharaj as he is pictured in a photograph poster. The legend may be loosely translated "The saint of action free from desire." 225

"Remember that! Otherwise you'll say. . . . "

"We won't say anything, Baba."

"All right, I'll come."

"Don't worry, Baba. We'll send a car."

The police car came. By the time Baba reached Bandra there were lights and decorations strung and thousands of people had gathered.

Everyone had heard about Baba's health. At first they were all disconsolate. But hearing that Baba was coming, not only all Bandra but all the way from Byculla, Dadar, and Mahim to Borivili the devout gathered in front of the police station.

No great expectations, but Baba was coming. We'll feast our eyes on him.

Men—young and old—women with babies at their breast. Seeing the crowd of ten to twenty thousand, Baba said, "Where did you round up all these people?"

"We didn't round up anybody, Baba. The devotees heard you were coming, and they just gathered to take your *darshan*."

"Amazing. Do you have a *bhajan* group?"

"Yes, we do, Baba."

"Call them, I'll see if I can talk a few minutes. I'll say a few words."

The joy of the police knew no bounds. They said solicitously, "Baba, don't stand up. Sit on a chair and speak!"

Baba laughed and said, "Sit on a chair? For a *kīrtan*? You must be crazy. Who can sit on a chair and do a *kīrtan*?"

Taking a stick in his hand Baba stood in the center of the crowd. He was leaning on his stick. The *bhajan* group started singing. Once again it was there—the spirit of the *bhajan*, the throng of the faithful, the lights, the banners.

Experiencing once more the atmosphere he had striven to create all his life, Baba forgot his body's frailty. His voice burst forth. Again the old enthusiasm, the old fire. He began the *bhajan* that had given him incomparable joy all his life.

"Gopala Gopala, Devkinandan Gopala. . . . "[1]

Eager and excited the crowd surged and overflowed, their

voices making a great tumult. Baba was struggling against the noise of the crowd, "Be quiet! Who's talking there!"

Finally everyone was quiet. The stream of Baba's speech began to flow:

Tukaram Maharaj,[2] that saintly man, gives advice to the world—Brahmadev made the four Vedas, the fifth was made by Tukobaraya. That saintly man tells us what we must do after taking birth as a man. What should we do? Earn money, or take care of wife and children and then die, or build up a *meḷa* (happy throng) of relatives and spend all our lives in that? But Tukobaraya says he who is born as a man and does *bhajan* to God, he will become God—*God*! He gives his own example. Says,

> I went looking for God
> And I became God.

Tukoba says I'm a farmer, the son of a farmer, what do I know about devotion to God? I heard the testimony of the saints and I started on the path of bhakti, asking what is God like?

> I went looking for God. . . .

He didn't see God. Tukobaraya says *I* became God. Some people keep thinking about God and trying to imagine what God is like, when they will find God, when they will see God. Anyone with these kinds of ideas is plain crazy. Since the creation of the earth no one has seen God. God is not going to appear to anybody. God is not something that can be seen. The god in the temple, the god in the river, the god here, the god there, the god at Rameshwar, the god at Badrinarayan—this is the bazaar of the gods. He who is called God, who is called Parmeshwar, who runs the universe, no one has seen him and no one will see him. But in doing *bhajan* to him man becomes God. A man talks to his wife, to his daughter, to his son, to his friend, but he is ashamed to do *bhajan*. The man who is ashamed to do *bhajan* is not a man.

Gopala Gopala, Devkinandan Gopala

What is God like? He is like the wind. Listen to what Dnyaneshwar[3] says:

The wind lives everywhere
But has no dwelling-place.

Wind, you know, wind? There's wind all over this earth. In the house, in the trees, wind is everywhere. But nobody says last night the wind stayed at Bombay Station. Does anybody say that?

—No . . . oo! (the audience)

Does anybody say, "The day before yesterday the wind was at Satara Station"?

—No . . . oo!

So, just as we don't know if the wind is red, green, or yellow, and the wind has no dwelling place, so it is of Parmeshwar. And these gods in the *tīrthas*—Jagannath, Rameshwar—they are gods for making a living, they're not gods. People went to the *tīrthas* to worship the gods. Tukoba did.

I searched for God till my mind grew weary.

Tukoba says I went all over, looking for God. I grew weary. But I didn't see God. Then what did I see?

Water and stone, hither and yon!

Then what did I see? A stone god, the water of the Ganga! Water! I didn't see God. Kabir[4] says

Someone set up a stone at the temple fair
And proclaimed the river holy!

The priests sell the holy water—fifteen rupees for the whole pot—take a holy sip—two annas a sip—two annas a sip.

Tell me, what is the god in the temple fair made of?

—Of stone.

Right. Bravo. Of what?

—Of stone!...

Going to a *tīrtha* has nothing to do with God. It's a waste of money; it's useless.

Gopala Gopala, Devkinandan Gopala

Tukoba says,

How can a god made of stone speak?
Speech will never burst forth from him.

When you go to Jagannathpuri, is it because God has invited you? Does He ask you where you came from? Or how many there are of you or who else is with you? Or did you eat or not? Or would you have tea? Did God ask you these questions?

—No...oo.

That's why I say there's no God in *tīrthas.* Going there is just a waste of money. The people who go there are interested in spending money. Let's raise our hands and do a *bhajan.*

Gopala Gopala, Devkinandan Gopala

People are ashamed to raise their hands. But they will raise their hands to grab a little bit of *prasād* the size of a fly.... Let's raise our hands and do *bhajan.*

Gopala Gopala, Devkinandan Gopala

Raising your hand isn't bhakti—then why raise your hand? Because man is proud. Wherever a man goes he goes in his arrogance. He thinks, "I won't die. I won't even fall sick."

. . . . . . . . . . . . . . . . . . . . . . . . . . . . . . . . . . . . . .

Tukoba says:

He whose pride has vanished
Tuka says he's become God.

. . . . . . . . . . . . . . . . . . . . . . . . . . . . . . . . . . . . . .

Nobody has seen God. God has appeared to no one and is not going to appear to anyone. Somebody says, last night I saw Parmeshwar in my dreams with all his baggage—conch, disc, mace. No, you didn't see Him.

> What ever is in your mind
> Is what you see in dreams.

Have you seen my father in your dreams?

—No . . . oo!

So what you haven't seen won't appear in your dreams. So if somebody looks at a picture of a god, he'll see the god in the picture, he won't see God. God is not a thing to be seen. So God is not in the *tīrtha.* Now we set up a Ganpati,[5] don't we?

—Ye . . . s!

There's no bhakti in the setting up of a Ganpati. It's just a custom. What is it?

—A custom!

No, there's no bhakti in setting up Ganpati. When you bring a Ganpati home you hire a band, arrange a *bhajan,* and bring him with music, shouting—

Morya . . . Morya . . . Mor. .ya . . .

You bring him in and set him on a throne. You do *pūjā* to him—*naivedya, modak, āratī.* Then the last day you take him out, don't you?

—Yes!

Then where do you put him?

—On our head!

And where do you carry him?

Morya . . . Morya . . . Morya

(Baba puts his hand on his throat.) In water this deep—Morya! Get going! This isn't bhakti. You decorated him, did *āratī* to him, you throw him in the water and drown him? Somebody could file a criminal suit against you. This isn't bhakti. *Bhajan* is bhakti.

Gopala Gopala, Devkinandan Gopala

And what's here today? At the police station?

—A *pū . . . jā*!

It's a Satyanarayan.[6] What?

—Satyanarayan!

A Satyanarayan isn't God's bhakti. Who does a Satyanarayan? People who want something. I don't have a son—Oh, Satyanarayan, give me a son. We don't have a car—we'll do a Satyanarayan. We don't have any money— we'll do a Satyanarayan. When will we get that house?—we'll do a Satyanarayan. Greedy people. A Satyanarayan isn't God's bhakti. It says in the Satyanarayan *pothī* (text) that Sadhuvani didn't take *prasād* and didn't do Satyanarayan and his ship worth millions of rupees . . .

—Sank!

He did a two-and-a-half rupee Satyanarayan, distributed *prasād,* took *prasād,* and his ship worth millions of rupees came . . .

—Up!

What? Up?

—Yes, up!

No, no, it's not true. During the war years ship after ship sank to the bottom—each worth five hundred million rupees. Completely lost. Tell one of these priests doing Satyanarayan, why do you take two and a half rupees and babble so much. Take two and a half lakhs, take two and a half crores. Do a Satyanarayan on the ocean shore and make one ship come up.

Gopala Gopala, Devkinandan Gopala

God is not in the temple.

Not in the mosque, not in the temple.

He's not in the Muslim mosque nor the Hindu temple.

. . . . . . . . . . . . . . . . . . . . . . . . . . . . . . . . . . . .

When a temple is ready we have to bring an image, don't we?

—Ye . . . s!

Say it!

—Yes!

Then is the image free or purchased?

—Pur . . . chased!

Can you purchase God? Tell me. Rather than that you'd better buy the sun. Let it cost what it will, and set it up in the house! Can you buy God? Is he spinach? Or potatoes or onions? The man who thinks he can buy God, how can he be a man? Okay, you brought the god and set him up in the temple. Can your god wash himself?

—No . . . o!

Anyone who hasn't enough brains to wash himself, how can he be a god? Can your god put on a dhoti?

—No!

Anybody who can't put on his own dhoti—how can you call him a god? You put *naivedya* before your god and a dog grabs it. Can your god drive the dog away?

—No!

He hasn't the strength to drive a dog away and you call him a god? Well, then, does your god give enough light to light his temple?

—No!

The light goes out and the people have come. Bapurao,

light the lamp. People have come for *darshan*. Bring a lamp. What lit up the temple?

—The lamp!

Then who is greater—the lamp or the god?

—The lamp!

God isn't in the temple. Where is God? God is in this world. Serve the world! Let's raise our hands and do *bhajan*.

Gopala Gopala, Devkinandan Gopala

The British government brought a great calamity on us. Then did the people carry on a *satyāgraha* or not?

—Yes!

Did the god of any temple come to help? Did anyone see there the Ram of Bandra or the Vithoba of Dadar?

—No!

Did anyone see the Māhadev of Walkeshwar there?

—No!

Then who did *satyāgraha*? Men! Who did it?

—Men!

Who did it?

—Men!

And who said "Quit India"? Gandhiji! Gandhiji! Who said "Quit India"?

—Gandhiji!

Then call Gandhiji a god. He said to those who ruled for hundreds of years, he said in a word, "Quit India." And did they go or not?

—They went!

Call Gandhiji a god. With a great shout, with great love, say, "Mahatma Gandhi *kī jay*, Mahatma Gandhi *kī* . . ."

—*Jay!*

He lived on bread and water . . . suffered imprisonment for the people, endured the blows of the police—stayed in solitary confinement. . . . Let's give a shout for him like the thunder of a cannon! Mahatma Gandhi *kī* . . .

—*Jay!*

. . . . . . . . . . . . . . . . . . . . . . . . . . . . . . . . . . . .

In ten minutes, in ten minutes the news spread all over the world—Gandhiji has been murdered! Mahatmaji has gone, Mahatmaji has gone! In ten minutes. And as for the rest of us, if we die, the guy living in the house next door won't know about it for six months. What happened? That Ganpatsingh died last night. Oh, dear! I didn't know. Like it was a goddamn dog that died. A man's wealth is not his money, it's not gold, it's not a car. A man's wealth is a good name. Kabir says:

> A good name is better than a beautiful face
> Because it flies without wings.
> Beauty fades, a good name never.

As long as the sun and moon remain on this earth Gandhi will not die. Gandhi is alive. We are the ones who die, not Gandhi.

> Tuka says that death is certain.
> Good reputation lives on.

Death will carry everyone off. Death does not spare anybody, is not going to spare anybody. Will the peons (office boys) in the office die one day or not?

—Die!

And will their boss some day go that road?

—Yes!

Then death will do everyone in. But fame doesn't die. Let's raise our hands and do *bhajan.*

Gopala Gopala, Devkinandan Gopala

Where is God? In the world. God is in the world. Serve the world. Have pity on the poor.

Do your dharma with humility.
There's danger in pride.
If you say, "I'm the giver,"
Then where did you get the goods?

Who gives rain for four months? Paramatma. Then the earth brings forth fruit. If it doesn't rain for four months will the earth produce?

—No!

Thousands, crores of people will die. Do *bhajan* to God. Do you offer flowers or not?

—Yes!

Who made the flowers?

—God did!

Your grandfather or great-grandfather didn't. Then they are *His* flowers, *His* rain. We give Him what is His. Then what should we give Him? Raise your hands nice and high and clap.

Gopala Gopala, Devkinandan Gopala

God is in the earth. Janardan is in the world. What is the proof of this?

God is in man, God is in man
The saints have told us this.

Yes, the saints testify that God is in the world. Build a women's hospital for the poor. Give medicine to the poor. Give the poor a yard or two of cloth. Give them a pound or half-pound of rice. Have pity on the poor.

God is in man, God is in man
The saints have told us this.

Who is great on this earth? The saints are, the saints. This is proven. There was a meeting. The subject came up—who was the greatest of all? Who was the greatest of all?

One said, "The earth is the greatest." Another asked, "Why is the earth greatest?" "Oh, she's standing on the head of Shesha (the holy snake)." "You call the earth greater than Shesha? She's standing on his head." So the first said, "Shesha is better!" The other asked, "Why is Shesha great? He's just an ornament around Shiva's neck." So the first said, "Shankar (Shiva) is the greatest." Another said, "Why is Shankar the greatest? He's sitting on Nandi (the bull)." (Gadgebaba goes on with Nandi stands in heaven, heaven owed three boons to Ravana, Ravana defeated Vali, Ram killed Vali.) So . . . so . . . Ram is greatest. One said, "How is Ram the greatest? He is in the custody of the saints' minds." Who is the greatest? The saints! The saints!

. . . . . . . . . . . . . . . . . . . . . . . . . . . . . . . . . . . . .

We are dupes! Why, Narayan built a house in his village. For five thousand rupees. Two or three people said God gave it to him. Who gave it?

—God!

Go die in the monsoon or the hot season! God doesn't give houses. Go ahead and die. Who builds houses?

—Man!

God gave it? You dummies! Who has the most wealth in Bombay? Marwadis, Gujaratis, priests, and Brahmans! In Bombay who's considered worthless? Marathas, Malis, Telis, Nhavis, Dhobis, Chambhars, Kolis, Kumbhars, Lohars, Wadars, Beldars, Kaikadis, Gonds, Gavaris, Mangs, and Mahars![7] They live like animals! Only three men live well—the Gujarati, Marwadi, and Brahman! Every day they have *shirā* with ghee (clarified butter). Ask any Maratha, have you had dinner today? Yes. The main dish? *Āmṭī* (thin lentil soup)! The damned stuff sneaked into their house in their grandfather's and great-grandfather's time and has never left!

Gopala Gopala, Devkinandan Gopala

. . . . . . . . . . . . . . . . . . . . . . . . . . . . . . . . . . . . .

Why have the people stayed poor? One reason is they have no education. What don't they have?

—Education.

A man without education you might as well call a cart-drawing . . .

—Ox!

Now, at least, do better. Now, at least, educate your children. If you don't have any money sell your dishes, live from hand to mouth. Give your wife a cheaper sari. Cut out having guests. But send your children to school.

—Don't fail!

Learning is great wealth. Learning is great wealth. People with learning give speeches in Delhi. And our people lift sacks at Boribandar Station. The first are men. What are ours? They're not oxen are they? What are they?

—Men!

Learning is a great thing, a great thing. Before, if you didn't educate a child, he would have to do manual labor; but from now on your child won't get a job at all, he'll have to polish boots. "Come on, fifteen paise, come on." He'll have to polish boots. How great learning is! Dr. Ambedkar's[8] family were sweeping the streets for generations. Ambedkar's father had the good sense to send him to school. And Ambedkar didn't just make a little money. He made the Constitution of India. And if he hadn't gone to school and gotten an education, his fate would have been sweeping the streets. Learning is great wealth. Sell your dinner plate, give your wife a cheap sari. Live in a brokendown house, but send your children to school . . .

—Don't fail!

And the other kind of education is devotion to God.

Gopala Gopala, Devkinandan Gopala

Household economy! Marwadis, Gujaratis, Brahmans,

priests—why can these people eat *shirā* every day? Because they keep accounts! Keep what?

—Accounts!

They know how much they make and how much they spend. And our Marathas, Telis, Malis, Nhavis, Dhobis don't know anything about accounts. What do they do? They make seventy-five rupees and spend eighty or ninety. Live it up in January and sit on their ass moaning and groaning in February. You need to economize. You need to keep accounts. A lot of people say our salary isn't...

—Enough!

You've got to be able to say there's some left over. In a house where the husband and wife are intelligent and sensible there's always some left over. They put aside the balance. Who can't make ends meet?

Whose strength is little, whose anger great.

A man is weak, but tops in picking quarrels. He starts something and gets hit in the face, and goes home yelling. Nothing saved, expenses huge.... In daily life, cleanliness, economy, and the greatest thing—compassion! What is the big thing?

—Compassion!

You may go to *tīrthas*,
you may go to Kashi, to Gaya if you want.
Kabir says to Kamal,
compassion is greater than all.

The master who has compassion in his heart is a man of virtue—a man of virtue! You Marathas, do you go to Jejuri?

—Yes!

Do you take a goat?

—Yes!

Do you take your rightful cut?

—Yes!

Do you spice it and cook it and eat it?

—Yes!

All your generations of Jejuri-goers will die! Will your lot improve?

—Never!

Gopala Gopala Devkinandan Gopala

. . . . . . . . . . . . . . . . . . . . . . . . . . . . . . . . . . . .

Do you feed the goat grass?

—Yes!

Do you give it water?

—Yes

If the goat is lost, do you look for it and bring it back!

—Yes!

If it starts to rain, do you tie it in the house?

—Yes!

You treat it like your own child, and then you spice it and cut it up and eat it? You aren't men. If somebody called you a wild boar he wouldn't be...

—Wrong!

Gopala Gopala, Devkinandan Gopala

In a wedding do you have a *gondhal*[9] or not?

—Yes!

Do you kill a goat in the yard and splash the blood about?

—Yes!

Does anybody shed a tear that this is a sin? That we're

doing wrong? That we won't do it anymore? Does anyone say that?

. . . . . . . . . . . . . . . . . . . . . . . . . . . . . . . . . . . .

It's a sin, damn it, a sin! He whose knife cuts another's throat, who takes another's life to feed himself—is he a man? He does not have a trace of humanness in him.

Gopala Gopala, Devkinandan Gopala

Are there chickens in a Marwadi's house?

—No!

Are there chickens in a Gujarati's house?

—No!

Are there chickens in a Bhat's house?

—No!

Well, then, how did they get into your houses? Every house filled up with the damned chickens! *Ko ko ku ku ku!* There's sin in your belly. In the morning you give it water in the trough, and in the evening you kill and eat it. Kill it? Tell me what *shāstra* (holy law) this is.

Some people go to the bazaar. The dried fish shop smells so far off that as soon as a person gets near it he has to hold his nose. But those who eat it have lost their sense of smell. Our women—all except Brahmans, Gujaratis, Marwadis, and Jains—go straight to the shop. Dried fish is such a filthy thing that even a dog wouldn't eat it. But these women are such that just two of them can finish off the head of a fish this big! . . . Are these women? They were demons in a previous birth. They are goblins. Why, put a piece of *bombīl* by a Marwadi or Brahman woman's nose and she'll die puking—aagh, aagh! And these women finish off a head! I've never seen women like them! . . . Let's raise our hands and do *bhajan.*

Gopala Gopala, Devkinandan Gopala

Get an education and help the poor to get an education.

Give a poor kid a pair of pants, a khadi cap. Give him a pencil and a slate. Give him a notebook. You plan to send your own children to England and damn it, you don't think of giving a one or two-anna notebook to a poor child. You're not men.

Tuka says do at least a little good to others.

You don't have to send him to England. But will you give him a yard of rough cloth? . . . At Diwali when you've made a basketful of *lāḍūs* (sweets) you give the kids of the house all they want—till they get the runs. But when a couple of poor kids come to the door you don't give them each even two little ones. Do something at least. You'll die without ever having done anything more than take care of your wife and family. This life will be a waste, a waste. A bitch feeds her young. A sparrow brings food to her young. Dumb animals do this. Then having taken birth as a man, what should a man do? Only if you do good to others are you a man. He who thinks only of his wife and children is not a man, he's an ox. You built a house, got a car, brought that, did this, got married! What does Tukoba say?

Tuka says an ox hauled water all his life,
And died hauling water.

Women, your husband may go to a holy place, let him go. Your husband's god may be in the mountains but your god is in the house. Serve your husband. Fall at his feet every day. Garland your husband's neck with flowers. Light incense before him.

A faithful wife has the faith
Her husband is her god.

Marathas, Nhavis, Dhobis, Koshtis, and Kumbhars will say, "Boy, this is great. If a wife falls at her husband's feet, it would be really great." What will they say?

—It's really great!

Yes, really great! But shouldn't the husband have the qualities of a god?

—Yes!

Otherwise the damn husband comes home drunk and pukes in the house and should the wife put the incense stick by his face or up his rear end? Tell me. If she has a husband like that the wife should do *mahāpūjā* to him—take a basketful of hot ashes from the stove and throw them in his face. Here's your *mahāpūjā*.

Gopala Gopala, Devkinandan Gopal

When Mirabai[10] got taken up with *bhajan* she left the palace, gave up fine clothes, and started to wear coarse cloth. She threw away her bangles and tied a string of *tuḷsī* beads on her wrist. The woman who will do *bhajan*, who will serve her husband, is fortunate, very fortunate.

Gopala Gopala, Devkinandan Gopala

. . . . . . . . . . . . . . . . . . . . . . . . . . . . . . . . . . . . . . .

Take care of your husband, take care of your kids, take care of your work all day long. But for a while do *bhajan* to Govinda.[11] In the evening, when all your work is done, you don't need cymbals, drum, or harmonium. But everyone should sit together and do *bhajan* for ten minutes, taking the name of God in whatever way you can. The house where *bhajan* is done—the door of that house is guarded by Parmeshwar. There is a Gurkha[12] at the door, a Gurkha. The house where there is idle gossip, abuse, this and that, Yamraj, the god of death, is at that door, Yamraj! *Bhajan* to God is a great thing!

Gopala Gopala, Devkinandan Gopala

In the houses of the rich, there are women doing the pots and pans. The women of the house wear saris worth hundreds of rupees, and the woman doing the pots and pans has a sari torn on all sides. She has to lay her children on the floor. And she has to lift such a huge stack of pots. Take pity on her. She's poor and she's probably pregnant. How will she manage her delivery? You help her. You don't have to give her wheat. Give her *jawār* flour. Don't give her ghee, give her oil. Don't give her a new sari, give her an old one. Do something before you die. If you do nothing but wear nice clothes and eat until you die, you'll have lived your life in vain, in vain!

Gopala Gopala, Devkinandan Gopala

There's a great blot on our Hindustan, a great blot. Try to wash that blot away. What blot is that? Untouchability! What is it?

—Untouchability.

What is it?

—Untouchability.

Asking about a person's caste—who are you? The person full of pride is the one who asks about caste—who are you? Is the person he asks a man like the one who asks?

—Yes, he is!

Is it that one has four hands and the other one and a half? Tell me.

—No!

Is it that one has four eyes and the other only two? Tell me.

—No!

Does the one have four legs and the other only one? Is that the way it is?

—No!

Then why ask who are you? If anyone asks who you are say, "I'm a man, who are you?" A man! Or are you a buffalo?

—No!

Who are you?

—A Man!

. . . . . . . . . . . . . . . . . . . . . . . . . . . . . . . . . . . . . . . .

The person who asks about caste is shameless. He is just like you and still he asks who are you. Are you like him or is there something wrong with you?

—No!

What?

—No!

Show what is different for us. Is your earth and theirs the same or different?

—The same!

Is your sky and theirs the same or different?

—The same!

Is the sun the same or different?

—The same!

Is the train the same or different?

—The same!

Is the taxi the same or different?

—The same!

Is the court the same or different?

—The same!

Is the plague or cholera the same or different?

—The same!

Are eating and shitting the same or different?

—The same!

Show what's different, then talk about untouchability. Say what is different. We have all been born by the same route. Or did some come out of a mother's womb and some out of a mother's mouth and armpit? Tell me. There are only two castes of mankind—two. How many?

—Two!

Male and female. Just these two castes. There is no third.

. . . . . . . . . . . . . . . . . . . . . . . . . . . . . . . . . . . . . . . .

Gopala Gopala, Devkinandan Gopala

How many teeth do you have?

—Thirty-two!

How many does the Harijan[13] have? Thirty-two. Or do you have thirty-two and he only ten?

—No!

How many days are you in your mother's womb? Nine months and nine days. How long is the Harijan in his mother's womb? Four months? Six months?

—No!

What did you say?

—No!

Show how we're different. You practice untouchability without any justification! This won't do. Show how we're different. Then say something. Somebody will mention the Scriptures. The Scriptures you can teach to anyone. Gather together fifty kids from any caste, teach them, have them recite the Vedas, have them listen to the Bhagwat, whatever you like. But show me what is different originally, from birth. Is your Ganga and theirs the same or different?

—The same!

The Marathas' river comes out from here and the Mangs' from there—is this how it is?

—No!

There is a blot on Hindustan. It is the blot of untouchability. Is there untouchability in England? No. Is there in Russia? No. In Japan? No. In China? No. In London? No. In America? No. Among the Parsees? No. Among the Christians? No. Among the Muslims? No. Did Hazrat[14] ever say the water's polluted, the bastard's polluted it? Did he say that?

—No.

Hey, fellow! You've polluted good water! Do you ever say that?

—Yes!

The Muslims' or Christians' water doesn't get polluted, so what in the hell is wrong with yours? Why does it get polluted? Does a water pot get polluted? Do you purify it or not?

—Yes!

How do you purify it? Speak! When a hand has touched the pot, how do you purify it? How? By burning it. By burning it with fire? Yes. And does a man get polluted or not?

—Yes!

Then pile grass on the bastard's body and light a match. Let him burn. Do you let a Harijan sit in your bullock cart?

—No!

Then have you taken leave of your senses at the bus stand? Narayan Patel comes—please sit down. Ganappa—please sit down. Shivrya Mang, please sit down. Then why doesn't anyone say the bus is polluted, we won't sit in it! Hollow! Where does a rat burrow? A hollow place! A hollow place! If he strikes rock he's turned back. . . . Get rid of untouchability! Be sensible and become human. Because of untouchability lakhs of people have become Christians. Lakhs have become Muslims. This untouchability has dealt a blow to Hinduism, a blow. Let's raise our hands and do *bhajan.*

Gopala Gopala, Devkinandan Gopala

In Bombay a rich man—one man—built ten buildings. And another man doesn't have sense enough to build a goddamn hut for his wife and kids. If you called him a Dhangar's sheep it'd be

—Okay!

Now the government's advice is don't drink. Whose advice? The government's. Do not stand in the shadow of that drink that has ruined the millionaire's house, killed the prince, made the palace desolate. Friend, do you set up a still and drink? Young people, if your father drinks—your who?

—Father!

And if he is found drunk—break off your relationship with him. He's not a father. He's an enemy. Run at him, grab his topknot, and take off his shoes. Beat him up and don't let him go till he shits in his dhoti. Only then are you sons. Otherwise if anyone called you dumb sheep it'd be

—Okay!

Gopala Gopala, Devkinandan Gopala

The government shouldn't have to give advice about drinking. But children should become police—children! Who should become police?

—Children!

If your father is found drunk, beat him up and cool him off, like nobody in his family has ever seen. Tell him, give up drinking. Are you going to leave off liquor or are you going to drink? Are you going to drink or have you given it up? Then let him go. Sons are sheep. Who is that babbling? Father—he's drunk. Don't let him go without beating him up. Don't show him any respect. Beat him up if you will. Besides, turn him over to the police. He's been making liquor. Arrest him. Anybody who drinks is no father. Lakhs of rich men have wasted their ancestral estates and ended up as coolies, coolies!

. . . . . . . . . . . . . . . . . . . . . . . . . . . . . . . . . . . . . . . .

These blasted drinkers—wrestlers, Marathas, Malis, Telis, Nhavis, Dhobis, Chambhars, Koshtis, Kumbhars, Beldars, Kaikadis, Gonds, Gavaris, Vinkars, Dhangars, Mangs, and Mahars! Have you ever seen a Marwadi lying drunk in Bombay?

—No!

Have you ever seen a Gujarati lying drunk in Bombay?

—No!

Have you ever seen a Brahman lying drunk in an office?

—No!

The man who drinks liquor will not fail to ruin his house...

—And home!

Gopala Gopala, Devkinandan Gopala

Today you have made me happy. The police are my gurus. I have had *darshan* of so many people today. I would have stayed in bed but my mouth made me take the name of God. For this I am indebted to our police friends. Let's do *bhajan* once more and then go.

Gopala Gopala, Devkinandan Gopala[15]

## EDITORS' NOTES

1. "Gopala Gopala, Devkinandan Gopala," the chanted refrain of this *kīrtan*, means "Hail to Krishna, son of Devki!"

2. Tukaram Maharaj, also called affectionately Tukoba and Tukobaraya (King Tukaram), in respect, is a beloved saint-poet of the bhakti

movement in Maharashtra. A seventeenth-century village Shudra, his songs are considered superb poetry, as well as religious advice as direct and unorthodox as that of Gadge Maharaj himself.

3. Dnyaneshwar, thirteenth-century author of the *Jñāneśvarī*, a commentary on the *Bhagavad Gītā*, is the founder of the bhakti movement in Maharashtra.

4. Kabir, a fifteenth-century Hindi poet, decried symbolic piety and ritual in the same manner as Tukaram. Gadge Maharaj here recites Kabir's *dohā* in Hindi, a language understood by the Marathi-speaking people in cosmopolitan Bombay.

5. The elephant-headed Ganpati or Ganesh is one of the most popular gods in Maharashtra. In an annual festival, Ganpati images are brought into homes or community-sponsored booths built for the occasion to the chant of "Morya . . . Morya." Offerings, including the sweet *modak*, are made to him, lights are waved before him, and on the last day the clay image is ceremoniously and publicly carried to a river and immersed. See Paul Courtright's article in this volume.

6. Satyanarayan *pūjā* is commonly performed for the well-being of a person, the success of a particular occasion, or the fulfillment of a wish. Gadge Maharaj here makes fun of Satyanarayan, even though the original occasion for his appearance was a Satyanarayan *pūjā* at the Bandra Police Station, probably for the well-being of the establishment in the coming year.

7. Marwadis, originally from Rajasthan, and Gujaratis comprise the primary business communities of Bombay and are high caste Vaishyas. Brahmans dominate positions related to education. The castes on Gadge Maharaj's "worthless" list are Shudra castes generally; the last two—Mangs and Mahars—as well as the ritually higher Chambhars, are ex-Untouchables. These Marathi-speaking low castes dominate the labor force of Bombay. Note that Gadge Maharaj praises the thrift and the vegetarianism of the high-caste Marwadis, Gujaratis, and Brahmans, but does not refer to their ritual status.

8. Dr. B. R. Ambedkar, an Untouchable Mahar by birth, became the Law Minister in independent India. Gadge Maharaj exaggerates the poverty of his background here—Ambedkar's father was a schoolmaster in a British Army school.

9. A *gondhal* is a ceremony performed in song by Gondhalis, traditional singers for the devi. See R. C. Dhere's article in this volume.

10. Mirabai, a Rajput princess in the sixteenth century, left her husband to become a devotee of Krishna.

11. Govinda, like Gopala, is a name for Krishna.

12. Gurkhas from Nepal are now commonly found as highly-respected guards at the doors of many establishments in Maharashtra. They are better known world-wide as fierce and effective soldiers.

13. Harijan (people of God) is a synonym for Untouchable made popular by Mohandas K. Gandhi.

14. Hazrat is a title commonly used for the Prophet Mohammad.

15. For an assessment of Gadge Maharaj' place in the radical tradition, see Eleanor Zelliot, "Four Radical Saints in Maharashtra," in *Religion and Society in Maharashtra*, ed. by Milton Israel and N.K. Wagle (Toronto: University of Toronto Centre for South Asian Studies, 1987).

KUMAR SAPTARSHI
TRANSLATED BY MAXINE BERNTSEN

# 17

# *Orthodoxy and Human Rights: The Story of a Clash**

## Editors' Introduction

Yukrand is a shortened version of Yuvak Kranti Dal (*Youth Revolution Force*). Founded in 1967, by Saptarshi and the late Arun Limaye, Yukrand has used the Gandhian method of *satyāgraha* to bring about revolutionary change in rural Maharashtra, but outside both Gandhian and Marxist organizations. The following account of one of Yukrand's campaigns shows with remarkable clarity the clash between two opposing philosophical viewpoints—the orthodox Hindu view that men are graded on a hierarchical scale with some men permanently outside the pale, and the view of *māṇuskī*, the idea that each person is entitled to be treated as a full human being. The concept of *māṇuskī* has been central to all modern Hindu reform movements. (*E. Z. and M. B.*)

* This article first appeared in Marathi in the *Maharashtra Times* (August 4, 1977).

## *The Datta Temple at Shedgao*

In 1975, Yukrand chose an area near the town of Rashim in Karjat Taluka of Ahmednagar District for intensive work. For the last two years (1975-1977) Yukrand has been constantly in touch with the people of this area. Shedgao, one of the villages we have been working in, is very famous for its Datta temple. It is believed that possession by ghosts can be cured by staying in the temple and serving the god. As a result, one can always find forty or fifty possessed people staying there. From a scientific point of view, of course, these people are mentally ill.

In this temple the role of the doctor is played by a *sannyāsī* called Akhandanand Maharaj. Of course he doesn't deliberately take the role of a doctor. He strictly observes traditional ascetic practices and religious vows. The Datta temple is not old; Akhandanand started it from nothing nineteen years ago when he first came there to devote himself to the reading of the scriptures. Gradually the temple grew, and increasing numbers of people supposedly possessed by ghosts came to be cured. At present, *āratī* is performed three or four times daily, numerous festivals are celebrated in the course of a year, and *yadnyas* and other such ceremonies are performed from time to time. These activities have grown to the point where almost everyone in the village participates in them. Moreover, devotees of the Shedgao Maharaj are found all over Maharashtra. The fame of the temple as a place for curing ghost possession is spread through the *gurusampradāy*—the network of gurus and their followers. Devotees come to Shedgao from many different places. As a result, the local economy has flourished. The Maharaj has firmly convinced the townspeople that service to Datta has worldly advantages beyond imagination. For that reason, they have surrendered their minds and souls to the Maharaj and put themselves completely in his power.

The population of Shedgao is twenty-five hundred. Here, unlike elsewhere in western Maharashtra, the Maratha caste is in a minority. The majority of the population are Malis. There are one hundred houses of Untouchables; that is, about five or six hundred people in all. Thus, one-fourth of the population is Untouchables, the largest proportion of them Mahars. Some Mahars have become Buddhists, but on the level of their daily life the conversion to Buddhism has not resulted in any change. They are still considered untouchable. Moreover, in order to obtain educational concessions these Buddhists list themselves in the government register as "Hindu-Mahar."

When the rest of the townspeople go every day to do *āratī* at the Datta temple or join together to celebrate festivals, or when the whole town is alive with the celebation of the birthday of a god or a *yadnya,* the Untouchables feel left out. Other townspeople can go to the Maharaj when they are in difficulty; sometimes they even get financial help. But the Untouchables get nothing from the Maharaj. On the contrary, when they stand wistfully at the temple door, the Maharaj asks them their caste and turns them away. The Maharaj regularly violates the Untouchability Offenses Act. So the Untouchables of Shedgao feel a suppressed, smoldering anger toward Akhandanand. They are convinced that if they express it they will be subjected to social boycott. They also know that in case of a boycott no political party is going to come to their aid, because the Maharaj is indirectly a political force. Opposing the Maharaj means losing the votes of ten to fifteen villages and incurring the active opposition of dedicated campaigners throughout Shrigonda Taluka.

On June 10, 1977, Yukrand workers from Rashim went to Shedgao to hold a public meeting. At that time the Untouchables of Shedgao told Prakash Bajaj, the Yukrand leader from Rashim, that they were barred from the Datta temple. When Prakash Bajaj and the Untouchables went to meet the Maharaj, the Maharaj asked all the local Untouchables their caste and refused to admit them into the temple. When he found out the caste of the Untouchable Yukrand workers from Rashim, he refused to admit them as well. Then Bajaj discussed this situation with the local people.

As a result of Yukrand's activity in the area, political antagonism had intensified. Consequently, it was hard for the Yukrand workers to understand the need for persuasion. It was only for my sake that the local workers were exercising restraint. On July 8, they went again to meet the Maharaj of Shedgao. This time even Prakash Bajaj and Shivaji Suravase, both caste Hindus, were denied entrance into the temple on the grounds that they did not observe untouchability.

By that time the Untouchables of Shedgao were frightened. They feared they would be subjected to social boycott. All the vital arteries of their existence—water supply, grocery store, and agricultural work—were in the hands of the caste Hindus. If these arteries were blocked, the Untouchables would find it difficult to live. So, although they were in favor of the *satyāgraha* planned by Yukrand, they were put off committing themselves to taking part in it as a group. The patience of the Yukrand workers was strained to the limit.

### *Declaration of Satyāgraha*

As they were convinced that the Maharaj's adamant position would not change,the Yukrand workers from Rashim argued, "First *satyāgraha,* then persuasion." I had already planned to tour that area from July 12 to 14. A visit to Shedgao had been scheduled for the evening of July 13. My program had been planned by the Yukrand workers from Rashim. They brought out a leaflet publicly announcing that on July 13, Kumar Saptarshi, along with a group of Untouchables, would enter the Datta temple in Shedgao. At that, hectic political activity started among the townspeople, the police, and political workers. They were all looking for ways to avert the *satyāgraha.*

The Shrigonda Taluka sub-inspector of police said that he was going to give an order banning public meetings. In the early morning of July 12, Prakash Bajaj phoned me in Pune, saying that the *satyāgraha* had been announced and that tension had increased. He also told me what the sub-inspector had said.

I took the morning bus to Ahmednagar on July 12. I phoned the District Superintendent of Police and told him that if there was an order banning public meetings, it would mean that the police were obstructing the Harijans' efforts to gain entrance into the temple. I told him that I would take responsibility for maintaining law and order, that Yukrand had no quarrel with the townspeople, that we would keep using persuasion until we succeeded, etc., etc.

On the evening of July 13, there was a public meeting in Bhambora, a village eight miles from Shedgao, where Yukrand has a great deal of influence. At Bhambora it was decided that everyone would hold a meeting and afterwards about a hundred of them would go by tractor-drawn trailer to Shedgao. A follower of Datta warned the tractor driver that he would bring on himself the wrath of the god, so the driver ran away in the dark, taking the key with him. Even the owner of the tractor had no idea where he had gone. Everyone in our group was discussing how to get to Shedgao. There was no vehicle available. The bus to Jalalpur had left at six. Ten Yukrand workers from Rashim had already gone on that. They were going to go on foot the three miles from Jalalpur to Shedgao. Seeing our confusion, the follower of Datta who had started it all began spreading the story, "Look, Datta has made the driver and the tractor key disappear. This is just a hint of the wrath of Datta and the Maharaj. If Kumar Saptarshi goes with the Harijans into the Shedgao temple, the Maharaj will destroy the Yukrand organization in this area." On the one hand he was propagandizing against us and on the other he was requesting me not to go ahead with the plan. Finally Prakash Bajaj and I set out on a motorcycle for Shedgao.

As we approached the village we saw many people walking towards it in small groups. On the main road there was a large crowd. From the surrounding area about ten thousand people had gathered in that small town. Every person in the village was there on the road. The crowd wasn't supporting us, but it wasn't in an aggressive, violent mood either. Everyone looked serious. No one was talking. They respected both the Maharaj and us, in our separate spheres.

If the Maharaj had opposed us in the political sphere, the people would perhaps have even gone against him. But now the Maharaj had created a crisis for them, saying, "If you approve of these people, if you approve of their program, our nineteen-year relationship is at an end. The very moment the Harijans touch the temple, the power of the temple will be destroyed. At that moment Datta Maharaj will leave the temple. And immediately, without even taking a drink of water, I will leave Shedgao, never to return. Our relationship will be completely severed." Because of the Maharaj's ploy they had to make a decision soon. They had to choose between the Maharaj and us.

The local leaders said, "In politics we support you. We voted for your Janata Party.[1] Understand our situation and cancel your agitation. As far as admitting Untouchables into the Datta temple we don't have any position one way or the other. We don't object to their entering. If they want to go into the other temples in town (Bahiroba's, for example) we will let them. The Maharaj has taken a completely inflexible position about this, and we are anxious to see that he does not leave the town. We ask you not to pursue this."

I told the leaders that if Baba's inflexibility was the only difficulty I would persuade him to change his mind.

After that discussion we set out for the Datta temple to talk to the Maharaj. Just then we were called by the police. Those present included the Ahmednagar District Deputy Superintendent of Police, four or five subinspectors, the *māmlatdār* of Shrigonda Taluka and his assistant, the regional and district level members of the Central Intelligence Division, and some stenographers to transcribe the speeches. There was a force of sixty to seventy police in the town. Including jeeps and vans they had four or five vehicles. I talked to them and asked them not to intervene in the conflict. I assured them that I would handle the situation properly. Then the Deputy Superintendent said, "As far as possible we will not interfere. We will entrust the situation to you. But if anyone breaks the law, we will have to intervene. I am warning you that if you break the law, we won't listen to you." If the police had clumsily interfered and violence had broken out, there would have been a *lāṭhī*-charge and firing and many people would have been killed. Credit for averting this must be given to the reasonableness of the townspeople and the police. Not a single person in town picked up the stone that could have set off the conflict. Similarly, the police avoided an unnecessary show of force and handled the situation delicately. Generally, this is not what happens.

The police officers had been encamped in town since morning. The crowd started forming at four in the afternoon and continued to grow. The widely-dispersed crowd milling about on the road could at any moment have turned violent. So the police told me, "Call everyone together and say something. Then they will sit in one place. They are anxious to hear what you have to say. They haven't even gone home to eat."

By then it was nine o'clock. We called a meeting on the open ground near the Datta temple. In a few minutes everyone gathered there. The Untouchables were waiting in their quarter of town, for earlier I had sent a message for them to gather there. However, after seeing the situation I thought it would be unwise to leave the crowd by itself, so I sent a message asking the Untouchables to come to the meeting. I told the seated crowd that I would go talk to the Maharaj and then come back, and asked them to remain seated until then.

### *The Maharaj's Viewpoint*

I requested the Maharaj to be broad-minded and allow the Harijans into the temple. I asked him why the Hindu religion, which saw *brahman* in everything, was not ready to regard the Harijans as men. Then he said, "Kumar, do you think that I am not humane? A separate temple should be built for the Harijans. I will give financial help. Neither steam nor any other power can be put to effective use unless it is kept under strict control. You have to enclose it in a steam engine and use it when and in the amount you want it. Only when strictly controlled is it of any use to anyone.[2] Datta Maharaj is able to help people in their difficulties because the spiritual power here is controlled by strict rules. You are raising the hue and cry that only Harijans are denied entrance here for political purposes. In this temple I have defined limits by caste. If these limits are broken, the power of the temple will go, just as steam escapes from an engine. You have come to destroy a power that is useful to the people, a power that has been created through great effort. If you are really interested in serving the people you will preserve this power intact. But if you only want to pull off a political stunt, you will destroy this power and deprive thousands of people of its benefits.

"The limit for the Harijans is outside the temple. Those non-Brahmans who are not Harijans are allowed inside the sanctuary. Inside the sanctuary is a smaller sanctuary where the image is. In front of this smaller sanctuary there is a small area enclosed by a wooden railing. Non-Brahmans who are not Harijans can come as far as the railing. Only Brahmans are allowed inside. But not all Brahmans are allowed to go all the way in to the inner sanctuary where the image is. Those Brahmans who drink tea or smoke cigarettes must stop just inside the railing. Only true Brahmans who do not drink tea are allowed all the way inside. It is because such strict rules are followed that Datta Maharaj stays here."

Then I asked him where in the most ancient Hindu scriptures (before the Laws of Manu were written) there is any support for untouchability. He cited the support of the *Gītā* and the *Gurucaritra*.[3] He quoted the verse from the *Gītā*:

> *cāturvarṇyaṃ mayāśṛṣṭaṃ guṇakarma vibhāgaśaḥ*
> The four-fold caste system has been created by me, based on a division according to characteristics and functions.

The Maharaj said, "This is correct. I am a true Hindu, so I am going to observe untouchability even at the risk of my life. The R.S.S., who claim to be Hindus and then say there is no untouchability in the Hindu scriptures, are hypocrites.[4] These people lie because the Harijans have votes. Your insistence on their entering the temple is out of political motives. For the same reason the R.S.S. doesn't believe in untouchability."

This discussion with the Maharaj took place in the porch of the temple. The door of the temple was locked. Normally the door was never locked. When I asked the Maharaj to open it, he said, "It will be opened at four in the morning for *āratī*. If you want to enter now you can break the lock. If you take the Untouchables and enter the temple, I will give the keys to the townspeople and leave."

After all this discussion we realized that there was no common ground, and so we got up to leave. According to the Gandhian method one should not leave a single avenue of persuasion untried. So we decided to conduct the *satyāgraha* only when we had exhausted all the avenues at our disposal. As we were getting up I asked him one last question, "Maharaj, do you acknowledge the law which has come out of democratic process?" He thought that the point of my question was that untouchability was against the law, so he said, "I don't mind if I'm arrested. But I am not going to give permission for Harijans to enter the temple. I do not acknowledge the power of the state and government. I acknowledge only the power of dharma, for I am a true Hindu."

Then we namaskared to him, requested him not to be angry with us for doing *satyāgraha,* and left.

In the public meeting I said, "If you are going to support the obstinate demand of this Brahman *sannyāsī,* I want to point out that I too am a Brahman. I have given up the medical profession and fought alongside you for ten or twelve years. So whose demand are you going to meet? My demand is that the Harijans be allowed entrance into the Datta temple. After that, let us all go together and request the Maharaj not to leave Shedgao. Let us close him in with love.

"This *satyāgraha* is not really for temple entry. There must be a place for us, for our thoughts, for *māṇuskī* in your minds. Because of customs and traditions thousands of years old you have closed the doors of your minds. On those doors human feeling is knocking. So the question is whether you are going to open them. You, Untouchable friends who are gathered here, must be humiliated that such a battle should be fought over your entry into the temple. You have to be fearless. Human rights are not won easily. So I ask you not to be afraid and to join me in the temple entry *satyāgraha*."

### *Entrance into the Temple*

Twenty-two of us, after introducing ourselves, left the meeting, and, raising cheers to Mahatma Gandhi and Dr. Ambedkar,[5] we entered the temple courtyard. The Maharaj said that those who were Harijans or Buddhists should go out. He forbade them from even coming on the porch. But crossing the limits he had set, we joined hands and silently sat cross-legged on the porch. I asked the Maharaj to open the door of the sanctuary. He refused. He said that the door would be opened at four in the morning for *āratī*.

We stayed outside the door until five in the morning. At eleven-thirty the night before—that is, when the Maharaj said that the Harijans should not come in—the police were going to arrest him. For, once he had forbidden the Untouchables to come into the temple, the crime had been committed.[6] But we had asked the police not to make the arrest. Until early morning the police were still trying to decide what to do. Both they and the townspeople had stayed up all night. The Harijans were standing outside in the dark on a slight rise, watching what was going on in the temple, giving their silent support.

At five in the morning the police told the Maharaj to open the door, warning that if he didn't do so they would have to arrest him. Then the *sarpanch* (village headman) called the Maharaj aside. The Maharaj turned the key over to him, saying he could do as he saw fit, but if the Harijans went into the temple, from that moment on he would break off relations with the townspeople. The *sarpanch* was on the verge of tears. He didn't know what to do. He called several other townspeople. The police waited for another half hour and then at five-thirty gave him an ultimatum: "Are you going to open the door or not? Make it clear once and for all." Then the *sarpanch* opened the door. The *satyāgrahīs* went in, with cheers for Mahatma Gandhi and Dr. Ambedkar. We all stayed in the temple for five minutes and then came out. At the door of the temple there were a police jeep and van. We were told to get into the van and the Maharaj into the jeep. At six-thirty we arrived at the Shrigonda police station. The police treated the Maharaj and us well. The Maharaj was freed on bail. The twenty-two of us gave our statements and were released after two in the afternoon.

When the police had left Shedgao with the Maharaj, the thirty or forty "possessed" women residents of the temple set up a great lament. Seeing this I too felt bad.

Slowly people from Daund and Shedgao were coming by bus and gathering in front of the Shrigonda police station. In front of them we appealed to the Maharaj to advise people not to start a boycott against the Untouchables. His answer was, "Now the relations between Shedgao and me are broken. The people are free to do whatever they want."

Namaskaring, I said publicly to the Maharaj that I hoped he would not be angry with me. In response he said to the crowd, "I am not angry with Kumar. He has just provided the occasion. For the last nineteen years I have been telling the Untouchables not to come into the temple. I have been asking those people who come what their caste is. I thought that someone would object, but nobody did. I wanted to court arrest under the anti-untouchability act. Today that has happened. In court I am going to say that I observe untouchability and am going to keep on observing it. I want to use this case to bring about a public discussion. I am going to say to the Indian government, 'I want to live as a true Hindu. A true Hindu cannot live without practicing untouchability. This is a conflict of principles. These people cannot live without giving Harijans entry into temples. I also cannot live without observing untouchability.' Then is the Indian government going to let me live according to my religion or not? I know that according to the law I am going to have to serve six months' imprisonment at hard labor. I am ready for that."

## CODA

*Akhandanand Maharaj did not serve his jail sentence. The Datta temple of Shedgao is still closed.*

—*Editors*

## EDITORS' NOTES

1. The Janata Party was formed in 1977 to battle the Congress Party ruled by Indira Gandhi. Saptarshi and other liberals entered parliamentary politics under the banner of this coalition, along with more conservative groups which had also been stifled during the Emergency, 1975-77.

2. Note that the Maharaj uses the same metaphor of steam and a steam engine that the Brahman woman used in Scattered Voices 2. In both instances, control produces power: personal control, in the case of women, and social control, in the case of priestly or religious power.

3. "The *Gītā*" always refers to the *Bhagavad Gītā*. The *Gurucaritra* is the life of two early Datta *avatārs*; it serves as a basic text for Maharashtrian Datta worship. See the article on Datta by Charles Pain with Eleanor Zelliot. Note that the four-fold caste system does not include untouchability.

4. The R.S.S. (Rashtriya Swayamsevak Sangh), although basically a conservative Hindu nationalist organization, has been very careful to balance its Brahman image with a defense of the idea of equality of all castes. Sirsikar's article on the R.S.S. in this volume does not deal specifically with this point.

5. Dr. Ambedkar (Bhimrao Ramji Ambedkar, 1892-1956) was the most prominent Untouchable leader in India; he was responsible for much social legislation and the Buddhist conversion as well as an awakening among the Untouchables themselves. He actually opposed Gandhi's use of the word "Harijan" (People of God) and the patronizing attitude that indicated, but here the Yukrand group claims both men as legitimizers of its action.

6. The Untouchability (Offenses) Act of 1955 made the practice of untouchability punishable by law.

ANNE FELDHAUS

# 18

# The Orthodoxy of the Mahanubhavs

## Editors' Introduction

The thirteenth century in Maharashtra saw the beginning of Marathi literature and the establishment of two still living religious movements, the well-known bhakti movement of the Varkari sect centered in Pandharpur and the less well-known bhakti sect of the Mahanubhavs—"those of the great experience." Considered heterodox at best, the Mahanubhavs rejected caste and the worship of idols, refused to acknowledge the ritual and scriptural authority of Brahmans even though many early converts were Brahmans, created an order of women *sannyāsīs* as well as one of men, and acknowledged the reality of only one god, Parmeshwar, who has five major incarnations: Krishna, Dattatreya (see the article on Datta in this volume), and three sect figures. Although the Mahanubhavs seem to have been popular at first, spreading chiefly north of the Godavari River even as the Varkari sect spread south, they came to be considered suspect sometime in the next two centuries. They adopted a secret script in which to preserve their sacred texts, and slipped into an inconspicuous position outside the mainstream of Maharashtrian society. There is currently considerable scholarly interest in the Mahanubhavs, and a renewed sense of their historic importance. The way in which this long-lived heterodox sect has accommodated itself to Hindu society shows us a still different facet of Maharashtrian religion. (*E. Z. and M. B.*)

### *The Difference of the Mahanubhavs*

It was in the year Irawati Karve died, 1970, that I first visited Maharashtra. The English translation of her "*Vāṭcāl*"[1] was one of the few things I had read in preparation for my visit, and it was in part that essay that led me to Paṇdharpur on Ashadha Ekadashi to watch the pilgrimage arrive. We stood for hours that evening on the Wakhari-Pandharpur road, watching the groups of pilgrims dance their way, one after the other, into the town. It was entrancing: the light of torches, the rhythmic sounds of drums and hand cymbals. The faces of the Varkaris impressed me most. They held a joy that was not that of schoolchildren on holiday or of mystics lost in another world, but something else. Theirs, I thought, was the joy of people dancing in to see their god.

Four years later, when I returned to India to write a thesis on Maharashtrian religion, it was not contemporary practice that I was to study, but medieval literature, and not the Varkaris but the Mahanubhavs.[2] It was not the mainstream bhakti sect of Maharashtra but a less well-known bhakti movement that had begun in the same medieval period, the thirteenth century.

In the course of my travels in search of manuscripts and interpretations of the Mahanubhavs' *Sūtrapāṭha*, I had occasion to meet many present-day Mahanubhavs—monks, nuns, and lay men and women. I saw monasteries and temples, worship services called *pūjās* and *āratīs*, a celebration of Krishna's birthday, and an initiation ceremony; and I heard much talk about nonviolence (*ahimsā*) and asceticism (*sannyās*). These are all things and topics common enough in the religious lives of ordinary Maharashtrian Hindus. Yet most of the Mahanubhavs I met seemed to think of themselves as significantly different from other Maharashtrian Hindus. And non-Mahanubhav Maharashtrians with whom I talked about the Mahanubhavs seemed to regard them as unusual or strange, if not downright untrustworthy.

What is the basis of this perceived difference? And is it really so great as everyone seems to think?

One kind of approach to these questions has been presented elsewhere.[3] If we take as the criterion of Hindu orthodoxy acknowledgement of the authority of the Vedas, the Mahanubhavs are probably heterodox. But none of the Mahanubhavs I met seemed particularly concerned about the sect's orthodoxy or heterodoxy with respect to the Vedas. What they seemed much more concerned about was defining their relationship to present-day popular Hindu belief and practice.

The basis of their difference along these lines is as follows: Mahanubhavs do not deny the existence or—within certain limits—the powers of the numerous gods (*devatās*) of the Hindu pantheon. But they do believe that there exists a single ultimate being, called Parmeshwar, who is heterogeneous to the many gods, and who alone has the power to liberate men. Parmeshwar brings about man's liberation (*moksha, uddharaṇ*) by descending to Karmabhumi (India) and giving his presence (*sannidhān* or *sambandha*) to men there: this presence is necessary for liberation. There have been numerous descents (*avatārs*) of Parmeshwar, but the relevant ones are those in which Parmeshwar has taken on human form. We know of five of these: Krishna; Dattatreya; Chakradhar, the founder of the sect; Govindaprabhu, Chakradhar's guru; and Changadeva Raula, Govindaprabhu's guru.[4]

The devaluation of normal popular Hindu practice involved in such beliefs is rather strikingly expressed in one of the short chapters of the *Sūtrapāṭha*.[5] This chapter, called "*Yūgadharma*," presents a hierarchy of religious activities (dharmas) arranged according to the four classical ages (yugas). The dharma proper to the Krita yuga is introspection (*ātmopāsti*); that proper to the Treta, devotion (bhakti);[6] that proper to the Dvapara, sacrifice (*yāga*); and that proper to the Kali, the religion of pilgrimages, vows, and almsgiving (*tīrtha-kshetra-vrata-dāna*). Performance during a given yuga of the dharma proper to that yuga leads to one of the hierarchized series of rewards, the better rewards corresponding to the better yugas and to the more worthy dharmas proper to them. But, the chapter ends, none of the dharmas proper to the different yugas leads one to know or attain Parmeshwar. Thus, none of these dharmas leads to liberation.

Since it is the Kali yuga in which Mahanubhavs since the time of their founder have lived, it is the dharma of *tīrtha-kshetra-vrata-dāna*, popular Hinduism, with which the religion of Parmeshwar, the pursuit of the means to liberation, must compete. In "*Yūgadharma*," *tīrtha-kshetra-vrata-dāna* is devalued in two ways: not just by pointing out its qualitative difference from the means to liberation, but by ranking it as the least of the non-liberating dharmas. Contemporary Mahanubhavs adhere to the spirit of "*Yūgadharma*" and other parts of the *Sūtrapāṭha* when, without condemning *devatā*-worship for others, they try not to participate in it themselves.

In some cases, at least, this abstinence is quite self-conscious. For example, the *Sūtrapāṭha* contains an explicit prohibition against visiting Mahur and Kolhapur,[7] the sites of temples to Renuka and Mahalaksmi, two of the most important Maharashtrian goddesses. Accompanied by a party of Mahanubhavs, I traveled once to one of these places, Mahur, in search of manuscripts. On the hills of Mahur, there are, besides the temple of Renuka, a temple of Dattatreya, a temple of Atri and Anasuya, and a Mahanubhav monastery reputed to have a good manuscript collection.

Our business at the monastery completed, we proceeded to visit the other important sites of the place. We went to the Dattatreya temple and to the temple of Atri and Anasuya on the further hill, and then returned to the tea-and-holy-picture stalls at the foot of the steps to the Renuka temple. There was some discussion among my Mahanubhav companions—a *sannyāsī*, two laymen, and the recently-converted wife of one of the laymen—as to whether or not to visit the temple. As clearly as I can remember, the recent convert and her rather easy-going husband finally went up to the temple—she but not he making an offering—while the other layman and the *sannyāsī* remained behind. At the booths at the foot of the hill we bought some sweet *prasād* of the goddess. On the way home, all ate the *prasād* with pleasure; apparently, no one had qualms about eating food supposed to have been offered to the proscribed deity.

Besides the uncertainty about visiting the Renuka temple, there was even some discussion, in the course of this trip, of the inappropriateness of going to Mahur at all, or of there being a Mahanubhav monastery there; but the fact that there is a monastery there seemed to excuse our trip.[8]

### *The Mahanubhav Monks and Nuns*

Although the one *sannyāsī* who accompanied me on this trip lived alone rather than in a monastery, and my three other companions were lay people, the vast majority of Mahanubhavs I met were *sannyāsīs* living in monasteries or camped in tents pitched for a few days' rest in the course of peregrination. The men were dressed in pink or grey, the women in black saris, their heads shaved. The appearance of these people, especially the women, impressed me tremendously. Their food, when I was asked to share it, seemed no worse than that of others in the surrounding countryside—except that the Mahanubhavs made such a big point about theirs never including meat.[9] In the large rooms which serve as sleeping chambers in the monks' quarters and the nuns' quarters, each ascetic is allotted three feet or so of wall space and six feet of floor space extending out from the wall. The wall space is used for storing belongings, and the floor space for sleeping.

All the Mahanubhav monasteries and camps I saw included both male and female *sannyāsīs*. In the Aurangabad Mahanubhav Ashram, I was shown the line separating the men's from the women's quarters, and I was shown the toothless old man who, I was told, is the only one to cross that line; he acts as a messenger and at mealtimes he carries food from the kitchen, located in the women's quarters, to the men's side of the ashram. The care with which the line and the old man who crosses it were pointed out indicated some anxiety, I thought, to dispel the suspicion that celibacy cannot be maintained in a monastery housing both men and women.

I visited only one monastery whose inhabitants did not claim to be celibate. This was a monastery whose head (*mahant*) is an active and respected leader in Mahanubhav circles. He is referred to, by himself and others, as a *sannyāsī*. Of the several Mahanubhav ashrams I visited, his was the only one where I had been invited to stay at the monastery itself rather than being put up with a local family of lay Mahanubhavs or in a lodge. I was grateful for the invitation, and anticipated my stay with a mixture of fear and excitement, picturing myself sleeping on the floor in a row of black-saried nuns, finding out by experience about a life of severe asceticism. I was surprised, then, on my arrival, to learn that, besides the Mahant, the only other "*sannyāsīs*" living in the monastery were his wife, his son, and his nephew. I was given a soft bed in a room that I shared with only a modern refrigerator, and I was well cared for by the Mahant's wife, who is a good cook as well as a sweet-tempered person.

The Mahant himself is kindly and unassuming, despite his high place in the order, and he was generous with manuscripts and information. After a couple of days I felt I knew him well enough to ask him about the types of lifestyle that are found among Mahanubhavs. There are *sannyāsīs*, I said, who do not marry, and laymen—and what other ways of life are there? He explained that there are also some Mahanubhavs who, although they are married, are called *sannyāsīs* because they have vowed to give up the householder's life when they reach their mid-fifties. The Mahant looked as if he was approaching his mid-fifties himself, but I did not ask his age. From the fact that I met no other householder *sannyāsīs*, I would guess them to be fairly rare, though R. E. Enthoven[10] mentions a type of Mahanubhavs, called *angvaṇshils* or *gharbārīs*, who "put on the dress of the order and live in monasteries," but who "marry by the *gāndharva* or love marriage form."

### *Mahanubhav Practice*

Most Mahanubhavs live as ascetics, and most refuse to take part in the worship of *devatās*. From this it might appear that the Mahanubhavs, intent on liberation, puritanically deprive themselves of all the concrete forms which fill other Maharashtrians' religious lives. In fact, however, Mahanubhavs have no dearth of things to do: ritual worship, pilgrimage places to visit, festivals to celebrate. They relate all of these—the things to which they do *pūjā*, the places they go on pilgrimage, and the festivals they celebrate—to the five human *avatārs* of Parmeshwar.

Of the objects to which Mahanubhavs do *pūjā*, they are careful to state that none of them is Parmeshwar. The objects are, rather, relics of Parmeshwar, reminders of his former presence in one of his *avatārs*. They include things touched by *avatārs* of Parmeshwar, and stones marking places Parmeshwar-*avatārs* visited during the period of their descent on earth.

The relics which are things touched by Parmeshwar *avatārs* are generally portable. These are stones, called *sambandhī pāshāṇs* or *visheshas*, believed to have been touched by one or another of the *avatārs*.[11] The most numerous of these stones seem to be ones touched by Chakradhar or by Krishna—notably those from Mount Govardhan, which the child Krishna is said to have lifted and held on one finger. Often the stones are encased in silver, and some of the larger ones are carved in the shape of Krishna, Chakradhar, or

Dattatreya. Usually several are displayed together in the common shrine of the monastery or the kitchen shrine of a private home, and part of the regular worship service consists in passing the stones among those present, each person rubbing each of the stones between his hands, touching it to his face, and passing it on to the person next to him. Most *sannyāsīs* have a number of these stones, and often a significant part of the wall space allotted to each of the residents of a monastery is taken up by a shrine housing his own *sambandhī pāshāṇ* collection.

It is often carefully pointed out that the *sambandhī pāshāṇs* carved in the shape of Krishna, Dattatreya, or Chakradhar are nothing more than stones—that is, they are not gods, or images containing gods (*mūrtis*). In Phaltan I was told that carved stones are displayed for worship so that the non-Mahanubhav townspeople can understand what is going on. In other places it was suggested that some Mahanubhavs, too, need images to remind them of the forms that have been taken by the Parmeshwar they worship.

Besides *sambandhī pāshāṇs*, the other kind of stone worshipped by Mahanubhavs is a pedestal, called an *oṭā*. These are raised to mark places where an *avatār* of Parmeshwar is remembered to have visited and to have done something or other. What exactly was done is often not clearly remembered, but that something was done here and that it was done by Parmeshwar is confidently believed. *Oṭās* are generally rectangular blocks about three feet high, whitewashed and sparingly decorated with red-lead designs. *Pūjā* is performed to them, *āratīs* are sung and lights waved in front of them, and individuals bow to them, touching them with their foreheads or their hands. Again, Mahanubhavs are careful to make it clear that they do not understand themselves to be worshipping the *oṭā* as a god, or to be worshipping a god present in the *oṭā*, but to be honoring the stone as a marker of the place where a Parmeshwar-*avatār* once did something.

There are also examples of honor being paid to a type of object which shares some of the characteristics of both *sam-*

12. The head of the Mahanubhav monastery at the site of the Ellora cave temples. *Photography by Eleanor Zelliot.*

13. Mahanubhavs bow in worship before an *oṭā*, a stone marking a spot visited by an avatar of the great god Parmeshwar. *Photography by Anne Feldhaus.*

*bandhī pāshāṇs* and *oṭās*. Once, when I was returning from another expedition with a small group of Mahanubhavs, we stopped at a Shiva temple on the outskirts of a small town. Everyone took *darshan* of the Shiva *linga* and touched it in homage. I asked what was going on: why had we stopped here? One member of the party remembered that this was a temple at which Mahanubhavs worship. No one knew the exact story, but all were sure that they were worshipping there not to honor Shiva but to honor a place where Chakradhar had been—had himself, one of them suggested, done *pūjā* to the *linga*.

The existence of *oṭās* and of other objects worshipped in a specific location gives rise to the phenomenon of pilgrimage. There are numerous Mahanubhav pilgrimage places in Maharashtra, all connected with the lives of the Parmeshwar-*avatārs*. In contrast to the Varkaris' pilgrimage places, which are mostly clustered in the part of Maharashtra to the south and west of the Godavari River, Mahanubhav holy places—as shown, for example, on the map entitled *Pañca avatāra caraṇāṅkita Mahārāṣṭrātīla tīrthasthāne* prepared by Mahant Dattaraj Shevalikar[12]—are most numerous along both banks of the Godavari and to the north and east of it, with a thick cluster in Amraoti District. The popular handbook *Sthāna-mārga-darśaka*, also prepared by Mahant Dattaraj Shevalikar,[13] lists and describes briefly 259 Maharashtrian pilgrimage places by District: one in Satara, sixty-five in Ahmednagar, twelve in Nasik, ten in Jalgaon, seventy in Aurangabad, twenty-four in Bhid, twelve in Buldhana, seven in Akola, six in Nanded, forty-six in Amraoti, one in Wardha, three in Nagpur, and two in Bhandara.[14] It also lists eleven Mahanubhav pilgrimage places outside of Maharashtra: Warangal, Broach, Dvarka, Gomati Dvarka, Mathura, Gokul, Govardhan, Vrindavan, Kurukshetra, Badrikashrama, Kashi, and Ujjain.

I have no information about the frequency of pilgrimage among the Mahanubhavs, nor about special practices their pilgrimages may involve. Neither do I have much information about Mahanubhav festivals, though I was told that the principal ones celebrate the birthdays of the five *avatārs*. In 1975, I attended the celebration of Krishna's birthday, Krishnajanmashtami, at the Mahanubhav temple in Ganesh Peth in Pune, and then went on to a celebration in a Brahman household in Narayan Peth. Superficially, at least, the similarities between the two celebrations were greater than the differences. If anything, the chaotic jubilation was more intense at the Mahanubhav temple than in the Brahman home; but then Ganesh Peth is generally more chaotic than Narayan Peth.

This much description should suffice to establish that the Mahanubhavs do not have a purely ascetic religious life. They, too, like other Maharashtrian Hindus, have their festivals and their pilgrimages, as well as concrete objects which they worship. Neither is their religious life completely separate from the popular religion of their fellow Maharashtrians. Besides sharing with the other Hindus of Maharashtra such festivals as Krishna's birthday and such pilgrimage places as Paithan (connected, for most Maharashtrians, with the saint Eknath, but for Mahanubhavs with their founder Chakradhar), as well as an occasional Shiva *linga*, Mahanubhavs also have their own roles in the wider Maharashtrian religious life. They are known in the Maharashtrian countryside as one of the many types of wandering religious mendicants,[15] and their monasteries and temples are frequented by persons seeking to be cured of ghost possession.[16]

If modern-day Mahanubhavs have popular religious practices like those of other Hindus, and if they also have their own place in Maharashtrian popular religion as a whole, then how seriously are they taking their scriptures' devaluation of the religion of *tīrtha-kshetra-vrata-dāna*? Worship of inferior deities they certainly try to avoid; but, having avoided this worship, they then take its forms and apply them to the relics of Parmeshwar's former presence on earth: the things he touched, the places he lived, and his birthdays.

Mahanubhavs claim that the things to which they do

*pūjā* are not *mūrtis*: they do not call their stones gods. But how different, really, is what the Mahanubhavs do from what other Maharashtrian Hindus do? An adequate answer to this question would involve a clear understanding of what Mahanubhavs and other Maharashtrians think about what they do. For example, what exactly do Mahanubhavs think is the relationship between Parmeshwar and his *oṭās* and *sambandhī pāshāṇs*? What exactly do other Hindus think a *mūrti* is? To answer such questions would require a great deal of field- and/or text-work.

### *The Mahanubhavs and Liberation*

Even without additional study, though, I can point out one factor which distinguishes the Mahanubhavs from other Maharashtrian Hindus. The exclusivism of the Mahanubhavs' attention to objects, places, and days of worship connected for them with Parmeshwar contrasts sharply to the eclecticism of most other Maharashtrians. For these, devotion to Khandoba, for instance, will not necessitate avoiding the temples or festivals of Datta, Krishna, or Vithoba; whereas for the Mahanubhavs the worship of things connected with Parmeshwar necessitates—in theory, at least—ignoring all lesser deities.

But Mahanubhavs' exclusive concentration on the worship of things connected with Parmeshwar does not seem to involve an exclusive concentration on liberation. Even when directed to things connected with Parmeshwar, the religion of *tīrtha-kshetra-vrata-dāna* cannot, according to their beliefs, produce liberation. For that, the presence of Parmeshwar himself—not just of something he touched or some place he walked—is necessary. My guess is that Mahanubhavs are very much like other Maharashtrian Hindus in that they rarely, if ever, think of their *pūjās*, their pilgrimages, or their festivals as conducive of liberation.

The two Mahanubhavs who expressed to me the most reflectiveness about liberation and the means to it were also the Mahanubhavs who were most aware of their difference, not just from the rest of Hindu Maharashtra but from other Mahanubhavs. These most reflective Mahanubhavs are not *sannyāsīs*, they are not vegetarians, they do not even call themselves Mahanubhavs, since that term is not used in the *Sūtrapāṭha* of Chakradhar. They are a pair of brothers who live together, with their father and the wife of one of them, in a comfortable bungalow in a Maratha housing colony on the outskirts of Pune. C. K. P.[17] by caste, they feel ill at ease with their Maratha neighbors; I cannot tell whether or not caste differences have anything to do with their alienation from the Maratha-dominated Mahanubhavs. At any rate, they are put off by what they perceive as the complacency and cliquishness of the orthodox Mahanubhav leaders, and they sought me out, late in my stay in India, to get a disinterested opinion on their questions and problems concerning Mahanubhav doctrines.

Their perplexities were intense and their opinions vehement, and much of what they were bothered about I did not understand. But their most pressing question was clear: how do we get liberation? The main problem, as they saw it, is that whereas the *Sūtrapāṭha* teaches that the presence (*sannidhāna*) of an *avatār* of Parmeshwar is necessary for liberation, there has not been an *avatār* of Parmeshwar since the end of the thirteenth century. So what are we in the twentieth century to do?

I suggested all the substitutes I could think of: the words of Parmeshwar's *avatārs*, the places they visited, the things they touched, even the community of their disciples and the life of asceticism taught by Chakradhar. But none of these was enough; it was all irrelevant. The brothers begged me to be on the lookout for the new *avatār*, the one for our times. And to let them know when I find him.

I did not see evidence of similar Messianic longings among other Mahanubhavs I talked with, though these young men's dilemma was based, as nearly as I can tell, on a sound interpretation of Mahanubhav scripture. Perhaps other Mahanubhavs interpret the scriptures differently. Or perhaps they do not really worry about such things. Perhaps for them, as for so many other religious people, the forms of their religion—their worship and even their monastic life—have become, over the centuries, ends in themselves, or, at least, means to things other than liberation.

For the past six or seven centuries, Mahanubhavs[18] have had no place like the Varkaris's Pandharpur, no place where they could go to meet their God. Yet they seldom seem to feel their deprivation.

## NOTES

1. "On the Road: A Maharashtrian Pilgrimage," *Journal of Asian Studies*, 22(1962):13–29. See also the version in this volume, pp. 142-171.

2. I am grateful to the American Institute of Indian Studies for supporting my stay in India during 1974–75, as well as to the scholars and Mahanubhavs who facilitated my work there.

3. See V. B. Kolte, "Mahānubhāva panthāce avaidikatva," *Mahānubhāva saṃśodhana 1* (Malkapur: Arun Prakasan, 1962), 59–76; also A. Feldhaus, "The Mahānubhāvas and Scripture," *Journal of Dharma* (Bangalore), 3.3 (1978): 295-308.

4. For further information about Mahanubhav beliefs, see I.M.P. Raeside, "The Mahānubhāvas," *Bulletin of the School of Oriental and African Studies*, 39(1976): 585–600; and Anne Feldhaus, *The Religious System of the Mahānubhāva Sect: The Mahānubhāva Sūtrapāṭha* (New Delhi:Manohar, and Columbia, Mo.: South Asia Books, 1983): 3–68. An almost contemporary biography of Chakradhar's guru, Gobindaprabhu, has been translated by Anne Feldhaus as *The Deeds of God in Ṛddhipūr* (New York: Oxford University Press, 1984).

5. The *Sūtrapāṭha* is a collection of sayings (sutras) attributed to the Mahanubhavs' founder, Chakradhar. The edition of the *Sūtrapātha* referred to here is that in A. Feldhaus, *Religious System of the Mahānubhāva Sect.*

6. To *devatās*, not to Parmeshwar.

7. 12 (Ācāra).25: *mātāpūrā kolhāpūrā na vacāveṃ. teṃ sābhimāniem sthāneṃ sādhakāsi vīghna karīti.* "Do not go to Matapur [i.e., Mahur] or Kolhapur. Those proud places create obstacles for those practicing religion."

8. The ambiguity about Mahur dates back to the early period of Mahanubhav literature, for, counter to Chakradhar's prohibition, is Govindaprabhu's reversal of it in *Govindaprabhucaritra* 322: *āvo melā mātāpurāsi jāe mhaṇe*, rendered delightfully by Raeside: "Damn it all, why don't you go to Mahur!" ("The Mahānubhāvas," 594).

9. The Mahanubhav emphasis on *ahimsā* is such that even lay families strain their water; all are strict vegetarians.

10. *The Tribes and Castes of Bombay* (Bombay: Government Central Press, 1922), vol. 2:430. The information for the article on "Manbhavs" was obtained from R.D. Bhandarkar.

11. I do not remember seeing other sorts of relics—clothes, for example—but the Mahanubhav text *Prasādasevā* lists many such relics; and Dr. S.G. Tulpule tells me he has been shown a fingernail worshipped as Govindaprabhu's.

12. Pune: Chitrashala Press, 1973.

13. Ghogargaon, Ahmednagar Dist., 1970.

14. The large number of pilgrimage places listed in Ahmednagar and Aurangabad Districts is to be accounted for by the fact that the Godavari River, the site of most of Chakradhar's activity, runs between these two districts; the large number in Amraoti District is explained by the location in that district of Riddhipur (Ritpur), the thirteenth-century residence of Govindaprabhu.

15. They were known, for example, in the village in Satara District which Lee Schlesinger studied in 1975–76.

16. See John Stanley's article in the present volume, pp. 26–59.

17. Candraseniya Kayastha Prabhu, a caste which considers itself to be Kshatriya. They are generally ranked above the Marathas and just below Brahmans.

18. It is impossible to find an accurate count of those who consider themselves Mahanubhavs, since they are counted among the Hindus in the Census. R.E. Enthoven in *The Tribes and Castes of Bombay*, 3 vols. (Bombay: Government Central Press, 1920–22) estimated their number as 22,000. A figure of 100,000 to 200,000 today seems likely, although the numbers at pilgrimage places and one's subjective impressions indicate more.

# 19
# *The Birth of a Rationalist*

## Editors' Introduction

K.N. Kadam, now a retired government official, writes here of his childhood faith, including the many diverse intertwined Hindu-Muslim practices which marked the religion of the lower classes fifty years ago. Born a Mahar Untouchable, Kadam has now become a Buddhist. His story is drawn from a collection of essays he wrote for private circulation entitled "Buddhism as Rationalism and Humanism," and indeed in later essays Kadam finds only the purest and earliest Buddhism to be without irrational or mystical overtones. Although his questioning of Hinduism and of religion in general seems to have come in his childhood chiefly on other grounds, his later experiences as an Untouchable reinforced his complete disavowal of all Hinduism. We have not included these passages from Kadam's writing here since, as it stands, Kadam's experiences as a child tell us much about religion in Pune in general in his day. And his entrance into the world of rationalism was a process not confined to Untouchables, but shared by a number of high-caste intellectuals in Maharashtra. The atheist strain is not out of place in a volume which is concerned with the reality of the religious scene in Maharashtra. Nor is the mention of the widespread conversion to Buddhism among Untouchables, a phenomenon with an impact on both the converts and on Hinduism itself. (*E. Z. and M. B.*)

### *The God-Fearing Boy*

It was in 1939, when I was about nineteen years old, that questions relating to the existence of God, gods and goddesses, ghosts and other supernatural beings, began to vex my mind. I have not always been the atheist and irreligious skeptic that I am today. There was, in fact, a time in my life when it could be said that I was a god-fearing boy and practiced with devotion the religion in which I had been brought up. That was the state of my mind almost until I ceased to be a schoolboy.

I was born into a family which shared the beliefs and superstitions of the benighted Mahar community. My grandfather, who had died a little while before my birth, was a simple and kind old man. My grandmother was a dominating woman. And perhaps precisely because she herself lived in the fear of her gods and goddesses, she demanded the same adoration and awe from her daughters-in-law and other junior members in the family. She performed, of course, with scrupulous care the religious duties enjoined upon her by the Hindu religion. She observed the fasts and the feasts; she and the rest of the family used to go on pilgrimage to Jejuri, Pandharpur, and Tuljapur, and on one occasion the family had even been to far-off Kashi. My grandmother used to offer sacrifices of sheep, goats, and fowls to the deities in fulfillment of the promises and vows made to them by her. The *jāwaḷ* (the first haircutting ceremony of a newly-born in the family) invariably required a sheep or a goat to be sacrificed to the family deity. I remember, as a child, shuddering at the sight of the poor creatures slaughtered in the courtyard, and I ran away tremblingly from the scene of horror to watch the awesome proceedings from behind partially closed doors. Incidentally, I believe this is one of the reasons why I am a vegetarian today.

My uncle was a devout, honest, and god-fearing man. He was interminably praying to the gods, so it seemed to me. He used to pray before meals and after meals. As he was about to set out to his office, he would stand for eternity, it seemed, before the picture of Vitthal and Rakhumai, and offer his silent prayers, gesticulating gently with both his hands, while his lips moved as if articulating inaudibly the prayers he offered. As a child, I used to watch him during his prayers and could almost hear his communication with the deities.

From the infant class up to my matriculation examination, I attended a Jesuit missionary school, with its regular prayer hours, and its transparently religious atmosphere. It is therefore evident that both at home and at school, I was steeped to the gills in religion.

Breathing as I was the religious atmosphere wherever I went, it was, I think, but natural that I should also become religious. It would, I suppose, be unnatural if I did not become so, while the strong religious influences lasted. In my early years, I had taken it upon myself to perform certain religious rituals. At regular intervals, and as occasion demanded, I used to worship with devotion the family deities. Before the *pūjā*, I would reverently collect all the household deities and other religious articles in a large copper dish, and scrub them all with ash from the family hearth. Then I washed the gods till they shone brightly. I washed the little pieces of colored cloth on which the deities reposed, after their divine bath, in the sacred corner assigned to them. Then I applied to them the yellow turmeric and the red *kunkū* powders, offered them fresh flowers, lighted a piece or two of camphor, tinkled the little brass bell long and loud, then joined my hands and offered my prayers. I do not now remember precisely the contents of the prayers, but I believe they must have been chiefly to win the deities over to my side in arithmetic, my worst enemy at school. The deities, however, appear to have ignored my prayers, and I continued to do as badly as ever in the subject. In these early religious practices, I think I must have unconsciously imitated my uncle, hoping one day to outdo him in piety.

My family used to worship not only Hindu gods, but Muslim "gods" as well. (May Allah forgive me my blasphemy!) There was a big effigy of a white horse in the city of Pune. It was called the Ghode-Pir, or "Horse-Saint." My grandmother appears to have made a vow to the Ghode-Pir before I was born, in her anxiety to have a grandson. And she appears to have vowed in all solemnity that if a male grandchild were born, she would make him a fakir at the feet of the Horse-Saint every Muharram;[1] he would wear the sacred shailies (a fakir's braided cloth). In response to her prayers, and by the grace of the Ghode-Pir, I was born a male child. And so for several years, until I was about eight years old, if I remember right, I used to accompany my grandmother to the Ghode-Pir every Muharram, and don the shailies and become a fakir for the day. I should thank my grandmother she did not vow to turn me into a "Muharram-Tiger," or else I would have had the black and yellow stripes painted on my body, and performed the weird dance of the "Muharram-Tiger," to the wild beat of a drum!

Again, while my family was living in Bhawani Peth, one of our houses was said to have been the haunt of a *pīr*, a Muslim saint, long dead and gone, but supposed to be still haunting the place. He must have been, however, a benevolent soul, and all that his spirit expected of the occupants of the place was an act of simple worship, a few fresh flowers, some incense burnt at a specific spot, and some sweets offered to him on Thursdays. I volunteered to take upon myself to officiate as the little high-priest to the ancient *pīr*. Every Thursday, without fail, I used to go to the market and buy flowers, incense, and sweets for the ancient *pīr*. In the evenings on Thursdays, I used to gather my younger brothers and sisters, clean the "sacred" spot in the rear

14. (L) The horse-saint (*ghoḍe-pīr*) of Pune described in K. M. Kadam's childhood memories. The proprietor of the Ghode-pir (and the colt, which Kadam does not describe) is a Hindu, the *pujārī* a Muslim. *Photography by Eleanor Zelliot.*

15. (R) The *samādhī* of Cokhamela, the Mahar Untouchable devotee of Vithoba, at the foot of the great temple in Pandharpur. *Photography by S. Y. Waghmare.*

verandah of the house, and perform the *pūjā*. We used to enjoy the weekly ritual, because after leaving some five *batāsās* or *rewaḍīs* for the *pīr*, we used to distribute the remaining sweets amongst ourselves and the other members of the family who would respectfully accept the *prasād* from us.

I used to accompany my grandmother on pilgrimages. I remember the places we visited on such occasions. Jejuri, Pandharpur, and Chaturshringi in Pune are those I remember best. At Pandharpur, I recollect we had no access into the temple of Vithoba, on account of the sacred Hindu cult of untouchability. We had to rest content at the shrine of Chokhoba, the Mahar saint, outside the main temple of Vithoba. Of course, we sent our offerings of flowers, and coconuts and the priests' fee, laying these articles on the doorstep of the temple for the agent of the priests to pick up and take away. This was one of my earliest experiences of untouchability, as far as I can recollect. I had similar experiences when I accompanied my uncle to the Maruti temple every Saturday, and when I accompanied my elders to the Chaturshringi temple on the outskirts of Pune.

I remember I had once been to the Chaturshringi temple accompanying my relatives, among whom was my father's maternal uncle, a devotee of the goddess. He came down each year from Bombay and stayed with us during the Navratra or Nine-Night Festival. On this particular occasion, my elders selected a spot under a shady tree, at the foot of the Chaturshringi hill. I cannot now recall all the religious proceedings that were taking place in our midst. But all of a sudden, I noticed my father's maternal uncle in wild ecstatic convulsions. I discerned he was "possessed" by the goddess Chaturshringi. I must have held my breath, and stared at him in awe. Soon he picked up the fowl he had brought there with him, and with a shout of "Jai Chaturshringi!" (victory to the goddess Chaturshringi), he caught the living cock's leg between his teeth, and tore the poor bird in two. Jai Chaturshringi! indeed. Needless to say I was extremely horrified at the spectacle of wanton cruelty, though it may have been sanctified by religion. My childish mind did not approve of these disgusting proceedings, and I have avoided going on such pilgrimages, as far as possible, ever since.

The Mahars of the locality where I was born used to worship another goddess named Mariai. The little shrine of the goddess still stands in Synagogue Street. It was then believed that this goddess had to be appeased to prevent the outburst of the dread diseases of smallpox and the plague. Once when I was at school, during the rainy season, it was decided by the women of the community to take out a procession to the Sangam, the sacred confluence of the Mula and the Mutha rivers, after worshipping at the shrine of the goddess Mariai. I joined the procession, and off we started, led by a colorful but awesome *potrāj*,[2] in his quaint costume, dancing to the wild beat of a rustic drum. At the Sangam, there were some religious proceedings, and *pūjā* in which apparently I did not take much interest. But during the holy proceedings, the *potrāj*, "possessed" by the goddess, went into what may be called a trance. And while in that "blessed" state, what the *potrāj* uttered was supposed to be the voice of the goddess herself. Thus spake the goddess through the *potrāj*: "I am very angry, because people are neglecting my worship. And that is why I have let loose the disease of smallpox, to remind you of your duties to me." Thereupon, a woman devotee asked the goddess prayerfully, "O goddess! What should we do to appease you, and mitigate your terrible anger?" To which the goddess replied through the medium of the *potrāj*: "Listen. I want a young unmarried boy from among you to bathe me every day, for a certain number of days." (I forget the exact number.) "The boy should have his bath and bathe me with wet clothes on.... Is there any boy willing to do it?" Someone asked me whether I would volunteer to obey the deity's behest, and I agreed. After all, I must have thought, I must do something for my gods, my religion, and my people! I remember I did keep my word, and I would have my daily bath with my clothes on and walk, with wet clothes on, right from Bhawani Peth to Synagogue Street (a distance of about a mile-and-a-half), with a pot of water in my hand, to bathe the terrible goddess. I do not know for how many days I underwent this ordeal, but I think I must have fulfilled my vow. And Pune owes it to me, if the dread diseases of smallpox and the plague have since been averted!

At school, I was under the influence of the Jesuit fathers and Roman Catholic teachers. Although non-Catholic boys were not made to sit for Catechism lessons, we had our moral lesson classes. We were taught to believe in God as the Creator of the universe, and we were instructed in our duties and moral responsibilities to Him. We were taught the value of prayer; and we had to learn simple prayers like "Our Father Who art in Heaven," "Grace before Meals," "Grace after Meals," the prayer on waking up in the morning, and the prayer before going to bed at night. I think I must have taken all those prayers very seriously. I never went to sleep without saying my prayer, and if I did at times fall asleep without offering it, I would awake suddenly in the middle of the night, sit up and say the prayer, and then lie down again to sleep.

### *The Development of Doubt*

From the foregoing paragraphs, it would appear that I was well-launched on the way to spirituality and sainthood. I shall now proceed to tell you the story of my "downfall," and how I lost my faith in God and religion.

It is difficult to give a precise date on which I lost my faith in God and religion, for in the nature of things, a precise date perhaps cannot be. Transition from one state to another, especially when it involves ideas and beliefs, is a process, a gradual process. But I recollect certain incidents in my early childhood that help show the direction in which the wind was blowing. The first incident relates to the day when my cousin (the only son of his mother) died in the prime of his youth, leaving behind his widowed mother, his wife, and two daughters. It was a sad blow to my family, too. I remember my pious uncle's reaction on the occasion. In that moment of intense affliction, he rushed to the wall, and gave a blow to the picture of Vitthal-Rukmini hanging on it. Perhaps that very blow must have also smashed the image of God in my mind.

In my early childhood, I must have compared the crude religion of the family with the more sophisticated religion of the Christians. One of my uncles had been converted to Christianity. I could not have failed to observe how he was freed from the shackles of untouchability on his conversion to Christianity. At the same time, I was viewing with skepticism the attitude of the Catholic priests who taught me at school. I wondered why they ridiculed Darwin and science. To me, it seemed so obvious that man was descended from the monkey, and there was no point in trying to disown our ancestors!

During my school days, I was a "devout" boy scout. I still have profound respect for the Scout movement, for the discipline it inculcates in young boys and girls, and for the "religion" of youth that it gives to youth. However, back to my story: I remember the occasion when I was returning from the Scout Jamboree at Delhi, in 1937. On the way our scout troop halted a while at Nasik for a dip in the holy Godavari. Everybody, except I, "cleansed" body and soul in the sacred river. But I feigned indisposition, and my scoutmaster, who incidentally was a medical man, did not press me to take the holy bath.

While speaking about scouting, I must make some observations about the Scout Oath. As a boy scout, in those days, one had to take the following oath: "On my word of honor, I promise to do my duty to God, King, and Country, etc." All went well, and I was a good scout until towards the end of my school career, when I told my scout-master that I could not bring myself to continue to take the Scout Oath. For apart from my hesitation to voice my allegiance to the King, I objected to the portion relating to the Almighty God Himself, having by then completely lost my faith in Him. So unless the Scout Oath and the relevant

Scout regulations were amended, I could not consent to continue as a scout.

While at college, especially in philosophy class, I must have been a source of continual annoyance to my professors, whenever God happened to be discussed. I would not concede to God the position of Prime Mover, or even the position of the Principle underlying the phenomenon of cosmic existence. I would always attempt to ridicule the deist argument, saying that "the Venerable Old Man with His inordinate lust for power and propitiation has now, after all, dwindled down to a dubious principle."

Thinkers and writers like Dr. B.R. Ambedkar and Bertrand Russell had quite a devastating impact on my mind, while I was still at college. Dr. Ambedkar's *Annihilation of Caste* was the first of his books that I read with care. Though Hindu caste still survives, Dr. Ambedkar's book annihilated completely my faith in Hinduism. Of Russell's books, it was his *Marriage and Morals* that I read first. It was followed by his *The Scientific Outlook*, *Skeptical Essays*, *Problems of Philosophy*, and *What I Believe*. Descartes and Russell taught me the philosophy of doubt. "Is there any knowledge in the world which is so certain that no reasonable man could doubt it?" asks Russell at the very outset, in his *Problems of Philosophy*. In his *Skeptical Essays*, he advocates the doctrine of doubt, and says that "it is undesirable to believe a proposition when there is no ground whatever for supposing it to be true." His *Marriage and Morals* blasted the traditional ideas about sex and marriage that were then taking root in my mind.

Other books like Grant Allen's *The Evolution of the Idea of God* and Joseph McCabe's *The Existence of God* helped destroy my beliefs in God and gods. And Charles T. Gorham's *Religion as a Bar to Progress* persuaded me to put all religions into the dock. Such then was the impact of my contact with the master minds that I came across in the world of books.

Such then in outline (as if in a capsule) is the story of the mental processes that helped shape and define my outlook on the subject. Such are the glimpses I get into my past, as I look inward and stir my memories. These experiences and memories are as real to me as the table at which I am presently sitting. They are an integral part of me; they have made me what I am. I cannot obliterate them, I cannot wipe them out of my mind, from my existence.

## EDITORS' NOTES

1. Muharram, the first ten days of the first month of the Muslim year, is associated with the memory of the martyred Husain, grandson of the Prophet, killed in battle at Karbala. The Shi'ia community observes this in various ways, some solemn and silent, some dramatic. See *Fairs and Festivals in Maharashtra*, Census of India, 1961, vol. 10, Maharashtra, Part 7-B (Delhi: Managers of Publications, 1969), pp. 38–39, for a description of Muharram as it is observed in Maharashtra.

2. The *potrāj* is the servant of the goddess of epidemic, Mariai. Until the conversion of the majority of the Mahar Untouchable caste to Buddhism in 1956 and after, the *potrāj* was almost invariably a Mahar.

# 20
# *Scattered Voices: Refuge in the Buddha*

## Editors' Introduction

One of the most dramatic rejections of Hinduism was the mass conversion to Buddhism initiated by Dr. B.R. (Babasaheb) Ambedkar in 1956. There are now almost four million Buddhists in India, the majority of them converts from the Untouchable caste of Mahars in Maharashtra, but others from urban areas throughout India. The way in which the conversion is seen by two middle-aged women, educated up to the seventh grade and the fifth grade respectively, indicates the depth of conviction which many of the former Untouchables feel as well as the way in which Buddhist doctrine is interpreted by the unsophisticated.

The following statements are drawn from an interview conducted by Maxine Berntsen, in which Bebi Kamble and Ulpabai Chauhan first discuss the story of the fourteenth-century bhakta and saint-poet Chokhamela, who came from their own caste, and then tell the story of the Buddha in such a way that one can feel the power of the oral tradition used in a modern cause. (*E. Z. and M. B.*)

### *Refuge in the Buddha*

There was a Mahar couple in a village who had no children. They were devotees of Vitthal and every day did *pūjā* to him. One day the woman was walking down the road. She met a sadhu and touched his feet. "Woman, what do you want?" he asked. "We are content with what we have," she said, "but we don't have a child." So he placed a mango in the *padar* of her sari and the woman went home. A son was born from that mango and they named him Chokha.

The boy grew up and about the time he was nineteen or twenty there was an Asura, a kind of demon, who caused the nectar of the gods to spoil. The gods began arguing among themselves about who could purify the nectar. They couldn't do it themselves. Then the sage Narada said that there was only one person on earth who could purify the nectar, a boy in the Maharwada named Chokha. He was born without the intercourse of his father and mother and so was pure (*ċokh*) as his name implies, and he could purify the nectar. Chokha did purify it and so was called Chokhamela. He was a member of our community.

Now we feel—before we didn't—that nobody can be born from a mango. That much is definite. And we don't put any faith in this story. There probably was a saintly man named Chokha and he probably did good works. But he wasn't born from a mango, and we don't believe that he was taken up to heaven where he purified the gods' nectar. There's no point to the story. The Brahmans probably covered up the real facts.

Buddha came from a kingly family. He was the king's son. Then why did he take up this new dharma? Do you know where he spent all his time? In the house. He never felt the scorching sun outside. He didn't know the wind or the birds or the animals. He didn't know all the troubles and difficulties of men. He would sit on his throne and say,

"Since I am happy the whole world must be happy." One day he asked his father, "Baba, may I go out for a walk?" His father said, "No, don't go. A guru told me not to let you go out for twelve more years, so don't go." But without telling his father the prince went out.

He went in a tonga with his servant. Just after they had left the house they saw a corpse. "What is that?" the prince asked.

"A man has died."

"Do men die? What does *die* mean?"

So the servant explained, "Now here are you and me. We've been born, we've grown up, we're alive. Now you are nineteen or twenty. Soon you'll be forty, then fifty. Your hair will all turn gray, you'll get tired, you'll sit wasting away. Finally you'll die and people will carry you away and bury you. That's how it is in the world."

That was the first thing he learned. The tonga went on. They met a leper. The prince asked his servant what had happened to the man. The servant answered, "It's a kind of disease. It could happen to you or to me. God sent this sickness to him and he could send it to us. That's the way the world is. The whole world is rotting." That shocked the prince.

They went forward a third time, and saw an old man with a bent back. The prince asked, "What is this?"

"When we get old, when we get past forty, sometime before we're eighty, we get bent like this. Our hair becomes gray. All of these things are bad."

The prince had never seen any of these things. He went back to his house, to his lovely wife and his son Rahul. All day long he sat thinking, and at midnight he took leave of his wife and his son and went into the forest. There he remained, doing *tapashcharyā* all night, but he didn't find God. He did this according to Hindu dharma, mind you. He did *tapashcharyā* but he didn't see God. So what did he do next? He fasted until he was skin and bones and ready to die. Then some passers-by came, gave him some milk, and brought him back to consciousness. So he decided that one cannot find God by fasting. Then he went down by the river and sat under a banyan tree. He sat meditating on the world and the mind. Nobody has seen the gods so why do people say that they exist?

After meditating on all this he wrote his thoughts down. He wrote that men—we ourselves—are God. There is no God in the world and nobody should put any hope in him. Nobody should feel that if he fasts or does such things he will see God. A man should honestly follow his own path. The *ātmā* is God. As for us, *sangham saraṇam gacchāmi*—I go for refuge to the *sangha*. That is what the Buddha taught. Be a friend to all and never hope in what we cannot see.

Nobody pays Chokhamela any respect nowadays. Not at all. But Babasheb Ambedkar is always before us. The things he has done are written on our hearts. He was born a Mahar but didn't die a Mahar, mind you. We don't believe what anybody else has said about our community and our dharma the way we believe what he has said.

The Mahars used to worship all the Hindu gods. They worshipped and served them all, but they never got any good out of it. They would do *bhajans* to Vitthal. They would just barely get along on what little they had, and they would spend their time doing *bhajans*. They would even beg from others, saying "Vitthal Vitthal" all day long. That was their culture. It did them no good. They didn't even try to spread it to others.

Now we know the way. *Buddham saraṇam gacchāmi*—I go for refuge to the Buddha. *Sangham saraṇam gacchāmi*—I go for refuge to the *sangha*. *Dhammam saraṇam gacchāmi*—I go for refuge to the *dhamma*. This at last is the way.

*—Bebi Kamble and Ulpabai Chauhan*
*Translated by Maxine Berntsen*

# *IV.*

# *CODA*

ASHOK R. KELKAR AND SADASHIV S. BHAVE

# 21

# *Bhakti in the Modern Mode: Poems and Essays*

## Editors' Introduction

A selection of seventeen poems by twelve contemporary Marathi poets, chosen by S.S. Bhave and translated and annotated by A.R. Kelkar, is presented first, so that the reader may deal directly with the poetry. This selection is followed by an essay by Bhave, linking the poems to age-old Hindu ideas. A response by Kelkar challenges some of Bhave's statements and widens the perspective to one which goes beyond Indian/Hindu poetry. Bhave, with his stress on the strength of tradition, has the last word. The result of this "coda" is not only the presentation of traditional Hindu ideas in modern Marathi poetry but also insight into the differing attitudes and interests of two contemporary Maharashtrian intellectuals.

Although Kelkar and Bhave originally prepared "Bhakti in the Modern Mode" for this volume, we gave permission for slightly different versions of it to appear in *Vagartha* 21, (1978):13–39, and in the *South Asian Digest of Regional Writing* 6 (1977):3–28. Bhave's death on October 5, 1986, as this volume was being edited has unfortunately brought an end to Kelkar and Bhave's dialogue. (*E. Z. and M. B.*)

## *The Poems*

### B.S. Mardhekar[1]
### *Let the Hardness in Me Break*[2]

Let the hardness in me break,
Let the sourness clear from my mind,
And let my voice sing
The notes of my love for you.

Let the taint in my known
Intention clear; and
Cast your seeds in the unknown
Font of my inspiration.

Let my freedom extend
Only to speaking forth,
Let the letters intone the shape[3]
Sent forth by your lungs.

Let the greed of my tongue burn,
Let all hatred freeze, and
Let the quality of Draupadi herself[4]
Grace the body of my speech.

Let the me-centered meanness vanish,
Let all into my embrace,
Let my feeling rival the test
Of the precision balance.

Let my ambition vaunt of
The pillars of your virtue,[5]
Let my ambition throb to
The beats spoken by your heart.

Let my hands feel for and grasp
The rudder of your remembrance,
Let great patience pervade my temper
Readying itself for the great effort.

I swear by the desire for you,
I swear by the devoid of luck,
I swear by my eyes
To keep my eyelids in vigil.

Grant me the courage, the humility
To see all that I must,
Let my intellect bend
Like heated steel,

And take through the senses
The impact of the world,
And burn to the core for that
Which lies beyond the senses.

You are the master of meaning:
This beggar is but the bearer of the word.
The asking knows no end
And the giver is the Lord.

But what possibly can I ask for?
What possibly can you give?
In a world where you alone are the giver
And you yourself the taker!

### *When the Heart Fills to the Brim*[6]

When the heart fills to the brim
And sweat is wrung from the body
When words take the bit—thy bit,
Which digs firmly into their flesh,

Then may this sinful hand
Work some white on black—
Only then! Else, the selfsame
Black writ on white!

### *If Only Thy Stone-still Brow*[7]

Have I not hurled names at thee? Even so
I come prostrate to thy feet,
Head laid low I look thee
In the eyes, letting my eyes scald.

When was the earth born? And
When did the blue fumes jell
Over massively?
When did this stillness
Quicken with mind joined to mind?

As a blue champak might bloom
Out of a blue conduit of fire

So bloomed a bed of sensings
And feelings from the joined consciousness—
But when?
What is discernible
Across the fire?
Or who, rather?
This hapless one sears his
Feckless feet over the coals.

Why the distress? Will the sky ever
Be laid low? I'll live on, afire,
If only they stone-still brow
Stir before my eyes the least little!

Have I not hurled names at thee? Even so
I come prostrate to thy feet,
Head laid low I look thee
In the eyes, letting my eyes scald.

B. B. Borkar[8]

## *From across Five Red Hibiscus Flowers*[9]

From across five red hibiscus flowers
Death greeted me: Aren't they
Dainty? And luscious? I mean
These cups I've filled among these trees.

The wounds of Jesus came to my mind[10]
Sweet honey welling up from them:
A moment saw my mind thrilled
To see the Cross drenched in fragrance and nectar.

## *Just Back from Mother's Home to Find*[11]

Just back from Mother's home to find
My home washed away
And my man gone I dunno where
Any my belongings mud
And my children gone their separate ways.
The line's all open leaving
Me out on a limb, a lightning tree
Scaling the endless sky.
No home here or there: but their caresses
I now hug in the air.

### Sharadchandra Muktibodh[12]
### *No Yearnings*[13]

No yearnings
And no regrets,
Under the blue sky
Laughs the quiet sea.

Storms gather.
Strange to relate,
Storms are led away
Bowing silently.

Roses in bunches,
Rosebuds growing,
Sprinkling joy
The evening retires.

No yearnings
And no regrets.
Now abides in me
Your boundless glory.

### P.S. Rege[14]
### *Hari on the Lips Spends the Night*[15]

Hari on the lips
Spends the night
The selfsame Hari
The name is Hari
    Hari Hari
Wooing this maid of the forest[16]
The livelong night, saying Hari.

Light in the heart
The livelong night
Light of the heart
Who else? The same Hari
    Hari Hari
This flowering maid of the forest[17]
The livelong night, the flame in the heart.

Light of the limbs
The livelong night
Hari's the night
Hari's the limbs
    Hari Hari

Blooming Radha, maid of the forest
The livelong night, limb by limb.

Kusumagraj[18]

*An Earth House*[19]

An earth house this, but it's yours
Make it bright and strong and fair!

To this day I felt it was mine
Under the blind sway of self,
I stood guard at the doors
Bolting me in from surrender!

In my heart of hearts I now see
I am but of your retinue,
The riches of life within
Are but a shaft of your glory!

The glory that fills the stars
And lights up night and day
And brings life to this earth—
A speck of which lights me indoors!

What blooms in the flowers, thunders from the clouds,
Flows down the river, blows in the winds—
That same being of yours abides here,
No house of mine, it's but your temple!

Not here either grandeur or splendour:
Your throne stands within all the same,
Tarry here a moment, call it your own
To let songs bloom songs over the void within!

In this dark recess for a moment
Light up the pure flame,
Light up the walk that'll bear
Your shadow as long as they stand!

Arati Prabhu[20]

*The Travelling Bed*[21]

For god's sake pull
The covers over my legs,
And don't you, Lord, let
Vultures feast on this life
Cowering in your hands.

The moments writ to my account
Hunger for the water of mercy,
The quilt, Lord, is held
Together by seams threaded
With my nerves.
The blood of Jatayu[22]
Is treasured by some lone vein,
Which in this tangled skein
Refuses to get lost—
It will give pain.
Snuff out these cupped hands
And make a clean sweep,
Maybe then some time, Lord,
I'll quit the travelling bed
To be on my way.

Dilip Purushottam Chitre[23]

*Down the Paths of Lightning*[24]

1. Down the paths of lightning tumble the moments
   free,
   Through the darkness plunges the arrow unknown.
   Let one come to your house down the paths of
   lightning[25]
   At the precise moment when cosmic knowledge
   strikes.
   The heartbeats hammer away at themselves,
   So the lifebreaths escape into the storm.
   Let one come to your house seeing it all,
   Shedding the burden of a mind.
2. Let one come to your house down the paths of
   lightning
   That are seen for a moment from the darkness.
   It's not for the feeble voice to sustain the notes
   In octaves past the spheres of the compass.
   Let one rather come to your house wreathed in
   rivulets,
   Lapsing into dust the while.
   When all streams of melody are lost,
   It's not for anyone to bear the pity of it.
   Let one come to your house on the crest of the

melody
Battering the doors of desire.
Let the spirit expend itself in a burst of surrender
And the cosmic knot come undone.

3. Down the paths of lightning tumble the moments
free,
Through the darkness plunges the arrow unknown.
Rapt in the driving patter of melodic feet
And burnt up in the enveloping moistness is
my mind.
Let one come to your house down a different path
Stricken by a different malaise
. . . Across the sands the cloud-shade-water
To the brim ablaze, the fire within.

Grace[26]

*Fragrance of Snow*[27]

Don't measure my steps
Along the path of deliverance:
The doors of the Cosmic Ovum
Have closed.

My tears sprout
The fragrance of snow—
Dammed on either side
By the eyelids.

N.D. Mahanor[28]

*Life Begins in Sorrow, Fills with Sorrow*[29]

Live begins in sorrow, fills with sorrow,
Sorrow may stay to the end for aught I know and care.
The whole body burns on the pyre to see the others
through.
The near and dear ones too keep their distance.
Even gathering rosebuds turns out to be a chore
With life's burden weighing you down—
With the eyes shutting the darkness in.
Then my farmland—[30]
Where the trees spread me a bed of roses.

### Vasant Sawant[31]

### *Thou Art the Retreat*[32]

Thou art the retreat,
I am the wilderness,
Send me the
Flower-wafting wind.

Not the thorns,
Send the bud.
Not the words
But are charged anew.

From afar
(O so far)
I begin to see
The city of Pandharpur.[33]

### *Fear Touches Not My Mind*[34]

My mind ever
Longs for sandalwood[35]
Whose grace
Happiness or sorrow
Never disturbs.

This longing
Is but a trance,
Transcendent its rhythm;
There fear touches not
My mind.

### *He's the One*[36]

He whom I walk around and who walks around with
me,
He's the one that walks men around.
The roads don't matter,
Each one has his own pace, treads his own soil.
The words on their lips may be of Krishna, Buddha,
Christ
Or Tukaram—
He's the One they're about.
Those who bring down the wall, build up the wall
Be it in Berlin or in China.
In the end it is the word alone that lives,

That goes for me too: only when I write a poem,
Then alone am I truly living.

Padma[37]

*You See I Am Not around Here These Days*[38]

You see I am not around here these days
Though I do drop in once in a while—
Well, of course, I have my folks
Though I must say I find it difficult to keep track of things
You see I am not around here these days—
Where do I live? You ask
As if you don't know!
Well, it's possible you don't
Nobody visits that town—
A house? Certainly
So big, so big—the house hasn't got any walls.
Ceiling? Yes, the ceiling of it is and isn't
And a threshold of the same sort.
A river crosses the threshold
In the river play moon and starlets.
Me? You must have seen the flowers discarded after *pūjā*
Floating at the water's edge—I'm among them somewhere
In them—well, and in the fresh dreams of the flowers.
Of course I have company
(What d'you call him—sure, he has a name
But it escapes me)
The silk thread is giving way slowly—
It has been digging
Around the throat, which is just finding its freedom.
The song has come up to my lips—shall I?
The song of the time when the Katyayani Vrata was performed in the Yamuna:[39]
The robes have long been draping the *kadamba* branches
Like the *antarpāṭ—sāvadhān*![40]
I'm turned into the blue song
Flowing down the blue river—along with the discarded flowers.

I am not around here these days
Though I do drop in once in a while.

Arun Kolatkar[41]

*At the Holy Sepulchre of Shri Dnyaneshwar*[42]

Clear blue void of the sky
Narada, Tumbara, the clouds scattered
Gone is the halo brought on by the Gandharvas[43]
The moonchild plays by himself
Scattered is the devout Vaishnava throng
The fever of the drum has ebbed away
The *vīṇā* strings stand still, as do the cymbals
The cowherds are back in their homes
The wreath stays, the petal withers
Entangled is the rib in the withered skein.[44]

## NOTES

1. Bal Sitaram Mardhekar (1909–56) was a poet, critic, and literary theorist who also wrote novels and operettas.
2. From *Āṇkhī kāhī kavitā* (Bombay: Mauj, 1951):3–5.
3. "Intone the shape": the original word is *ākār* "shape," whose other sense, "the vowel aa, often used by singers to sustain a note," is also relevant here.
4. "Draupadi": the wife shared by the Pandavas who won the Mahabharata war; in a famous episode Dushshasan tries to disrobe her, but Krishna covers her nakedness in answer to her prayer; she is fiery in speech and purpose (in consonance with her birth from the sacrificial fire).
5. "Virtue": the original word *tap* (Sanskrit *tapas*) means power, especially power accrued through single-minded austerities: the element of penance or self-mortification may or may not be present.
6. From *Āṇkhī kāhī kavitā*:1.
7. From *Maṛdhekarāncī kavitā* (Bombay: Mauj, 1959):160–61.
8. Balkrishna Bhagavant Borkar (1910–84) was a poet and speaker. He also wrote personal essays and a novel. He wrote both in Marathi and his native Konkani and translated from English.
9. From *Caitrapunav* (Bombay: Mauj, 1970):84.
10. It will be recalled that the stigmata marking Jesus' wounds were five in number.
11. From *Caitrapunav*, 1970:17.

12. Sharadchandra Madhav Muktibodh (1921–85) was a poet, novelist, and Marxist critic; he was the younger brother of Gajanan Madhav Muktibodh, who wrote poetry in Hindi.

13. From *Yātrik*, 1957:134.

14. Purushottam Shivram Rege (1910–78) was a poet, novelist, short story writer, literary theorist, playwright, and economist.

15. From *Priyāḷ* (Bombay: Mauj, 1972):73.

16. "Maid": the original word *gaurī* means "the fair-skinned maid," also an epithet of the mother goddess.

17. "Flowering": the original word *phulavit* refers to the flowering of a bud as well as the growth of a flame.

18. Kusumagraj (Vishnu Waman Shirwadkar, b. 1912) is a poet, playwright, novelist, and speaker.

19. From *Kinārā* (Pune: Deshmukh, 1952):75.

20. Arati Prabhu (Chintamani Tryambak Khanolkar, 1930–76) was a poet and song writer, a novelist, short story writer, and playwright.

21. From *Jogavā* (Bombay: Mauj, 1959):39.

22. "Jatayu": the vulture in the *Rāmāyaṇa* that fights courageously by himself for Rama against Ravana.

23. Dilip Purushottam Chitre (b. 1939) is a poet, translator of poetry from and into Marathi, critic and commentator, dramatist, filmmaker, and writer of short stories and literary travelogues.

24. From *Kavitā* (Bombay: Mauj, 1960):40.

25. "Your": this poem could also be read as a love poem.

26. Grace (Manik Godghate, b. 1937) is a poet who has also edited literary reviews and written personal essays.

27. From *Sandhyākāḷcyā kavitā* (Bombay: Popular, 1967):17.

28. Namdeo Dhondo Mahanor (b. 1942) is a poet who also collects folklore when he is not tending his farm.

29. From *Rānātlyā kavitā* (Bombay: Popular, 1967):60.

30. "My farmland": the original word *rān* also means woodland in other contexts; a farmland may have trees in it.

31. Vasant Ladoba Sawant (b. 1935) is a poet and the author of a forthcoming study of the Marathi travelogue.

32. From *Svastik* (Bombay: Popular, 1973):52–53.

33. "Pandharpur": with its temple of Vithoba, it is the City of God visited by the Vaishnava pilgrims of Maharashtra.

34. From *Svastik*:53.

35. "Sandalwood": yields a lasting fragrance as it is ground to a paste, which is applied to the icon in a *pūjā*.

36. From *Svastik*:78–80; this is the fifth out of the six stanzas in the original.

37. Padma (Padmavati Gole, b. 1913) is a poet.

38. From *Ākāshveḍī* (Bombay: Mauj, 1968):67.

39. "Katyayani Vrata": allusion to an episode narrated in the *Bhāgavata Purāṇa*; the Gopis are bathing in the Yamuna on a religious occasion of this name; Krishna playfully makes away with the milk-

maids' clothes, hangs them on a nearby *kadamba* tree, and watches their discomfiture from the tree as he plays the flute.

40. "The *antarpāṭ*": the cloth held curtain-like between the bride and the groom by the priests reciting the wedding mantras, whose refrain is *sāvadhān*! (alerting the couple and the others that the two are entering into the blessed union).

41. Arun Kolatkar (b. 1932) writes poetry in Marathi and English and translates Marathi poetry (some of it his own) into English; he is also a graphic artist.

42. From *Aruṇ Kolaṭkarcyā kavitā* (Bombay: Pras, 1977):49.

43. "Gandharvas": the court singers of Indra, the god of thunder, Tumbara being one of them. The *rishi* Narada, along with Tumbara, sings in attendance on Vishnu. The Gandharvas beclouded the night sky to deceive Pururavas into losing Urvashi.

44. Dnyaneshwar had himself immured, sitting in a trance. The term *samādhī* refers to the mystic trance and metonymically to the holy sepulchre where a *sannyāsī* is buried. (*Sannyāsīs* are not cremated.) There is a tradition that he urged the poet Eknath in a dream to disentangle from his bones the roots of the tree planted on the spot. Eknath, who did so, also edited the text of *Jñāneśvarī*, the poetic exegisis of the *Bhagavadgītā*.

## ACKNOWLEDGEMENT

*Thanks are due to the poets and their heirs who were generous with their permission and to those who commented on the translations and offered suggestions (Borkar, Rege, Sawant, Bhave on their respective work and Nissim Ezekiel, Vrinda Nabar, James Beveridge, Maxine Berntsen, Eleanor Zelliot, Vinay Hardikar, and Bhave on the translations of the poems.)*

—*Ashok Kelkar*

## *Bhakti in Modern Marathi Poetry: An Essay*

These poems are not just modern but contemporary, spread over the last twenty-five years or so. "Modern poetry" in Marathi is about a century old. Marathi critics generally date it from the poet Keshavsut (1866–1905). Earlier Marathi poetry—in contrast to modern—is (it is held) renunciatory, other-worldly, spiritual, and devotional. The British connection brought people into contact with values like liberty, equality, and fraternity. With them came also rationalism, secular humanism, nationalism, the integrity of the individual, love of nature, the dignity of womanhood, and social reform. "Modernity" (or *navmatvād* as it is sometimes called in Marathi) came to be identified with the composite of all these values. The Marathi poetry of the last hundred years is modern or *navmatvādī* according to the critics.

A finer exploration of the century's poetry, however, would not wholly bear out this assessment. True, modern values gradually "arrived" and modernity was recognized as important. But the older values were by no means displaced, and did not suffer any real loss of prestige. There has been a constant effort to achieve a synthesis of the two value systems, to accept the new without destroying the old, indeed to accommodate the new within the older framework. This urge was in evidence in the poetic personality of Keshavsut as much as in that of Kusumagraj forty years later. Keshavsut cherished the notion of *advaita* (non-duality), the interpenetration of *prakṛiti* and *purush* (the female principle of active energy and the male principle of passive knowingness). Not too different is the pull underlying these lines of Kusumagraj:

> But then comes to mind (rousing even longings)
> The still small lamp flame near the hearth.

The union of the individual person and the Cosmic Person, the sense of one's own incompleteness, and other such older ways of thought are still very much there. The simple and direct expression of these beliefs—*bhakti*, in other words—is apparent in the poems of all the following major Marathi poets of this century—Keshavsut, Narayan Waman Tilak (a Christian minister), Vinayak, Balakavi, Govindagraj, Tambe, "Bee," Yashvant, Madhav Julian, Savarkar, Anil, Kusumagraj, and Borkar.

The poetry written after the Second World War accepted the revolutionary lead of B.S. Mardhekar and is held to be even more modern than the earlier poetry. This is not to be denied. One can certainly characterize the "new" modern poetry (*navkavitā*) in terms of a revolt against established values, a stance against the tradition (even against the notion of tradition itself), an excessively individualist view of life, a need to take a stand against any sort of establishment, and an acute sense of frustration engulfing any sort of optimism.

One wouldn't have been surprised to have found no room for the old bhakti theme in this new modernity. But, notably, the devotional theme of the Indian tradition has a place in this poetry. Let's go over the selected poets and poems.

Each poet has made a reference, mostly direct, to God or Godhead—Lord (*murārī*), by Mardhekar; Jesus, by Borkar; Hari, by Rege; Lord (*prabhū*), by Arati Prabhu; Dynaneshwar, by Arun Kolatkar. Then there is a direct address (the Marathi *tū*) in the poems of Muktibodh, Kusumagraj, Chitre, and Sawant. Sawant also specifically speaks of Him (the Marathi *to*). Borkar has an indirectly suggestive mention: Mother's home (*māher*), i.e., God's house. Padma alludes to Krishna's Katyayani Vrata games. Mahanor sees Godhead in his farmland (*rān*).

The wholeness of God, the less-than-wholeness of oneself, and consequently the hoping for and begging of divine grace—these are the three important constituents of bhakti. And they are all there in these poems to a greater or lesser extent.

> Let the quality of Draupadi herself
> Grace the body of my speech.

These lines are from a Mardhekar poem that has all the three elements. It goes on to say:

> You are the master of meaning:
> This beggar is but the bearer of the word.

Lines which are not too different from the seventeenth-century saint-poet Tukaram's:

> Breaking into the storehouse—
> All this is the Lord's property—
> Me but a lowly porter

> Bearer of loads.

The poem is overfull of the sense of the less-than-wholeness of oneself—one has only to look at the harsh words Mardhekar hurls at himself: hardness, sourness, taintedness, greed, hatred, meanness, vaunting ambition, and (in the third poem) haplessness. In contrast, Muktibodh speaks of God's wholeness as:

> Your boundless glory.

(Glory is what the Almighty has—*aishwarya* (lordship) is the attribute of Ishwar.) Kusumagraj refers to the body as earth house. Arati Prabhu expresses an acute sense of the tangled skein and the abject hunger of existence, as does Dilip Chitre of the feeble voice. Mahanor speaks of life's sorrow and burden. Padma has chosen the image of discarded flowers, and Sawant spots the soil on everyone's feet.

The essential worthlessness of this world and the worth of union with God—or at least some treasured moments of realization "in this very body, with these very eyes" (in Tukaram's phrase); life as the progressive winning over (*sādhanā*) of this goal; the need of God's grace to fulfill and complete this progress—this characteristic spiritual progression of the Indian tradition can be seen in the poems selected. Arun Kolatkar writes:

> The fever of the drum has ebbed away.

The drum (*mṛidang*) is the earth (*mṛid*) that is body (*anga*). The ebbing of the fever of *māyā* (the magical illusion-creating energy) marks the fulfillment of *sādhanā*, the liberation from the hold of illusion.

> Make it bright . . .
> Tarry here a moment . . .

Such is the prayer of Kusumagraj.

> Even so I come prostrate to thy feet . . .

so confesses Mardhekar. Chitre has neatly expressed the traditional devotional image in

> Let the spirit expand itself in a burst of surrender
> And the cosmic knot come undone.

The power of surrender (*lāchārīt shaktī*) is very much in the spirit of the medieval Marathi saint-poets. The bhakta (devotee) is the child—nay, the babe. God is mother. Wherein does the power of the baby lie? In its total dependence on the mother. What is left for the baby to do? To express openly and unreservedly this powerlessness, to send out a piercing howl without budging an inch, eyes shut tight and mouth stretched wide. The mother runs down, picks it up, clasps it to her bosom. And she is doing no favor to the baby. It's her duty. It's the baby's privilege—this is bhakti, Marathi style. Chitre's poem is in august company. Grace wants

> The doors of the Cosmic Ovum

to open. That can't be so long as the worldly bond has not snapped.

> The silk thread is giving way slowly.

To realize this image of Padma's is also to recall another breaking of the thread—the seventeenth-century sage, Ramdas's:

> For God's friendship's sake
> May I break with the near ones.

The realization and the approach to realization—as described in these poems—is quite in line with the bhakti tradition. Rege hints at the experiential progression in "Wooing . . . Flowering . . . Blooming."

> The robes have long been draping the *kadamba* branches
> I am turned into the blue song

says Padma.

> The trees spread me a bed

testifies Mahanor.

> To the brim ablaze, the fire within

so runs Chitre's line.

> Me out on a limb, a lightning tree

this is Borkar's variation; and

> Sprinkling joy

being Muktibodh's.

> I look thee
> In the eyes letting my eyes scald.

Such is the searing experience of Mardhekar, who has felt the power of that moment in:

> Then may this sinful hand
> Work some white on black—
> Only then!

Suffice it, I should think. Exploring the expanding circles of meanings through all these poems is letting oneself in for unending delight. But that's not what this essay is for. The point, the question rather, is: why does this traditional bhakti theme appear in this ultra-modern poetry? Mardhekar, Borkar, Kusumagraj, and Muktibodh belong almost to the same generation, but nobody can accuse them of belonging to the same school!—the individualistic, pessimistic Mardhekar; the socialistic, radical Muktibodh; the incorrigibly romantic Borkar; the idealistic Kusumagraj. The generation of Chitre, Khanolkar, and Sawant is again a different story. Padma, Arun Kolatkar, and P.S. Rege do not admit of any labels. With all these differences, what is the source of this common affinity with the bhakti tradition?

It is not for me to offer a complete answer—or even to choose from among the varied answers that might be forthcoming from sociologists, social psychologists, or ethnologists. Maybe I can, however, suggest one for consideration—something "felt" along the way, so to speak.

I think that, broadly, almost to a man, the Indian consciousness has remained just where it has been for centuries. It accepts the idea of the other world, rebirth, the fruit of karma of past births, karma, God, nonduality, renunciation, *sādhanā*, realization, liberation. Indeed these ideas are ingrained in it. Howsoever the context of life may alter, howsoever modern it may become, the Indian preserves his detachment. Once the life here is taken to be secondary, unreal, something to be quickly gotten through, one cannot really be excited about changes in it. Maturity in age and attitude only confirms an Indian in this wisdom.

Wisdom—am I not begging the question in so calling it? Wisdom or folly, knowledge or ignorance—who can say? A comparison with other peoples and times may be to our disadvantage. But then which other attitude can support an individual into self-sufficient contentment irrespective of circumstance and society? None that I know of.

*—Sadashiv Bhave,*
*translated by Ashok Kelkar*

### *A Response to Sadashiv Bhave's Essay*

It may seem curious that Bhave repeatedly speaks of the Indian tradition consisting of a worldview and a simple and direct expression of it in bhakti. This, for him as for us, provides perspective for bhakti in contemporary Marathi poetry. But the perspective needs to be broadened further.

It is not so much a question of a pedantic correction, namely for "Indian" read "Hindu," for are not all the poets selected Hindus (in any case for census purposes)? In point of fact, Bhave does mention the precontemporary modern Marathi poet Narayan Waman Tilak, born a Hindu and converted to Protestant Christianity, and Jesus, who makes his appearance in one of Borkar's poems. (Sadanand Rege is another contemporary Marathi poet who uses the Christ theme without being a Christian. One may also recall the Indian Sufis or *premamārgī* (path of love) *bhaktas* among Muslims.)

Indeed, "Hindu" may not be enough of a correction to satisfy the exact historian. After all Bhave's account of the worldview is unmistakably Vedantic, and Vedanta is not the whole of Hinduism despite popularized accounts of it. Hinduism is not a "book faith" (to borrow a convenient term from Islamic theology); rather it is like the ancient Greek complex of myth, ritual, philosophy, and morals which impinges on the life of a family or rather a person.

Historically, Hinduism is far from a complete fusion of (at least) three elements:

(1) The Vedic religion centering around the sacrifice (*yadnya*) to the pantheon (with unmistakable family resemblances to the Greek, Latin, Norse, and Celtic pantheons) and displaying its orderly and orgiastic elements.

(2) The family of pre-Vedic religions centering round notions of pollution (*ashaucha*) and oblation (*pūjā*) to the local (*grāma*), familial (*kula*), and above all personal (*ishṭa*) god—these partially crystalized into the cults of Shiva, of the epic heroes Ram and Krishna, and the Mother Goddess (devi), and the cycle of festivals.

(3) The ferment of speculative and meditative philosophy attempting philosophical cosmology and a definition of dharma (the proper ordering of one's personal or social life) and thus "containing" and transcending the polytheistic and tribalistic thrust of both Vedic and pre-Vedic religions—this ferment being associated with the Upanishads, the rise of Buddhism and other views and more recently, the absorbing of Islamic and Christian pressures.

The Hindu world views draw both on other-worldly and this-worldly, pessimistic and optimistic, non-materialistic and materialistic ways of looking, in different proportions and combinations. The Brahman priest supporting ritual, segregation, and rigid order; the wandering sadhu whose special strength lies in his renouncing both the benefits and the constraints of the Hindu social order (segregating caste from caste, village from village, sex from sex); and the poetizing and singing *bhakta* seeking an ecstatic and loving union with one God and making light of the ritual proprieties, without, however, renouncing a worldly life—all claim veneration from the populace, though the last is probably closest to their hearts. India has then its orgies of religious hatred and sectarian persecution, but the dominant tendency is one of peaceful coexistence, informal organization, and multiple commitments. Vedanta and bhakti is only one rather well-trodden path cutting through this maze.

Moreover, this way has close affinities to pre-rational and mystical ways everywhere. It is not for nothing that Protestant missionaries enthusiastically translated Tukaram into English or that Borkar or Sadanand Rege appropriate Jesus. Indeed some phrases from these poems may strike the reader as parallel to Christian or Sufi phrases. Of course, there are unmistakable differences. Bhakti as interpreted by the medieval Marathi saint-poets (consider Bhave's striking image of the howling babe) is in important ways different from bhakti as interpreted in other parts of India. (One may note in passing that P.S. Rege has greater affinity with Jayadeva's Sanskrit *Gītagovinda* than with Tukaram's Marathi poetry.) If the howling babe image is inappropriate for an understanding of, say, Rege or Tulsi Das, it is of course even more so for the Christian bhakta not daring to hope for divine grace and mercy.

But, speaking of affinities and divergences, what do we make of Bhave's central question: Why does this traditional bhakti theme appear in this modern poetry, not to speak of ultra-modern poetry? In the first place, the marriage of religious, mystical, devotional consciousness and the modernist perspective is not confined to India—one has only to think of William Blake, Kierkegaard, and T.S. Eliot, among others. The sense of anxiety brought on by the scientific perspective has obvious religious intimations. Think of A.E. Housman's haunting lines:

> I, a stranger and afraid
> In a world I never made.

Surely the point is not so much that

> Even so I come prostrate at thy feet

But that the condition is going to remain unfulfilled—

> If only thy stone-still brow
> Stir before my eyes the least little!

To realize that

> The doors of the Cosmic Ovum have closed

is not necessarily to pine for deliverance and snapping of

worldly bonds. The sense of anxiety has religious intimations, but not necessarily religious consequences.

A second and perhaps more important point has already been hinted at when I spoke of Borkar and Sadanand Rege "using" the Christ theme. Sawant's lines are quite explicit:

> In the end it is the word alone that lives,
> That goes for me too: only when I write a poem
> Then alone am I truly living.

Here is a poet using the religious perspective for a poetic purpose, and not a *sādhak* (religious seeker) using the poetic stance to convey a spiritual quest. The important thing is that one could read Muktibodh's poem as a mood poem and Chitre's poem as a love poem. One doesn't have to, but one could. But this already means that one doesn't have to read either of them as a religious poem, though one certainly could and Bhave obviously has. The modernist poets in Marathi pointedly reject a good deal of the inter-war poetry, which is their immediate heritage, as factitious and recognize a true lyricism in the medieval *bhaktas*—it is a poetic rather than a religious affinity.

To write a bhakti poem in the modernist mode is perhaps to write a modernist poem in the bhakti mode. Of course contemporary modernist Marathi poetry has many other modes; and Bhave of course is not denying that in confining his attention to a specially-made selection out of it.

*—Ashok Kelkar*

### *A Response to Ashok Kelkar's Response*

"Indian" of course is not an exact rendering of *bhāratīya* (of or belonging to Bharat) in my original Marathi version. (The Constitution of India, to be sure, speaks of "India, that is Bharat.") "Bharatiya" reminds us, as "Indian" does not, of the Hindu tradition. Buddhists, Jains, Muslims, Christians, nay, even the Marxists, of today's India cannot help partaking of it—they are all Hindu-Bharatiya at heart.

What is it to be a Hindu-Bharatiya? What does it involve?

Chiefly, the accepting of the other world as well as this world, the attempt to reconcile the two. But between the two, the other world comes first. *Brahman* and *māyā* are both real, but *brahman* is the ultimate Reality, *māyā* being the provisional reality. This ultimate/provisional duality has best been resolved into a unity in the Vedanta of non-duality (*advaita*).

In the world of Hindu thought Advaita Vedanta is the most dominant. In Maharashtra, moreover, all the bhakti sects, with the exception of the Mahanubhavs, are Advaita Vedantist and Veda-accepting. And the Mahanubhavs were never accepted by the Marathi people, whose aversion to them became evident as early as the latter half of the fourteenth century. Not only is bhakti in Maharashtra Vedantist, but many other sects have been either brought into the bhakti fold or have disappeared. Dnyaneshwar brought the Nath Sect into the Varkari fold in the thirteenth century, and Eknath the Datta Sect in the sixteenth century. The Ramdasi Sect of the seventeenth century had no future after the death of its founder, Ramdas. The highway of the Varkari sect has always remained the most frequented ever since the thirteenth century. I should account for this fact on the following lines:

(1) The unification of the Shaivas and the Vaishnavas in the Varkari sect—thanks to Dnyaneshwar, its thirteenth-century founder—constituted its strength.

(2) To see God, Vithoba, in the image of a mother is the distinctive feature of bhakti in Maharashtra, which saved it from the excesses and the morbid possibilities of *madhur* (sweet) *bhakti* which sees God in the image of the beloved.

(3) Another feature of bhakti in Maharashtra is the wonderful reconciliation of the spiritual and the temporal. In the thirteenth and fourteenth centuries the saints' way of seeing the practical life as but an aspect of the spiritual was innovative. Besides, this came in handy for coming to terms with the Islamic invasion. Even Savta Mali, the humble gardener, could declare:

Onions, radishes, greens—
They're all mother Vithoba to me.

To spiritualize the practical life, to think of the allotted necessities of life as a form of *sādhanā*—this bold step did not remain limited to Dnyaneshwar in the thirteenth century. That everybody, a goldsmith, a tailor, a barber, a lowly Mahar, a humble serving maid, even a Muslim Varkari, came to realize this difficult abstraction is as much a token of the prior dissemination of *advaita* Vedanta to all strata of the Hindu-Bharatiya Society as it is of Dnyaneshwar's achievement.

So, when the Advaita insight (*dnyān*) of Dnyaneshwar was joined to the passion for God's name (*nām*) in Namdev in Maharashtra, the way of bhakti proved to be not only the easiest way but the chief way—the Varkari sect becoming the principal vehicle.

Naturally, in Maharashtra no less than in the rest of Bharat, the *bhakta* is no mere bard dreaming of union with God. In his personal life he is a social worker. This twofold urge is as present in the poetry of Keshavsut in the nineteenth century as in the contemporary poetry of Kusumagraj or Muktibodh. Mardhekar's poetry presents a clear retreat from the twofold stance, but most of the contemporary intellectuals of Maharashtra display this dual stance in their critical activity.

So, therefore, the quivering unease of modernist Marathi poetry relates not only to the artist's restlessness but also to the Hindu-Bharatiya tradition. That's why it is not possible to read Chitre's poem as a simple love poem. There are word-images in that poem that definitely transcend the sentiment of love.

*—Sadashiv Bhave*
*translated by Ashok Kelkar*

# V.

# APPENDICES

# Appendix A

## Glossary

*NOTE: Separate lists of the Hindu months; Gods, Goddesses and Festivals; and Castes follow the glossary. The first spelling indicates Marathi pronunciation; standard transliteration, when different, follows in parentheses. Proper nouns have not been italicized. Please refer to our initial "Notes on the Writing of Marathi Words." We are indebted to Philip Engblom and Anne Feldhaus for their comments on the Glossaries, but neither is responsible for our errors.*

*abhanga:* (abhaṅga) (Lit. unbroken, inviolable); a particular metrical composition used by the Varkari saint-poets
*advaita:* Non-dualism; *advaita vedānta* is a prominent school of monistic philosophy
*āī:* (Anglicized as aee) Mother; appended to the name of a god seen as mother
*ahimsā:* (ahiṃsā) Non-violence
*amāvāsyā:* No-moon (new moon) day
Āmbeḍkar, B.R.: (1891–1956) Affectionately known as *Bābāsāheb*; a statesman, writer, and leader of the Untouchables
*āmṭī:* Thin lentil soup
*angāt (aṅgāt) ālelā / ālelī:* One who is possessed
*angāt (aṅgāt) yeṇe:* (Lit. to come into the body); possession of a person by a god

*āratī:* The ceremony of circling a tray of lights before a deity
Ashṭavināyak: (Aṣṭavināyaka) The eight pilgrimage places of the Ganpati Sect
*āshram:* (āśrama) A stage of life; used also for the retreat of a guru and his disciples
*ātmā:* The individual soul; identical with *brahman*, the universal absolute
*audumbar:* *Glomerous* fig tree
*āvaḷī:* *Phyllanthus emblica*; a tree
*avatār:* An incarnation of a god

*bābā:* Holy man, father
Bābāsāheb: (Lit. father-master); respectful name given to Ambedkar around 1930
*bābhūḷ:* Gum *arabica*, an acacia tree
*bāī:* Woman; a respectful form of address
*bakūḷ:* *Mimusops elengi*; a flowering tree and its flower
*bel:* *Cratoeva religiosa;* a tree sacred to Shiva
*Bhagavad Gītā:* (Lit. the song of god); often called simply the *Gītā*; Krishna's message to Arjuna in the *Mahābhārata* epic
*Bhāgavata Purāṇa:* A *purāṇa* devoted to Krishna; often called in Marathi simply the *Bhāgwat*
*bhajan:* Devotional group singing, usually accompanied by instruments; also the devotional song sung by such a group
*bhākrī:* Flat unleavened bread made of sorghum, millet, or maize flour; the staple food of rural Maharashtra
bhakti: Devotion, usually a personal devotional relationship to one particular god; the "Bhakti movement" refers to the historic presence of numerous schools of bhakti saint-poets and teachers in the various linguistic regions
*bhaktimārg:* (bhakti mārga) The path of devotion
*bhāratīya:* Indian; an adjective
*bhārūḍ:* Allegorical story presented in dramatic form
*bhūt; bhūt bādhā:* Ghost; possession of a person by a ghost
*bhutyā:* A religious mendicant who sings for the goddess Jagadamba
*bombīl:* *Bommelow*, a type of fish
*buwā:* (buvā) A religious leader; a respectful form of address

*çauk:* (cauk) (Anglicized as chowk), an intersection of roads
Chakradhar: (Cakradhara) The historic founder of the Mahan-

ubhav sect in the thirteenth century; see also the Gods and Goddesses list

*chilla:* Memorial to a Muslim saint

Chokamela: See Çokhāmeḷā

Çokhāmeḷā: (Cokhāmeḷā) A fourteenth century Mahar saint-poet

*dalit:* Downtrodden, oppressed; now current among ex-Untouchables as an acceptable word for themselves and all oppressed peoples

*dargā:* Tomb of a Muslim saint, often a center of healing

*darshan:* (darśan) Seeing an idol or a person with divine power

Dasnāmī: (Dasanāmī) An order of monks, followers of the philosopher Shankara

Desh: (Deś) A country or region; in Maharashtra, the area east of the ghats from the Godavari River south to the Karnataka region

*devasthān:* (Lit. place of the god), temple

*devatā:* Deity

*devṛishī:* (devarṣī) Shaman

*dinḍī:* (dinḍī) A group, usually with a specific leader, participating in a pilgrimage

Dnyāneshwar: (Jñāneśvar) The thirteenth century author of the *Jñāneśvarī*, formally titled the *Bhāvārthadīpikā*, a commentary on the *Bhagavad Gītā*; considered to be the founder of the Varkari tradition

*dohā:* A couplet form used by Hindi bhakti poets

*dvādashī:* (dvādaśī) The twelfth day of the lunar fortnight

*ekādashī:* (ekādaśī) The eleventh day of the lunar fortnight

Eknāth: (1533–99) One of the major saint-poets; a linking figure who edited the *Jñāneśvarī* and prepared the way for later bhaktas

*gaṇa:* Multitude or troops; a composition in praise of Ganpati (lord of the ganas)

Gāṇpatyas: (Gāṇapatyas) The *sampradāy* or formal tradition of the Gaṇesh sect

Gandharva: Heavenly singer in Indra's court

*gānjā:* (gāñjā) Hemp

*gavḷaṇ:* A song in honor of Krishna playing with the milkmaids

*ghī:* (Anglicized as ghee), clarified butter

*Gītā:* See *Bhavagad Gītā*

*gondhaḷ:* A folk-art form consisting of narration presented through songs, accompanied by instruments and pantomime.

Gondhaḷī: A *gondhaḷ* performer

*gopura:* The tower of a Hindu temple

*gosāvī:* An ascetic or a sect of ascetics

*gulāl:* Bright red powder scattered on festive occasions

*Gurucaritra:* A religious text of the Datta tradition; the life of Narasimha Saraswati, written around 1538 by Saraswati Gangadhara

*guru dakshiṇā:* (*guru dakṣiṇā*) An offering made by a disciple to his teacher

*guru sampradāy:* A network or lineage of gurus, past and present, and their followers

*haḷad:* Turmeric powder, used in many rituals

Harijan: (Lit. people of God); a synonym for Untouchable initiated by Mohandas K. Gandhi

*jāgṛīt:* (jāgṛta) Wakeful, used for an especially potent, awake god

Jain: A member of a religion organized around the fifth to sixth century B.C.; now chiefly found among merchants in Gujarat and Gujarati-speaking merchants in Maharashtrian cities, also among a small community of agriculturists still present in southern Maharashtra

Janābāī: (1260–1363) The maid servant of Namdev who was also a saint-poet

*jatrā:* A religious fair

*jay; kī jay:* Victory; victory to . . .

*jīv:* Life or soul

*jawar; jawārī:* *Holcus sorghum*; the staple grain of Maharashtra

*kaḍak:* harsh, hard

*kadamba:* *Nauclea cadamba*; a tree

Kailās: The heaven of Shiva

Kali yuga: The fourth age of the fourfold cycle of the universe; the "dark age" in which we now live

*karṇī:* Black magic

*kheḷ:* A game or sport; a Dhangar ritual dance

*kheḷiyā:* A song sung during Holi or in fun at weddings

*kīrtan:* A religious discourse accompanied by *bhajan*, q.v.
*kunkū:* Vermillion powder, usually used as a mark of auspiciousness

*lāḍū:* A sweetmeat ball
*lagorī:* A game played with a ball
*lalit nibandh:* An artistic or light essay
*lāṭhī:* A heavy stick carried by the police
*lāwaṇī:* (lāvaṇī) A type of love song
*leḻīm:* (lejīm) A group dance performed with sticks to which metal discs are attached
*linga:* (liṅga) The phallic symbol of Shiva
Lingāyat: A person of the Virashaiva faith; see the Caste list

*madhur; madhur bhakti:* Sweet; the bhakti in which the devotees see themselves to be the female beloved of Krishna
*Mahābhārata:* The great epic of the Pandava and Kaurava clans and the war at Kurukshetra
*mahant:* Head of a monastery
Mahānubhāv: (Mahānubhāva) A member of a religious sect begun in the thirteenth century as protest against image worship and Brahmanical orthodoxy
*mahāpūjā:* An elaborate form of ritual worship
*mahārāj:* (mahārāja) A title used for royalty, some holy men, and some gods
*māher:* Mother's house
Mahīpati: (1715–90) Author of the *Bhaktalīlāmṛta* and other texts on the saint-poets
*māmā:* Maternal uncle; father-in-law
*māmledār, māṁlatdār:* Taluka revenue officer
*manḍal:* (maṇḍaḷ) Association
*māntrik:* Practitioner of magic
Manu: The traditional first man; the law giver
*māṇūs; māṇuskī:* Man; humaneness; the view that each person is entitled to be treated as a full human being
Marāṭhā kingdom: The kingdom ruled by Shivaji, and later his son and grandson, and the Peshwas, existing from 1660 to 1818
*maṭh:* Hermitage, monastery
*māulī:* Mother; used as a term of endearment especially for Vithoba
*māyā:* Illusion, the power to cause illusion

Mīrābāī: (Anglicized as Meera), a sixteenth-century Rajput princess, poet and devotee of Krishna
*meḷā:* A gathering, assembly; fair, often for religious purposes
*modak:* A sweetmeat held to be beloved by Ganpati
*moksha:* (mokṣa) Final liberation
Moryā: A shout at the time of the Ganpati festival; a name of Ganpati
*mṛidang:* (mṛdaṅga) A long horizontal drum, played at both ends
Muktābāī: (1279–96) The sister of Dnyaneshwar and a saint-poet in her own right
*mujāvar:* An attendant at a Muslim shrine
*murḷī:* (*muraḷī*) A female dedicated to the service of Khandoba
*mūrti:* An image; in this volume, the image of a god or goddess

*nāg:* A snake
*naivedya:* Food offered to a god
*namaste, namaskār:* A greeting with the palms pressed together
Nāmdev, Nāmdeo: (1270–1350) A contemporary of Dnyaneshwar; a saint-poet held to be the originator of many of the practices of the Warkari tradition
Nandī: The bull which is the vehicle of the god Shiva
Nāth: (Lit. lord); member of a sect of Shaiva ascetics
*navas:* A vow to a god, often involving the promise of an offering in return for the granting of a request
*nived, nivedya:* Dialect variants of *naivedya*, q.v.

*oṭā:* A stone block worshipped by the Mahanubhavs as a place hallowed by an action of one of the *avatārs* of Parmeshwar
*ovī:* A poetic stanza form, often used for religious songs

*padar:* The end of a piece of cloth or a sari
*pādukā:* Raised impression of the feet or the sandals of a saint or a god
*paisā:* A coin worth one hundredth of a rupee
*pālkhī:* A palanquin
*pān:* (Lit. leaf) the leaf of *piper* betel, rolled with spices and lime as a chew
*panchāyat:* (pañcāyata) The council of a caste or a village
Panḍharī: (Panḍharī) A religious name for the town of Pandharpur

*panjā:* (pañjā) A wooden pole capped by a hand representing a *pīr*, used at the time of Muharram

*panth:* (pantha) (Lit. road or way); a religious group or persuasion; often translated sect or cult

Pārsī: A member of the Zoroastrian faith; a small group of highly educated and successful people, originally from Persia, now concentrated in Bombay

*pati:* Lord

*pāṭīl:* The village headman

*pāylī:* About eight pounds

Peshwā: (Peśvā) Prime minister; the *de facto* rulers of the Marāṭhā Empire from the early 1700s until 1818, when the Peshwa's armies were defeated by the British

*peṭh:* A section of a city, originally demarcated by a market

*pīr:* A Muslim saint in the Sufi tradition

*pishāça:* (piśāca) A ghost, a spirit

*pothī:* A holy text or manuscript

*potrāj:* Servant of the village goddess of epidemics, Mariai, generally a Mahar before the Buddhist conversion

*povāḍā:* A ballad recounting heroic deeds

*prabhu:* Lord

*prachārak:* (pracāraka) A missionary, one who spreads doctrine; the basic R.S.S. leadership category

*pradakshiṇā:* (pradakṣiṇā) Circumambulation of a god or a holy place

*prakṛiti:* (prakṛti) The female principle of active energy in the Sankhya system of philosophy

*prasād:* Anything received as a gift from the deity; often a portion of the offering a worshipper has made

*pret:* Corpse, ghost

*pūjā:* Ritual worship

*pujārī:* Temple priest

*purāṇas:* The most voluminous body of all Sanskrit texts, composed chiefly in the first millennium of our era; mythic histories of gods and kings

*pūrṇima:* Full moon day

*purush:* (puruṣa) The male principle of passive knowingness in Sankhya philosophy

*rāg:* (rāga) A series of notes which denote a mode of music

*rākshas:* (rākṣas) A demon

*Rāmāyaṇa:* Epic of the ideal king, Ram, and the ideal woman, Sita, his wife

Rāmdās: (1534–81) A *bhakta* of Ram who founded a religious order and began the "Maharashtra dharma" idea of a special ethos for a Hindu state

*rangaṇ:* (raṅgaṇ) (Lit. a playing field); in the Varkari tradition, a ceremony of horses circling the *pālkhī* in a large field

Rāshṭriya Swayamsevak Sangh: (Rāṣṭrīya Svayaṃsevaka Sangha) Known as the R.S.S.; an organization of volunteers for a Hindu nation

*sādhanā:* Practice; study toward a goal of release from bondage; a *sādhak* is one engaged in religious exercises to obtain *moksha*

Sakhū: The eighteenth century devotee of Vithoba punished for joining the pilgrimage without her mother-in-law's consent, who was rescued and reconciled to her husband's family by Vithoba

*samādhī:* A monument built over the remains of a Hindu saint; entrance into a state of union with *brahman*

*sambaḷ:* A kind of drum

*sampradāy:* (sampradāya) Custom, practice; a system of religious doctrine; a systematized tradition

*samskār:* (saṃskāra) Life cycle rituals

*sangam:* (saṅgam) A confluence of rivers

*sannyās; sannyāsī:* The ascetic life; one who lives the ascetic life

*sant:* (santa) Close to the English word saint in meaning, but with no etymological connection; usually used for the bhakti saint-poets of the Marathi and Hindi speaking areas

*sarpanch:* (*sarpañca*) The head of the village panchayat

*sat:* The real, the essential

*sattva:* Moral goodness, virtue

*satyāgraha; satyāgrahī:* The technique of non-violent direct action developed by Mahatma Gandhi; a participant in *satyāgraha*

*saumya:* Benign, gentle

*Sāvitrī:* A princess whose devotion and cleverness saved her husband from death.

Sāvtā Māḷī: A Varkari saint-poet of the fourteenth century from the gardener caste

*shākhā:* (śākhā) (Lit. branch or bough); a section or subdivision of the R.S.S.

*shaktī:* (śaktī) Power; the principle of female power

*shāligrām:* (śāligrāma) Black stones found in rivers, worshipped as sacred to Vishnu

Shankara, Shankarācharya: (Śaṅkarācārya) An 8-9th century philosophy; founder of the Dasnāmī order and chief formulator of the Advaita Vedānta school of philosophy; a Shaiva bhakta

*shānta:* (śānta) Calm, peaceful

*shāstra:* (śāstra) A Hindu text or treatise, considered to be of divine origin

*shirā:* (śirā) A sweet dessert

Shivājī: (Śivājī) (1630–80) The first Chhatrapati or King of the Marathas, founder of the Maratha empire and most important hero of the Marathi speaking people

*shrī:* (śrī) An honorific term

*siddha; siddhi:* One who has attained extraordinary powers through ascetic practice; that extraordinary power

*Sītā:* Wife of the god-king Ram, symbol of ideal womanhood

*sovḷa:* Ritual purity; ritually pure clothing

*Sūtrapāṭha:* Sayings attributed to Chakradhar, founder of the Mahānubhāv sect

*tāī:* Older sister; used as a respectful term of address to another woman

*ṭāḷ:* A pair of small cymbals

*tālukā:* A division of a district, somewhat like an American county

*tamāshā:* (tamāśā) Marathi folk drama

Tamil: The language of Tamilnadu, a large state on the southeast coast of India

*tapashcharyā:* (*tapaścaryā*) Devout austerities

*tarūṇ:* Young

Telugu: The language of the state of Andhra Pradesh, adjoining Maharashtra to the east and southeast

*tilak:* A spot or line on the forehead which sometimes has religious meaning

Ṭiḷak, Bāḷ Gangādhar: (1856–1920) A fervant nationalist, founder of the public Ganpati festival, and an important politico-religious influence today

*tīrtha:* Holy water; holy place

*tīrtha-kshetra-vrata-dāna:* The religion of pilgrimages, vows and almsgiving

Tukārām: (1608–49) (Also called Tukā, Tukobā and Tukobarāyā); a saint-poet of Dehu near Pune, one of the most beloved poets in the Marathi tradition

*tuḷshī:* (tuḷśi) *Ocymum sanctum*; a plant sacred to Krishna; holy basil

*tuṇtuṇ:* A one-stringed drone

Upanishads: (Upaniṣads) Philosophical and mystical texts, from around 650–200 B.C., very important in the development of Hindu thought

*(Note: v and w are interfiled)*

*wāḍā:* An area of residence, often by caste; a traditional joint family home

*vāghyā:* A man dedicated to lifelong service of Khandoba

*vahinī:* Brother's wife, used by extension for a friend's wife

Vārkarī: (Lit. one who keeps a regular time); the name for the pilgrims to Pandharpur

*varṇāshram:* (varṇāśrama) The traditional four-fold division of *varṇas*: Brahman, Kshatriya, Vaishya, Shudra; also the four stages of life for the three highest *varṇas*

Vāsudev: A religious performer or mendicant, marked by a hat of peacock feathers, who sings of Krishna

*vedānta:* (Lit. the end of the Vedas); the philosophical systems based on the Upanishads; the advaita vedanta is dominant in Indian intellectual circles today

*Vedas:* The four Vedas form the earliest literature of the Indo-European peoples, dating roughly 1200–1000 B.C.; the Rig Veda is considered the holiest of texts by the orthodox.

*vīṇā:* The Indian lute

*virodh-bhakti:* Devotion through opposition

Yādava kingdom: Centered at Devgiri, near modern Aurangabad, the dynasty of the Yadavas in the eleventh and twelfth centuries saw the beginnings of Marathi literature and the foundation of the Mahanubhav and Warkari traditions

*yadnya:* (yajña) Vedic sacrifice

*yātrā:* Pilgrimage; among the Nandiwalas, this word is used to mean a group sacrifice

*yuga:* An age; classically four ages form a cycle in the life of the universe

Zoroastrianism: The religion of Zoroaster of sixth century Persia, practiced in India by a small but influential group of Parsis

# *Appendix B*

## Gods, Goddesses, and Religious Festivals

*NOTE: Names are given first as they are pronounced in Marathi. Standard transliteration is given in parentheses. See the "Notes on the Writing of Marathi Words" for our formula.*

| | |
|---|---|
| Ambā, Ambābāī | A goddess whose name means "Mother," at times associated with Durga. Also known as Bhavani. |
| Ambājī-Limbājī, or Bāpū Sāheb | A Nandiwala god. |
| Atri and Anasūyā | The parents of Datta. |
| Bābīr | A Shaiva god, born a Gavli cowherd. |
| Bahirobā | A spirit or deity said to prevent disease. |
| Bālkrishna (Bālakṛṣṇa) | The child Krishna. |
| Bāṇāī, Bāṇabāī | The Dhangar wife of Khandoba. |
| Bhavānī | A great goddess, worshipped by Shivaji, King of Maharashtra in the seventeenth century. Bhavani of Tuljapur is one of four major Maharashtrian goddesses. |
| Bhoḷānāth (Bhoḷānātha) | A name of Shiva, "the innocent lord." |
| Bhūtamātā | "Mother of ghosts," an early goddess incorporated into Renuka. |

| | |
|---|---|
| Birobā | A Dhangar Shaiva god, at times called brother to Vithoba. |
| Brahmā | Together with Shiva and Vishnu, Brahma constitutes the Hindu trinity. To be distinguished from the Absolute, *brahman*, and the Brahman caste. |
| Chakradhar (Cakradhara) | Considered by the Mahanubhavs to be an avatar of Parmeshwar. |
| Champāshashṭhī (Campāṣaṣṭhī) | The last day of the Khandoba festival during which Vaghya boys and Murli girls are dedicated to the god. |
| Çāngdev Rāul (Cāṅgadeva Rāüḷa) | Considered by the Mahanubhavs to be an avatar of Parmeshwar; the guru of Govindaprabhu. |
| Chaturshṛingī (Catuśṛṅgī) | The goddess of "four peaks" on the outskirts of Pune; analogous to Saptashringi—"seven peaks"—near Nasik. |
| Chaturmās (Cāturmāsa) | The four months of rainy season, a time of fasting and other special religious activities. Considered inauspicious for marriages and other such ceremonies. |
| Dasarā | See Vijaya Dashmi. |
| Datta, Dattātreya | Lord of ascetics; in Maharashtra popular as an incarnation of Shiva, Vishnu, and Brahma who in turn is incarnated time after time. |
| Dev (deva), Devatā | God. |
| Devī | Goddess. |
| Diwālī (Divāḷī), Dipāvaḷī | A major festival involving the worship of wealth and Lakshmi, the celebration of Vishnu's victories and the expression of brotherly and sisterly affection. |
| Durgā | An all-India goddess, wife of Shiva. |
| Ekvīrā (Ekavīrā) | Goddess of the Koli and C.K.P. castes. Also another name for Renuka. |
| Firisti (Phiristi) Māribā | A Nandiwala god, evidently with Muslim associations. |
| Gaṇpati, Gajānan, Ganesh, Ganarājā (Gaṇapati, Gaṇeśa) | All names of the elephant-headed god who is beloved throughout Maharashtra. |

| | |
|---|---|
| Gaṇesh Chaturthī (Gaṇeśa Caturthī) | The birthday of Ganesh on the 4th of the bright half of Bhadrapad. |
| Gaurī | A goddess of the harvest and protector of women. A name for Parvati before her marriage to Shiva. |
| Giridharī | A name of Krishna. |
| Gopāḷa, Govinda | Names of Krishna. |
| Gopāḷkālā (Gopāḷakālā) | The feasting which concludes a Krishna festival. |
| Govindaprabhu | Considered an avatar of Parmeshwar in the Mahanubhav sect; the guru of Chakradhar. |
| Grāmdaivat (Grāmadaivata) | The patron deity of a village. See Ishtadaivat and Kuldaivat. |
| Gumustā Dev | A Nandiwala god. |
| Hanumān | Also known as Maruti. The monkey devotee of Ram. |
| Hari | A name of Vishnu. |
| Hoḷī | A popular festival held on the full moon of Phalgun in which a bonfire is lit and behavior is the opposite of normal decorum. |
| Indra | A Vedic god, the king of gods. |
| Īshwar (Īśvara) | A general name for god. Often used in combination, as in Parmeshwar. |
| Ishṭadaivat (Iṣṭadaivata) | A god chosen by an individual as a special deity. See Gramdaivat and Kuldaivat. |
| Jagadambā | "Mother of the world." See Amba. |
| Jagannāth | "Lord of the world," the name of the great god at Puri in Orissa. |
| Jamadagni | Husband of the goddess Renuka and father of the Parashuram incarnation of Vishnu. |
| Janārdan | A name of Vishnu; also the name of Eknath's guru. |
| Jogābāī (Jogābāī) | A goddess, probably the same as Jogeshwari (Jogeśvarī), the patron goddess of Pune. |
| Jyotibā, Jotibā | A god identified with Shiva whose pilgrimage site is at Vadi Ratnagiri (Kolhapur District). |

| | |
|---|---|
| Kāḷ Bhairav | A terrible form of Shiva. |
| Kālī | A terrible form of Shiva's wife. |
| Kāḷubāī | A goddess who is sometimes the patron goddess of a village. |
| Khanḍobā (Khanḍobā) | A popular Maharashtrian god whose home is the temple at Jejuri. |
| Kṛishṇa (Kṛṣṇa) | A popular all-India god, an avatar of Vishnu. |
| Kṛishṇajanmāshṭamī (Kṛṣṇajanmāṣṭamī) | The birthday of Krishna. |
| Kuldaivat (Kuladaivata) | The god of a family. See Gramdaivat and Ishtadaivat. |
| Lakshmī (Lakṣmī) | A major all-India goddess. See Mahalakshmi. |
| Mahādev (Mahādeva) | "Great god." A name for Shiva. |
| Mahālakshmī (Mahālakṣmī) | One of the four great goddesses of Maharashtra. Her home is the temple in Kolhapur. |
| Mangaḷmūrti (Maṅgaḷamūrti) | "Auspicious image." A name for Ganpati. |
| Marīāī | A village goddess, formerly in the care of the Untouchable Mahar caste. Goddess of epidemic disease. |
| Māruti | The usual Marathi name for Hanuman. Every village has a temple to him, and many forms of Māruti are found, such as Bhangya Maruti and Chinnal Maruti in Karve's article "Town Without a Temple." |
| Mhāḷsā | The first wife of the god Khandoba, from the Lingayat community. |
| Mhaskobā | A Shaiva deity represented by a rock, with a major shrine at Vir, near Jejuri. Probably evolved from Mhasoba, q.v. |
| Mhasobā | The buffalo demon as a god; the deity of boundaries, represented by a stone covered with red. |
| Moreshwar (Moreśvara) | A name of Gaṇpati. |
| Muharram | The first ten days of the first month of the Muslim year; associated with the memory of the martyred Husain, the Prophet's grandson. |
| Mumbāḍevī | The goddess who probably gave the city of Bombay its original name. |

| | |
|---|---|
| Murukan (Murukaṉ) | A Tamil god. |
| Nāgpanchmī (Nāgapañcamī) | A festival in which Nags or serpents are worshipped. Said to celebrate the return of Krishna from his triumph over the snake Kaliya. |
| Nānā Sāheb | A Nandiwala god, probably, like Ram Mama, a former powerful human being. |
| Nandī | The sacred bull of Shiva. |
| Narahare | An invocation to Narasimha (Narasiṃha) or Narahari, the man-lion avatar of Vishnu. |
| Nārāyaṇ (Nārāyaṇa) | A name for Vishnu. |
| Navnāth, Nao Nāth (Navanātha) | The nine legendary Nath ascetics, worshipped as a group as well as under their individual names. |
| Navrātra (Navarātra) | Nine nights consecrated to the worship of the Devi, culminating in the festival of Dasara. |
| Pāṇḍurang (Pāṇḍuraṅga) | A name for Vithoba. |
| Paramātmā | The soul encompassing all souls, a name for the abstract God. |
| Parshurām (Paraśurāma) | Ram with an axe, the Brahman avatar of Vishnu. |
| Parmeshwar (Parameśvara) | An abstract name for God. For the Mahanubhavs, the only real God. |
| Pārvatī | The consort of Shiva. |
| Rādhā | The lover of Krishna. |
| Rakhumāī | Rukmini, Vithoba's wife; Krishna's wife. |
| Rām (Rāma) | The hero of the *Rāmāyaṇa*, avatar of Vishnu. |
| Rām Māmā | The newest god of the Nandiwalas. |
| Ranābāī | A goddess of the Nandiwalas. |
| Reṇukā | One of the four great goddesses of Maharashtra; her home is in Matapur or Mahur. |
| Rudra | A Vedic god, prototype of Shiva. |
| Rukmiṇī | Vithoba's wife; Krishna's wife. Also called Rakhumai in Maharashtra. |
| Sāhebrāo (Sāhebarāva) Dev | A Nandiwala god, probably previously a dead hero. |

| | |
|---|---|
| Saptashṛingī (Saptaśṛṅgī) Devi | One of Maharashtra's four major goddesses. Seven hills or horns on a hill near Nasik are her home. |
| Saraswatī (Sarasvatī) | The classical Indian goddess of music and learning. |
| Saṭwāī (Saṭavāī) | The goddess who writes a baby's future on his forehead. |
| Satyanārāyaṇ Pūjā | A very modern popular rite performed when some new undertaking or journey is begun (often when a son or daughter is going overseas) or to insure good fortune in the coming year. |
| Shankar (Śaṅkara) | A name for Shiva. |
| Shesha (Śeṣa) | The cosmic thousand-headed snake king who forms Vishnu's couch and canopy during his sleep between intervals of creation. |
| Shiva (Śiva) | The great god of destruction, of the reproductive power of nature, and of ascetics. |
| Shivnāth Mahārāj (Śivanātha Māhārāja) | A Nandiwala god. |
| Shivrātrī or Mahā-Shivrātrī (Śivarātrī) | The "great night" of fasting, worship of the *linga* with *bel* leaves, and recitation of Shiva's thousand names. |
| Sītā | The wife of Ram. |
| Skanda | The brother of Ganpati. |
| Somvatī (Somavatī) Amāvāsyā | The conjunction of sun and moon on a Monday. |
| Tuḷjā Bhavānī | The goddess at Tuljapur, one of the four great Maharashtrian Devi temples. |
| Umā | A wife of Shiva. Another name for Parvati. |
| Vetāḷ (Vetāḷa) | The lord of spirits, king of ghosts. |
| Vighneshwar (Vighneśvara), Vināyak | Names of Ganpati. |
| Vijayā Dashmī (Daśamī) | Also called Dasara. Chiefly a men's festival involving worship of the implements of a trade or profession, including those of war. Formerly included buffalo sacrifice. |
| Vishṇu (Viṣṇu) | A great god, protector and preserver of mankind, who descends to earth in various incarnations. |

| | |
|---|---|
| Viṭṭhal, Viṭhobā, Viṭhāī, Viṭhu, Viṭhurāyā | All names of the god of Pandharpur. |
| Yam, Yamarāj (Yamarāja) | The god of death. |
| Yamāī, Yellammā | Names of Renuka |

# Appendix C

## The Hindu Calendar

*NOTE: The month is given first in Marathi pronunciation, then with traditional diacriticals in parentheses.*

| | |
|---|---|
| Chaitra (Caitra) | March-April |
| Vaishākh (Vaiśakh) | April-May |
| Jyeshṭha (Jyeṣṭha) | May-June |
| Āshāḍh (Āṣāḍh) | June-July |
| Shrāvaṇ (Śrāvaṇ) | July-August |
| Bhādrapad | August-September |
| Āshvin (Āśvin) | September-October |
| Kārttik | October-November |
| Mārgashīrsha (Mārga-śīrṣa) | November-December |
| Paush (Pauṣ) | December-January |
| Māgh | January-February |
| Phālgun | February-March |

# *Appendix D*

## Castes

*NOTE: The caste name is given first as it is pronounced in Marathi. A second name in parentheses indicates standard transliteration.*

Beldār: Stone and earth workers, also called Waḍār.
Bhaṭ: A generally used name for any Brahman priest.
Brāhmaṇ: The four most important Brahman castes in Maharashtra are Chitpāvan, Deshastha, Karhāḍā and Sāraswat, q.v.
Cāmbhār (Cāmbhār): Usually written Chambhar in English. The Marathi version of Cāmār or Chāmār, the leather worker in the Hindi-speaking area.
Chāndrasenīya (Cāndrasenīya) Kāyastha Prabhu: A "writers" caste, ranked below the Brahmans but as well educated.
Chitpāvan (Citapāvan): A Brahman caste that dominated the political scene from the eighteenth century until the death of Tilak in 1920 and the intellectual scene until recently. Also known as Konkanasthas (from the Konkan, their place of origin).
Deshastha (Deśastha): The Brahmans of the Desh. Most numerous and dominant until the rise of the Chitpāvans.
Dhangar (Dhanagar): A shepherd caste.
Gavārī: Cowherds, not a specific caste.

Gavḷī (Gavaḷī): A cowherd caste.
Goṇḍ: A tribal group in Eastern Maharashtra.
Gurav: A Shudra caste, often priests of Shaiva temples. Also musicians.
Harijan: "People of God." Gandhi's name for Untouchables, often rejected by the followers of the Untouchable leader, B.R. Ambedkar, as patronizing.
Hāṭkar: A sub-caste of the Dhangar caste cluster.
Jain: A religion, now found chiefly among Gujarati merchants, with a smaller group of adherents among agriculturists in Southern Maharashtra, which took organized form about the time of the formation of Buddhism (6–5th centuries B.C.) Both groups are treated as castes in the Maharashtrian context.
Kaikaḍi: A caste that makes twig baskets.
Karhāḍā: A small Brahman caste, originally from the Konkan.
Koḷī: Fishermen and watermen.
Konkaṇastha (Koṅkaṇastha): Name for Chitpāvan Brahmans, q.v.
Koshṭī (Koṣṭī): Weavers.
Kumbhār: Potters.
Lingāyat: A member of the Vīrashaiva sect, originally from Karnataka; they are treated as a caste in Maharashtra.
Lohār: Ironsmiths.
Mahār: The largest of the Untouchable castes in Maharashtra, chief participants in a movement for equality which culminated in a large Buddhist conversion.
Māḷī: A gardening caste.
Māng (Māṅga): An Untouchable caste, still rope makers.
Marāṭhā: The dominant agricultural caste of Maharashtra.
Mārwāḍī: Money lenders and businessmen, from Marwar originally.
Nandīwālā: (Lit., one who works with bulls), a nomadic tribe, originally from Andhra Pradesh.
Nhāvī: Barbers.
Parīṭ: Washermen.
Rāmoshi (Rāmośi): Watchmen, formerly tribal.
Sāḷī: Weavers.
Sāraswat (Sārasvata): A Brahman caste with a mythic origin in the North, religious centers in the South.
Shūdra (Śūdra): The fourth order of the varṇas. Some Brahmans

hold that all castes in Maharashtra except Brahmans and Untouchables are Shūdra.

Telī: Oil pressers.

Untouchable: The three most important Untouchable castes in Maharashtra are Chambhar, Mahar, and Mang, q.v. Since the practice of untouchability was barred in the Indian Constitution, the term "Ex-Untouchable" has been used where appropriate.

(*Note: v and w interfiled*)

Waḍār (Vaḍāra) or Beldār: Stone and earth workers.

Vanjārī, Banjārī (Vañjārī, Banajārī): Carriers of grain and salt, now often settled farmers.

Wārik (Vārik): Barbers.

Viṇkar (Viṇakar): Weavers.

# Contributors

*Maxine Berntsen, now an Indian citizen, lives in Phaltan, Maharashtra, where she has founded two schools, one in the poorer area of the town. She has produced beginning and advanced Marathi material which is available from the South Asia Regional Studies Department of the University of Pennsylvania and her Ph.D. in linguistics is from that University. She teaches Marathi to Associated Colleges of the Midwest students during their U.S. orientation in alternate years, and has tutored many American scholars.*

*Sadashiv S. Bhave, who died in 1986, was a member of the historic Deccan Education Society and taught Marathi at various of the Society's Colleges, most recently Fergusson College in Pune. A much published critic in Marathi, he also taught Marathi literature in the Associated Colleges of the Midwest's India Studies program in Pune and in 1984 at Carleton College in Northfield, Minnesota.*

*Paul B. Courtright, a Ph.D. in the History of Religions from Yale, is now teaching at the University of North Carolina, Greensboro. He has recently published his major study on* Gaṇeśa *(Oxford, 1986) and is now at work on the life and teaching of the seventeenth century politico-religious saint Ramdas.*

*Ulpabai Chauhan is a housewife in Phaltan, Maharashtra. Her father owned a shop which made hats, an unusual advance in status for an Untouchable of his day, and also became one of the leading Buddhists in the area, in spite of a severe physical handicap. Ulpabai Chauhan continues his interest in Buddhism.*

*G.N. Dandekar is a noted and popular novelist in Marathi. He lives in Pune, and travelled with Gadge Maharaj for some time.*

*R.N. Dandekar, now almost eighty, goes to his office at Bhandarkar Institute of Oriental Studies every day. A major contributor to the Bhandarkar edition of the* Mahābhārata, *Dandekar also taught Sanskrit at the University of Poona for many years. He has published much on Hinduism (see the Selected Bibliography) and many of his scholarly articles were republished in* Vedic Mythological Tracts *(Delhi: Ajanta, 1979).*

*R.C. Dhere, who has a doctorate from the University of Poona, is one of the most prolific writers in Marathi on Maharashtrian religion. His work on folk religion and such topics as Muslim saint-poets in the Maharashtrian bhakti tradition is unique. His most recent work is on the Varkari tradition, the God Vithoba and Pandharpur (see the Selected Bibliography).*

*Philip Engblom, a Ph.D. from the University of Minnesota, has just published a major work on the Varkari movement, a translation with introduction of D.B. Mokashi's* Palkhi. *He has also co-edited the Marathi Sampler issue of the* Journal of South Asian Literature. *He is at work on translations of an important Marathi poet, P.S. Rege, and planning a related study on modernism in Marathi and Indo-English poetry in contemporary Bombay.*

*Anne Feldhaus, a Ph.D. in Religious Studies from the University of Pennsylvania, teaches at Arizona State University. She has published two books on the Mahanubhav tradition, a number of articles (see the Selected Bibliography), and is now at work on a major study of pilgrimage places in Maharashtra.*

*Vitthalrao Ghate (Viththal Dattatraya Ghate) (1895–1978) was a major writer in Marathi, with books of history, poetry, drama, light essays, and geography, as well as a well-known autobiography to his credit.*

*K.N. Kadam is a retired officer of the Social Welfare department in Maharashtra. Educated in Jesuit schools and Wadia College in Pune, he has written a number of privately circulated ar-*

*ticles in English on his life, Buddhism, and Dr. B.R. Ambedkar. He lives in a Pune housing society, where he has founded a Buddhist study circle.*

*Bebi Kamble and her husband run a small store in the Maharwada (ex-Untouchable quarters) of Phaltan, Maharashtra. Her brother is a poet in the Dalit Sahitya (literature of the oppressed) movement and her own autobiography,* Jiṇa amuca *(our life), has just been published as a book after being serialized in the Marathi magazine for women,* Strī. *Her oldest son is well educated and serves as an agricultural officer in a bank.*

*Irawati Karve (1905–1970) was born in Burma (hence her unusual first name), educated at Fergusson College and the University of Bombay, and received her Ph.D. from the Kaiser Wilhelm Institute for Anthropology in Berlin. She taught at the Deccan College Postgraduate and Research Institute from 1939 on, with a year at the University of California. Her personal help as well as her writing has been an inspiration to the editors and to many of the contributors of this book.*

*Jayant Karve, now a computer programmer in San Diego, has worked with Eleanor Zelliot on many translations, including the famous Tendulkar play,* Ghashiram Kotwal *(Calcutta: Seagull, 1984). His knowledge of Marathi colloquialisms and Pune cultural life is unobtrusively reflected in various ways in this volume.*

*Ashok Kelkar, Professor of Applied Linguistics at the Deccan College Postgraduate and Research Institute, is an internationally known linguist who also writes on literary and cultural matters. His Ph.D. is from Cornell University, and his home in Pune is a haven for intellectuals of many countries.*

*Shankarrao Kharat, who lives in Pune, has been a lawyer and a government official in many capacities. His greatest claim to fame is as the first recognized* dalit *writer, with some twenty books to his credit. He has edited Dr. Ambedkar's newspaper, written on the Buddhist conversion, published his autobiography, and continues to produce short stories on the lives of the rural poor in a gentle, sometimes humorous fashion.*

*Anasuyabai Koratkar (1911–1983) was a Marathi-speaking housewife who lived in Hyderabad. Her home served as the first Indian experience of Maxine Berntsen.*

*K.C. Malhotra was a student of Irawati Karve's and taught anthropology at the Deccan College Postgraduate and Reseasrch Institute in Pune. He has also taught in the United States, and is now with the Indian Statistical Institute, Calcutta.*

*D.B. Mokashi (1915–1982) has been one of the formative forces in Marathi literature, often writing on the rural scene. A short story dealing with the bhakti faith among farmers, his journal of participation in the Varkari pilgrimage, both translated by Philip Engblom, and his moving novel of the removal of the household gods from a village home, translated by Pramod Kale, are noted in the Selected Bibliography.*

*Jai Nimbkar, born in Pune to D.D. and Irawati Karve, now lives in Phaltan where she pursues the double career of writing and market gardening. Her novel* Temporary Answers *was published by Orient Longman, and a collection of short stories,* Lotus Leaves, *was published by Writers Workshop, Calcutta.*

*Charles Pain, a graduate student in Sanskrit at the University of California, Berkeley, has returned to India several times after his initial study under the auspices of the Associated Colleges of the Midwest's India Study program in 1969. He is a graduate of Carleton College.*

*Kumar Saptarshi became a founder-member of Yukrand, the Revolutionary Youth Organization in his student days. He practiced medicine from 1969–74, leaving that to found a commune in an Untouchable area of Rashim, where he now has founded the Indian Institute for Social Development and Research. After a year and a half in jail during the Emergency, he won a seat in the Maharashtra Legislative Assembly as a Janata Party member in 1977.*

*V.M. Sirsikar, Mahatma Gandhi Professor of Politics and Public Administration at the University of Poona before his retirement, is now joint director of the Centre for Development Studies and Activities in Pune. He is the author of several highly respected books on the behavioral aspects of voting in India. He has served as Director of the Certificate Course offered by the University of Poona to the Associated Colleges of the Midwest's India Studies program, taught twice at Carleton College, and aided many American scholars and groups.*

*Carolyn Slocum, a Carleton graduate of 1982, is now in seminary studying liberation theology. She participated in the Associ-*

*ated Colleges of the Midwest's program in India, where her independent study was on the meaning of* shakti *in women's lives. She has also worked for a social concerns group developing grass roots farm leadership.*

*Gunther-Dietz Sontheimer studied at Tubingen and the University of Poona Law College, and obtained his Ph.D. from the School of Oriental and African Studies, University of London. Since 1965, he has been head of the South Asia Institute of the University of Heidelberg, teaching in the Department of Religion and Philosophy. He publishes in both German and English, and has founded the English journal,* South Asia Digest of Regional Writing, *at Heidelberg. He divides his year between Germany and India.*

*John M. Stanley is Ellen C. Sabin Professor of Religion at Lawrence University, Appleton, Wisconsin. A graduate of the University of Colorado and the Pacific School of Religion, he secured his Ph.D. from Columbia University. He has frequently led the Associated Colleges of the Midwest's India Studies group to Pune, and has written on the Khandoba cult and on the god Hanuman (see Selected Bibliography), and the Pandharpur pilgrimage. He is now deeply involved in studies on medical ethics.*

*Narayan Surve is a poet, schoolteacher, and Marxist. Raised as an orphan on the streets of Bombay, he is identified with the Dalit Sahitya (literature of the oppressed) school of writing.* On the Pavements of Life, *a collection of his poetry translated by Krishna Chaudhari and P.S. Nerurkar, has been published by Lok Vangmaya Griha, Bombay, 1973.*

*Anutai Wagh has founded a center for the education of Warlis, a tribal people of Thana district, which is considered a model of its kind. Her autobiography describes her social and religious concerns, and those of her distinguished family.*

*Eleanor Zelliot, a University of Pennsylvania Ph.D., teaches the history of India at Carleton College in Northfield, Minnesota. She has travelled periodically to Maharashtra since 1963, pursuing her research on Dr. B.R. Ambedkar and the bhakti saint-poets Eknath and Cokhamela, or as director of the Associated Colleges of the Midwest's India Studies program, most recently in 1986 under the auspices of the Western India Regional Language Centre.*

# *Selected Bibliography on Religion in Maharashtra*

Partially Annotated

*NOTE: The editors would like to acknowledge the help of John M. Stanley and the Ames Library of South Asia at the University of Minnesota in the creation of this bibliography. Because the volume is intended for the general reader, only a few Marathi sources have been included. The edition used is indicated first; if the most recent edition of the volume is given first, it is followed by the first date of publication in parentheses.*

Bibliography Contents


| | | |
|---|---|---|
| I. | General | 351 |
| II. | The Bhakti/Varkari/Pandharpur Tradition | |
| | Texts | 354 |
| | General Literature | 355 |
| III. | Caste Practices | 356 |
| IV. | Gods and Goddesses | 357 |
| V. | Gurus and Other Religious Teachers | 358 |
| VI. | Festivals and Rituals | 361 |
| VII. | Religion in Literature | 362 |
| VIII. | Religions Other than Hinduism | |
| | Buddhism | 363 |
| | Christianity | 364 |
| | Islam | 365 |
| | Judaism | 365 |
| | Tribal Religions | 365 |
| | Zoroastrianism | 366 |
| IX. | Reform and Rejection | 366 |
| X. | Statements of Personal Views | 367 |
| XI. | Temples and Holy Places | 369 |

## I. General

Abbott, John. *The Keys of Power*: A Study of Indian Ritual and Belief. London: Methuen, 1932. Reprinted in 1974 by University Books, Seacaucus, N.J.

Amar Chitra Katha (classic picture stories), India Book House Education, Bombay, has published a number of comics on saints of the Varkari tradition and other religious figures which accurately reflect current public knowledge and attitudes. Among them are *Pundalik and Sakhu, Eknath, Tukaram, Ahilyabai Holkar*, and *Tales of Sai Baba*.

Bambawale, Usha. *Inter-religious Marriage*. Introduction by V.G. Pundalik. Pune: Dastane Ramchandra, 1982. Much information on Hindu-Muslim marriages and religious life.

Bhandarkar, Ramkrishna Gopal. *Vaiṣṇavism, Śaivism and Minor Religious Systems*. Varanasi: Indological Book House, 1965 (1913).

*Bhāratīya Saṃskṛtikośa* (Encyclopedia of Indian Culture). Edited by P. Mahadevshastri Joshi. 10 vol. Pune: Bharatiya Sanskiritikosh Mandal, 1962–82.

Damle, Y.B. "Harikatha: A Study in Social-Education." In *New Quest* 49 (Jan.-Feb. 1985): 23–29.

Deleury, G.A. "The Religion of the Hindu Village." In *Religious Hinduism by Jesuit Scholars*. 3rd ed. Edited by R.V. De Smet. Allahabad: St. Paul Publications, 1968.

Deshpande, Kamalabai. "Great Hindu Women in Maharashtra." In *Great Women of India*. Edited by Swami Madhavananda and Ramesh Chandra Majumdar. Mayavati, Almora: Advaita Ashrama, 1953.

Dixit, Prabha. "The Ideology of Hindu Nationalism." In *Political Thought in Modern India*. Edited by Thomas Pantham and Kenneth L. Deutsch. New Delhi: Sage, 1986. A discussion of Savarkar and Golwalkar of Maharashtra, among others.

Enthoven, R.E. *The Folklore of Bombay*. Oxford: Clarendon Press, 1924. All sorts of folk beliefs and notes on religious life as gathered from schoolmasters.

Feldhaus, Anne. "Maharashtra as a Holy Land: A Sectarian Tradition." In the *Bulletin of the School of Oriental and African Studies*, University of London 49:3 (1986): 532–48.

*Gazetteer of Bombay Presidency*. Bombay: Government Central Press, 1877–1904. District Series. The districts covered which are now in Maharashtra are Ahmadnagar, Khandesh (now Jalgaon and Dhulia), Kolaba and Janjira, Kolhapur, Nasik, Poona, Ratnagiri and Savantvadi, Satara, and Sholapur. See *Maharashtra State Gazetteers* for revised editions.

*Gazetteer of the Central Provinces of India.* Various presses, including Government Presses in Bombay, Calcutta, and Allahabad, 1906-11. District Series. The relevant districts are Akola, Amraoti, Bhandara, Buldana, Chanda, Nagpur, Wardha and Yeotmal. See *Maharashtra State Gazetteers* for revised editions.

Jagalpure, L.B. and K.D. Kale. *Sarola Kasar: Study of a Deccan Village in the Famine Zone.* Ahmadnagar: L.B. Jagalpure, 1938.

Kale, Pandurang Vaman. *History of Dharmashastra.* 5 vols. in 7 tomes. Poona: Bhandarkar Oriental Research Institute, 1930–62. International Publications Services reprinted a 1968 edition in 1973. Kane's personal notes and references to Maharashtra throughout make this a volume useful for contemporary Hinduism in Maharashtra as well as the history of religious law.

Karandikar, V.R. and M.R. Lederle. "Philosophy in Marathi." In *Philosophy in the Fifteen Modern Indian Languages.* Edited by V.M. Bedekar. Pune: Continental Prakashan for the Marathi Encyclopaedia of Philosophy, 1979.

Karve, I. *Maharashtra: Land and Its People.* Maharashtra State Gazetteer, General Series. Bombay: Directorate of Government Printing, Maharashtra State, 1968. Contains a chapter on "Religion and Gods" as well as many relevant notes.

Karve, Irawati and J.S. Ranadive. *The Social Dynamics of a Growing Town and Its Surrounding Area.* Poona: Deccan College Postgraduate and Research Institute, 1965.

Kosambi, D.D. *Myth and Reality: Studies in the Formation of Indian Culture.* Bombay: Popular Prakashan, 1962.

Lederle, M.R. *Philosophical Trends in Modern Maharashtra.* Bombay: Popular Prakashan, 1976.

Lyall, Alfred C. "Religion of an Indian Province." In *Asiatic Studies: Religious and Social.* 2nd ed. London: John Murray, 1884. Dated and prejudiced but an unusual perception of the com-

Dated and prejudiced but an unusual perception of the complexities of religion in one region (Berar, now part of Maharashtra).

*Maharashtra State Gazetteers, District Series*. Bombay: Directorate of Government Printing, Maharashtra State, 1962–77. 24 vols. The volume on Poona District in this revised series was published in 1954 by the Government of Bombay State. All volumes are revisions of the earlier *Gazetteers* (q.v.), except those for districts which were in the State of Hyderabad.

Paranjpe, Ashok G. and D. Nadkarni. "Folk Performances of Maharashtra." In *The Performing Arts*. Edited by Narayana Menon. Bombay: Marg Publication, 1982. Over a dozen folk performers, most of them with religious connections, are described, with several pictured.

Ranade, Mahadeo Govind. *Rise of the Maratha Power*. Delhi: Publications Division, Ministry of Information and Broadcasting, Government of India, 1961 (1900). Also published in 1961 by Bombay University Press, with a critical essay by R.V. Orturkar. Included here because Ranade's evaluation of Shivaji and of the Bhakti movement's impact in forming Maharashtrian ethos has determined much of contemporary thought.

*Religion and Society in Maharashtra*. Edited by Milton Israel and N.K. Wagle. South Asian Studies Papers, no. 1. University of Toronto, Centre for South Asian Studies, 1987. (Gunther D. Sontheimer, "Rudra and Khaṇḍobā: Continuity in Folk Religion"; Charlotte Vaudeville, "The Shaivite Background of Santism in Maharashtra"; John M. Stanley, "Niśkāma and Sakāma Bhakti: Pandharpur and Jejuri"; Anne Feldhaus, "The Religious Significance of Ṛddhipūr"; David N. Lorenzen, "The Social Ideologies of Hagiography: Śaṅkara, Tukārām and Kabīr"; Jayant Lele, "Jñāneśvar and Tukārām: An Exercise in Critical Hermaneutics"; Eleanor Zelliot, "Four Radical Saints in Maharashtra"; and N.K. Wagle, "Ritual and Change in Early Nineteenth-Century Society in Maharashtra.")

Zelliot, Eleanor and Anne Feldhaus. "Marathi Religions." In the *Encyclopedia of Religion*. General Editor: Mircea Eliade. New York: Macmillan, 1986.

## *II. The Bhakti/Varkari/Pandharpur Tradition*

### Texts

*Bahina Bai. A Translation of Her Autobiography and Verses* by Justin E. Abbott. The Poet-Saints of Maharashtra, no. 5. Poona: Scottish Mission Industries, 1929. Reprinted by Motilal Banarsidass in 1985 with an introduction by Anne Feldhaus.

Dnyaneshwar. *Jñaneshvarī: A Song-Sermon on the Bhagavadgītā.* Translated by V.G. Pradhan. Edited by H.M. Lambert. Albany: State University of New York, 1986. Previously published by George Allen and Unwin in two volumes, 1967–69.

Kolatkar, Arun. "Translations from Tukaram and other Saint-Poets" (Namdeo, Janabai, Muktabai). *Journal of South Asian Literature* 17:1 (Winter-Spring 1982): 111–14.

Mahipati. *Eknath, a Translation from the Bhaktalilamrita* by Justin E. Abbott. The Poet-Saints of Maharashtra, no. 2. Poona: Scottish Mission Industries, 1929. Reprinted by Motilal Banarsidass in 1981 with an introduction by G.V. Tagore.

——. *Nectar from Indian Saints.* Translations from the *Bhaktalilamrita* by Justin E. Abbott, N.R. Godbole, and J.F. Edwards. The Poet-Saints of Maharashtra, no. 11. Poona, 1935.

——. *Stories of Indian Saints.* An English translation of Mahipati's Marathi *Bhaktavijaya*, vols. 1 and 2. Translated by Justin E. Abbott and Narhar Godbole. The Poet-Saints of Maharashtra, nos. 9 and 10. Poona, 1933–34. Reprinted in one volume by Motilal Banarsidass in 1982.

——. *Tukaram.* Translation from Mahipati's *Bhaktalilamrita* by Justin E. Abbott. The Poet-Saints of Maharashtra, no. 7. Poona, 1930. Reprinted by Motilal Banarsidass in 1980 and 1986.

*Śrīsakalasantagāthā.* (A collection of all the saints' work.) Compiled by Shrinanamaharaj Sakhare. Edited by Kashinath Anant Joshi. Pune: Shrisantwangmay Prakashan Mandir, 1967 (1923). A new edition began appearing serially in 1985. This is the basic collection of the saint-poets *abhangas* in Marathi.

*Stotramālā: A Garland of Hindu Prayers.* A Translation of Prayers of Maratha Poet-Saints, from Dnyaneshvar to Mahipati by Justin E. Abbott. The Poet-Saints of Maharashtra, no. 6. Poona: Scottish Mission Industries, 1929.

Tukaram. *Psaumes du pelerin*. Translated by G.A. Deleury. Connaissance de l'orient; collection UNESCO d'oeuvres representatives. 2nd ed. Paris: Gallimard, 1956.

——. *The Poems of Tukarama*. Translated by J. Nelson Fraser and K.B. Marathe. Vol. 1. Delhi: Motilal Banarsidass, 1981. First edition in three volumes. Madras: Christian Literature Society, 1909–15.

## General Literature

See also Durga Bhagwat, D.B. Mokashi, and Vijay Tendulkar's work in the *South Asian Digest of Regional Writing* issue and D.B. Mokashi's short story in the *Journal of South Asian Literature* issue listed under Religion in Literature (VII). Also see Iravati Karve's "On the Road" in this volume.

Belsare, K.V. *Tukaram*. New Delhi: Maharashtra Information Centre, Government of Maharashtra, 1967.

Dandekar, S.V. *Dnyanadeo*. New Delhi: Maharashtra Information Centre, Government of Maharashtra, 1969.

Deleury, G.A. *The Cult of Vithoba*. Poona: Deccan College Postgraduate and Research Institute, 1960. The first and still basic study of the Varkari tradition.

Deshpande, P.Y. *Jnanadeva*. Makers of Indian Literature Series. New Delhi: Sahitya Akademi; Sterling Publications, 1973.

Dhere, R.C. *Śrīviṭhṭhal: ek mahāsamanvaya*. (Vitthal, a great integrator.) Pune: Shrividhya Prakashan, 1984.

Edwards, J.F. *Dnyānesvar, the Outcaste Brahman*. The Poet-Saints of Maharashtra, no. 12. Poona: United Theological College of Western India, 1941.

Feldhaus, Anne. "Bahiṇā Bāī: Wife and Saint." In *The Journal of the Academy of Religion* 50 (1982): 591–604.

Karandikar, M.A. *Namdev*. New Delhi: Maharashtra Information Centre, Government of Maharashtra, 1970.

Kulkarni, Shridhar. *Eknath*. New Delhi: Maharashtra Information Centre, 1966.

Lele, Jayant, ed. *Tradition and Modernity in Bhakti Movements*. Leiden: E.J. Brill, 1981. Also appeared as the *Journal of Asian and African Studies* 14:3 and 4 (1980). (Includes Jayant Lele, "The Bhakti Movement in India: A Critical Introduction" and "Community, Discourse and Critique in Jnanesvar"; Jayashree B. Gokhale-Turner, "Bhakti or Vidroha: Continuity and Change in Dalit Sahitya"; Bhalchandra Nemade, "The Revolt of the Underprivileged: Style in the Expression of the Warkari Movement in Maharashtra"; and Eleanor Zelliot, "Chokhamela and Eknath: Two Bhakti Modes of Legitimacy for Modern Change.")

Mokashi, D.B. *Palkhi*. Translated by Philip Engblom. Introductory essays by Philip Engblom and Eleanor Zelliot. Albany: New York State University Press, 1987.

Nemade, Bhalacandra. *Tukaram*. New Delhi: Sahitya Akademi, 1980.

Ranade, Ashok D. "Keertana: an effective communication." In his *On Music and Musicians of Hindoostan*. New Delhi: Promilla and Co., 1984.

Ranade, R.D. *Mysticism in India: The Poet-Saints of Maharashtra*. Albany: State University of New York Press, 1983. First published in 1933; then as *Pathway to God in Marathi Literature* in 1961.

Sardar, G.B. *The Saint-Poets of Maharashtra: Their Impact on Society*. Translated by Kumud Mehta. Bombay: Orient Longmans, 1969.

Skyhawk, Hugh van. "*Eknāthī Bhāruḍe* as a Performance Genre." In *South Asian Digest of Regional Writing* 10 (1981): 48–56. Issue on "Drama in Contemporary South Asia," edited by Lothar Lutze.

Tulpule, Shankar Gopal. *Mysticism in Medieval India*. Wiesbaden: Otto Harrossowitz, 1984.

Vaudeville, Charlotte. "Pandharpur, the City of Saints." In *Structural Approaches to South India Studies*. Edited by Harry M. Buck and Glenn E. Yocum. Chambersburg, Pa.: Wilson Books, 1974.

Zelliot, Eleanor. "Eknath's Bharuds: The Sant as Link Between Cultures." In *The Sants: Studies in a Devotional Tradition of India*. Edited by Karine Schomer and W.H. McLeod. Berkeley: Religious Studies Series; Delhi: Motilal Banarsidass, 1987.

## *III. Caste Practices*

Conlon, Frank F. *A Caste in a Changing World*: The Chitrapur Saraswat Brahmans, 1700–1935. Berkeley: University of California Press, 1977. Includes changes in religious attitudes and organizations.

Enthoven, R.E. *The Tribes and Castes of Bombay*. 3 vol. Bombay: Government Central Press, 1920–22. Volumes 1 and 3 reprinted by Cosmo Publications, Delhi, 1975.

*Illustrated Weekly of India* (Bombay). Feature stories on various castes and their current caste practice appeared in this publication during 1970–73. Included were the Chitpavans (February 22, 1970); the Saraswats (June 28, 1970); the Kayastha Prabhus (July 26, 1970); the Marathas (May 2, 1971); the Mahars (April 2, 1972); and the Karhada Brahmans (February 4, 1973).

Ketkar, Shridhar Venkatesh. *History of Caste in India*. Jaipur: Rawat Publications, 1979 (1909). Ketkar's work is so filled with personal opinion that it stands as a liberal view of the times.

Kosambi, D.D. "The Living Prehistory of India." In *Scientific American* 216 (1967): 104–14. Refers to the Dhangars and other nomads.

Robertson, Alexander. *The Mahar Folk*. London: Oxford University Press and Calcutta: Y.M.C.A. Publication House, 1938.

Russell, Robert, assisted by Rai Bahadur Hira Lal. *The Tribes and Castes of the Central Provinces of India*. 4 vol. London: Macmillan, 1916.

## *IV. Gods and Goddesses*

Cashman, Richard. "The Political Recruitment of God Ganapati." In the *Indian Economic and Social History Review* 7 (1970): 347–73.

Courtright, Paul B. *Gaṇeśa: Lord of Obstacles*. New York: Oxford University Press, 1985.

Gadgil, Amerindra. *Śrī Gaṇeśa Kośa*. (Encyclopedia of Ganesh). Pune: Shriganesh Kosh Mandal, 1967.

Ghurye, G.S. *Gods and Men*. Bombay: Popular Prakashan, 1962.

Joshi, Pralhad Narahara. *Śrīdattātreya-jñānkośa*. (Encyclopedia of Datta). Bombay: Surekha Prakashan, 1974.

Joshi, Purushottam Balkrishna. "On the Household and Village Gods of Maharashtra." In the *Journal of Anthropological So-*

*ciety of Bombay* 2 (1889–90): 202–07. Still valid as a list of village gods and goddesses and as a delineation of various categories of worshipped deities.

Mate, M.S. *Temples and Legends of Maharashtra*. Bombay: Bharatiya Vidya Bhavan, 1962. Includes Ganesh, Mahalakshmi, Bhavani, Dattatreya, Parshurama, Bhimashankar, Tryambakeshvar, Khandoba, Vitthal.

Sontheimer, Günther-Dietz. *Birobā, Mhaskobā und Khaṇḍobā: Ursprung, Geschichte und Umvelt von pastoralen Gottheiten in Mahārāṣṭra*. Wiesbaden: Franz Steiner Verlag, 1976.

## *V. Gurus and Other Religious Teachers*

*NOTE: Dates of the guru or religious teacher are given, when available, after the first reference. Not all gurus are Maharashtrian, but all have or have had important ashrams in Maharashtra.*

Apte, S.S. *Shree Samartha Ramdas, Life and Mission*. Bombay: Vora and Co., 1965. History of Ramdas (1608–81) by a Ramdasi.

Belfrage, Sally. *Flowers of Emptiness: Reflections on an Ashram*. New York: Dial Press, 1981. Notes on the ashram of Rajneesh (1931–) in Pune.

Dandekar, R.N., ed. *Ramakrishna Gopal Bhandarkar as an Indologist*. Pune: Bhandarkar Oriental Research Institute, 1976. Essays include Dandekar's own evaluation of the work of Bhandarkar (1837–1925) on Vaishnavism and Shaivism.

Date, V.H. *R.D. Ranade and His Spiritual Lineage*. Bombay: Bharatiya Vidya Bhavan and Jodhpur: Adhyatma Sahitya Vikas Sanstha, 1982. A biography of R.D. Ranade (1886–1957), author of *Mysticism in Maharashtra*, by one of his many disciples.

Donkin, William. *The Wayfarers: An Account of the Work of Meher Baba with the God-Intoxicated, and also with Advanced Souls, Sadhus and the Poor*. San Francisco: Sufism Reoriented, 1969 (1948). Includes descriptions of the ashrams of Meher Baba (1894–1969) at Ahmadnagar, Mahabaleshwar, and Satara in Maharashtra.

Duncan, I.R. "A Western Anthropologist's Experience under One

Form of Yogic Initiation." In *Theoria to Theory* 4 (1970): 78–80. About Swami Muktananda, 1908–86.

Hopkinson, Tom and Dorothy. *Much Silence: Meher Baba, His Life and Work*. London: Victor Gollancz, 1974. Much on the life of Meher Baba in Pune.

Joshi, P.L. "Saints of Vidarbha." In *Political Ideas and Leadership in Vidarbha*. Edited by P.L. Joshi. Nagpur: Silver Jubilee Committee, Department of Political Science and Public Administration, Nagpur University, 1980. Includes Gulabrao Maharaj, Gadge Maharaj (d. 1956) and Tukdoji Maharaj (1909–68).

Kane, Padmakar Sidhanath. *The Rashtrasant: the Socio-political Thought of Sant Tukdoji Maharaj*. Foreword by V.B. Kolte. Nagpur: Ameya Prakashan, 1973.

Kirtane, Mrs. Sumati. "Educated Women and the Cult of Gurubhakti." In *Bulletin of the Deccan College Research Institute* 31, 32 (1970–72): 353–59. Dr. Irawati Karve Commemoration Volume.

Kulkarni, B.R., editor. *Critical and Constructive Aspects of Prof. R.D. Ranade's Philosophy*. Belgaum: Academy of Comparative Philosophy and Religion, 1974. Kulkarni's introduction is instructive on the life and religious teaching of this important Maharashtrian scholar.

Mangalwadi, Vishal. *The World of Gurus*. New Delhi: Vikas, 1977. Includes Shri Dattabai Desai of Kolhapur as well as the better known Rajneesh and Muktananda.

Meher Baba. *Listen, Humanity*. Narrated and edited by D.E. Stevens. New York: Dodd, Mead and Co., 1971 (1957).

Muktananda (Swami Muktananda Paramhansa). *Chitshaktivilas: The Play of Consciousness*. New York: Harper and Row, 1971.

Narasimha Swami, B.V. and S. Subbarao. *Sage of Sakuri*. Life story of Shree Upasani Maharaj (1870–1941). 4th ed. Sakuri: Shri Upasani Kanya Kumari Sihan, 1966. An important guru in the Sai Baba of Shirdi tradition.

Narayan, Shriman. *Vinoba: His Life and Work*. (Vinoba Bhave, 1895–1982.) Bombay: Popular Prakashan, 1970. Good on the background and home life of this Marathi-speaking "successor" of Mahatma Gandhi.

Nargolkar, Vasant. *The Creed of Saint Vinoba*. Bombay: Bharatiya Vidya Bhavan, 1963.

Osborne, Arthur. *The Incredible Sai Baba.* London: Rider and Co., 1958 (1957). Sai Baba, one of the most important gurus in the Maharashtrian tradition, lived at Shirdi until his death in 1918.

Prajananda, Swami. *A Search for the Self: The Story of Swami Muktananda.* 3rd ed. Ganeshpuri: Gurudev Siddha Peeth, 1979.

Rajneesh, Bhagwan Shree. *Hammer on the Rock: a Darshan Diary.* New York: Grove Press, 1979. Illustrated.

Sahukar, Mani. *Sai Baba: The Saint of Shirdi.* 2nd ed. Bombay: Somaiya Publications, 1971 (1952).

——. *Sweetness and Light: an Exposition of Sati Godavari Mataji's Philosophy and Way of Life.* Foreword by Lal Bahadur Shastri. Bombay: Bharatiya Vidya Bhavan, 1966. A woman guru, born in 1914, in the Shirdi/Sai Baba/Upasani Baba tradition.

Sham Rao, D.P. *Five Contemporary Gurus in the Shirdi (Sai Baba) Tradition.* Bangalore: The Christian Institute for the Study of Religion and Society. Published by the Madras Christian Literature Society, 1972. (Sai Baba, Upasani Baba, Kanya Kumari Sati Godavari Mataji, Meher Baba, Satya Sai Baba.)

Shepherd, Kevin. *Gurus Rediscovered*: Biographies of Sai Baba of Shirdi and Upasni Maharaj of Sakori. Cambridge: Anthropographia Publications, 1985.

Tipnis, S.N. *Contributions of Upasani Baba to Indian Culture.* (Poona University Ph.D. Thesis.) Sakuri: Shri Upasani Kanya Kumari Stan, 1966.

Tope, T.K. "Bombay University Honours Laxmanshastri Joshi." In *The Radical Humanist* 39:4 (1975): 21–24. A note on Maharashtra's most important humanist religious spokesman.

Tukdoji Maharaj. *The Gramgeeta: an Epic on Indian Village Life.* Translated by R.S. Kadwe. Vol. I. Wardha: Rashtrasant Sahitya Prachar Mandal, 1979.

Tulpule, S.G. *Ranade: a Modern Mystic.* Translated from the Marathi by S.R. Sharma. (Sharma is noted as the author on the spine and the title page.) Poona: Venus Prakashan, 1961.

White, Charles S.J. "The Sai Baba Movement." In *The Sai Baba Movement: Study of a Unique Contemporary Moral and Spiritual Movement.* New Delhi: Arnold-Heinemann, 1985.

——. "The Sai Baba Movement: Approaches to the Study of Indian Saints." In the *Journal of Asian Studies* 31:4 (1972): 863–78.

——. "Swami Muktananda and the Enlightenment through Śakti Pāt." In *History of Religions* 13:4 (1974): 306–22.

Zweig, Paul, ed. *Muktananda: Selected Essays.* New York: Harper and Row, 1976.

## *VI. Festivals and Rituals*

Apte, Mahadev L. and Judit Katona. "The Significance of Food in Religious Ideology and Ritual Behavior in Marathi Myths." In *Food in Perspective.* Edited by A. Fenton and T.M. Owen. Edinburgh: John Donalds, 1981.

Babar, Sarojini. *Folk Literature of Maharashtra.* New Delhi: Maharastra Information Centre, Government of Maharashtra, 1968.

Barnouw, Victor. "The Changing Character of a Hindu Festival." In the *American Anthropologist* 56 (1954): 74–86. The Ganpati Festival in Pune.

Courtright, Paul B. "On This Holy Day in My Humble Way: Aspects of Puja." In *Gods of Flesh, Gods of Stone: the Embodiment of Divinity in India.* Edited by Joanne Punzo Waghorne and Norman Cutler in association with Vasudha Narayanan. Chambersburg, Pa.: Anima, 1985.

Gupte, Balkrishna Atmaram. *Hindu Holidays and Ceremonials.* Calcutta: Thacker and Spink, 1966 (1919).

India (Government of). *Fairs and Festivals in Maharashtra.* Census of India 1961, volume 10. Maharashtra. Part 8-B. Prepared by the Maharashtra Census Office, Bombay, 1969. A very detailed listing of the celebrations of all religions in the state with figures on attendance—a most useful volume.

Jackson, A.M.T., collector, and R.E. Enthoven, editor. *Folklore of the Konkan.* Delhi: Cosmo, 1976 (1915). A great variety of material collected from school teachers.

Skultans, Vieda. "Trance and the Management of Mental Illness among Maharashtrian Families." In *Anthropology Today* 3:1 (1987): 2–4. Good pictures of healing ritual at the Mahanubhav temple in Phaltan.

Stanley, John M. "Hanuman Wrestles on Saturday: An Examination of the Conceptualization of the Special Power of Certain Days." In *Contemporary India: Socio-Economic and Political Processes*. Poona: Continental Prakashan, 1982: 458–68.

——. "Special Time, Special Power." In the *Journal of Asian Studies* 37:1 (1977): 37–48. The Khandoba festival at Jejuri.

Underhill, Murial Marion. *The Hindu Religious Year*. Calcutta: Association Press, 1921. Still an excellent compendium of information on festivals and fairs, chiefly in Bombay Presidency.

## *VII. Religion in Literature*

Bharucha, Perin. *The Fire Worshippers*. Bombay: Strand, 1968. A novel on Parsi life.

Chitale, Venu. *In Transit*. Bombay: Hind Kitabs, 1950. A novel of a Chitpavan Brahman family in Pune, with much on ritual and custom.

*Journal of South Asian Literature* 17:1 (1982). "The Marathi Sampler" issue edited by Philip Engblom and Eleanor Zelliot. Contains short stories by D.B. Mokashi, "An Experience of Immortality," and Shankarrao Kharat, "Potraj"; and two semi-religious poems by Bahinabai Chaudari, "The Mind" and "What It Should Not Be Called."

Kolatkar, Arun. *Jejuri*. Bombay: Clearing House, 1976. A poem cycle on the town of Jejuri, which is a religious center.

Mokashi, D.B. *Farewell to the Gods*. Translated by Pramod Kale. Delhi: Hind Pocket Books, 1972. A novel on the removal of a family's godhouse from a village home.

McMurry, George H. *The Call to Murralla*. New York: Harper and Brothers, 1960. A novel on a young boy's life in a missionary family in Maharashtra.

*South Asian Digest of Regional Writing* 3 (1974). Edited by Gunther D. Sontheimer, University of Heidelberg. Includes Sontheimer's "Religion in Modern Maharashtrian Literature"; Durga Bhagwat's "The Vithoba of Pandhari"; and Vyankatesh Madgulkar's "The Pilgrimage."

Tilak, Lakshmibai. *I Follow After; an Autobiography*. Translated by Josephine Inkster. Madras: Oxford University Press, 1950. Considered a literary masterpiece and recently made into a television drama, this is the autobiography of a Brahman woman who followed her husband, Narayan Waman Tilak, into Christianity.

Tulpule, Shankar Gopal. *Classical Marathi Literature.* (A History of Indian Literature 9:4). Wiesbaden: Otto Harrassowitz, 1979. A history of the pre-1818 literature, essential for understanding the background of religion today.

## *VIII. Religions Other than Hinduism*

*See also the volume by Bambawale listed under the General Section (I) and the Castes and Tribes volumes under Caste Practices (III).*

### Buddhism

*See also Bebi Kamble and Ulpabai Chauhan's statement in this volume.*

Ambedkar, B.R. *The Buddha and His Dhamma.* Bombay: Siddharth College Publication: 1, 1957. The basic bible for those who followed Ambedkar into the Buddhist conversion movement in 1956 and after.

Kharat, Shankarrao. *Dā. Bābāsāheb Āmbeḍkarāñce dhammāntar.* (Dr. Babasaheb Ambedkar's conversion.) Pune: Thokal Prakashan, 1966.

Ramteke, D.L. *Revival of Buddhism in Modern India.* New Delhi: Deep and Deep Publications, 1983.

Sangarakshita. *Ambedkar and Buddhism.* Glasgow: Windhorse Publications, 1986. A memoir by an English Buddhist who knew Ambedkar personally and has established several Buddhist teaching and service centers in western India.

Wilkinson, T.S. and M.M. Thomas, editors. *Ambedkar and the Neo-Buddhist Movement.* Bangalore: The Christian Institute for the Study of Religion and Society. Published by the Christian Literature Society, Madras, 1972.

Zelliot, Eleanor. "Buddhism and Politics in Maharashtra." In *South Asian Politics and Religion.* Edited by Donald E. Smith. Princeton: Princeton University Press, 1969 (1966).

——. "The Psychological Dimension of the Buddhist Movement

in India." In *Religion in South Asia*. Edited by G.A. Oddie. New Delhi: Manohar, 1977.

——. "The Buddhist Literature of Modern Maharashtra." In *South Asia Digest of Regional Writing* 11(1985): 134–49. Issue on "Minorities on Themselves," edited by Hugh van Skyhawk, Heidelberg University, 1986.

## Christianity

*NOTE: There is surprisingly little material on the Christian community in Maharashtra, except for the well known nineteenth century woman social reformer Pandita Ramabai and the poet Narayan Waman Tilak. See also the* Tribes and Castes *volumes under Caste Practices (III.), the* Fairs and Festivals *volume under Festivals and Rituals (VI), and the autobiography of Lakshmibai Tilak under Religion in Literature (VII).*

Adhav, S.M. *Pandita Ramabai*. Bangalore: Christian Institute for the Study of Religion and Society; Madras: Christian Literature Society, 1979.

Hivale, Ruth. *The Wings of the Morning*. Edited and translated by Sarala Barnabas. Bombay: The Bombay Tract and Book Society, 1984. On the life of Dr. B.P. Hivale of the very influential Ahmednagar College, with much emphasis on relationships with the West.

Jacob, Plamthodathil S. *The Experiential Response of N.V. Tilak*. Bangalore: Christian Institute for the Study of Religion and Society; Madras: Christian Literature Society of Madras, 1979.

Moulton, Joseph Langdon. *Faith for the Future: the American Marathi Mission, India, sesquicentennial 1963*. New York: United Church Board for World Ministries, 1967.

Pandita Ramabai. *The Letters and Correspondence of Pandita Ramabai*. (1858–1922). Compiled by Sister Geraldine; edited and with an introduction by A.B. Shah. Bombay: Maharashtra State Board for Literature and Culture, 1977.

Shirsat, K.R. *Narayan Waman Tilak: Poet and Patriot*. Bombay: Bombay Book and Tract Society, 1979.

Staelin, Charlotte. "The Influence of Missions on Women's Education in India: The American Marathi Mission in Ahmadnagar, 1830–1930." Ph.D. dissertation, University of Michigan, 1977.

## Islam

*NOTE: Material on Muslims in Maharashtra is even more sparse than that on Christians. See the* Tribes and Castes *and* Fairs and Festivals *volumes as above. See also detailed bibliographies for occasional articles on the Gujarati-speaking merchant Muslim communities, Bohras and Khojas, chiefly found in Bombay and the cities of the area.*

Dalwai, Hamid. *Muslim Politics in Secular India*. Delhi: Hind Pocket Books, 1972. A statement on communal problems by the late Muslim secularist and reformer.

Shakir, Moin. *Muslim Attitudes: A Trend Report and Bibliography*. Aurangabad: Parimal Prakashan, 1974.

——. *Secularization of Muslim Behavior*. Calcutta: Minerva, 1973. Professor Shakir teaches at Marathwada University in Aurangabad; his many books represent a liberal Nationalist Muslim voice.

van Skyhawk, Hugh. "The Heart of Religion: A Sufi's Thoughts on the Relations between Religious Communities." In *South Asian Digest of Regional Writing* 11 (1985): 117–33. Issue on "Minorities on Themselves," edited by Hugh van Skyhawk, Heidelberg University, 1986.

## Judaism

Abraham, A.S. "The Jews of India." In the *Illustrated Weekly of India* 90:42 (October 19, 1969): 6–11, 18–19.

Israel, Benjamin J. *Religious Evolution among the Bene Israel of India since 1750*. Bombay: author, 1963.

Kehimkar, H.S. *The History of the Bene Israel of India*. Tel-Aviv: Dayag Press, 1937.

Strizower, Schifra. *The Bene Israel of Bombay: A Study of a Jewish Community*. New York: Schocken Books, 1971.

## Tribal Religions

Chapekar, Laxman Narayan. *Thakurs of the Sahyadri*. 2nd ed. Bombay: University of Bombay, 1966.

Kale, D.N. *Agris; A Socio-Economic Survey*. Bombay: Asia Publishing House, 1952.

Naik, Thakorlal Banabhai. *The Bhils, a Study*. Delhi: Bharatiya Adimjati Sevak Sangh, 1956. Includes Khandesh in Maharashtra as well as the Bhil community in Gujarat.

Punekar, Vijaya B. *The Son Kolis of Bombay*. Bombay: Popular Book Depot, 1959.

Save, K.J. *The Warlis*. Bombay: Padma Publications, 1945.

## Zoroastrianism

Bharucha, Sheriarji Dadabhai. *A Brief Sketch of the Zoroastrian Religion and Customs*. 3rd ed. Bombay: D.B. Taraporevala, 1928.

Bulsara, Joel F. "The Parsis." In the *Illustrated Weekly of India* 90:35 (August 31, 1969): 9–29 *passim*.

Duchesne-Guillemin, Jacques. *Symbols and Values in Zoroastrianism: Their Survival and Renewal*. New York: Harper and Row, 1966.

Hinnells, John R. *Zoroastrianism and the Parsis*. London: Ward Lock Education, 1981.

Kulke, Eckehard. *The Parsees in India: a Minority as Agent of Social Change*. Munchen: Weltforum Verlag, 1974.

Masani, Rustom Pestonji. *The Religion of the Good Life, Zoroastrianism*. London: G. Allen and Unwin, 1954 (1938).

Modi, Jivanji Jamshedji. *The Religious Ceremonies and Customs of the Parsis*. 2nd ed. Bombay: J.B. Karanis & Sons, 1937 (1922).

## *IX. Reform and Rejection*

*See also Buddhism under Other Religions (VIII) and the essay by Kadam in this volume.*

Ghugare, Shivprabha. *Renaissance in Western India: Karmaveer V.R. Shinde, 1873–1944*. Bombay: Himalaya Publishing House, 1983. Shinde was an educator and reformer who worked chiefly for the depressed classes.

O'Hanlon, Rosalind. *Caste, Conflict and Ideology: Mahatma Jotirao Phule and Low Caste Protest in Nineteenth-century Western India*. Cambridge: Cambridge University Press,

1985. Phule's Satyashodak (truth-seeking) Society is no longer engaged in religious reform, but Phule's underlying thought is still important in Maharashtra.

Phadke, H.A. *R.G. Bhandarkar (1837–1925)*. New Delhi: National Book Trust, 1968. Contains a chapter on the importance of Bhandarkar's religious reform.

Phadke, Y.D. *Social Reformers of Maharashtra*. 2nd ed. New Delhi: Maharashtra Information Centre, Government of Maharashtra, 1975. Includes Balshastri Jambhekar, Gopal Hari Deshmukh (Lokahitawadi), Jotirao Govindrao Phule, Ramkrishna Gopal Bhandarkar, Mahadeo Govind Ranade, Gopal Ganesh Agarkar, Dondo Keshav Karve, Vitthal Ramji Shinde, Chhatrapati Shahu Maharaj, Bhaurao Paigonda Patil, Bhimrao Ramji Ambedkar. For most of these social reformers, religious reform was also an issue.

*Rationalists of Maharashtra*. Dehradun: Indian Renaissance Institute, 1962. Includes essays on "Gopal Deshmukh, Lokahitawadi," by N.R. Phatak; "Jyotirao Fule," by Tarkateertha Laxman Shastri Joshi, and "Gopal Ganesh Agarkar," by G.P. Pradhan.

*Social and Religious Reform Movements in the 19th and 20th Centuries*. Edited by S.P. Sen. Calcutta: Institute of Historical Studies, 1979. Includes articles by J.V. Naik, N.H. Kulkarnee, S.R. Hanmante, Mani Kamerkar, Vasanta D. Rao, M.P. Kamerkar, and S.R. Shirgaonkar on Maharashtra.

Shah, A.B. *Religion and Society in India*. Bombay: Somaiya Publications, 1981. Essays by the late leading secularist of the India Secular Society in Pune.

## *X. Statements of Personal Views*

Bedekar, D.K. *Towards Understanding Gandhi*. Edited by Rajabhau Gawande. Bombay: Popular Prakashan, 1975. A thoughtful, revealing analysis by a leading Marxist intellectual.

Bhave, Vinoba. *Talks on the Gita*. London: George Allen and Unwin, 1960.

Damle, N.G. "The Faith of an Idealist." In *Contemporary Indian Philosophy*. Edited by J.H. Muirhead and S. Radhakrishnan. 2nd ed. London: George Allen and Unwin, 1952 (1936).

Dandekar, Ramchandra Narayan. *Insights into Hinduism*. Delhi: Ajanta Publications, 1979.

——. *Some Aspects of the History of Hinduism*. Poona: Poona University, 1967. Includes a chapter on Hinduism and Modern Culture.

Deshpande, Mahadeo. *Socio-Linguistic Attitudes in India*. Ann Arbor: Karoma Publications, 1979. The place of Sanskrit in affecting caste attitudes is one of Deshpande's interesting and personal analyses.

Joshi, Tarkateertha Laxmanshastri. "Caste System and Hindu Theology." In *The Radical Humanist* 42:5 (Aug. 1978).

Apa, Pant. *Mandala: An Awakening*. Bombay: Orient Longman, 1978.

——. *A Moment in Time*. Bombay: Orient Longman, 1974. Apa Pant is the influential heir of the princely house of Aundh.

Paradkar, M.D., ed. *Studies in the Gita*. Bombay: Popular, 1970. Includes statements by a number of Maharashtrians.

Paranjpe, Anand C. *In Search of Identity*. New York: John Wiley and Sons, 1975. Includes lengthy interviews with students on their beliefs and attitudes.

Ranade, R.D. *Bhagavadgita as a Philosophy of God-Realisation*. Bombay: Bharatiya Vidya Bhavan, 1982 (1959).

——. *Essays and Reflections*. Compiled by B.R. Kulkarni. Bombay: Bharatiya Vidya Bhavan, 1964.

——. "The Evolution of My Own Thought." In *Contemporary Indian Philosophy*. Edited by J.H. Muirhead and S. Radhakrishnan. 2nd ed. London: George Allen and Unwin, 1952.

Rege, M.P. "Gandhi, Dharmashastra and Untouchability." In *Quest* 84 (Sept.-Oct. 1973): 9–17. A report on the thought of Lakshmanshastri Joshi in an interview with Gandhi.

——. "Some Reflections on the Indian Philosophical Tradition." In *Quest* 44 (Jan.-Mar. 1965): 9–24.

Tilak, Bal Gangadhar. *The Hindu philosophy of life, ethics and religion. Om-tat-sat, srimad Bhagavadgita rahasya*: or Karma-yoga-sastra, including an external examination of the Gita, the original Sanskrit stanzas, their English translations, commentaries on the stanzas, and a comparison of Eastern with Western doctrines, etc. (Short title: *Gita Rahasya*.) Translated by Bhalchandra Sitaram Sukthankar. 5th English ed. Poona: J.S. Tilak and S.S. Tilak, 1983 (1935; Marathi original, 1915).

Tulpule, S.G. "Spiritual Autobiography in Marathi: a Tradition Lost and Renewed." In *South Asian Digest of Regional Writing* 5 (1976): 57–68. Includes a discussion of the work of G.V. Tulpule and K.V. Belsare, among others.

## *XI. Temples and Holy Places*

*See also the essential* Fairs and Festivals *(VI); Feldhaus under General (I); and the listings on Pandharpur under Bhakti/Warkari/Pandharpur Tradition (II). The reader should also note that while the magnificent cave temples of Maharashtra—Ajanta, Ellora, Elephanta, Karla, Bhaja, Kanheri and many others—are no longer used as religious structures, they are an important part of Maharashtra's religious past. There are Hindu temples now in use near the sites of the Karla and Ellora cave temples, ashrams of Hindu and Jain sadhus near Kanheri, and a new Buddhist retreat center near Bhaja.*

Dave, J.H. *Immortal India*. 4 vols. Bombay: Bharatiya Vidya Bhavan, 1957–61. Vol. 1 includes Pandharpur and Nasik; vol. 2, Kolhapur, Ambarnath and Bhimashankar; vol. 3, Alandi and Paithan; vol. 4, the Godavari, Krishna, and Bhima rivers and the Sahyadri mountains.

Dingre, Gajanan Vithalrao. "Study of a Temple Town and its Priesthood." Ph.D. dissertation in Sociology and Anthropology, Deccan College, 1968. The town is Pandharpur, but Dingre concentrates on the priesthood, not the Varkaris, and on all the temples of the town, not only those visited by Varkaris.

*Gazetteer of the Bombay Presidency*. District Series. Edited by James M. Campbell. Bombay: Government Central Press, 1877–1904. Each volume contains material on holy places important to that district. Revised versions, often shorter, have been published by the Government of Maharashtra in the *Maharashtra State Gazetteer* series beginning in 1970 which include districts originally in Berar and the Central Provinces and the state of Hyderabad. The revised versions began in the 1950s under the Government of Bombay State.

Huble, S.K., Traude Vertschera, and Sudhakar Khome. "The Sacred Complex of Mahdi." In *Man in India* 56:3 (Jul.-Sep. 1976): 237–62. A rare look at the place of Kanifnath, one of the nine Naths.

Mate, M.S. *Temples and Legends of Maharashtra*. Bombay: Bhavan's Book University, 1962. Includes Morgaon, Kolhapur, Tuljapur, Gangapur, Pedhe, Bhimashankar, Tryambak, Jejuri and Pandharpur.

# Index


Adbanginath: in Dagadu Halwai Datta Mandir, 108n. 14

*Ahimsā*: as Mahanubhav principle, 265, 279n. 9

Ahmednagar: Ganesh festival in, 87, 88

Akhandanand Maharaj: and Shedgao Datta temple, 252; breaking of Untouchability Offenses Act by, 253, 260, 261, 263n.6

Alandi: Dnyaneshwar's *samādhī* at, 145; Dyaneshwar pilgrimage from, 143, 145

*Amalikāgrāma Māhātmya*: on *gaundalī*-dance, 181

*Amāvāsyā*: *bhūt*-excorcism on, 37

Amba, 180

Ambaji-Limbaji: as principal Nandiwala god, 134, 135; *navas* to, 135; overshadowing of, by Ram Mama, 136, 137

Ambedkar, Dr. B. R., 294; and mass conversion to Buddhism, 291; and religious skepticism, 288; Gadge Maharaj's extolling of, 224, 237, 249n.8; invocation of, by Yukrand satyagrahis, 260, 261, 263n.5

Amraoti District: concentration of Mahanubhav pilgrimage places in, 274, 279n.14

Ancestor deification: by Dhangars, 115

Ancestor-worship: by Hatkar Dhangars, 114–16, 119, 127, 128; by Nandiwalas, 133, 134

Andhra Pradesh: origin of Nandiwalas in, 132

*Angāt ālelā*: exorcism of *bhūts* by, 30

*Angāt ālelī*: as mediums of gods among Nandiwalas, 135; as mediums and healers, 46–47; as temple of god, 52; common hyperactivity of, 42; "mighty works" done by, 45; power of, felt as gift of god, 51; respected social standing of, 47, 50; rivalry among, 136

*Angāt yene*: and age, educational, and caste distributions, 42–43; as common to Hindus and Muslims, 40–41; as distinct from power infusion, 44–45; as prototype of religious experience, 51;

comparison of, with *bhūt bādhā*, 26–27, 48–53; great variation in symptoms of, 41–44. *See also* Possession by the divine
Anti-Muslim Sentiment in the R.S.S., 195, 201
*Āratī*: as occasion for *angāt yene*, 51; as religious experience for healed *bhūt* victims, 56–57; *bhūt*-exorcism during, 35, 37; by Mahanubhavs, 265, 271; for Dnyaneshwar *pādukās*, 149: in Ganesh worship, 209, 230, 231; in temple worship of Datta, 101, 105, 106, 252, 259; of Jagadamba, in *gondhaḷ*, 182; Untouchables excluded from, 253
Arati Prabhu (Chintamani Tryambak Khanolkar), 302, 308n.20, 311, 312
Arjuna, 164
Ashadhi Ekadashi: Arrival of Dnyaneshwar pilgrimage on, 145, 265
*Ashṭavināyaks*, 77
Atheism: among Maharashtrian intellectuals, 281
Ātmā: identification of, with God, 294; transcendence of duality by, 222
*Avadhūta* ascetic: Datta as type of, 99, 105
*Avatār*: Datta as, of Brahma, Shiva, Vishnu, 95
*Avatārs*: as object of Mahanubhav devotion, 266, 270; birthdays of, celebrated by Mahanubhavs, 275; of Datta, 98–99, 103

*Bābā*: god or *pīr* at healing center known as, 37–39, 53, 54–55; bonds to, of healed *bhūt* victims, 56
Babir: annual *jatrā* for, 122; story of, in Dhangar *ovīs*, 123
Badrinarayan, 227
Bahinabai, 4, 6n.1
Bahiroba, 256
Balakrishna, 205; Yashoda's right to, as son, 6
Banabai: possession by, of high court judge's wife, 47
Banai: Khandoba's second wife, as Dhangar, 124
Bards: Gondhalis as, 181, 186–87
Barodekar, Hirabai: annual concert by, to Dattatreya, 103
Bathing: and *sovḷa*, 207
*Bel* leaves: offering of, to Shankar, 206–07
Berads, 15n.1
Betasur: *tuṇtuṇ* formed from head of, 177
Bhadrapad: major Ganesh festival in, 77, 86
*Bhagavad Gītā*: as rendered by Dnyaneshwar, 144; as sacred book of Varkaris, 164; cited in support of untouchability, 258–59
*Bhāgavata Purāṇa*, 245, 308n.39
Bhagwat. *See Bhāgavata Purāṇa*
*Bhajan*: all-importance of, to Mirabai, 242, 249n.10; as nuisance to middle class, 70; at Dagadu Halwai Datta Mandir, 105, 106; in Datta and Varkari cults, xvii; in Ganesh festival, 87, 88; preparation by, for possession, 41; recommendation of, by Gadge Maharaj, 227, 242; sung by Gadge Maharaj, 226. *See also* Devotional singing.
Bhakta: 315, 316, 317, 318; and practical life, 320; as baby to mother, 313; of Biroba, 119; of Datta, 98, 102
Bhakti: as key to readiness for *angāt yeṇe*, 51, 52; as most potent factor in relation to god, 63; as one of many Hindu ways, 316; as reinforcement of *karnī*, 32; in poems of modern Marathi poets,

310–14; through opposition, 219; true meaning of, in *bhajan*, 230–31; Tukaram's pursuit of God through, 227
Bhangya Maruti temple: as locality marker in Pune, 71
Bharat Mata: glorification of, by R.S.S., 195
*Bhārūḍ*, 175; performance of, on Pandharpur pilgrimage, 161, 166; place of *gondhaḷs* in, 180
Bhavani of Taljapur: as *kaḍak* deity, 17; as religious base for Maratha empire, 175, 178; official emphasis on benevolent aspects of, 24–25; photograph of, as sword, 173; possession by, of high court judge's wife, 47; power of, localized in Tuljapur, 18; submission of *bhūt* victims to, 55; worhip of, by Kadamrai Gondhalis, 177
*Bhaviṣya Purāṇa*: on celebration of Bhutamata festival, 178
Bholanath, 123
Bhutamata: origin of *gondhaḷ* in cult of, 178–79
*Bhūt bādhā*: as cause of illness, 29, 33: as neurosis, 34; as religious experience, 53–57: comparison of, with *angāt yeṇe*, 26–27, 48–53; diagnosis and cure of, 35–40; experience of, as "wrongness," 50; healing from, as *rite de passage*, 57; traditional Maharashtrian beliefs about, 27–29; worsening stages of, 35–36. *See also* Possession by a ghost
*Bhūt* exorcism, 38–40, 54–55, 57; by *angāt ālelī*, 47
*Bhūts*: and Bhutamata festival, 178; and origin of *gondhaḷ*, 179; as seen by *angāt ālelā*, 44; traditional Maharashtrian beliefs about, 27–29. *See also* Ghosts
*Bhūt* victims: description of, at healing centers, 37–40, 54–55; ritual pollution as key to susceptibility of, 32
Biroba: annual *jatrā* for, at Arevadi, 117–18; as brother of Vithoba, 114; devotion to, by Dhangar *devṛishīs*, 116; Dhangar *jatrās* for, 118–20: possession by, 127–28; temples of, 118; worship of, in *kheḷ*, 126–27
Body-temple-cosmos homology of *angāt ālelā*, 52
Borkar, Balkrishna Bhagavant, 300, 307n.8, 310, 311, 313, 317
Bose, Subhash Chandra, 197, 202n.2
"Boy-friend": as term for Vithoba, 3–6
Brahma: and four Vedas, 227; incorporation in Datta of, 95
*Brahman*: and Varkari devotionalism, 164; attainment of, through indifference, 219; *dalit* poet's ironic identification with, 64–65; Ganesh as symbol of, 76; humanity of Harijans provided in, 257
Brahman: as guru in pilgrim *dinḍī*, 144; Datta as, 106; in Dhangar *ovī*, 122
Brahmanical sacrifices: erotic representations in, 161
Brahmans: Akhandanand and Saptarshi in conflict as, 259; as chief patrons of Dagadu Halwai Datta Mandir, 105; authority of, not acknowledged by Mahanubhavs, 264; disdaining by, of water brought by Maratha, 154; Ganpatyas confined to, 76; houses of, to be lower than king's palace, 71; rituals of, not encouraged in R.S.S., 193; separation from Marathas at mealtimes, 143–144, 151–53; virtues of, 236, 237, 240, 248, 249n.7
*Bṛhadāraṇyaka Upaniṣad*: on love of self, 214–15

Buddha, 169, 291, 305; and legitimation for Untouchables, xix; story of, by Mahars, 292; taking refuge in, 294
Buddhism, 316; and propagation of ascetic life, 164–65; conversion of Untouchables to, 281, 291
Buddhists: former Untouchables as, 280; in Shedgao, 253, 260. *See also* Mahars

Campbell, Sir James: on Maharashtrian beliefs about *bhūts*, 27
Caste: deemphasis on, in Ganesh festival *maṇḍaḷs*, 88; divisions of, in pilgrim *diṇḍī*, 151–55. *See also Varṇāshrama*
Celibates: support of, by women, 163
Celibacy in Mahanubhav sect, 269
Chaitra: Mariai fair on full-moon day of, 8, 9
Chakradhar, 266, 270, 274, 275, 278n.5
Chambhars, 185; Gadge Maharaj on failings of, 236, 248, 249n.7; new position of, in Pandharpur pilgrimage, 170n.3
Chandraseniya Kayastha Prabhus (C.K.P.), 277
Changadev Raula, 266
Chaturmas: as time of self-restraint, 207-208
Chaturshringi: Mahar pilgrimage to, 285
Chhinal Maruti temple: as locality marker in Pune, 71
Childbirth: and *bhūt*-susceptibility, 32
Chinchwad: Ganesh cult center at, 76, 77, 210
Chitre, Dilip Purushottam, 303, 308n.23, 311, 312, 313, 318
Chokamela, 291, 294; devotional song of, 155; Mahars at Pandharpur shrine of, 285; Mahar story of birth of, 292; photo of *Samādhī* of, 284
Chokhoba. *See* Chokhamela
Christ, 305, 318. *See also* Jesus; Christianity; Roman Catholicism
Christianity: and Hinduism, 316, 318; and missionaries, 159–60; and translation of Tukaram, 317; conversion to, by Mahar, 288; Narayan Waman Tilak and, 310, 315. *See also* Christ; Jesus; Roman Catholicism
Circumcision: as preventative of *bhūt bādhā*, 33
C.K.P. *See* Chandraseniya Kayastha Prabhus
Cowdung and *sovḷa*, 207
Cow-slaughter ban and R.S.S., 200
Crooke, William: on Maharashtrian beliefs about *bhūts*, 27

Dagadu Halwai Datta Mandir, 102, 104–06
Dagadu Halwai Ganpati, 104
*Dargā*: as healing center for *bhūt bādhā*, 35, 36, 37
*Darshan*: at Dagadu Halwai Datta Mandir, 104, 105: at temple of Swami of Akkalkot, 104; by Gadge Maharaj of crowds, 248; in Datta temples, 101; of *bābā* by healed *bhūt* victims, 56; of Gadge Maharaj, 226; of Ganesh in Morgaon, 209; of Khandoba, in Degaon, 14; of *linga*, by Mahanubhavs, 274; of Vithoba, by Irawati Karve, 4
Darwin, Charles, 288
Dasara, xvii; and Ganesh celebration at Morgaon, 210
Dasnamis and Datta tradition, 97, 98
Dasopant, 98
Datta. *See* Dattatreya
Datta *jayantī*: celebration of, in Pune, 106

*Datta Māhātmya*, 106
*Datta Prabodh*, 106
Dattatreya: as archetypal guru, 98; as Mahanubhav *avatār* of Parmeshwar, 97, 264, 266, 271; as patron god of prostitutes, 105; as ultimate syncretistic god, 95; as wandering ascetic, 96; Brahmanness of, 106; as guru of *naonāth*, 103; importance of music to, 107n.12; in Varkari Panth, 319; photo of temple image of, 100; temple of, in Mahur, 267; temple of, in Shedgao, 252; Untouchables excluded from temple of, 253; varying emphasis on Shaiva or Vaishnava aspects of, 102
Dattatreya temples: as healing centers for *bhūt bādhā*, 36; in Pune, 101. *See also* Dattatreya
*Dāvaṇ* and Dhangar sheep sacrifice, 120
de Beauvoir, Simone: on saint possession in Brazil, 49
Deccan College Postgraduate and Research Institute, xv, 140
Defecation and susceptibility to ghost-possession, 116–17
Defilement: as religious experience of *bhūt* victims, 54–57
Deification: of Dhangar ancestors, 115, 117; of Ram Mama, 131–32, 138–40
Deoras, Balasaheb, 190, 198
Desh, xvii, xx n.5
Deshastha Brahmans: as patrons of *gondhaḷ*, 174, 176; as principal constituent of Ganesh cult, 77; as *pujārīs* in Datta temples, 101, 105
*Devasthān*: as center of divine power, 18
Devi: *kaḍak* form of, at Degaon, 17; possession by, as uniquely rapturous, 42. *See also* Bhavani of Tuljapur; Bhutamata; Jagadamba; Kali; Mahalakshmi of Kolhapur; Mariai, Renuka of Mahur
Devotionalism: harmony of, with monistic idealism, 61–62; in pre-modern Marathi poetry, 309
Devotional singing: during Dnyaneshwar pilgrimage, 144, 149, 150, 160, 162, 165–66. *See also* *Bhajan*
*Devṛishī*: as medium of Dhangar ancestors and gods, 116–17; cause of *bhūt bādhā* attributed to, 29, 30, 58n.4
de Waal Malefijt, A: on voluntary and involuntary possession, 58n.7
Devwalas, 132, 139
*Dhamma*: taking refuge in, 294
Dhangars, xviii, 185, 186, 248; and influence of Shaivism, 113–14; and *jatrās* for Biroba and Mhaskoba, 117–20; and Khandoba, 124–25; and *Kheḷ*, 125–28; ancestor worship by, 114–16, 119, 127, 128; *devṛishī* as ancestor medium for, 116–17; monsoon camps of, 109–11; *ovīs* of, 120–24; photo of, 112
Dharma, 235; as applicable to each yuga, 267; evocation of, by Akhandanand Maharaj, 259; independence of, from god-propitiation, 20; in Dhangar *ovīs*, 124; of R.S.S. ethos, 192; of the Buddha, 292
*Dinḍī*: pilgrimage in, by Irawati Karve, 144, 145, 155, 165, 168, 170; separation of Brahmans and Marathas in, 153
Dnyaneshwar, 170n.2, 307, 309n.44, 311; *advaita* insight of, 320; and Nath Sect, 319; cult of Vithoba antecedent to, 144–45; devotional song of, 165; in Gadge Maharaj's *kīrtan*, 228, 249n.3; Gondhali simile for

*prakṛiti* by, 179; in temple of Swami of Akkalkat, 104; regarded as god, 142, 143; taking of *samādhī* by, 74–75, 75n, 145. *See also* Jñāneśvarī
Draupadi, 298, 307n.4, 311
Drums: importance of, in possession, 119; in *gondhaḷ*, 176, 177, 182
Dualism: as heuristic, not essential in man-god relation, 61; of *brahman* and *māyā*, 319
Dushshasan, 307n.4
Dvapara yuga and dharma of sacrifice, 267

Eclecticism in common Hindu religious practice, 276
Eichmann, Adolf: from Upanishadic viewpoint, 216, 220, 222
*Ekadāshī*, 4, 145, 265
Eknath, 150, 275, 309n.44; and Datta Sect, 319; *gondhaḷs* in *bhārūḍs* of, 180; performance of *bhārūḍs* of, 161; recognition of God by, in Datta, 97
Eliade, Mircea, 52, 53
Emergency and banning of R.S.S., 190
Enthoven, R.E.: on Maharashtrian beliefs about *bhūts*, 27; on married Mahanubhav *sannyāsīs*, 270; on number of Mahanubhavs, 279
Ethics: as aspect of dharma, not god-worship, 20
Evil-eye: screen against, at food offering to Dnyaneshwar, 149

Fascism and the R.S.S., 200–201
Fasting: as active measure for influencing *kaḍak* deities, 23; as preparation for *angāt yeṇe*, 51; by Brahman women on pilgrimage, 148; gaining of *shaktī* by, 208; of the Buddha, 293
Feldhaus, Anne: on "Marathi Religions," xxi n.7
Fire walking rite: and religious dimension of *angāt yeṇe*, 52; by *panjā* bearers at Muharram, 45
Firisti Mariba, 134, 135
Freud, Sigmund: on opposition as sign of agreement, 219
Full-moon day and vow to Mariai, 7, 8, 9. *See also Pūrṇimā*

Gadge Baba: as modern saint, xviii; as Varkari reformer 223–24; *darshan* of, by thousands, 226; extolling by, of education, 237, 240–41; illustration of, 225; on evil of Untouchability, 224, 240, 243–46; vegetarianism promoted by, 224
Gadge Maharaj. *See* Gadge Baba
Gaekwads of Baroda: patronage by, of Gondhalis, 187, 189n.18
Gandharvas, 307, 309n.43
Gandhi, Mahatma: assassination of, 190, 198, 221; extolled by Gadge Maharaj, 233–34; invocation of, by Yukrand satyagrahis, 260, 261
Gandhian method and Yukrand, 251, 259
Ganesh: as protector of democracy, 210; distribution of temples of, 77; in role of trickster, 84; invocation of, in *gondhaḷ*, 182, 183; iconography and names of, 78; mediatory function of, 85; origin of, as related in *Śivapurāṇa* and *Skandapurāṇa*, 79–81; photos of images of, 89, 90; worship of, in Morgaon, 209. *See also* Ganpati
Ganesh *chaturthī* celebrated in Morgaon, 209
Ganesh festival: ambiguous modernity of, xviii; as largely an urban phenomenon, 86; criticized by Gadge Maharaj as lacking bhakti, 230–31; liminality of so-

cial relationships during, 91–92; procession of images on last day of, 87–88; promotion of, by Lokmanya Tilak, 77, 92; sponsorship of, by Peshwas, 77
Ganesh *sampradāy*, 76
Gangapur, 98
Ganpati, 249n.5; as protector of democracy, 91; installment and exhibition of *mūrti* of, 86–87; near Dagadu Halwai Datta Mandir, 104. *See also* Ganesh
Ganpati festival. *See* Ganesh festival
*Gānpatyas* as Maharashtrian Brahman sect, 76
*Gauḷaṇīs* in *gondhaḷs, 183*
*Gaunḍalī, gaunḍalīnṛitya* as variants of *gondhaḷ*, 179, 181
*Gazetteer of the Bombay Presidency*: on Maharashtrian beliefs about *bhūts*, 27, 28
Ghode-Pir, 283; photograph of, 284
Chosts: little fear of, by Dhangars, 116; Nandiwala's belief in, 134; textual connection of Gondhalis with, 179. *See also Bhūts*
Ghurye, G.S.: on enumeration of Pune temples, 101
Giridhari as Meera's "lover," 4
Girnar: meditation at, by Datta, 96
*Gītārṇava* on *gondhaḷ's* connection with ghosts, 179
Godavari River: common reference to as Ganga, 157; Datta's morning bath in, 96; Mahanubhav pilgrimage places along, 274, 279n.14; ritual bathing in, 288; spread of Mahanubhavs north of, 264
God-house: photo of, in Brahman home, 100
Gokul, 184–85, 274
Golwalkar, M.S., 195; change of R.S.S. under, 197–98
*Gondhaḷ*: animal sacrifice at, 239; as type of folk literature, 182; at wedding and thread ceremonies, 176; modernization of, 175; on Varkari pilgrimage, 160; origin of, in cult of Bhutamata, 178–79
Gondhalis: government patronage of, xix; in performance, 176, 181–82; as bards of Maratha kingdom, 181, 186–87; patronage of, 174–75; textual connection of, with ghosts, 179; under the Peshwas, 180–81
*Gopāḷkālā*, 4
*Gopura* as symbol of town's presence, 71
Gorakhnath, 97
Govardhan, 270, 274
Govindaprabhu, 266, 278n.4
Grace (Manik Godghate), 304, 308n.26, 313
Great Tradition: in *ovīs* of Dhangars, 121, 123–24; interpenetration of, with Little Tradition, 60
*Guru dakshiṇā* and R.S.S. funds, 193–94
Guru: care for, by women, 163; Datta as archetype of, 98; in *dinḍī* of Irawati Karve, 144, 145, 152; Mother Goddess as, 180; M.S. Golwalkar in role of, 198
*Gurucaritra*, 98; cited in support of untouchability, 258–59; public reading of, on Datta *jayantī*, 106

Hari Singh Nalwa eulogized by R.S.S., 195
Harijans, 245, 249n.13; of Shedgao, 255, 257, 258, 260. *See also* Untouchables
Hatkar Dhangars, *See* Dhangars
Hazrat, 246, 249n.14
Hedgewar, Dr. K.B., 193, 197
Hindu dharma and R.S.S. ethos, 194
Hinduism: and nationalistic ethos of R.S.S., 191; and practice of untouchability, 258–59, 262; as fusion of myth, ritual, philoso-

phy, morals, 315; god-consciousness of, 61–63; Shaivism and Vaishnavism synthesized in, in Maharashtra, xvii; regional diversity of, vii; Untouchables' complete disavowal of, 280; weakening of, by Untouchability, 246
Hindu Mahasabha and the R.S.S., 198
Hindu-Muslim interaction: xvi-xvii, 280; in history of Datta and Varkari sects, xvii; in K.N. Kadam's experience, 283
Hindu nation and R.S.S. ethos, 192, 193, 195, 198, 200
Hindu scriptures on untouchability, 258–59
Hitler, Adolf: from Upanishadic viewpoint, 220, 222
Horses with Dnyaneshwar palanquin, 147, 150, 160–61
Hospitality: as cardinal virtue in Dhangar *ovīs*, 122
Householder: as *sannyāsī* in Mahanubhav sect, 269–70; devaluation of, as compared to renunciation, 164–65
Humanism: basis for, in Hinduism, x. *See also Māṇuskī*

Illiteracy: as no bar to effective culture, 159–60
Indra: in myth of Ganesh's origin, 84
Indian National Theatre and *gondhaḷ*, 175
Inquisition in Goa, 218
*Ishṭadaivat*: Ganesh as, 76
Islam: and *angāt yeṇe*, 45–46, 52–53; and Hinduism, xvi-xvii, 280, 316, 318, 320; and Muharram, 40–41, 283; and R.S.S., 191, 195, 200, 201; healing centers of, 27, 35, 36, 49. *See also* Muharram; *Dargā*; *Pīr*

Jagadamba invoked in *gondhaḷ*, 180, 182, 183
Jagannath, 228, 229
Jainism and propagation of ascetic life, 164–65
Janabai, 5, 6n.2; songs of, preparation for *angāt yeṇe*, 51
Janardan Swami, 97
Janata Party: R.S.S. affiliation with, 190–91; Yukrand affiliation with, 256, 262n.1
Jani. *See* Janabai
Jan Sangh and R.S.S., 190, 199
Jatayu, 303, 308n.22
*Jatrā*: contrast of, with *kheḷ*, 126; for Biroba and Mhaskoba, 177–78; in honor of deified *devṛishī*, 117. *See also Yātrā*
Jejuri: animal sacrifice at, 238–39; localized power in, of Khandoba, 18; Mahar pilgrimage to, 281, 285; taking of Banai to, by Khandoba, 124, 125
Jesus, 300, 307n.10, 311, 315, 317. *See also* Christ
*Jñāneśvarī*: on Gondhali as *bhut* and *pishāça*, 178. *See also* Dnyaneshwar
Joshi, Bhimsen: as patron of *gondhaḷ*, 174–75

Kabir: in Gadge Maharaj's *kīrtan*, 228, 234, 238, 249n.4
*Kaḍak* (harsh) deities: anxiety in people's relations to, 20–21; animal offerings to, 19; possession by, most frequent, 24
Kailas, 80, 114–15
Kal Bhairav: assimilation of Mhaskoba as, 118; temples of, as healing centers, 36
Kali: possession by, of high court judge's wife, 47
Kaliya depicted in *gondhaḷ*, 183–185
Kali yuga: and dharma of *tīrtha*-

*khsetra-vrata-dāna*, 267; decline of *shaktī* in, 208
Karbala, saints of: as precedent for fire walking rite, 41, 52–53
Karma, 314; as applied to *bhūts*, 28; god as dispenser of, 62–63; in Dhangar *ovīs*, 124
*Karṇī*: as cause of *bhūt bādhā*, 29, 30, 31; by *māntrik*, *devṛishī*, or *navas*, 32
Kartik: ancestor ceremony of Dhangars in, 115; Varkari pilgrimage from Konkan in, 158
Karve, Irawati, 140, 265; insight of, in "On the Road," xv; as scholar and Marathi essayist, xvi, xx n.3
Kashi, 274, 281
*Kattal kī rāt* and fire walking rite, 45
Katyayani vrata, 306, 308n.39, 311
Keshavsut: and modern Marathi poetry, 309, 320; cherishing of *advaita* by, 310
Khandoba, 14, 276; as Dhangar god, xix, 124–25; as *kaḍak* deity, 17, 22; as represented in *khel*, 128; as version of proto-Indian god Rudra/Shiva/Murukan, 124; official emphasis on benevolent aspects of, 24–25; photograph of *pujārī* of, 43; possession by, 42, 47, 51, 52; power-infusion by, 45, 125; power of, localized in Jejuri, 18
*Kheḷ*, 126–28; and Dhangar ancestor-possession, 115; healing of ghost-possession during, 117
*Kīrtan* in performance by Gadge Maharaj, 226–48
Kolatkar, Arun, 307, 309n.41, 311, 312, 314
Konkan, xvii, xx n.5; Dhangars' annual migration to, 113; Varkari pilgrimage from, 158
Konkanastha Brahmans and Ganesh cult, 77
Krishna, 305, 307n.4, 308n.9; as Mahanubhav *avatār*, 264, 266, 270; as Vithoba, 164; stories of, in *gondhaḷs*, 183–85; unfamiliarity of, to Hatkar Dhangars, 114
Krishnajanmashtami, 275
Kriti yuga: and dharma of introspection, 267
*Kuladaivat*: as generally a *kaḍak* deity, 18–19, 21; Ganesh as, 76; mother goddesses as, 175; source of, in pre-Vedic religions, 316
Kurus and Panchalas, sacrifices of, 164
Kusumagraj (Vishnu Waman Shirwadkar), 302, 308n.18, 311, 312

*Lāchārīt shaktī*: of medieval Marathi saint-poets, 313
Lakshmi: in Dhangar sheep pens, 125
*Lalit nibandha*, xvi, xx n.4
*Lāwaṇī*, 175
Liberation, 312, 314; *avatārs* of Parmeshwar necessary for, 266, 277. *See also Moksha*
Limaye, Arun, 251
Lime: as offering against *bhūts*, 31; purification by, before possession, 41, 52
Liminality of Ganesh festival celebration, 91
Lingayats, 129n.3; effects of, on pastoral groups, 114
Liquor: as offering to *angāt ālelā*, 135; offering of, to Ram Mama 137–138
Literacy: as distinct from culture, 159–60
Lord of Divine Hosts, 78
Lord of Obstacles, 77, 78, 84

Madalasa: in song of renunciation, 162–63
*Madhur* bhakti, 6, 319

*Mahābhārata*: in *ovīs* of settled Dhangars, 121
Mahalakshmi of Kolhapur, 175; daily begging by Datta at temple of, 96; Mahanubhavs forbidden visit to, 267, 278n.7
Mahanor, Namdeo Dhondo, 304, 308n.28, 311, 312, 313
Mahanubhavs, 279n.18, 319; as medieval bhakti movement, 265; first Marathi reference by, to Datta, 97; heterodoxy of, 264, 266; *maṭhs* and temples of, as healing centers, 36, 37, 54, 275; on meaning of "*gondhaḷ*," 179; perception of, as different, 266; photographs of, 272, 273; pilgrimage places of, 274; visit by, to Mahur, 268, 278n.8
*Mahāpujā*: at Dagadu Halwai Datta Mandir, 105; by wife, to husband, 242
Maharashtra: as bridge between Aryan and Dravidian, xix, 92; definition of, by Pandharpur pilgrimage, 158; deities of, that do and do not possess, 40, 58n.6; pilgrimage as education in language and culture of, 159; thirteenth-century bhakti movements of, 264
Mahars, 236, 248, 249n.7; access denied to, at Vithoba temple, 285; and worship of Mariai, 286–87; in Shedgao, 253; mass conversion of, to Buddhism, 291; rituals of, in household shrine, 282–83; story of Chokamela's birth by, 292. *See also* Buddhists
Mahur: Gondhali's origin at, 177, 181; Mahanubhav temple in, 267; sleeping of Datta at, 96
Malis, 236, 237, 238, 248; dominance of, in Shedgao, 253
Mangalmurti, 78
Mani and Malla, 52
Manikprabhu: Datta incarnation as, 98
*Māntriks*: as cause of *bhūt bādhā*, 29, 30, 58n.4
Manu on begetting of progeny, 164
*Māṇuskī*: as modern corollary of non-duality, x; in conflict with orthodox Hindu view, 251, 260
Maratha kingdom: Gondhalis as bards of, 181, 186–87
Marathas, 186; as dominant caste among Mahanubhavs, 277; as patrons of *gondhaḷ*, 174, 176; Gadge Maharaj on failings of, 236, 237, 241, 248; in minority in Shedgao, 252-53; and separateness from Brahmans in *dinḍī*, 143–44, 147, 151–53
Marathwada, xvii, xx n.5
Mardhekar, Bal Sitaram, 298, 307n.1, 310–311, 312, 313
Mariai, 175; annual fair at Degaon for, 8–9; as *kaḍak* deity, 9; offerings for, 9, 13, 15; possession by, of Dhangar *devṛishī*, 127; ubiquity of, 15n.2; vow to, 15; worship of, by Mahars, 286–87; worship of, in *kheḷ*, 126
Maruti, 69–70, 285
Marwadis: Gadge Maharaj on virtues of, 236, 237, 240, 248, 249n.7
Marx, Karl, 169
Matapur: as name of Mahur, 177
Mate, M.S.: on syncretism in Maharashtrian temple *pūjā*, 101
Matsyendranath, 97
*Māulī*: as epithet of Dnyaneshwar and Vithoba, 143
Mediums: function as, by *angāt ālelī*, 47
Meenakshisundaram temple, 71
Meera (Mira), 4, 5, 6n.1, 242
Meher Baba, xvii
Menstruation: and *bhūt* susceptibility, 32

Metraux, A.: on possession as pleasure for the poor, 49, 58n.7
Mhalsa, 124
Mhaskoba, 120; fourteen-day *jatrā* for, at Vir, 118
Mira. *See* Meera
Mira Datar Chilla: as healing center for *bhūt bādhā*, 34–35, 49, 56, 57
Mira Wali Darga; as healing center for *bhūt bādhā*, 35, 56
Modernity: ambiguous manifestations of, in Ganpati festival and R.S.S., xviii; and future of Gondhali, 175; in Marathi poetry, 309–10
Mokashi, D. B.: on Pandharpur pilgrimage, 171n.6
Mokashi-Punekar, Shankar: on diversity of Datta tradition, 99
*Moksha*: in Mahanubhav system, 266. *See also* Liberation
Monasteries: of Mahanubhavs, 267, 268–69
Monistic idealism: harmony of, with passionate devotionalism, 61–62
Monotheism and intolerance, 159–60
Monsoon: and Dhangar's pastoral cycle, 109–11
Morgaon, 76, 209–10
Moreshwar, 78
*Mṛidang*, 146, 151, 160, 312
Muharram, 290n.1; and fire walking rite, 45; and vow to Ghode-Pir, 283; possession by Shi'ia *pīrs* during, 41
Muktabai: devotional verses of, 165; palanquin of, 163
Muktananda, xvii
Muktibodh, Sharadchandra Madhav, 301, 308n.12, 311, 312, 313, 318
Murli, 176; photo of, 43
*Mūrti*: exhibition of, in Ganpati festival, 86–87; communication of diety to devotee through, 116; of Dhangar ancestors, 115; difference of, from *sambandhī pāshāṇs*, 271

Nagpanchmi, xvii; in Gondhalis' songs, 185
Nagpur: as main R.S.S. center, 190, 191, 195
*Naivedya*, 230, 232. *See also Nived*
Namdev: devotional songs of, 150; way of bhakti established by, 320
Nandi: of Shiva, 236; of Nandiwalas, 132
Nandiwalas: and possession, 134, 135–36; deification of Ram Mama by, 136–40; deities worshipped by, 134; ethnology of, 132–33; sacrifice of pigs by, 137–38
*Nao-nāth*: depiction of Datta as guru of, 103. *See also* Nath Panth
Narada, 80, 292, 307, 309n.43
Narasimha Saraswati, 98, 103, 104
Nasik, 288
Nath Panth: ascetics of, at Datta temple in Pune, 103; close connection of, with Datta tradition, xvii, 97, 99, 103; effect of, on pastoral groups, 114; in Maharashtra, xxi n.6, 129n.2; in Varkari sect, 319
*Navanāthabhaktisāra*: Datta as founder of Nath *sampradāy* in, 97
*Navas*: and offerings to Mariai, 9, 15; as active measure for influencing *kadak* deities, 23; connection of, with many cults, xvii; to Ambaji-Limbaji, 135; to *kuladaivat* to remedy barrennes and *karṇī*, 19; to Ram Mama, 139. *See also* Vow
*Navmatvād* in Marathi poetry, 310
Navratra, 285

Nazis: from Upanishadic viewpoint, 216
Neurosis: and *bhūt bādhā*, 34, 48–49
*Nived*: at Dhangar ancestor shrine, 115, 120. *See also Naivedya*
Nonduality; 314; as basis for Hindu ethics, x
Nontheism, 61
*Nṛtyaratnāvalī*: on *gondhaḷ* as part of Bhutamata festival, 178

Obscenity: in *bhārūḍ* performances, 161–62
Offerings: annual demand for, by *kuladaivat*, 19; at Dhangar ancestor shrine, 115; of food to Dnyaneshwar, 149; of liquor to *angāt ālelā*, 135; of pig, liquor, and *gānjā* to Ram Mama, 137; of rice balls, lime, and *kunkū* against *bhūts*, 31; to Mariai at annual fair, 9, 13
Officer Training Camps of R.S.S., 195
*Oṭā*: as relic for Nahanubhav worship, 271; photograph of, 273
Overcomer of Obstacles, 77
*Ovī*: of the Dhangars, 120–24

Padma (Padmavati Gole), 306, 308n.37, 311, 312, 313
*Pādukās*: in Datta worship, 102; of Dnyaneshwar, 143, 149; of Swami of Akkalkot, 104
Paithan, 275
Palanquin: of Dnyaneshwar, 144, 145, 146, 147, 149, 150, 160–61; of Ganesh in procession, 210; of various Varkari saints, 145, 163. *See also Pālkhī* of Khandoba
*Pālkhī* of Khandoba: possession or power infusion induced by, 42, 45
*Panchāmṛit*: as *prasād* at Dagadu Halwai Datta Mandir, 105
*Panchāyat*: dispute settlement by, among Nandiwalas, 133, 140n.2
Pandhari, 4, 6n.1, 156. *See also* Pandharpur
Pandharpur, 6n.1, 305, 308n.33; as place of pilgrimage, 143, 145; Irawati Karve's connection with, 3–6; Mahar pilgrimage to, 281, 285; pilgrimage to, as definition of Maharashtra, 158. *See also* Pandhari
Pandurang: as epithet of Vithoba, 155, 166, 167, 168, 169, 170n.1
*Panjā*: and possession at Muharram, 41, 44
*Paramahamsa*: Datta as type of, 99
Parashuram: creation of *gondhaḷ* by, 177
Parmeshwar, 227, 230, 242; as paramount Mahanubhav god, 264, 266, 267, 270, 277; attributes of, 64; devotion to, by Gadge Maharaj, 223; exclusivism of Mahanubhavs' devotion to, 276; incarnation of, in Dattatreya, 97
Partition: role of R.S.S. in, 202, 202n.5
Parvati, 79–81, 84
Pasodya Vithoba temple: as locality marker in Pune, 71
Peshwas: patronage of *gondhaḷs* by, 180–81; support of Ganesh cult by, 76–77
Pigs: sacrifice of, by Nandiwalas, 134, 137–38
Pilgrimage: by Mahars, 281, 285; Mahanubhav places of, 274
*Pīr*: as a haunting ghost, 283; as power of exorcism at *dargās* and *chillas*, 36; possession by, 41, 53. *See also* Ghode Pir
*Pishācas*, 28, 29; and Bhutamata festival, 178
Poona: *See* Pune
Possession by ancestors: among Nandiwalas, 134; and Dhangar ancestor shrines, 115

Possession by the divine: among the Nandiwalas, 135–36, 139; and fire walking rite, 45; as most personal experience of *kadak* deity, 23–24; at Chaturshringi temple, 285; description of, 40–47; importance of drums to, 119; of Dhangars at Mhaskoba *jatrā*, 118; of *portrāj* in Mariai procession, 286; sociological causes of, 49, 58n.7. *See also angāt yeṇe*
Possession by a ghost: Mahanubhav temples as places for cure from, 275; Shedgao Datta temple as healing center for, 252; similarity of, to Christian conception of sin, viii; sociological causes of, 49, 58n.7. *See also Bhūt bādhā*
*Potrāj*, 286, 290n.2
*Povāḍās* and Gondhalis, 180, 182, 187
Power: as key to Hindu concept of divinity, 18
Power infusion: as distinct from *angāt yeṇe*, 44–45; by Khandoba, at Dhangar chain-breaking, 125
*Prachārakas*: as life-blood of R.S.S., 196, 199
*Prasād*: as poor substitute for *bhajan*, 229; at Ram Mama *yātrā*, 138; from *pūjā* of dead *pīr*, 285; in Ganesh worship, 209; of Renuka, 268; sacrificial animal as, 19
Pressler, H.H.: on correlation of *ṭonā vidyā* and poverty, 49
Prets, 28; and Bhutamata festival, 178
Pre-Vedic religions: as one constituent of Hinduism, 316
*Pūjā*: and *sovḷa*, 207; as characterized by syncretism of Maharashtra, 101; as pre-Vedic notion, 316; in Datta temples, 101, 105; of Dnyaneshwar *pādukās*, 149; by Mahanubhavs, 265, 270, 271; to ghost of *pīr*, 284–85; to household gods, 205–06, 282; to Mariai, 286; to Vitthal, 292
*Pujārīs*, 101, 102, 104, 117; photograph of, 43
Pune, 160, 216; bias toward, in this volume, xvii; Datta temples of, 101–06; historical center of Ganesh festival in, 86; K. N. Kadam's early life in, 280–87; Krishnajanmashtami in, 275; new Maruti temple in, 69
Puranas: on Bhutamata festival, 178
*Purush*, 310
*Pūrṇimā*: as powerful time for *bhūt*-exorcism, 37. *See also* Full-moon day

Quit India Movement: and R.S.S. non-participation, 198, 202n.3; extolled by Gadge Maharaj, 233

Radha, 6, 302
Raeside, I.M.P.: on complexity of Datta cult, 96
*Rāgas*: in pilgrimage singing, 160
Raidas *diṇḍī*, 170n.3
Rakhumai, 147, 161, 163, 164; Mahar worship of, 282, 288
Ram, 133, 236; as benign deity, 18
Rama Gondhali: and *Tamāshā* in Peshwa Period, 187
Ramakrishna Mission, 197
*Rāmāyaṇa*, 308n.22; in *ovīs* of settled Dhangars, 121
Ramdas, 313; place of, in Varkari pilgrimage, 163, 171n.5
Rameshwar, 227, 228
Ram Mama, 132, 133, 134; history of, 136–37; overshadowing of other Nandiwala gods by, 136, 139
Ramoshis, 15n.1; death of Babir attributed to, 122, 123

Rana Pratap: eulogizing of, by R.S.S., 193, 202n.1, 195
*Rangaṇ*, 160–61, 166
Rashtriya Swayamsewak Sangh (R.S.S.): ambiguous modernity of, xix; and political socialization, 199–200; anti-Muslim sentiment in, 195; banning of, in Emergency, 190; criticism of, for not upholding untouchability, 259, 262n.4; Hindus and nationhood defined by, 198; military drill of, 191–92; *prachāraks* as lifeblood of, 196
Ravana, 236
Refuge in the *Buddha*, *sangha*, and *dhamma*, 294
Rege, Purushottam Shivram, 301, 308n.14, 311, 313; affinity of, with *Gītagovinda*, 317
Rege, Sadanand, 315, 317
Relics worshipped by the Mahanubhavs, 270–71, 279n.11
Renunciation, 314; and devaluation of householder, 162–64
Renuka of Mahur, 96, 175, 178; Mahanubhavs prohibited from visit to, 267, 278n.7; worship of, by Renukrai Gondhalis, 177
*Reṇukā Māhātmya*: on origin of *gondhaḷ*, 177
*Rite de passage*: in healing from *bhūt bādhā*, 57
Ritual: as fabric of daily life, 204–10; as means of mollifying *kaḍak* deities, 23; gaining of *shaktī* by, 208; invocation of Ganesh at beginning of, 85; of Mahars in house shrine, 282–83; preceding possession by the divine, 41; to control Ganesh's trickster tendencies, 84; R.S.S. non-support of, 200
Ritual garments: and *sovḷa*, 207; wearing of, by Brahmans at mealtime, 143, 144
Ritual pollution: as key variable to *bhūt*-susceptibility, 32–33; as pre-Vedic notion, 316; intolerance of, by *kaḍak* deities, 19–20; variation in codes of, by caste, 20; water and, 154. *See also Sovlā*
Roman Catholicism, 287, 289. *See also* Christianity
R.S.S. *See* Rashtriya Swayamsevak Sangh
Rudra, 80, 124
Russel, Bertrand, 289

Sacrifice: as center of Vedic religion, 316; of bird or animal to *kaḍak* deities, 19; of sheep, goats, fowl by Mahars, 281–82, 285; of pigs by Nandiwalas, 134, 137, 138; of sheep by Dhangars, 117, 119, 120, 127. *See also Yadnya*
*Sādhanā*, poetry as, 312, 314
Sadhuvani and Satyanarayan *pūjā*, 231
Sahasrarjuna in mythic origin of *gondhaḷ*, 177
Sai Baba of Shirdi: as Datta incarnation, 99
Saints: as greater than gods, 235–36; dust on road of, sacred, 145–46; rebellion of, against purity-pollution, 154
Sakhu, 4, 6n.1
*Samādhī*: as healing center for *bhūt bādhā*, 36; of Dnyaneshwar, 145, 309n.44
*Sambaḷ*-drum, 176, 177, 182
*Sambandhī pāshāṇs* in Mahanubhav worship, 270–71
*Sangha*: refuge taken in, 294
Sankara: paradox of monistic idealism and devotionalism in, 62
*Sannyāsīs*: burial of, in *samādhī*, 309n.44; of Mahanubhav sect, 264, 266, 268, 269
Sanskrit: in R.S.S. prayers, pledges, and drills, 191–92, 194

Saptarshi, Kumar, 251
Saptashringi, 175
Saraswati, 85
Sardar Shitole, 147
*Sat*: temple as symbol of, 72
*Satyāgraha*, 233; as practiced by Yukrand, 251, 254, 259, 260, 261
Satyanarayan *pūjā*: as part of Ganesh festival, 87; Gadge Maharaj's last *kīrtan* at, 224, 231, 249n.6
Satyayuga: in Hatkar Dhangar *ovīs*, 121
Savitri, *shaktī* of, 208
Sawant, Vasant Ladoba, 305, 308n.31, 311, 312,318
Seven water goddesses: worship of, at Dhangar sheep shearing, 125
Sexual intercourse and *bhūt*-susceptibility, 33
Shabaraswami: on limits of celibacy, 164
Shaivism: large effect of, on pastoral communities, 113–14; Maharashtrian synthesis of, with Vaishavism, xvii, 319
*Shaktī*, 208, 209
Shaligram, S.T.: on *gondhaḷs* in Peshwa Period, 180–81, 187
*Shālīgrāms*, 205
Shankar, 206
Shesha, 236
*Shids*: and Mhaskoba-possession at Vir, 118
Shi'ia Muslims: possession by saint-heroes of, 41
Shiva: as leper in Dhangar *ovī*, 122; crystalizing of pre-Vedic religion in, 316; incarnated as Babir, 123; incorporation in Datta of, 95; mediatory functions conferred on Ganesh by, 81, 82; role of, in myths of Ganesh's origin, 79–81, 84
Shiva *linga*: worship of, by Mahanubhavs, 274, 275
Shivaji: eulogizing of, by R.S.S., 193, 195, 202n.1; illustration of, 173
Shripad Shrivallabha: Datta incarnated as, 98, 103
Sickness: as punishment by *kaḍak* deity, 20: as result of *bhūt bādhā*, 29
*Siddhis*, 118
Sita, *Shaktī* of, 209
*Śivapurāṇa*: myth of Ganesh's origin in, 79–80
Skanda: in contest with Ganesh, 84
*Skandapurāṇa*: myth of Ganesh's origin in, 80–81; on dramatic performances in Bhutamata festival, 178
Somavati-Amavasya: Dhangar chain-breaking rite on, 125
Sopankaka, palanquin of, 163
*Sovḷa* in daily ritual, 207–08. *See also* Ritual garments; Ritual pollution
Stalin, Joseph: from Upanishadic viewpoint, 220, 222
Suicide, 74; and Dnyaneshwar's taking of *samādhī*, 75, 75n.
Sunni Muslims: in Shi'ia processions, 41, 46
Surve, Narayan, 61, 64–65
Surya: in Dagadu Halwai Datta Mandir, 104
*Sūtrapāṭha*, 265, 277; devaluing by of popular Hindu practices, 266 67, 278n.5
Syncretism: of Brahma, Vishnu, Shiva in Dattatreya, 95; of temple *pūjā* in Maharashtra, 101
*Svānubhavadinakara*: on Parashuram and first *gondhaḷ*, 177
Swami of Akkalkot: Datta incarnated as, 98; Pune temple of, 101, 103–04

*Tamāshā*: and Gondhalis, 187; in Ganesh festival, 87

*Tapashcharyā* of the Buddha, 293
*Tarūṇ manḍaḷs*: for Ganesh festival, 88–93
Tilak, Bal Gangadhar: and Ganesh festival, 77, 92
Tilak, Narayan Waman, 310, 315
*Tīrtha-kshetra-vrata-dāna*: as dharma of Kali yuga, 267, 275, 276
*Tīrthas*: Gadge Maharaj's scorn for, 228, 229, 230, 238
Treta yuga: and dharma of bhakti, 267
Trickster, Ganesh as, 84
Tukaram, 5, 6n.3, 170n.2, 305; iconography of Datta given by, 95–96; in Gadge Maharaj's *kīrtan*, 227, 228, 229, 234, 241, 248n.2: on individual less-than-wholeness, 311–12; palanquin of, 163; self-identity of, with God, 227; devotional songs of, 150
Tuljapur: localized power in, of Bhavani, 18; Mahar pilgrimage to, 281
Tulpule, S.G., 176; on Mahanubhav relics, 279
*Tuḷshī*, 207
*Tuṇtuṇ*-drone, 176, 177, 182
Turmeric: ritual use of, 125, 126, 282; presence of Biroba in, 119

Uma, 81
University Training Corps: as model for R.S.S., 193
Untouchables: disavowal of Hinduism by, 280; pilgrim *dinḍī* of, 150, 170n.3; fear of social boycott of, 254, 261; legitimation sought by, in Buddhism, xix; part played by, in Shedgao satyagraha, 253, 256, 257, 260
Untouchability: Gadge Maharaj's scorn for, 224, 240, 243–46; Hindu scriptures cited as support for, 258–59; viewed as necessary to true Hindu practice, 262
Untouchability Offenses Act: breaking of, by Akhandanand Maharaj, 253, 260, 261, 263.6
Upanishads, 316; and propagation of ascetic life, 164–65; and speculative "containing" of Vedic and pre-Vedic religions, 316; on oneness of self and universe, 214, 216

Vaghyas, 45, 176, 189n.16
Vaishavism: Maharashtrian synthesis of, with Shaivism, xvii
Varhad, 6, 6n.4. *See also* Vidarbha
Varkari Panth, 264; annual pilgrimage of, 145; Gadge Maharaj and social reform in, 223–24; connection of, with Datta, 97, 319; devotional songs of, 160; as rural and non-Brahman, xvii; saints of, against Brahman exclusiveness, 155;
Varkari pilgrimage: photograph of pilgrims on, 172, viewed as education, 160
Varkari tradition, 320; and renunciation, 162–63; and Tukaram, 6n.3; at odds with ritual purity-pollution, 154
*Varṇāshrama*: justification of, in R.S.S., 198. *See also* Caste
Vasudev, 175, 176, 189n.16
Vedanta, 161, 316
Vedas: and immortality through progeny, 164; as criterion of orthodoxy, 266; fifth attributed to Tukaram, 227; representation of, by Datta's four dogs, 95
Vedic religion: centering of, on sacrifice, 316
Vegetarianism, 282; Gadge Maharaj's espousal of, 224; of Mahanubhavs, 268, 279n.9
Vidarbha, xvii, xxn.5
Vighneshwar, 78, 79, 80

# Tropical Fish Otoliths: Information for Assessment, Management and Ecology

Reviews: Methods and Technologies in Fish Biology and Fisheries

VOLUME 11

Series editor:

Jennifer L. Nielsen

*U.S. Geological Survey,*

*Alaska Science Center*

*Anchorage, Alaska*

For further volumes:

http://www.springer.com/series/6481